Decolonial Feminist
Genealogies and Futures

DISSIDENT FEMINISMS

Elora Halim Chowdhury, Editor

*For a list of books in the series, please see
our website at www.press.uillinois.edu.*

Decolonial Feminist Genealogies and Futures

Edited by
ANNIE ISABEL FUKUSHIMA
and K. MELCHOR QUICK HALL

UNIVERSITY OF ILLINOIS PRESS
Urbana, Chicago, and Springfield

© 2025 by the Board of Trustees
of the University of Illinois
All rights reserved
1 2 3 4 5 C P 5 4 3 2 1
∞ This book is printed on acid-free paper.

Cataloging data available from the Library of Congress

ISBN 978-0-252-04689-6 (hardcover)
ISBN 978-0-252-08901-5 (paperback)
ISBN 978-0-252-04845-6 (ebook)

Contents

Foreword   Genealogies of Struggle and Scholar-Activist Journeys: On Democratizing Knowledge   *Linda Carty and Chandra Talpade Mohanty* vii

Introduction   *Annie Isabel Fukushima and K. Melchor Quick Hall* 1

PART I. SUBVERSIVE LABOR

1   Late Capitalism and Gender: Stories, Challenges, and Perceptions of Women Workers Who Train Artificial Intelligence on Amazon Mechanical Turk   *Amanda Jurno, Bruno Moreschi, and Monique Lemos*.............. 15

2   Cultivating a Decolonial Feminist Praxis through Testimonio and *Pláticas*   *Lynn Hampton and Sylvia Mendoza Aviña* 31

3   Embodied Precarity: Feminist Politics, Laboring Bodies of Color, and the Neoliberal University   *Azza Basarudin and Tina Beyene*... 49

4   The Emotional Labor of Reconciliation and Indigenization: Indigenous Women Creating Decolonial Feminist Praxis within the Academy   *Tricia McGuire-Adams and Janice Cindy Gaudet*... 64

PART II. SPATIALITIES AND TEMPORALITIES

5   Methods, Modes, and Mapping: The (Re)Construction of Palestinian Sites as an Act of Return   *Lydia Zakel* 85

6 Subaltern Ways of Knowing: A Critical Spatial
Analysis of Migrant Worker Knowledge Production
in Beirut, Lebanon   *Shireen Keyl* 103

7 Say, Who's Online? Building Feminist Futures through
South Asian Collectivity in Texas   *Rachel Afi Quinn*.............. 120

PART III. RESISTANCE

8 "I Am Not Oppressed! Give It a Rest!": *The Hijab
Project* As Resistance to Western Narratives about
Muslim Women   *Ana Carolina Antunes*........................ 143

9 Children's Bodies and the Sensual Disruptions of
Schooling in India and Turkey   *Akanksha Misra*................ 157

10 Decolonial Pedagogy: Resisting through Transnational
WGS Introductory Courses   *Esther Oluwashina Ajayi-Lowo*..... 175

PART IV. GENEALOGIES AND FUTURES

11 [A] Migrant Vernacular   *Eun-Jin Keish Kim
and Angel Sutjipto*... 203

12 Warrior Butterflies Walking with the Ancestors:
Xicanx Indigenous Youth Becoming Leaders of
Transformational Justice
*Cueponcaxochitl D. Moreno Sandoval,
Miriam G. Valdovinos, Elisa Contreras,
and Xochitl E. López Andrade*................................. 223

13 A Red Feminist Manifest: Meditations on Native
American Women, Sovereignty Protectors, and the
Liturgies of Colonial Violence   *Leece Lee-Oliver*................ 241

14 Not Only an Academic Field, but Also Movements:
Advancing Ethnic Studies with Decolonial Feminisms
Xamuel Bañales 269

Conclusion   *K. Melchor Quick Hall,
Annie Isabel Fukushima, Chandra Talpade Mohanty,
and Linda Carty*... 297

Contributors... 305
Index 307

FOREWORD

Genealogies of Struggle and Scholar-Activist Journeys
On Democratizing Knowledge

LINDA CARTY and
CHANDRA TALPADE MOHANTY

We begin with brief remarks on each of our individual scholar-activist collaborations, specifically collaborations at Syracuse University that led to envisioning the *Democratizing Knowledge: Developing Literacies, Building Communities, Seeding Change* project in 2009 (https://democratizingknowledge.syr.edu). The initial proposal to the Mellon Foundation for the Democratizing Knowledge Project (henceforth, the DK Project) described our vision in this way: "Confronting white privilege, hegemonic masculinity, heteronormativity, and colonial heritages, this project focuses on producing transformative knowledges and collectivities that result in inclusive publics in higher education, in the workforce, and in the larger national and global polity. The Project will draw on, provide greater support for, and bring together the interdisciplinary projects already in place, creating a culture on campus for the cross-fertilization of disciplinary and interdisciplinary knowledges and projects that bring intellectually marginalized work to the center." The core vision of the DK Project has always been institutional change for building inclusive futures. And from this arose the DK Collective—a group of individuals committed to this cause.

The DK Collective uses tools of the humanities and social sciences such as public ethnography, documentary filmmaking, and critical pedagogy to learn how community activists' framings of problems and challenges relating to the presence and impact of the university in the broader community constitute valuable forms of knowledge and latent political and ethical critiques that can and should be incorporated into curricula. We argue that these framings and representations, which are perhaps unique to the overlapping and intersecting spaces between communities and universities, are often ignored or subject to being dismissed by the academy because they don't emanate from or serve the university's interests. DK builds and promotes a model for engagement with local communities that eschews the notion of the scholar as sole legitimate expert who, inevitably following academic-disciplinary protocols, dictates how problems can be "fixed." And the DK collective rejects related understandings of universities as singular, preeminent sites for what can be known about problems and solutions and contends that using the methods of critical pedagogy leads to a more democratic approach to community-university partnerships and can result in the constitution of community groups that, through collaborations with scholar-activists, become newly empowered to engage the university and their own community challenges on a more equitable footing.

Along with colleagues in Lesbian, Gay, Bisexual, and Transgender (LGBT) and Latino/Latin American Studies (Margaret Himley and Silvio Torres-Saillant), we are the founding members of the DK Project, with a long and storied history of collaborations with different communities and with each other. We met in 1988 at the Third International Feminist Book Fair in Montreal, Canada. Our paths crossed multiple times in the 1990s—at Oberlin College, where we both taught, and at feminist conferences such as "I am Your Sister" honoring Audre Lorde. Of course, we have always participated in overlapping Black, South Asian, Caribbean, and women of color (WOC) communities in the United States and Canada. Since the early 2000s, we have both taught at Syracuse University. It is our belief that the intersection of political and intellectual journeys is significant to leading ongoing and ambitious collaborations facilitated by proximity and a common vision of epistemological praxis, pedagogy, and commitment to racial and gender justice. At Syracuse University (SU), we have been the primary instigators of three transnational scholar-activist projects: the *Future of Minority Studies* project, which led to over a dozen residential semester-long mentoring fellowships at SU for untenured scholars of color; the *Democratizing Knowledge* project, which was the genesis for this particular book; and the *Feminist Freedom Warriors Video Archive,* which documents intergenerational conversations about feminist politics, justice, solidarity, and hope (http://feministfreedomwarriors.org).

Linda's Story

I joined the academy as a teacher during graduate school at the University of Toronto in Canada in the mid-1980s, teaching at Seneca and Centennial Community Colleges in Toronto. During that time, I always referred to myself as a radical Black feminist activist. Back then, I was a member of the Toronto Black Women's Collective (BWC), a group of young Black feminists who fought many forms of injustice in Canada, specifically multiple police shootings of Black men and women in the greater metro Toronto area. I have long engaged in collaborative work as a feminist activist and in my academic writings because my activism has been an integral part of the same trajectory. My activism has always informed my scholarship because the two constitute my trajectory through the minefield that I have experienced in the academy and inform how I have navigated it. Understandably, on that path, I have a notable list of collaborative scholarship.

During my activism period in Canada, I learned that the Canadian state spent much time, energy, and resources denying Canada's history of institutional racism. Canada is a settler colonial society with a state that has remained in denial about its past. Neither the settlers' attempt to annihilate the First Nations peoples nor the state's support of chattel slavery in the United States was ever acknowledged. The state has always been proud of pointing out that Canada has never had slavery. But that overlooks the fact that after the War of 1812 between the United States and the United Kingdom, Canada allowed the Loyalists who moved north to bring with them their "pots and pans and slaves," and the latter had to remain slaves until their masters' or their own deaths. The first text to document this history and the role of Black women in Canadian history was a collaborative effort of mine with five other Black feminists that resulted in the publication of *We're Rooted Here and They Can't Pull US Up: Essays in African Canadian Women's History* (P. Bristow et al., 1994). So there was slavery in Canada, albeit not institutionalized as it was in the United States. In keeping with its pattern of denying racism, the state coined the term "visible minorities" to refer to Canadian Black people and immigrants of color. In the BWC, we regularly contested such practices. For example, Dionne Brand and I (both from the BWC) coauthored the article "'Visible Minority' Women: A Creation of the Canadian State," which was published in *We're Rooted Here and They Can't Pull US Up*.

Immediately after completing my PhD, I worked as a non-tenure-track Assistant Professor in the Women's Studies Department at the University of Toronto. The university was gifted almost $1 million to advance the department's curricular offerings, explicitly developing a focus on women and development courses and the department's connection to the community. I was the young professor hired to bring this initiative to fruition. In the first year, in collaboration with my BWC sisters, we developed a literary speakers' series that spanned three weeks. I invited five renowned feminist writers of color, including Barbara Smith (Black feminist pioneer and cofounder of Combahee River Collective), Anne Adams (Cornell University), Swasti Mitter (feminist British economist, University of Brighton), Ama Ata Aidoo (Ghanian author and poet), and Nancy Morejón (Cuban poet), who was given special permission by the US government to attend an event in the United States at the time but was not allowed a visa to travel to Canada. Hundreds of people from the community came out for every speaker. During that first year, 1989, I also developed and taught a senior seminar, Third World Feminisms, which was over-enrolled for the two years I offered it.

In the second year, 1990, again working with the BWC and other community members, we put on a First Nations women's conference, the first in the history of the University of Toronto. I invited twenty-five First Nations women writers representing many nations across Canada and some from the United States. Two of the most renowned authors included Bea Medicine and Lee Maracle. Maracle was instrumental in helping us compile the list of invitees. Some younger scholars in attendance included Donna Goodleaf and others from the Gananoque community on the Ontario-Quebec border. On the first day of the four-day conference, we had an approximate attendance of 700 for the opening plenary session. It was the largest First Nations gathering or event in the university's history. Following this conference, the BWC developed closer relationships with First Nations communities across Ontario and Quebec. In the fall, we hosted a conference, where I taught a graduate course at the University of Toronto's Ontario Institute of Studies in Education, incorporating some of Lee Maracle's texts.

Subsequently, I moved to the United States and continued my work of merging my activism and scholarship. At Oberlin College, in 1991, I got to know the Black community outside of the town and was later instrumental in mobilizing that community while helping to organize a march at the college. An estimated 2,000 people turned out to protest the brutal police beating of Rodney King in Los Angeles in June 1992. Later that year, I moved to the University of Michigan-Flint, and I taught two semesters at the University of Michigan-Ann Arbor. There, I worked with the Haitian community located in Ypsilanti, Michigan. They were experiencing intense discrimination on multiple levels by the Michigan state government.

I moved to Syracuse University in 2000. Immediately, I volunteered in programs in the public school system after learning that the SU School of Education, which was then ranked in the top three in the country, was turning out many teachers from white suburban and rural communities across the tri-state area. They were doing their practice training in Syracuse's urban schools with a majority Black and Latino student population. However, many of these young teachers had no experience working with these populations. For this reason, I was involved in challenging such racialized practices, and the school eventually stopped these practices.

Having a background in health care, I also was involved with the caring professions in Brooklyn, New York, volunteering with Caribbean and Latin American health clinics, primarily the Caribbean Women's Health Network. This center provides health and immigration services to the working-class communities in that borough. Related to all of the above, I have written what is known in the academy as "public scholarship" that is not counted in the quantification game of "legitimate" academic work. But such pieces, whether discussing behaviors prevalent in the community that could benefit many as an educational piece or just providing assistance with a grant proposal, are deeply appreciated by the organizations and deeply rewarding to the activists.

Chandra's Story

What does it mean to create a narrative of the life and commitments of one feminist of color from the Global South, just "doing her work," as Audre Lorde used to say? I see myself as a scholar, teacher, organizer, and social justice worker. For the past three-plus decades, my place of work has been the US academy—hence, the academy has always been a crucial site of struggle, engagement, and transformation for me. My story here touches on some of the highlights, what I see as turning points in my political and intellectual journey as a feminist of color "doing her work." My experience of collaboration and organizing began in the mid-1970s, organizing as an undergraduate student at the University of Delhi against the national emergency of then-Prime Minister Indira Gandhi.

But it was as a graduate student at the University of Illinois at Urbana-Champaign, in the context of initiating and collaborating with Ann Russo and several sisters and comrades around the *Common Differences, Third World Women and Feminist Perspectives Conference* (April 1983), that I truly understood what it meant to collaborate and organize around women's and gender issues across regional/national borders. I believe this was (one of) the first non-UN conferences of this scale to bring US women of color and feminists from the "third world" into conversation about the "common differences" in our feminist praxis. This was the beginning of my intellectual journey in the company of transnational feminists of color. Questions of intersectionality and relationality of structures of power and women's place-based resistance; the complexities of working across race, class, sexuality, and nationality in the context of multiple colonial legacies and imperial adventures of the United States; the centrality of economic issues, poverty, and class in envisioning and enacting gender justice; the significance of identity and community (who are the "we"?); and the theoretical and epistemological contributions of an anticolonial and decolonial feminist engagement were the multiple issues that emerged from this collective space—and that have stayed with me through all the work I have done and continue to do since then. My co-edited collection *Third World Women and the Politics of Feminism* (1991) emerged from this conference.

My work since the early 1980s has been with sister-comrades, including Jacqui Alexander, whom I met at a historic gathering of feminists of color initiated by Barbara Smith in the mid-1980s. Many of the feminist writers from the book *This Bridge Called My Back, Writings by Radical Women of Color*—one of the books that inspired my feminist commitments and the *Common Differences* conference—were at this gathering discussing the possibility of a Women of Color Institute for Radical Action. The institute never materialized, but the friendships and collaborations from this retreat in the Adirondacks have sustained me through these last many decades. My work with Jacqui Alexander led to another edited collection, *Feminist Genealogies, Colonial Legacies, Democratic Futures* (1997). Much of the feminist pedagogical work I have engaged in also has been profoundly collaborative—with Beverly Guy-Sheftall, Margo Okazawa-Rey, Angela Davis, and Linda Carty. In fact, it is my cross-cultural, cross-racial dialogues with friends and sisters across the globe that have taught me the meaning of solidarity and struggle across difference and power. I have engaged in and learned from sustained and ongoing place-based dialogues with feminist scholar-activists in India, Canada, Europe, South Africa, Colombia, Mexico, and Palestine. My understanding of the political significance of collaboration and solidarity as a profoundly political act of producing counter-hegemonic knowledge comes from these experiences.

Alongside my work in the academy, I have organized with grassroots communities since the 1980s, including Grassroots Leadership of North Carolina, an anti-privatization organization that has worked these many decades to confront and fight against the privatization of prisons and immigrant detention centers in the US South. It was from my comrades here that I understood and began to analyze the profound colonial impact of privatization and neoliberal practices normalized in the academy. My work with the Center for Immigrant Families in New York City taught me the power of immigrants of color organizing against school segregation in Upper Manhattan. Similarly, working with the Municipal Services Project, a research and policy-based international project, on the privatization of public services in the Global South took me to South Africa and Europe and fostered engagement with scholar-activists confronting the effects of privatization and global capitalism on a large scale. This work consolidated my understanding of an anti-capitalist global comparative feminist focus on policy and grassroots social movements. My most recent involvement with Freedom University in Georgia brought many of these experiences together by confronting academic and political repression, and imagining and creating political education courses for undocumented students denied access to public universities in the state.

Undergirding all of my scholarly work are my activist commitments to building radical, anti-racist transnational feminist communities in all of the spaces I have occupied over the last four-plus decades of living in the United States. None of this work would be possible without these dissident communities. And this, I think, is the key to living an insurgent life as an anti-racist, transnational feminist in these times. Building the "intellectual neighborhoods" (Toni Morrison) and communities of dissent that inspire and can sustain an insurgent feminist life. I learned very early in my intellectual journey that the best thinking and strategizing emerge through collaborations with diverse communities of people with similar commitments to and visions of justice. I have worked to build these radical intellectual neighborhoods in the service of social justice.

In addition to, or alongside, this work in the academy and with grassroots community organizations, I continue to be engaged with feminists of color, anti-racist feminists, and feminists from the Global South organizing and producing knowledge about feminist decolonial/anti-racist futures. My 2011 participation in the *Indigenous and Feminist of Color Solidarity* delegation to Occupied Palestine is an example of this kind of collaborative, political work across borders. Movements and communities that continue to inspire me in the DK Collaborative and beyond are movements that theorize care work as central to feminist futures; immigrant and refugee movements that problematize nation-state borders and questions of citizenship; anti-racist and anti-caste movements in the Global North and South; anti-imperial, anti-capitalist movements, Indigenous movements against settler-colonialism; Adivasi, tribal, Dalit movements in India; Palestine Justice struggles; and in the United States, No DAPL (fighting the Dakota Access Pipeline) movements; Mijente (Latinx) organizing; and Movement for Black Lives (MBL) and Black Youth Collective movements; and Justice for Muslims/Against Islamophobia. These are some of the movements and modes of collaboration and solidarity that I believe are necessary to envision and enact the most equitable feminist futures, and this is the work Linda and I believe the DK Project contributes to.

Concluding Reflections

A major achievement of the DK Project was the three Mellon-funded summer institutes titled *Just Academic Spaces: Creating New Publics Through Radical Literacies*. It was at these institutes that our paths crossed with the editors of this volume: Kia Melchor Hall and Annie Fukushima. Throughout the lifetime of the DK Project, we used the language of "democratizing" instead of "decolonizing," although, given our intellectual genealogies and commitments, we always meant "decolonizing." The success of these institutes is evident in the number of DK collectives that emerged in various colleges and universities—all spearheaded by the DK fellows attending the three institutes at Syracuse University, Rutgers-Newark, and Spelman College. Concretely, the three-year series of summer institutes (2016–18) brought together scholar-activists and community activists to articulate how these collaborations build new—sometimes unexpected—kinds of publics in the borderlands between critical academic scholarship and community-based knowledge and organizations.

Publics and communities both describe groupings of people. However, we use "publics" to denote the joined non-academic and academic populations who are producers of their own knowledge, and who are accountable to all participants and responsible for the legitimacy of the forms of knowing they produce. At the same time, we seek to identify the "radical literacies" generated in these collaborative borderlands, understanding them as place-based ways of reading power relations and generating alternative possibilities for making knowledge, history, and community. One of the key questions addressed by the institute concerns the ways these forms of radical literacies can be elaborated into methods and concepts that can travel beyond their original place, generating new publics in other academic and community sites. And this is exactly what has occurred—the generation of new collectives and publics in different sites across the United States. This collection on *Decolonizing Feminist Genealogies and Futures* is yet another offering in the tradition of the Democratizing Knowledge Project. We deeply appreciate the energy, dedication, and inspiration provided by our DK sisters and co-editors of this volume, Kia Melchor Hall and Annie Fukushima, in the crafting and birthing of this anthology. We could not have imagined a better legacy than the collaborative work of these two feminist scholar-activists. Our heartfelt gratitude and thanks for this volume of essays.

Introduction

ANNIE ISABEL FUKUSHIMA
and K. MELCHOR QUICK HALL

As we edit this book, multiple localized and global events have taken force in our communities, shaping politics and social life. The global pandemic of COVID-19 limited ways of connecting and was exacerbated by a "multi-demic" of issues from domestic violence, fatal deaths related to arms, racism, and ongoing colonialities. As the world grappled with inequities that intensified during the pandemic, the structures of coloniality—racism and modern colonial economic systems—persevered as they were meant to, even as millions of people died, were displaced, or continued to experience marginalization and oppression. The ongoing context of colonization of Native lands and structures of empire are palpable in the discourse surrounding national interests, protection of borders, and settler colonial logics. The settler colonial logics, manifest in the form of policing populations, land seizures, and automation, are examples of what Lloyd and Wolfe convey as "the fundamental continuity between the historical development of European settler colonialism and the present-day development of the neoliberal world order resides in the exigencies of managing surplus populations" (Lloyd and Wolfe 2015, 3). Integral to colonial structures is racism. Therefore, racism continues to be an ongoing violence around the world, shored up during the pandemic in the form of inequities in accessing health care, deprivation of basic needs, violence at the hands of the state (such as the police), and everyday racisms circulating as individualized "hate crimes." Twenty-first-century colonial structures are met with resistance from Indigenous communities, including examples of water protectors in South Dakota and Indigenous people protecting the rainforests in the Brazilian Amazon. Decolonial movements cannot be disconnected from anti-racist movements where a Black Lives Matter movement led to mass mobilization, Black communities stood in solidarity with other marginalized communities, and Asian mobilizations were reinvigorated to illuminate the deep structures of racism and anti-Blackness that affects communities. And endeavors for a better future manifested in how people took to the streets: global feminist movements such as "el violador en tu camino" / "the rapist in your way" anthem by Las Tesis circulated widely, with mujeres, women, and gender-non-conforming folks performing and chanting in the streets, and circulating videos via social media, to call out state violence. We are witnessing global movements to make visible the genocide of Palestinians. As movements address the current material conditions of people's lives, it is in the resistance that a particular future is being reimagined and articulated, one that hopes for and aspires toward decolonization.

Decolonial Feminist Genealogies and Futures grows out of a seed planted by feminist scholars Chandra Talpade Mohanty and Linda Carty, through a series of Democratizing Knowledge (DK) summer institutes. As foregrounded in the *Feminist Freedom Warriors* collaborative book (2018) and web archive of Chandra Talpade Mohanty and Linda Carty, feminist scholars, organizers, and activists must "sustain radical struggles against neoliberal, transnational capital, carceral, national-security-driven nation-states, and the rise of racist, right-wing, authoritarian regimes in the United States and around the world." Mohanty and Carty mark that "the urgency of a decolonial, anti-capitalist, anti-racist resistance" is one that builds "coalitions and solidarity across struggles." Mohanty and Carty (2018) highlight how feminist freedom warriors engage resistance and build coalitions with an imaginative and courageous spirit. Decolonial feminisms embrace this spirit of coalition as one that not only is about a relationality among people and their environments but also extends across time. To be in coalition is to bring into the fold the intellectual and community genealogies one carries.

Decolonial Feminist Genealogies

Decoloniality is an "unfinished project" that may be traced to a rich tradition of theory and practice furthered by Gloria Anzaldúa (1987), Aimée Césaire (2000), Enrique Dussel, Frantz Fanon, Lewis Gordon, Nelson Maldonado-Torres, Walter Mignolo, Emma Perez, Laura Perez, Chela Sandoval, Linda Tuhiwai Smith, and Sylvia Wynter, to name some of our interlocutors (and we recognize there are many, many unnamed). Examining coloniality is a theory and a practice, as put forth by Gloria Anzaldúa,

> The lines between oppressed and oppressor, white and colored, "them" and "us" are no longer so rigid because we have crossed over to become subjects in our own right. In becoming subjects, we look at them as objects, as Others, and they still look at us as objects, as Others. They are also implicated in our culture and our history and heritage. The term that I use is

"nos/otras." The "nos" is the "us" and "we"; the "otras" is the "them" or the "others." It's really all of us, Euro-Americans and people of color, in "nos/otras." (Hernández and Anzaldúa 1995)

The conditions of coloniality structure lives, and as Walter Mignolo reflected, "there is no modernity without coloniality" (2012, 43). Coloniality is the "long-standing patterns of power that emerged as a result of colonialism" (Maldonado-Torres 2007, 243). Coloniality is embedded in other systems of power, including gender. As conveyed by María Lugones, "coloniality of gender is still with us; it is what lies at the intersection of gender/class/race as central constructs of the capitalist world system of power" (Lugones 2010, 745). Resisting coloniality is complex, and here, we offer up the decolonial as an integral concept guiding this anthology. It is here that we pause to think with María Lugones, who offers up resistance as not the "end" of a political struggle, but rather the beginning of possibility (2010, 746). And with this possibility, resistance serves as a central calling for theory and praxis for decolonizing. Therefore, included in this edited anthology is an endeavor to suture together through a multiplicity of struggles, sites, embodiments, and locations a decolonial feminist theory and practice.

Decolonial feminisms build on this rich history of resistance. Drawing on the work of Grosfoguel and Fukushima, we situate decolonial feminisms as a praxis that centralizes anti-racist theory and reclaims intersectionality and alterity (Grosfoguel 2007; Fukushima 2019). Recognizing that that colonial project uses categorical construction of race as an instrument of social domination (Quijano 2000), the decolonial in decolonial feminisms is one of resistance. A decolonial feminist methodology "denounce[s] and transform[s] colonial relations of power and colonial ways of relating that continue to persist in our present, a concern that resonates with and builds on the work of many postcolonial thinkers as well as transnational and women of color feminists" (Mendez 2015, 49). If decolonial feminisms are method, they are also a practice, moving into the realm of how one goes about mobilizing a theory.

Decolonial feminisms work toward a deep coalition to create the possibility of an active subjectivity of multiple selves and realities (Moya 2006; Lugones 2003). Therefore, the tracings of decolonial struggles are difficult to pinpoint in time and place, where authors in this volume, scholars and practitioners who contribute to decolonial feminisms, delineate how decolonial struggles are ongoing. The sites of decolonial feminist genealogies are place and space specific, grounded in the specificity of a location. But space, place, and locations cannot be separated from time. Therefore, as decolonial feminist genealogies allow one to conceptualize a past and history of the present, to grapple with how we are using "futures" is to engage with

Elizabeth Grosz's notion of feminist futures as bound to a radical notion of time and consciousness. Grosz conveys how the future emerges through the conditions of a past, stating,

> [W]e need an account of time that enables us to have at least partial or mediated access to the resources of the past, those resources consecrated as history and retaining their traces or tracks in the present, which do not tie us to the past in any definitive way or with any particular orientation and which provide for us the very resources by which to supersede the past and the present—the very project of radical politics. (Grosz 2002, 18)

Thinking along with Aimee Bahng (2018), notions of "futurity" means communities and individuals contend with the conditions about the material present to make decisions and construct narratives about the "future."

In this collection, the contributors of decolonial feminist genealogies and futures collectively illuminate the tensions between transnational feminisms and decolonial endeavors. That tension exists between theories of praxis, where one necessitates the border crossing of boundaries sustained by the nations and states while acknowledging the roles of both, and the other seeks to imagine a future and present beyond the confines of nationalism. Therefore, here in this edited anthology there are slippages between and among decolonial, transnational, and women of color theories that are central to understanding how this collection defines decolonial feminisms. For scholars Ashwini Tambe and Millie Thayer (2021), decolonial feminism centers Indigenous epistemologies, where transnational feminism as practice embodies decolonial sensibilities. Contributions found in this collection locate displacement and diasporic relationship to land, and Native and Indigenous perspectives on decoloniality. And it is in these slippages that a liberatory theory is possible, where a theory of liberation cannot be contained or always captured through a monolithic definition. It is through the analysis of the colonial/modern gender system, made possible through decolonial feminisms, that coalition and the reconstruction of nonbinary subjectivities are made possible (Alarcon et al. 2020). Decolonial feminisms reject colonial systems and binaries, constituting an ongoing project that extends beyond individualisms.

A decolonial feminist project furthers coalition and an ongoing project of "activity of the self in metamorphosis" (Zaytoun 2019, 86). Many of the contributions found here draw on multiple voices, perspectives, and communities, without relinquishing the individuals who are part of collectives. That is, the coalition of the many individuals constituting decolonial feminisms illuminates that it is a theory bound to praxis, multiplicity, and collective action. Here readers will find autoethnography, *testimonio*, and lived experiences, where the invitation is to bring multiple communities and people together to foster opportunities to "enter into each other's worlds" (Lugones 2003).

As we look backward to move forward (embodying the *sankofa* idea), we reconcile how time as a construct means that the past is always a part of our present and futures; we find that the legacy of decolonial feminist theorists such as Gloria E. Anzaldúa (1987), Linda Carty (2003), Evelyn Nakano Glenn (2015), Cricket Keating (2005), María Lugones (1987), Chandra Talpade Mohanty (1984), Mariana Ortega (2017), Chela Sandoval (2000), and others manifests in a next generation of scholars, practitioners, activists, and mobilizers. We find that the rooting of decolonial feminist theory and praxis in the everyday keeps us grounded. The call to edit a collection on *Decolonial Feminist Genealogies and Futures* comes at a time when the praxis is needed in the face of multiple crises, disjuncture, forms of violence, repressive governments, calls for hope, resistance movements, and social innovations in our communities. Appeals for decolonial feminisms are an important turning point in scholarship and community activism. Genealogies have multiple meanings—in notions of genealogies, one's past is a central ideological feature of a national and cultural sense of belonging. Genealogies are also bound individual and collective invocations of legacies, where it is a "conscious thinking and rethinking and historicity, a rethinking which has . . . autonomy and self-determination at its core" (Alexander and Mohanty 1997, 58–59). Recognizing that each contributor of this edited anthology comes from a different location of examination and histories, including locations in Turtle Island, Asia, Latinidad, Africa, and Southwest Asia, this project has multiple genealogies. *Decolonial Feminism in Abya Yala* is an exemplar of an anthology that examines decolonial feminisms in the Caribbean, Meso, and South America, where Black, Indigenous, and racialized women in Latin America and the Spanish-speaking Caribbean resist dictatorships and colonialities through events that can be traced to the 1970s and 1980s struggles onward (Espinosa-Miñoso et al. 2022, x). As some genealogies may be traced with specificity in time and location, here we invoke the multiple of spatiality, place, land connection, and histories as the project of decolonial feminisms—that it is an invitation to conceptualize the multiple histories bound to individuals and collectives, specifically located.

The Formation of the Anthology

We began conversations in 2019 regarding the materialization of the Democratizing Knowledge fellowship narratives into a publication. Many of us were shaped by multiple precarities pre-pandemic as early-career scholars. After workshopping drafts at a Democratizing Knowledge Institute workshop hosted at Pendle Hill Quaker Study, Retreat, and Conference Center, outside of Philadelphia, Pennsylvania, in 2019, the co-editors facilitated virtual workshopping of submissions in 2021. *Decolonial Feminist Genealogies and Futures* is the manifestation of community conversations about a shared decolonial and transnational feminist praxis and vision. When we began this edited anthology, it was during a "pre-pandemic" moment, and as time continued it was during the pandemic. As the book nears publication, five years later, many of our contributors' worlds have changed—some continued in higher education through promotions, tenure, and completing doctoral degrees, as others ventured into the realms beyond the walls of the academe. Some contributors even chose to find their radical possibilities beyond the educational institution. Many of our contributors and editors experienced loss of loved ones, and the pains of supporting those living during a time of ongoing inequity due to the colonial capitalist structures. While there were many wounds experienced before the anthology and since its materialization, the nod toward a "future" invokes a politics of optimism that is so vital to our survival. As the violence of coloniality is named in this collection, it is the possibility of decolonization that drives, moves, and inspires this anthology.

Decolonial Feminist Genealogies and Futures is a visionary framing of radical feminist praxis, rooted in a unique history. Chapters challenge conventional boundaries of time and space around which labor and resistance are imagined to be organized. Methodological approaches engaged include participant observation, *pláticas*, critical participatory action research, spatial analysis, interviews, *testimonio*, grounded theory, and historical analysis. A feminist praxis of multiple modalities, the chapters are inspired by art exhibits, poetry, artifacts, sharing circles, and social movements. The anthology's chapters make visible radical struggles across four thematic areas: subversive labor; spatialities and temporalities; resistance; and genealogies and feminist futures. Within each of these areas, contributors engage a range of struggles.

A central subtheme of transnational feminisms is theorizing labor and imagining how decolonization may be enacted. Thinking with scholars such as Anibal Quijano, Sylvia Wynter, and María Lugones, we recognize that colonial systems are structured by systems of exploitation that further the organization of coloniality through wage labor systems that take the form of slavery, servitude, and racialized labor. Therefore, this edited anthology begins with a collaborative examination of the gender-based forms of labor in the modern colonial capitalist system, in Part 1. Amanda Jurno, Bruno Moreschi, and Monique Lemos contribute "Late Capitalism and Gender: Stories, Challenges, and Perceptions of Women Workers Who Train Artificial Intelligence on Amazon Mechanical Turk." The Group on Artificial Intelligence and Art (GAIA), at the University of São Paulo's Innovation Center (Brazil), surveys and interviews Amazon Mechanical Turk (AMT) women workers from Brazil, India, England, and France. We come to know this on-demand, 24-7 workforce through their conditions of precarious labor in a transnational context.

From the precarious conditions of the workforce in an ever-growing technological world, we return to a familiar condition of the academe. Through the cohering of decolonial feminisms with intersectionality, Lynn Hampton and Sylvia Mendoza Aviña's chapter, "Cultivating a Decolonial Feminist Praxis through Testimonio and *Pláticas*," takes the reader into the precarious and violent conditions that contingent faculty labor in. Through a methodology of witnessing as *testimonio*, the reader enters into the world of Hampton, who labors as a Black woman in the academe. Through witnessing Hampton's disclosure, specific themes emerge, such as how Black women's contingent labor, bodies, and knowledge are exploited in institutions; misogynoir makes its way from visual culture into the optics and practices of the everyday as the hatred and distrust toward Black women; and the resulting impact of misogynoir takes the form of spirit murder.

Azza Basarudin and Tina Beyene's chapter seeds the discussion of decolonizing knowledge through an "unapologetic feminist" reflection of their pedagogies during crisis in "Embodied Precarity: Feminist Politics, Laboring Bodies of Color, and the Neoliberal University." Through reflections on their own teachings during a global pandemic, they remind us of the ever-pressing nature of relinking racism with the structures that create precarious labor. Part 1 ends with an imagining and enacting of a decolonial feminist praxis through collaboration among Indigenous women scholars. Tricia McGuire-Adams and Janice Cindy Gaudet (chapter dedicated to Dr. Jennifer Ward), in "The Emotional Labor of Reconciliation and Indigenization: Indigenous Women Creating Decolonial Feminist Praxis within the Academy," craft a feminist Indigenous praxis through the exemplar of poetry and narrative derived from Canadian scholars. The authors demonstrate the expectations of reconciliation labor and the emotional labor associated with it; they created kind, loving spaces from which to generate support, and in so doing, crafted an Indigenous feminist praxis. Through a method of narrative and poetry, they enact a form of truth-telling and care, modeling a praxis of collaboration and what they refer to as "codes of wellness": the acts of caring among each other and for oneself.

Understanding the relationships among space, temporality, and decolonial feminisms requires grappling with land, bodies occupying space, migration, and (de)colonized space and place, which segues into Part 2 of the anthology: "Spatialities and Temporalities." Lydia Zakel's chapter "Methods, Modes, and Mapping: The (Re)Construction of Palestinian Sites as an Act of Return" enacts participatory action research (PAR) for "counter-mapping." Zakel uses modes of mapping to (re)construct three different villages in Palestine—Sataf, Miska, and Al-Nada. Counter-mapping then becomes a decolonial act for understanding displacement and envisioning returns. Exploring the relationship between displacement and capitalistic systems, Shireen Keyl's chapter, "Subaltern Ways of Knowing: A Critical Spatial Analysis of Migrant Worker Knowledge Production in Beirut, Lebanon," spatially grapples with a migrant center in Lebanon. Through methods of in-depth qualitative interviews coupled with participant observation, Keyl brings to the fore spatial (in)justice that incorporates a critical frame in its ontological analysis of the "triple dialectic": the social/societal, the temporal/historical, and the spatial/geographical. Keyl examines how migrant laborers resist spatial erasure and violence through creating a sense of community and educational support for migrant women laborers in Lebanon.

Temporality is deeply tied to space in decolonial visions; therefore, to conclude Part 2, we end "Spatialities and Temporalities" with Rachel Afi Quinn's chapter "Say, Who's Online? Building Feminist Futures through South Asian Collectivity in Texas." Through the exemplar of South Asian Youth in Houston Unite (SAYHU), a transnational feminist collective based in Houston, Texas, readers meet the SAYHU collaboration, which has roots in Bangladesh, Bhutan, India, Nepal, the Maldives, Pakistan, Sri Lanka, and other parts of the Indo-Caribbean diaspora. Quinn reflects on participatory research through the collective organizing of SAYHU. As the spatiality of Texas emerges, so too does the space of the Internet, where the reflections capture the work of collective solidarities in a time of global pandemic. Through a transnational feminist framework and praxis, the parking lot, the digital space, and the real-world fatigue of a Zoom connection all cohere to material transnational solidarities across time and space, as well as the related decolonial possibilities and challenges.

Part 3 explores the theme of resistance. Whether through the hijab and contemporary art, children's expressive bodies, or university curricula, feminist resistance responds to the boundaries and borders imposed by others. In this series of chapters, historiography, critical participatory action research, participant observation, and autoethnography are engaged to highlight resistance from the margins. Throughout these chapters, the relationship between local and transnational ties are highlighted.

In Utah, Ana Carolina Antunes introduces the *The Hijab Project* art exhibit in the chapter "'I Am Not Oppressed! Give It a Rest!': *The Hijab Project* As Resistance to Western Narratives about Muslim Women." Youth use creative collaborations to resist Islamophobia in a predominantly white state, where they are minoritized as being Muslim, migrant people of color. In the next chapter, Akanksha Misra's descriptive ethnographic voice takes the reader into classrooms of Istanbul (Turkey) and Hyderabad (India), where children's bodily curiosity and exploration are the focal point. "Children's Bodies and the Sensual Disruptions of Schooling in India and Turkey" centers children's bodies as sensual, filled with desire, and visceral, in a place where caste, race, gender, and religion all cohere. Part 3 concludes with Esther O. Ajayi-Lowo's chapter, "Decolonial Pedagogy: Resisting through Transnational WGS Introductory Courses." She is a Nigerian educator who develops curriculum for a university in Texas, appealing for the centering of transnational feminist pedagogies as a means to facilitate subversive teachings, where resisting colonial epistemologies and democratizing knowledge are made possible. Together, these chapters highlight possibilities for engaging feminist resistance in different locations, including in collective movement, art exhibits, nonconforming bodies, and university curricula.

The last section of the anthology, Part 4, moves the reader toward feminist genealogies and futures. We are invited to re-orient ourselves in relation to our histories by adopting a migrant vernacular; to learn how ancestral knowledge systems are inspiring Indigenous youth; to engage the long historical arc of Native American women's resistance; and to consider Ethnic Studies as part of a decolonial feminist movement. Through each of these chapters, history is instructive in informing a vision for the future. These chapters develop new glossaries, engage multiple languages, theorize Native women's hereditary voice, and invite a reinterpretation of academic disciplines.

Angel Sutjipto and Eun-Jin Keish Kim's "[A] Migrant Vernacular" redefines normative and legal definitions about migrants. Through this collaborative authorship, Sutjipto and Kim weave language, memory, and histories of exclusionary immigration policies to examine the violent structures of citizenship upheld through erasure of Black and Indigenous lives. This chapter reorients a collection of words that haunt the lives of migrant, undocumented, queer, feminist, anti-racist, anti-capitalist beings. In "Warrior Butterflies Walking with the Ancestors: Xicanx Indigenous Youth Becoming Leaders of Transformational Justice," Cueponcaxochitl D. Moreno Sandoval, Miriam G. Valdovinos, Elisa Contreras, and Xochitl E. López Andrade share a ten-year collaborative study that examines the intergenerational intention and action of unearthing what they refer to as ancestral knowledge systems (AKS) with youth leaders in an urban high school. The chapter describes a pilgrimage to Tenochtitlan and Teotihuacan (Mexico) in 2010, and the ongoing significance of returning to the past, to enact a decolonial praxis of the present. This authorship includes student participants and DK fellows.

Leece Lee-Oliver's "A Red Feminist Manifest: Meditations on Native American Women, Sovereignty Protectors, and the Liturgies of Colonial Violence" re-historicizes the Sand Creek Massacre through auto-ethnographic and archival methods that unearth a history of violence through storytelling, through what Lee refers to as a hereditary voice. We are reminded of the stakes of education and our context of the academe in Xamuel Bañales's "Not Only an Academic Field, but Also Movements: Advancing Ethnic Studies with Decolonial Feminisms." The chapter makes appeals for protest, refusal, and the adoption of a decolonial feminist praxis framework. These chapters are in the final section of the book because they represent new, yet historically rooted, feminist trajectories.

We write this introduction in a synthesized voice, albeit journeying into the project with different genealogies, orientations, methodologies, and lived experiences. As the reader will see, many of the contributions are coauthored or informed by multiple voices. We have endeavored to frame this introduction and anthology through the multiplicity of voices, perspectives, and multiple modalities of a decolonial feminist praxis. We invite the reader to enter into a feminist praxis that is grounded in decolonized visions and futures.

Bibliography

Alarcon, Wanda, Dalida María Benfield, Annie Isabel Fukushima, Marelle Maese-Cohen, eds. 2020. "World-Making and World-Traveling with Decolonial Feminisms and Women of Color." Special Issue. *Frontiers: Journal of Women Studies* 41(1).

Alexander, M. Jacqui, and Chandra Talpade Mohanty. 1997. *Feminist Genealogies, Colonial Legacies, Democratic Futures*. Routledge.

Anzaldúa, Gloria E. 1987. *Borderlands/La Frontera: The New Mestiza*. Aunt Lute Books.

Bahng, Aimee. 2018. *Migrant Futures: Decolonizing Speculation in Financial Times*. Duke University Press.

Carty, Linda. 2005. "Not a Nanny: A Gendered Transnational Analysis of Caribbean Domestic Workers in New York City." In *Decolonizing the Academy: Africa Diaspora Studies,* edited by Carole Boyce Davies, Meredith Gadsby, Charles Peterson, and Henrietta Williams. Trenton, NJ: Africa World Press.

Césaire, Aimée. 2000. *Discourse on Colonialism*. New York University Press.

DiPietro, Pedro, Jennifer McWeeny, and Shireen Roshanravan, eds. 2019. *Speaking Face to Face: The Visionary Philosophy of María Lugones*. SUNY Press.

Espinosa-Miñoso, Yuderkys, María Lugones, and Nelson Maldonado-Torres. 2022. *Decolonial Feminism in Abya Yala: Caribbean, Meso, and South American Contributions and Challenges (Global Critical Caribbean Thought)*. Rowman & Littlefield Publishers.

Fukushima, Annie Isabel. 2019. *Migrant Crossings: Witnessing Human Trafficking in the US*. Stanford University Press.

Glenn, Evelyn Nakano. 2015. "Settler Colonialism as Structure: A Framework for Comparative Studies of U.S. Race and Gender Formation." *Sociology of Race and Ethnicity* 1(1): 52–72. https://doi.org/10.1177/2332649214560440.

Grosfoguel, Ramon. 2007. "The Epistemic Decolonial Turn: Beyond Political-Economy Paradigms." *Cultural Studies* 21(2–3): 211–223.

Grosz, Elizabeth. 2002. "Feminist Futures?" *Tulsa Studies in Women's Literature* 21(1): 13–20.

Hernández, Ellie, and Gloria Anzaldúa. Fall & Winter 1995–96. "Re-Thinking Margins and Borders: An Interview with Gloria Anzaldúa." *Remapping the Border Subject* 18 (1/2): 7–15.

Keating, Cricket. 2005. "Building Coalitional Consciousness." *Hypatia* 17(2): 86–103.

Lloyd, David, and Patrick Wolfe. 2015. "Settler Colonial Logics and the Neoliberal Regime." *Settler Colonial Studies,* http://dx.doi.org/10.1080/2201473X.2015.1035361.

Lugones, María. 2003. *Pilgrimages/Peregrinajes: Theorizing Coalition Against Multiple Oppressions.* Rowman and Littlefield.

Lugones, María. 2007. "Heterosexualism and the Colonial/Modern Gender System." *Hypatia* 22 (1): 186–209, http://www.jstor.org/stable/4640051.

Lugones, María. 2010. "Toward a Decolonial Feminism." *Hypatia* 25(4): 742–759.

Maldonado-Torres, Nelson. 2007. "On the Coloniality of Being." *Cultural Studies,* 21:2–3, 240–270, https://doi.org/10.1080/09502380601162548.

Mendez, X. 2015. "Notes Toward a Decolonial Feminist Methodology: Revisiting the Race/Gender Matrix." *Trans-Scripts* 5:41–59.

Mignolo, Walter. 2012. *Local Histories/Global Designs: Coloniality, Subaltern Knowledges, and Border Thinking.* Princeton University Press.

Mohanty, Chandra Talpade. 1984. "Under Western Eyes: Feminist Scholarship and Colonial Discourses." *boundary* 2, Vol. 12/13, Vol. 12, no. 3–Vol. 13, no. 1, On Humanism and the University I: The Discourse of Humanism: 333–358.

Mohanty, Chandra Talpade, and Linda E. Carty, eds. 2018. *Feminist Freedom Warriors: Genealogies, Justice, Politics, and Hope.* Haymarket Press.

Moya, Paula. 2006. "María Lugones *Pilgramages/Peregrinajes: Theorizing Coalition against Multiple Oppressions.* Lanham, Md.: Rowman & Littlefield, 2003." *Hypatia*, 21(3), 198–202. https://doi.org/10.1017/S0887536700016561.

Ortega, Mariana. 2017. "Decolonial Woes and Practices of Un-knowing." *The Journal of Speculative Philosophy* 31(3): 504–516. https://doi.org/10.5325/jspecphil.31.3.0504.

Quijano, Anibal. 2000. ¡QUÉ TAL RAZA! Rev. Venez. de Economía y Ciencias Sociales 6(1), 37–45.

Sandoval, Chela. 2000. *Methodology of the Oppressed.* University of Minnesota Press.

Tambe, Ashwini, and Millie Thayer, eds. 2021. *Transnational Feminist Itineraries: Situating Theory and Activist Practice.* Duke University Press.

Zaytoun, K. D. 2019. "A Focus on the 'I' in the 'I→We': Considering the Lived Experience of Self-in-Coalition in Active Subjectivity." In *Speaking Face to Face: The Visionary Philosophy of María Lugones*, edited by Pedro DiPietro, Jennifer McWeeny, and Shireen Roshanravan, 47–64. SUNY Press.

PART I
Subversive Labor

1

Late Capitalism and Gender
Stories, Challenges, and Perceptions of Women Workers Who Train Artificial Intelligence on Amazon Mechanical Turk

AMANDA JURNO, BRUNO MORESCHI,
and MONIQUE LEMOS

Imagine waking up early in the morning and getting ready to work, and being expected to be willing to spend a day divided between tasks online and doing housework until late at night. Now, imagine having to do repetitive tasks on a computer, with a timer ticking on the screen, while your child cries in the background and lunch is still to be cooked. And imagine, after all this, having to hear from friends, family, and in public discourse, that all the tasks done are not considered "a job." In fact, one of these jobs, domestic labor, is not paid at all; and the other one is significantly underpaid—workers perform tasks online for pennies. Surreal and impractical but, paradoxically, a reality that is utterly aligned with the pillars of patriarchal capitalism.

This is the daily routine of many women who work on the Amazon Mechanical Turk (AMT), a platform where people from all over the world work remotely performing Human Intelligent Tasks (HITs). HITs are the small, but important, tasks responsible for making the so-called artificial intelligence (AI) feasible, such as labeling data or supervising the operation of an algorithm. By looking at the relationship between women and AMT, we discuss how AI automation is a complex and opaque architecture between humans and machines and not "caricatural 'alien minds' that self-reproduce in silico" (Pasquinelli and Joler 2020), as technology companies try to make us believe. The main objective of listening to women, who are part of the human layer behind these automation processes (the "turkers," as AMT workers are called), is to try to understand how gender permeates the processes enabled and inhibited by the platform's practices.

This focus on understanding the bodies and physicalities embedded in the machine learning process relates to the concerns of the Group on Artificial Intelligence and Art (GAIA), which we are part of in Brazil. GAIA is a network of humanities researchers, artists, programmers, and engineers located at the Artificial Intelligence Center (C4AI) of the University of São Paulo. The group develops projects to analyze and question contemporary digital infrastructures, considering their social implications and refuting the idea that technology is an abstraction (Donna Haraway 1988; see also Jenna Burrell 2016). Our interest in researching the turkers' work and experiences originated from the realization that a large part of Brazilian engineers and programmers, who are responsible for building the so-called "smart machines," knew almost nothing about turkers—even those who use their services.

Our choice to look at an AI path permeated by humans also relates to our context as Global South researchers, from Brazil, in Latin America. Technology was never just "magic" for us, as certain Global North promotional narratives describe. The layers of natural resources exploitation (53 percent of the world's lithium is in Argentina, Chile, and Bolivia—Hernandez 2017) and increasing labor precarity (Out of 5 million Uber drivers and delivery workers, one is in Brazil—Uber 2020) were always visible for us. Thus, to analyze technology from a Global South perspective is also to think about practices of extracting bodies and natural resources, in a logic historically consolidated by our intense colonial past (that is still present).

First, we contextualize AMT and its workers. Then, we explain our methodology that mixes bibliographic references and fieldwork, and we present the main results that emerged from our approach to women turkers. We conclude by showing how gender issues that appeared concerning the AMT platform should not be seen as specific to it, but as a strategy that is part of the so-called "late capitalism" (Crary 2016), which is to control and profit twice from the women labor force at home.

Work on AMT

Part of the US company Amazon, the AMT has as its slogan: "access a global, on-demand, 24×7 workforce" (Amazon Mechanical Turk 2020a), which directly relates to Crary's (2013) book title *24/7: Late Capitalism and the Ends of Sleep*—in which the author describes this model as "the imposition of a machinic model of duration and efficiency onto the human body" (see also Fernanda Bruno 2013) at the service of global and uninterrupted infrastructure.

AMT is a "crowdsourcing marketplace" that allegedly "makes it easier for individuals and businesses to outsource their processes and jobs to a distributed workforce who can perform these tasks virtually" (Amazon Mechanical Turk 2020a). These tasks can be anything, such as data validation, survey participation, or content moderation. In the words of one of our interviewees, the AMT is "a great job fair, where everything is allowed, or almost everything," which is confirmed by the list of some HITs done by mechanical turks: "Draw boxes on lab rats in different pictures"; "Mark body parts of people fighting"; "Locate hard-to-find business addresses on their original websites"; "Make facial expressions on the computer camera"; "Rate tweets on Twitter"; "Transcribe commercial receipts"; "Categorize images from pornographic sites" (Moreschi, Pereira, and Cozman 2020). Below, the image shows a dashboard of a mechanical turk account.

AMT was created in 2005, initially for Amazon's internal use, to exclude repeated product advertisements. Despite being the best-known online work

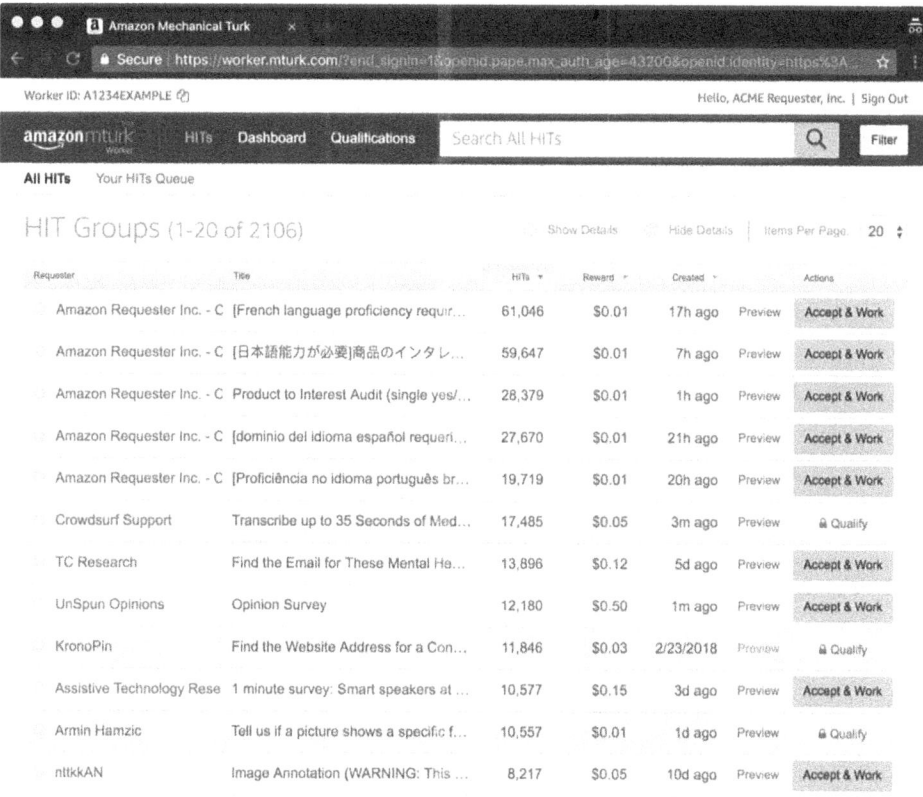

FIGURE 1.1. Representation of an Amazon Mechanical Turk (AMT) HITs page, designed based on an AMT's blog post (Link: https://blog.mturk.com/quick-update-another-improvement-to-the-mturk-worker-experience-9cfd0b1963e7). Source: Thiago Vinícius Adaltino Ferreira (2024)

platform on this new algorithmic conquest of capitalism, it is not the only one: Clickworker, Figure Eight, Fiverr, and JobBoy are some competitors. For Finn (2017), the mass of workers in these technological practices underground is "the final telos of algorithmic labor."

According to Difallah et al. (2018), 75 percent of turks live in the United States, 16 percent in India, and 9 percent in other countries. Although the total number of workers reported by AMT is generic, "about 500,000 registered" (Amazon Mechanical Turk 2020b), and has not been updated for more than two years, it is estimated that more than two thousand workers can be found simultaneously in the platform at any time (Difallah et al. 2018). This shows that we are not discussing something specific and residual, but a significant workforce that grows every day (Kuek et al. 2015). More than the increase in work in digital environments, this new force indicates an intensification of society's datafication (Bastin and Paola Tubaro 2018). These workers are part of what Ursula Huws (2003) calls "cybertariat," as well as Antunes (2019) and Grohmann (2018) name them "cyber-proletariat" (*authors' translation*).

FIGURE 1.2. "Home office," Source: Unknown author.

The proportion of women in this space lacks consensus: while Difallah et al. (2018) indicate that AMT is 51 percent women, Ipeirotis (2010) shows that women's participation in the workforce may be 70 percent. It is also important to highlight the dilemma of carrying out demographic investigations on the platform, where results vary between surveys, due to different time zones and the difficulty of checking responses. However, even if women are not underrepresented in AMT, it doesn't mean that conditions are equal in this digital work environment. When listening to women workers, it became evident that the logic that "the two sexes have never divided the world up equally" (Simone de Beauvoir 2011) remains true in the so-called gig economy.

Methodology

First, we did some bibliographic research to understand the specificities of digital work (Gillespie 2010; Woodcock 2019; Srnicek 2017; Gray and Suri 2019; Zyskowski and Milland 2018; Moreschi, Pereira, and Cozman 2020; Difallah et al. 2018; Irani 2015), gender and intersectionality (Federici 2012; Beauvoir 2011; Collins 1997; Davis 2016; Ribeiro 2017), and how these two topics—digital work and gender—intersect (Haraway 1988; Atanasoski and Vora 2015; Jarrett 2015; D'Ignazio and Klein 2020).

Then, to understand what women mechanical turks think about gender issues in their work routine, we interviewed fifty-one workers. We published a ten-question questionnaire on AMT, in English, filtered to receive only answers from women, and paid US $7 for the HIT—71 percent more than the average payment, which is US $2 (Difallah et al. 2018). A conversation was extended to participants who provided their emails in the questionnaire. These interviewees were paid another US $7 for agreeing to be interviewed.

Our approach to specific mechanical turks is based on the urgency to make technologic processes comprehensible (Winner 1977; Atanasoski and Vora 2015) and to give human life to abstract terms that are frequently used to categorize online platforms' workers, such as "ghost workers" (Gray and Suri 2019).

Approximations: Issues Raised

The age of the fifty-one participants ranged from twenty-one to sixty-seven years old, with thirty-seven participants being between the ages of twenty-five and forty-five (73 percent). Most of the mechanical turks interviewed lived in the United States (thirty-eight, or 75 percent), with the rest of the interviewees residing in Brazil (five), India (five), England (two), and France (one). Regarding their marital status, nearly two-thirds (thirty-one) declared being married (61 percent), twelve single (23.5 percent), and eight divorced (15.5 percent). The majority had children (thirty-two of them, or 63 percent)—fifteen had one, sixteen had two, and one had three children. Even though the AMT platform divides the tasks as a gender-binary, in the HIT task we wrote that we were looking for both cis and trans women.

General Problems

The first non-demographic question was about the platform's work situation and did not focus on gender issues. The answers related to previous non-gender-specific research, such as that with Brazilian turkers (Moreschi, Pereira, and Cozman 2020) and with people from the United States or India (Gray and Suri 2019). Rosa, a thirty-seven-year-old single woman from the United States, summarized the answers: "Terrible pay, long hours, requestors that never get back to you, unfair rejections, inconsistent hours and pay." Others complained about low payments:

> "Requesters posting HITs with very low pay and lack of available HITs";
> "Very low HIT payments only found";
> "Since the pandemic, it seems that it is harder to get decent work for decent pay."
> Or high competition on the platform: "Congested, there is too much competition";
> "I spend more time trying to catch HITs than actually doing the work."

As in other types of remote jobs, AMT workers are responsible for their work infrastructure. The costs of maintenance are not considered in their payment, making work instruments for Amazon and the requesters a "constant capital, without any risk and without the need to have their physical properties" (Antunes and Filgueiras 2020, 68, *authors' translation*). In the answers, the women talked about having to pay for faster internet and good computers to try to minimize competition for better-paid HITs. This situation is also part of a process that "abstract[s] physical and cultural infrastructure away altogether" (Finn 2017, 327) creating a "non-place" of work—that is, a territory as diluted as it is difficult to regulate. As Sueli, forty-three, and Lélia, fifty-three, both from the United States, explain, this cloud is not abstract but is the precarious worker's home and equipment: "I cannot seem to work on high paying HITs. I am qualified but then it seems like my computer is too slow to accept the HIT"; "I cannot catch HITs because I can only afford a slow internet."

Linda, also from the United States, detailed a recent problem when living with a man and with little domestic infrastructure:

The biggest thing holding me back is my really crummy laptop. I left a bad situation right before Covid happened, and the man who I kicked out of my home left his laptop. It's the only reason I'm even able to provide at all for my kids right now, but it's SO SLOW and awful and old. I don't have money for a new one, so it has to do for now.

Geopolitical issues also emerged in their answers: HITs that are specific for US workers. This makes mechanical turks of other nationalities feel somehow ignored by AMT since there are "many tasks only being available to US turkers," as told by Bell, a thirty-seven-year-old English woman.

Until September 2020, Amazon was not directly paying turkers of some nationalities, such as Brazilians and Indians (Moreschi, Pereira, and Cozman 2020). For Brazilians, the payment was made via a gift card exclusive to the US Amazon website, forcing workers to buy products in dollars and pay for international shipment—at the same company they work for! To avoid this, they looked for alternatives such as selling gift cards on online auctions, generally losing money due to fluctuating currency and commonly charged fee payments, leading to more precarity. The Brazilian mechanical turk Conceição, twenty-seven, summed up this situation as "very tiring and frustrating."

For nine mechanical turks (out of fifty-one) who answered our questionnaire, AMT has no problems. As for sixty-seven-year-old Maya, from the United States and new in the platform: "I haven't faced any difficulties at this time, although, I have only been doing this for 7 weeks."

Domestic Work:
Housekeeping and AMT at the Same Time

A recurring topic was the need to coordinate housekeeping and AMT work. According to Vilma: "I feel like right now I am working the equivalent of a full-time job or more on AMT yet also nearly having the responsibilities of a full-time homemaker and that is stressful." Erica, also from the United States, who was married and a mother, affirmed that this synchroneity of obligations relates to gender and made her work harder: "I think I have to prove my worth more than others and I have to spend more time turking than men do. I have to find a good balance and multitask and take breaks in between turking for household chores." This response relates to the assumption of domestic work being a responsibility of women, as it has traditionally been imposed on them, but also to the fact that "it has been transformed into a natural attribute of our female psyche and personality" (Federici 2012, 16). Silvia Federici argues that, because housekeeping is not considered a job, wages are denied, and housekeeping is transformed into "an act of love," the figure of the housewife was created to serve the male worker, leaving him free to perform his role in the capitalist system. This "peculiar combination of physical, emotional, and sexual services that are involved in the role women must perform" makes such work "so burdensome and at the same time so invisible" (Silvia Federici 2012, 17). This led some of the interviewees to separate specific days to do the housework: "I usually clean on Saturday, but work [Monday to Friday]. I might tidy up a bit here and there, but most of the time I just leave it for a non-working day." Another interviewee stated, "I get my domestic work and responsibilities for home done first thing in the morning so that I have plenty of time to work on AMT during the day."

Even though this juggling is not specific to AMT women, the work on the platform has a particularity: tasks can appear at any time. If workers want to get HITs that pay well and guarantee a good average payment, they must be always available. "A lot is about being fast enough and being on this platform at the right time," said Kimberlé, from the United States. This discourse materializes the concept of "heteromation" (Ekbia and Nardi 2017), a mechanism of capitalism that aims to place and maintain the largest possible number of humans in the circuit—the opposite of automation, which, theoretically, aims to free human beings from work. For Mary L. Gray and Suri (2019), this is the "paradox of the last mile of automation" that makes us think about whether there really will be a final stage, in which the automation process will be fully concluded. The paradox resides in the fact that the smarter the machines become, the more issues appear demanding human help. In fact, the utopia of humans being free from work, in practice, "produces platforms that must actively conceal the fact that other forms of 'miserable' work are still being done by human labor" (Atanasoski and Vora 2015, 20).

Given this unpredictability in the AMT, it becomes difficult to divide the work routine rationally, which generates anxiety, stress, and negative consequences on these workers' health: "I do almost all the housework. I live with constant anxiety and pressure and frustration. I am diagnosed with GAD and MDD." Another informed us that she had "arthritis in [her] hands and spine."

Some women reproduced the idea that they could "multitask" due to their gender. Like Audre, from the United States, for whom the housekeeping and childcare of her two children did not interfere with her performance: "Being a woman, I am very good at multitasking and am able to focus and concentrate on multiple things at the same time. Having my kids at home and working from home does not deter me from my AMT performance." Erica reinforced this stereotype but recognized the difficulties it imposed: "I have to take care of my son and also do another job and multitask so it makes it more difficult to turk and make the most of my time spent on here."

The turkers' responses highlighted the AMT overwork, but they also materialized the burden carried due to the housework routine. Like technological practices, housework routines are not abstractions and consume lives, especially among low-income women. On average, it is estimated that a housewife spends between 3,000 and 4,000 hours on housekeeping per year (Davis 2011; Oakley 1976).

AMT and Children

In previous GAIA research (Moreschi et al. 2020), we talked to Florynce, a Brazilian woman turker who has worked at AMT since 2018. Among her main motivations for working on the platform was the possibility of buying specific toys on the US Amazon website (like Baby Alive dolls and Legos not available in Brazil for her kids). In this research, by talking to other women turkers who are also mothers, we realized that Florynce is no exception. In the questionnaire, many women related their work on the platform to their children. Yet, while Florynce found in them a motivation to carry on, our interviewees highlighted the difficulties they faced when balancing work and childcare. For example, Bell, a British single mother, reported feeling guilty and having concentration problems caused by difficulties in dealing with the AMT and children (this difficulty is emphasized in her repetition of the verb "try"):

> Trying to fit it around childcare, difficulty concentrating sometimes due to this. I feel guilty if I'm completing work when my son is around and not paying him attention. . . . I try to fit my domestic tasks around work but it is hard and sometimes I sacrifice a tidy home to make money because we need money at the moment and that can feel quite stressful and I feel guilty.

Linda, who had two children, also talked about balancing responsibilities: "I have to take a lot of breaks having two kids. They need to have meals made, they fight, they need to be taught school and entertained. It's definitely a juggle." In other conversations, Linda said that one of the main difficulties was making her children understand that being at home does not mean that she was not working—"it's WORK time," she repeats to the children. Working as a turker for more than ten years, she said to us that working in one room at home while her children were in another, nearby, often made her feel sad.

Sueli, also from the United States and with two children, recognized that this situation put her at disadvantage. Consequently, the nights were a time with no child interruptions to work on the platform: "I feel I am productive enough but not that much because of my responsibility as a mother and as a woman I have very few spare-time to work at AMT. I have lots of work at home. I sometimes stay up at night to work. My kids are all asleep so I have time to work."

Sueli's working nights allow us to once again relate work conditions on AMT with Crary's (2013) reflections. According to Crary (2013), over the years, the US Defense Department has spent large amounts of money funding research on the brain activity of birds during prolonged sleepless periods, hoping to acquire knowledge applicable to humans, especially soldiers.

Contrarily, Vilma, a mother of an autistic adult from the United States, found an alternative for coordinating her daughter's care and continuing to work. However, she recognized that this context makes her routine difficult:

> It negatively affects my productivity somewhat because of having to cook dinner and attend to stuff around the house, and sometimes stuff with my daughter, who's an adult but on the autism spectrum so needs help with things sometimes and I sort of function as a caregiver to her often—that can impact my ability to do HITs.

In more conversations (via email), Vilma explained that AMT was a feasible job because it allowed her to take care of her family, but not only her daughter. She could also help her parents, who lived in another house and often needed her to prepare their meals.

Work Seen as Non-Work

Silvia Federici (2012) considers housework the "most pervasive manipulation" and "the subtlest violence" (42) that capitalism has ever perpetrated. By seeking to convince women that it is a "natural, unavoidable, and even fulfilling activity" (43), so that they would accept working without a wage, capitalism perpetuated the idea that domestic labor is not labor. This situation generates expectations and social functions that are imposed on women, said Judith, a thirty-seven-year-old French woman: "As a woman, you are expected to do all the household chores so I'm a little stressed in managing my time doing the housework and working this job."

This structural imposition is not a generic result of capitalism where the subjects act to make it concrete. Dandara and Kimberlé, two US women aged twenty-five and twenty-nine, respectively, justified their housekeeping responsibilities because their partners worked outside the home: "I do most of the housework because my fiancé works full time. It's a little difficult to balance both because I sometimes get distracted from doing HITs because I have to do laundry or start cooking dinner, etc." Another interviewee conveyed, "I take on the responsibilities for the home because my partner works not at home. There are times when I choose to get housework/errands done before I start to do work on here and other times I'll work here first, then housework later."

This takes us to another recurrence in the answers: the existence of partners who do not recognize the turking work as labor, perhaps because it is performed at home. In the cases of the French Judith and the British Bell, this denial of AMT work was described: "My husband does not consider this as work and expects me to do most of the household chores." Another interviewee stated, "I would ideally need to not need to sleep! Or failing that for my partner to be more understanding and take my AMT work seriously." The justification of the little, if any, help from partners because of their "full time" jobs seems to be a contradiction, since many of the women workers reported the necessity of being always available at AMT (see figure 1.2). To put it another way, AMT work in practice does not seem to require a full day, but is also a full-time job—with the aggravation that it has no starting or ending time and is concomitant with domestic labor because it is done at home. This is what thirty-seven-year-old Brazilian Grada, who is married and has a son, reported: "As a woman I have to take care of the home and family, as well as myself, and working at AMT requires us to stay in front of the computer all the time waiting for jobs or doing jobs."

Lélia, a US fifty-three-year-old, complained about this accumulation of domestic responsibilities: "I have to try and work and do a million other things over the course of a day and it is constantly stressful. There is never enough time because of the timers on HITs. I am guessing men do not have as many other responsibilities as women on the platform."

Dandara, who talked about her husband working all day outside the home, also agreed that accumulation of work was directly related to gender: "I feel like I have to do a lot more around the house than my fiancé, maybe just because I'm a woman, like cleaning, doing laundry, cooking, etc."

Two women (out of fifty-one) declared sharing housekeeping tasks with partners. Michelle, a thirty-five-year-old woman from the United States with two children, said: "My husband and I split the housework and kids' stuff evenly to allow me to be able to work so I don't have to work outside of the home." Berenice, a twenty-eight-year-old from the United States, also shared the responsibilities: "My boyfriend and I share the housework. If I am too busy, he will pick up for the most part. However, there are times where I will have to ask him to do things and I have to take time away from working to do chores."

Anonymity in the AMT as a Possible Advantage

Anonymity provided by AMT emerged as a counterpoint to gender problems faced on a daily basis. Because their bodies are not exposed, some women said they felt safer when working on the platform. For Vilma, a forty-eight-year-old from the United States, not being harassed as an AMT was an advantage:

"I like the fact that I don't have to do emotional labor at AMT like I would in an office job and like I do in my other part-time job. I also like that nobody yells or swears at me on AMT, like I've experienced at work sometimes. I like that I can wear whatever I want when working on AMT and nobody cares, and I'm free from harassment here so it feels safer."

Beatriz, a thirty-six-year-old from the United States, also pointed to anonymity as a positive feature on the platform: "It's really good, to be honest. Since I am behind a screen, my sex doesn't really affect anything and judgments on work are purely 'Did you do a good job?' I feel that it is more equal for men/women so it's good for me."

Other answers followed this direction:

"I have not received any sexism";

"I've never really thought about my gender in relation to turk. I don't think it's really relevant. My gender doesn't define my ability to turk";

"I don't really face any discrimination."

We were shocked that the women turkers considered the absence of harassment an advantage, but it is important to note that anonymity emerges as an unanticipated benefit in AMT. It is a positive effect that does not seem to have been thought to benefit the working woman. The lack of individualization of these workers directly relates to employers' profit pursuit. As Angela Davis (2011, 234) pointed out, in the capitalist system, the employer is not concerned with "the way labor-power is produced and sustained, he only is concerned about its availability and its ability to generate profit." In AMT, anonymity can make it hard to talk about labor regulation, because, as the English Virginia said: "We're all numbers and statistics here."

This positive effect of the AMT workers' separation and alienation makes way for a purposeful reflection for those who wish to build fairer online work platforms concerning gender, race, and nationality. Anonymity can be considered an important feature for these work relationships.

Women as Best Consumers for Market Research HITs

The consumerist women stereotype seems to lead some requesters to prefer the women turkers at AMT, according to some of the interviewees:

"I get some HITs that are specifically for women."

"I'd say it [being a woman in the AMT] almost affects it positively by receiving higher-paying surveys and more specific demographic questions";

"I feel like I qualify for as many opportunities or even more than males on AMT. A lot of opinions and surveys are targeted towards women and I believe that's because women have a lot of media and purchasing influence in US society."

In this case, and only in this case, having children became an advantage to some of these women: "I guess maybe we get more surveys asking about children or women's health." Market research in specific sectors also benefits women: "Cosmetics HITs are liked by women."

Yet, market-specific research HITs should not be considered a relevant advantage for women turkers. Answers about these services that are related to a "female universe" stereotype exemplify a movement that is emblematic of contemporary capitalism: bodies previously not welcomed in the system are included when they become potential consumers. The inclusion of racialized and gendered bodies in the capitalist system is part of liberalism's fantasies that hinder "revolutionary claims to remaking the human" (Atanasoski and Vora 2015, 30).

Conclusion

In this paper, we presented a set of practices carried out on the AMT platform that shows how gender remains a daily reality in this new kind of work. Our methodology mixed theoretical reflections on technology and feminism and, above all, listening to the women workers who face the issues we described on the platform.

Individualized approaches confirm the constitution of this group of people, which is essential for technologies and AI development that is heterogeneous and diverse. This approach also offered an outline of common issues these women faced. Besides general AMT difficulties (such as low wages and high competition), the workers pointed out balancing housekeeping and AMT work; the responsibility of doing childcare while working, which affects their productivity on the platform; and the lack of appreciation of the AMT work and the domestic labor. We also identified that the anonymity and HITs of market research, albeit not intentionally, benefit these women minimally.

Listening to the workers proved to be urgent and necessary to break the opacity of the AMT platform and understand the real problems they faced. We aimed to mark a "place of speech" for them to speak from their standpoint and to understand realities that are often erased in the face of "hegemonic normalization" (Djamila Ribeiro 2017). This exercise of listening to women and gathering common topics from their answers also contributes to the idea that "it is the common social location in hierarchical relations of power that creates groups and not the result of collective decisions made by individuals of these groups" (Collins 1997).

We learned about the structural challenges. AMT seems to be the prototype of a new work reality that, remotely, makes women and its other workers insecure. The platform also manages to do something precious to capitalism: keep the women labor power available for unpaid domestic services and, at the same time, make it profitable for several companies, especially those responsible for organizing and maintaining contemporary information flows (Castells 2008). Two excerpts of the interviewees echo this duplicity AMT is able to carry out, the last written by the woman AMT in capital letters: "Many women are at home, and it helps to generate a source of income if they are stay-at-home parents";

"YES, I WILL WORK ON MY FREE TIME."

To help break the abstract rhetoric of Silicon Valley technology, studies on digital infrastructures that consider bodies and materialized processes are important to give women a rightful place in remote jobs like AMT. AMT workers show that the current processes of data training and regulation of the interconnected society are not only technical but also a cultural and social construction (Pasquinelli and Joler 2020). Technological perspectives that ignore this idea of construction, based on what is already determined by a patriarchal society, are pure sophism—typical of naive (or cynical) people who idealize an idyllic technological future, while ignoring the real problems of the present. As Pinto (2005, 72), a Brazilian technology theorist, considered by Paulo Freire as his great master, reminds us: The problem of understanding the machine, from the simplest to the most complex computers, does not begin with it, but with its natural background, the human being who creates it (authors' translation). In our case, it begins by understanding the women workers who are in precarious situations in their domestic and (real) online contexts.

As a way of personalizing these workers and to avoid possible retaliations from Amazon and requesters, all of the women AMT workers in this text had their names changed. We chose to replace them by the first name of important feminist thinkers, mainly Black women and intersectional perspectives' representatives. They are Sueli Carneiro, Lélia Gonzalez, Linda Bellos, Conceição Evaristo, Maya Angelou, Rosa Luxemburgo, Erica Malunguinho, Kimberlé Crenshaw, Audre Lorde, Florynce Kennedy, bell hooks, Judith Butler, Dandara dos Palmares, Grada Kilomba, Michele Wallace, Vilma Reis, Virginia Woolf, Berenice Bento, and Beatriz Nascimento. This was an attempt to honor the structures of resistance that each interviewee needs to have when working on platforms like AMT. We also intended to humanize them in all their power, going beyond the alpha-numerical sequences they use as personal identification in the platform.

Bibliography

Amazon Mechanical Turk. n.d. Accessed November 11, 2021. https://www.mturk.com/.

Amazon Mechanical Turk. n.d. *Welcome to the Amazon Mechanical Turk Requester*

User Interface Guide. Accessed November 11, 2021, https://docs.aws.amazon.com/AWSMechTurk/latest/RequesterUI/OverviewofMturk.html.

Antunes, Ricardo, ed. 2019. *Riqueza e Miséria do Trabalho no Brasil IV*. São Paulo: Boitempo Editorial.

Antunes, Ricardo, and Vitor Filgueiras. 2020. *Plataformas digitais, uberização do trabalho e regulação no capitalismo contemporâneo*. In Uberização, trabalho digital e Indústria 4.0. Arnaldo Mazzei Nogueira et al.; org. Ricardo Antunes. 1 ed. São Paulo, Boitempo.

Atanasoski, Neda, and Kalindi Vora. 2015. "Surrogate Humanity: Posthuman Networks and the (Racialized) Obsolescence of Labor." *Catalyst: Feminism, Theory, Technoscience* 1(1): 1–40.

Bastin, G., and Paolo Tubaro. 2018. "Le moment big data des sciences sociales." *Revue Française de Sociologie* 59(3): 375–39.

Burrell, Jenna. 2016. "How the Machine 'Thinks': Understanding Opacity in Machine Learning Algorithms." *Big Data & Society* 3(1).

Bruno, Fernanda. 2013. *Máquinas de ver, modos de ser: Vigilância, tecnologia e subjetividade*. Porto Alegre: Sulina.

Castells, Manuel. 2008. *A Sociedade em Rede*. São Paulo: Paz e Terra.

Collins, Patricia Hill. 1997. "Comment on Hekman's 'Truth and Method: Feminist Standpoint Theory Revisited': Where's the Power?" *Signs: Journal of Women in Culture and Society* 22(2): 375–81.

Crary, Jonathan. 2013. *24/7: Late Capitalism and the Ends of Sleep*. London: Verso Books.

Davis, Angela Y. 2011. *Women, Race, & Class*. New York: Vintage.

De Beauvoir, Simone. 2011. *The Second Sex*. New York: Vintage Books.

Difallah, Djellel et al. 2018. *Demographics and Dynamics of Mechanical Turk Workers*. Anais da 11th ACM International Conference on Web Search and Data Mining, Los Angeles, 5 a 9 de fevereiro de 2018.

D'Ignazio, Catherine, and Lauren F. Klein. 2020. *Data Feminism*. Cambridge, MA: MIT Press.

Ekbia, Hamid R., and Bonnie A. Nardi. 2017. *Heteromation, and Other Stories of Computing and Capitalism*. Cambridge, MA: MIT Press.

Federici, Silvia. 2012. *Revolution at Point Zero: Housework, Reproduction, and Feminist Struggle*. Oakland: PM press.

Finn, Ed. 2017. *What Algorithms Want*. Cambridge, MA: MIT Press.

Gillespie, Tarleton. 2010. *The Politics of 'Platforms.'* New Media & Society 12(3): 347–364.

Gray, Mary L., and Siddharth Suri. 2019. *Ghost Work: How to Stop Silicon Valley from Building a New Global Underclass*. Boston: Houghton Mifflin Harcourt.

Grohmann, Rafael. 2018. *Materialidades do trabalho digital no sul global e invisibilidades comunicacionais*. Comunicação & Educação 23(2): 153–163.

Haraway, D. 1988. "Situated Knowledges: The Science Question in Feminism and the Privilege of Partial Perspective." *Feminist Studies* 14(3): 575.

Hernandez, Oscar. 2017. "Lithium Batteries Won the Nobel Prize. How Is This an Opportunity for Latin America?" *Inter-American Development Bank*, accessed

November 20, 2020. https://www.iadb.org/en/improvinglives/lithium-white-gold-regions-development.

Huws, Ursula. 2003. *The Making of a Cybertariat: Virtual Work in a Real World*. New York: Monthly Review Press.

Ipeirotis, Panos. 2010. *Demographics of Mechanical Turk*. NYU Working Paper No. CEDER-10-01, New York, accessed July 15, 2019. https://papers.ssrn.com/sol3/papers.cfm?abstract_id=1585030.

Irani, L. 2015. "The Cultural Work of Microwork." *New Media & Society* 17(5): 720–739.

Jarrett, Kylie. 2016. "Feminism, Labour and Digital Media: The Digital Housewife." Routledge Studies in New Media and Cyberculture; 33. New York: Routledge, Taylor & Francis.

Moreschi, Bruno, Bernardo Fontes, Guilherme Falcão, and Gabriel Pereira. 2020. Exchanges w/ Turkers. Disponível em: Accessed on September 24, 2020. https://exchanges.withturkers.net/.

Moreschi, Bruno, Gabriel Pereira, and Fabio G. Cozman. 2020. Trabalhadores brasileiros no Amazon Mechanical Turk: sonhos e realidades de trabalhadores fantasmas. Contracampo, Niterói 39(1): 44–64. https://pdfs.semanticscholar.org/93cd/6ed572fa3211862b82138a3e9c04797a073b.pdf.

Oakley, Ann. 1976. *Woman's Work: The Housewife, Past and Present*. New York: Random House Inc.

Pasquinelli, Matteo, and Vladan Joler. 2020. "The Nooscope Manifested: Artificial Intelligence as Instrument of Knowledge Extractivism." Visual essay, KIM HfG Karlsruhe and Share Lab, 1 May 2020. http://nooscope.ai.

Pinto, Alvaro Vieira. 2005. O conceito de tecnologia 1. 2a. ed. Rio de Janeiro: Contraponto.

Ribeiro, Djamila. 2017. *O que é lugar de fala?* Belo Horizonte(MG): Letramento: Justificando.

Srnicek, Nick. 2017. *Platform Capitalism*. Cambridge: Polity.

Uber, Equipe. 2020. *Fatos e Dados sobre a Uber*. In Uber Newsroom. https://www.uber.com/pt-BR/newsroom/fatos-e-dados-sobre-uber/.

Winner, Langdon. 1977. *Autonomous Technology: Technics-out-of-Control as a Theme in Political Thought*. Cambridge, MA: MIT Press.

Woodcock, Jamie and Graham, Mark. 2019. *The Gig Economy: A Critical Introduction*. Cambridge: Polity.

Zyskowski, Kathryn and Kristy Milland. 2018. "A Crowded Future: Working against Abstraction on Turker Nation." *Catalyst: Feminism, Theory, Technoscience* 4(2): 1–30.

2

Cultivating a Decolonial Feminist Praxis through Testimonio and *Pláticas*

LYNN HAMPTON and
SYLVIA MENDOZA AVIÑA

Women of color, and Black women specifically, are disproportionately hired as contingent faculty at college and university campuses across the United States (Finkelstein et al. 2016; Nzinga 2020). This contributes to what Nzinga (2020) refers to as a "hyper-producer of inequity" within higher education, as contingent faculty are required to teach larger course loads in addition to coordinating departmental projects, are sometimes paid per class rather than on salary, may not receive work benefits, may have to teach at multiple college and university campuses in one semester, and live under the threat of not having their contracts or courses (if offered) renewed. For Nzinga (2020) this "graduate school-to-food stamps" pathway is an example of the neoliberalization and corporatization of higher education that reflects the calculated disposability of Black and women of color scholars, especially those associated with critical race, feminist, and postcolonial studies within higher education (Mohanty 2013). In this essay, we use women of color feminisms as our theoretical framework and methodology to name, expose, heal, release from, and theorize on our experiences as a Black and a non-Black Chicana lecturer laboring at a predominantly white institution (PWI) in north Texas as a decolonial feminist praxis.

We highlight our roles as contingent faculty to make clear that our value in the eyes of the institution was in the amount of labor that could be extracted from us at minimal cost and commitment (Nzinga 2020). We draw from Hoff's (2020) use of racial opportunity cost to highlight the cultural, psychological, and emotional costs Black, Indigenous, and people of color pay to pursue opportunities within historically white supremacist schooling institutions, to include feeling the need to continuously prove ourselves and feeling left with insufficient strategies to navigate academia outside of engaging with and upholding white norms and behaviors. Hoff (2020) uses racial opportunity cost as an analytical tool to reflect on an experience she had as a Black faculty member serving on a hiring committee when a Latinx candidate departed from white supremacist standards of professionalism during her job talk, by discussing her ancestors and showing emotion. Hoff wrestles with her hopes for this candidate to beat the institution at its own game by "proving" her smartness during this job talk.

> I rationalized that she just needed to get the job, play the game, after which she could be her whole self. However, there is an inextricable cost in playing the smartness game for people of color because ... smartness is socially constructed around the norms, values, and behaviors of whiteness. (Hoff 2020, 42)

Hoff's vulnerable reflection is useful here as it highlights how faculty of color are told by the institution that to get hired or advance in higher education, they must "play the game" by engaging in behaviors that do not align with our ancestral knowledge, spiritualities, and forms of solidarity. This is often perpetuated by mentors that advise grad students and junior faculty of color to keep their heads down, play the game, and wait until they defend or get their PhD, go up for review, or get tenure to speak out about acts of violence that occur within academia (Davis n.d.; Hoff 2020).

Racial opportunity cost then helps us to understand how some scholars of color, and particularly contingent faculty vying for tenure-track positions, can feel moved to: overproduce; remain complicit in colonial logics embedded within higher education that enforce white supremacist standards of professionalism and promote individualism and competition; and remain silent when one of our own experiences white supremacist violence by the institution, for fear of losing the precarious annual contract or facing professional retribution (Edwards 2018; Hoff 2020; Venzant Chambers 2011; Venzant Chambers and Huggins 2014). In the face of this danger and despite the fact that at the time, both of us had been contingent faculty and on the job market for years, we highlight some of the ways we refused colonial logics and chose to produce critical and transformative curricula and praxes with our students and each other. We also refuse/d to stay complicit and silent about the white supremacist violence of the institution.

We reflect on our experiences as visiting lecturers at a PWI in north Texas and the ways actors within this institution strategically attacked one of us, Lynn, who also identifies as a Black woman lecturer. The attacks furthered white civility under the white supremacist guise of professionalism after Lynn was invited to help develop a comparative ethnic studies course for the newly developed and white-led ethnic studies department. Through this course, Black students felt empowered to engage in campus activism that involved critiquing white leadership. As such, these students and their mentor, Lynn, were surveilled and slandered by faculty and administration for refusing to engage in behaviors associated with racial opportunity cost that normalize domination, colonization, and injustice (Hoff 2020).

Instead, Lynn and her students asked critical questions about the department's leadership and the historic and continued discrimination experienced by Black and students of color on campus. Lynn was portrayed as difficult and was accused of manipulating Black and students of color into campus activism. She and the group of mostly Black undergraduate students she mentored were portrayed as disruptors and agitators without legitimate concerns or criticisms about their experiences at this institution, despite the fact this university is known as a violent space for Black students and faculty (Johnson 2020a; Johnson 2020b; Harris 2020). Sylvia served as witness to this misogynoir (Trudy 2013) and learned with/from Lynn on how contingent faculty of color, in the face of our precarious positions, can and do embody agency.

For Sylvia, it became clear that despite aligning and identifying with social justice ideologies, listening to and centering Black women and students is a specific praxis. Sylvia recognized the ways non-Black Chicanx/Latinx folks in higher education can sometimes uphold and reproduce whiteness even while positioning themselves as anti-racist and/or social justice scholars, particularly in the ways non-Black faculty of color believe they are "playing the game." This caused Sylvia to reflect on what non-Black Chicanx/Latinx solidarity does materially for Black colleagues and students in higher education, and how to engage in a praxis of solidarity that offers more. We hope that our writing and sharing this essay is instructive, as it highlights not only the violence of the institution against women of color and Black women specifically, but also the strategies and solidarity we cultivated.

In the next section, we discuss our theoretical framework drawing from women of color feminisms, followed by our methodology that uses the Black/Chicanx/Latinx feminist method of testimonio and plática (Delgado Bernal et al. 2012; Pérez Huber 2009; Rose 2003). Through intentionally centering Lynn's testimonio, we invite witnessing (Villenas 2019) of the following themes: 1) the exploitation of Black women's knowledge, bodies, and labor; 2) misogynoir (Trudy 2013); and 3) spirit murder (Williams 1991).

We hope to provide insight into a decolonial and coalitional feminist praxis in process in which Black women are centered and affirmed. Our solidarity at this PWI looked like: listening to, believing, and affirming Lynn and her students; speaking up and engaging in action as the violence occurred, documenting it, and submitting to human resources, administration, and the office of inclusion; questioning administration and colleagues about their beliefs when they made comments rooted in white supremacy; moving through fear by acknowledging it and still choosing to engage in actions that support Black women; refusing labor and refusing silence.

Framework for a Praxis of Solidarity

We situate our essay within the epistemological foundations, activism, and solidarity of women of color feminisms (Mohanty and Carty 2018; Moraga and Anzaldúa 1983; Trudy 2013). We specifically draw from the Combahee River Collective and their groundbreaking statement to theorize on our solidarity as "sister-comrades" (Mohanty and Carty 2018) and to understand what it means to show up for Black and women of color in higher education and beyond, particularly within the context of Texas, which boasts its own brand of white supremacy.

The Combahee River Collective, comprised of radical Black feminist activists, writers, and scholars, including Barbara Smith, Beverly Smith, and Demita Frazer, outlined a politics of feminisms rooted in the "belief that Black women are inherently valuable, that our liberation is a necessity not as an adjunct to somebody else's may because of our need as human persons for autonomy." The Combahee River Collective is explicit that if communities organized around the liberation of Black women, this would necessitate liberation for everyone, as Black folks comprise all other identities and because the United States is founded on anti-Blackness.

Despite this, non-Black scholars have failed to center or account for Black communities in their analyses of structural oppression in the United States, focusing predominantly on non-Black Chicanx/Latinx communities, which, as Molina (2013) has cautioned, can be limiting in its production of a single-identity history. Molina (2013, 520) offers a relational analysis of racialization in the United States that "recognizes that the construction of race is a mutually constitutive process and demonstrates how race is socially constructed." Further, Black Latinx scholars have long critiqued Chicanx Studies, Latinx Studies, and Chicanx/Latinx feminisms for upholding and reproducing ideologies like Latinidad and mestizaje, constructs that perpetuate anti-Blackness and anti-Indigeneity and erase Black and Indigenous experiences and material realities in Latin America and the United States (Figueroa-Vásquez 2020; Hernández 2022).

As such, Lynn's testimonio is centered in this draft, with Sylvia's reflections focusing on what it means to witness and act. We recognize how differently we are racialized, sexualized, and read historically and presently as a Black woman and non-Black Chicana in contingent positions, and how this racialization presents different consequences for us when critiquing white supremacy. We expand on testimonio and Chicanx/Latinx feminista plática methodologies in the next section.

Testimonio and Pláticas

In line with our theoretical framework, we use testimonio (Delgado Bernal et al. 2012; Perez Huber 2009), as it is a "verbal journey of a witness who speaks to reveal the racial, classed, gendered, and nativist injustices they have suffered as a means of healing, empowerment, and advocacy for a more humane present and future" (Perez Huber 2009, 644). Testimonios are rooted in radical Latin American traditions of decolonial resistance within historically oppressed communities, particularly Indigenous communities and by women who refuse to remain silent about the violence they experience. Testimonios function as a way to speak up and back, to document injustices, and in the process, to heal by releasing any shame associated with the pressure of having to keep a secret about violence and oppression that happens—not just to the person giving their testimonio but to entire communities.

Latina feminists use testimonios in their edited book *Telling to Live: Latina Feminist Testimonios* to rupture silences within Latinx culture while at the same time highlighting the knowledge and strategies cultivated by Latinas navigating their everyday lives (Latina Feminist Group 2009, iv). Hamzeh, Flores Carmona, Hernández Sánchez, Delgado Bernal, and Bejarano (2020, 251) draw parallels between haki/pláticas and testimonios/shahadat as examples of an Arabyyat feminista decolonial praxis that functions as acts of linguistic and epistemic disobedience in academia. Haki/pláticas and testimonios/shahadat operate as a refusal, or "a process of unlearning, agitating," and resisting the master's tools (253).

Villenas (2019) draws from Latinx/Chicanx perspectives of witnessing "to articulate a grounded, tenuous praxis of relationality, and solidarity in everyday social movements" (153). She offers: "I qualify 'social movement' with the term 'everyday' to refer to the daily, (extra)ordinary, and intentional pedagogical work of creating spaces and conditions for critical witnessing and social change" (153). For Villenas, testimonio and witnessing offer to community organizing, social movements, and—we add here—solidarity in higher education, the pedagogical practice of encountering each other, testifying, and bearing witness "to each other's different accounts . . . to recognize each other as resistant and to move from recognition to a deciphering of each other's resistant codes. It is then possible to imagine common action in plurality and across diverse spaces of community" (156).

Pláticas have been written about as a Chicanx/Latinx feminist methodology, not only within qualitative research, but also as a praxis of solidarity (Fierros & Delgado Bernal 2016; Hampton & Mendoza Aviña forthcoming). Important within pláticas and testimonio, aside from being rooted in our ways of knowing and being as Black and Chicana contingent faculty, is the act of witnessing. We center Lynn's testimonio, while also acknowledging and theorizing from the many pláticas, or informal conversations rooted in our cultural traditions, that took place during this time that helped cultivate our relationship.

Testimonio and the pláticas we engaged in served as our decolonial praxis of solidarity in our refusal to engage in and reproduce white supremacist logics with each other that would otherwise have us ignore each other on campus, gaslight each other, or believe there is a right way to "play the game" against white supremacist violence in the workplace. Instead, we engage in critical care with and for each other through pláticas and witnessing, where we affirm each other, center Lynn and her students' experiences and listen to and believe what they say, make space for Black pain, rage, and joy, strategize on how to show up after encounters with white supremacist violence, and celebrate each other.

We center Lynn's testimonio first in this essay, inviting others to bear witness, before moving into a discussion on what we learned, with the hope that our experiences contribute to a larger discussion of solidarity. We end with a discussion of the implications of plática and testimonio as ways of bearing witness to each other's experiences through difference, and what was involved for us in moving from witnessing to solidarity in action.

Lynn's Testimonio

Exploitation of Black Women

In the spring of 2016, while serving in a one-year lecturer position at the politically conservative and racially homogeneous campus where I was teaching, I had the opportunity to develop a Black Lives Matter course. Despite the overwhelmingly white undergraduate population at the university, the class was immensely popular. This "special topics" course drew students from across the university, the majority nonwhite and representing nearly every academic college on campus. For two hours once a week, I engaged students in intense and thoughtful discussions about police brutality, racial inequality, mass incarceration, social justice reform, and the sustainability of the #BlackLivesMatter movement.

The level of student engagement and critical reflection in this course made clear that students, both Black and non-Black, had been waiting a long time to have conversations about racism and social justice. I was inspired by these students' activism and awareness of systemic inequality not just in our society but also on our campus. They had a sincere desire to create institutional change and wanted strategies to be more effective agents in their communities and at the university.

Throughout the semester, the students described their transformational experiences during the Black Lives Matter course to other faculty members at the PWI. After hearing from several of my students, a tenured white male professor, whom I will refer to as "white male administrator" (WMA) reached out to me and asked if I would be involved in developing a new comparative race and ethnic studies program. Since I was primarily serving as a one-year lecturer, I was a bit hesitant about taking on additional labor within the university because of the contingent nature of my employment. However, this WMA was persistent about my involvement and after finally hearing that my one-year contract was getting renewed for another year, I agreed to attend a few meetings.

I was recruited to develop the curriculum and the course design for the introductory course that would launch the new program in the fall of 2017. As a critical race scholar and a social justice educator, I saw an opportunity to develop curricula that could speak to the lived experiences of marginalized groups on campus and would simultaneously serve as a vehicle for institutional change. By the start of the fall semester, I was the instructor of record for the newly launched introductory course.

The student enthusiasm was remarkable. In the first semester, I taught over fifty students in the course, and by the spring term, I had taught fifty more. The program had generated so much momentum that it transitioned from a program into a full academic department within the first year of its launch. This increased level of racial consciousness and social justice awareness among marginalized students, and white students alike, posed a threat to the white leadership.

Misogynoir

Black women are frequently recruited into spaces for our academic knowledge, where we are scrutinized for challenging institutionalized structures of whiteness, white supremacy, and patriarchy. Anti-Blackness in institutions of higher learning is nothing new (Haynes et al. 2020; Nzinga 2020; Trudy 2013). When this anti-Blackness is coupled with patriarchy, this has a detrimental impact on the professional success of Black women in academia (Davis n.d.; Trudy 2013). Too often this violence is unchecked by university officials.

White men, many of whom occupy positions of power and influence in academic settings, frequently target lesser-ranked Black women colleagues with impunity, reifying Moya Bailey's concept of misogynoir. Misogynoir refers to the "specific hatred, dislike, distrust, and prejudice toward Black women" (Trudy 2013). Misogynoir was highly evident in my personal interactions, email communications, and professional dealing with this WMA.

Despite bearing the brunt of the labor, both physical and emotional, in terms of the teaching responsibilities and mentoring of students, my voice was never amplified, nor were my experiences centered. Whenever I attempted to offer suggestions for greater levels of support for faculty of color, or tried to raise legitimate concerns from students, I was repeatedly chastised and attacked. It became clear to me that my presence on that executive board was symbolic. My ideas, suggestions, critiques, and feedback were not wanted nor welcomed.

Additionally, the more that students of color taking the Comparative Race and Ethnic Studies (CRES) course gravitated toward me, the more the resentment and hostility from the white leadership grew. A group of students, organized primarily by Black female students, developed a student organization to raise awareness on campus about the program and facilitate campus-wide conversations on social justice. White fragility (DiAngelo 2018) materialized in the form of campus leadership shutting down the student organization. The CRES program leadership informed students that they were not to affiliate themselves, their activism, or their discussions with the program, even though many of them had switched their majors to CRES.

It was undeniable that when either Black students or I tried to challenge the oppressive structures of whiteness and white supremacy that we were witnessing, we were silenced. Black female students were reprimanded for desiring greater agency in curricular decisions and the hiring of more faculty of color. Also, I was blamed due to my role as the Black female faculty of record for this student organization, and subsequently punished for my alleged involvement in "riling up" students. When it became clear to the WMA that he would not be successful in silencing me—despite repeated attempts that involved inviting me to coffee to politely tell me "I talk too much"—he resorted to more drastic measures to "discipline" and embarrass me. The WMA's violent disciplinary tactics escalated.

At the conclusion of the 2017–2018 academic year, not only did I receive the "Excellence in Teaching Award" for my instruction of the introductory CRES course, but I also received a glowing letter of reappointment to the executive committee. In the letter below, taken from an email, the WMA wrote the following:

> You have helped CRES in many ways as a leader in the Honors College and frequent attendee at CRES events and Core meetings. I am especially grateful for your work developing and teaching our introductory courses, CRES 10103 Engaging Difference and Diversity in America. (WMA, June 2018)

Imagine my surprise when just a few short weeks after receiving this email, I began receiving a series of emails from the WMA pressuring me to attend a meeting to discuss my future in CRES. After responding that I was not available to meet in person but would be available via email, since I was not under contract by the university and needed these summer months to dedicate to my scholarship, I received another email demanding that I meet with the WMA to discuss my "problematic behavior" and to determine whether I was "suited" to continue teaching CRES 101.

My frequent requests for "documentation" or "evidence" as to why I was being summoned to this meeting (over the summer when I was a one-year contractual employee and under no obligation to hold meetings over the summer) were denied. At this mandatory meeting in August, the WMA went out of his way to portray me as "disruptive," ineffective, and unethical. He made comments about me wearing all black to an end-of-the-year banquet, and I was accused of "staging a protest" because I and other students were similarly dressed in black at this banquet celebration. Additionally, I was reprimanded for not smiling enough during this celebration and was even told that I was "scowling."

That mandatory meeting in August lasted two and a half hours. During it, I was never provided with support nor "protection" from my department chair, even though the WMA offered no evidence or documentation to substantiate his allegations of "problematic" behavior on my part. Needless to say, I felt many of the emotions that Hoff discussed related to psychological violence, degradation, and betrayal by the institution and this WMA. A few days after this meeting, I received another email from this WMA that was titled "memorialization of our August 7th meeting." In this "memorialization" email, the WMA wrote:

> At the meeting we discussed my concerns about your activities in CRES over the past year. While there was substantial disagreement about the nature of past events, we nonetheless reached some agreements regarding the future. I counseled you to exhibit high standards of professional ethics and collegiality in your capacity as an instructor of CRES 101 and a member of [the] Executive Committee. Specifically, we expect that you will. . . .

The WMA then enumerated six behavioral steps that I need to improve on, including acting as a "team player," "sharing my opinions in appropriate venues (CRES meetings), and "ultimately following the democratic will of majority decisions." He concluded the letter with the following statement:

> Based on our conversation, I was reassured that we could put past events behind us and that you would be able to continue teaching CRES courses and serving as a key ambassador for our Department. This letter does not represent a reprimand; indeed, I have no power over your employment at TCU. Instead, the goal is to ensure that we are all on the same page moving forward. (email communication)

However, it is worth noting that while he says this letter was not to serve as a "reprimand" because he has no power over my employment at the university, the intentional carbon copying (cc) of the college associate dean, department chair (white man), the Associate Vice Provost, and Dean of the School of Interdisciplinary Studies (white woman) who presided over the CRES department asserted his power.

In Moya Bailey's conceptualization of misogynoir, she discusses anti-Black and misogynistic representations of Black women in visual culture. However, this groundbreaking concept has since been applied to all the ways, structurally and socially, that Black women are denied our humanity by virtue of being both Black and women. Too often in academia, Black women, as Hoff (2020, 44) writes, have to "field questions about [our] hair, clothing, and accessory choices." Also, we are forced to "navigate perceptions that make us simultaneously hyper-visible and invisible, creating socio-psychological landmines on campus and in the surrounding community" (Hoff 2020, 44). Hoff purports that we are often required to challenge "beliefs that dehumanize and mark us as undeserving and unworthy of having the benefit of the doubt."

When misogynoir is reported, it is often dismissed and minimized by human resources and, in this case, even by the office of diversity. Even when evidence is provided, rarely do human resource officials or department and unit heads intervene. Sadly, this was the case for me.

Immediately after receiving the "memorialization" of the August 7 email, I wrote a rebuttal letter to this WMA in which I vehemently denied his characterization of the events. I also made it very clear in my rebuttal letter that I have acted with integrity throughout my tenure at the university and have given generously of my time in terms of mentorship and development of not only students, but also the curriculum in the CRES department. Furthermore, I stated that, as a critical race scholar, I am well aware of the dynamics of power and colonizing structures of patriarchal norms that reinforce and uphold standards of exclusion, whiteness, and fear to preserve and protect white supremacy.

I explicitly stated in my rebuttal, "you have consistently attempted to silence me when I have raised questions that don't align with your agenda. It's becoming clear to me that my failure to comply has led you to engage in hostile and malicious attacks that are clearly designed to hurt and harm my professional credibility. This is not acceptable." I concluded this email by stating that I would no longer engage in back-and-forth communication, and this would be my last correspondence with him on this matter, and that any further correspondence would include the university's Chief Inclusion Officer as well as the university's Vice Chancellor for Human Resources. I made sure to copy both individuals on this email and attached documentation of all previous correspondence, demonstrating a pattern of hostility and harassment from the WMA. Unfortunately for me, I failed to receive any acknowledgement from either the university's Chief Inclusion Officer or the university's Vice Chancellor for Human Resources.

Sadly, this lack of acknowledgement on the part of the university officials should not come as too much of a surprise, given what we know about the ways the norms of white supremacy and patriarchy are upheld within PWIs, often at the emotional, psychological, and professional expense of Black women academics. In her book *White Fragility,* sociologist Robin DiAngelo (2018) writes about white solidarity, "the unspoken agreement among whites to protect white advantage and not cause another white person to feel racial discomfort by confronting them when they say or do something racially problematic" (57). This solidarity is often referred to as white "racial bonding."

I witnessed firsthand white racial bonding during my tenure as the instructor of record of the introductory CRES course and while serving as a member of the Executive Board. However, what is often undertheorized in the literature on white fragility and white racial bonding within academic institutions is that when this behavior is specifically targeted at Black women academics, it often results in a form of psychic violence that becomes institutionalized and contributes to the removal of Black women from academic positions.

Spirit Murder

When we talk about the targeted violence toward Black women in academic settings—in other words, misogynoir—we also must attend to the ways misogynoir is internalized and the ways co-conspirators are complicit in the spirit murdering of Black female faculty. Legal scholar Patricia Williams (1987) defined spirit murdering, which was further explicated by and applied to education by scholar Bettina Love (2014) as "the personal, psychological, and spiritual injuries to people of color through the fixed, yet fluid and moldable, structures of racism, privilege, and power" (Love 2014, 302). What makes spirit murdering so troublesome is that it "denies inclusion, protection, safety, nurturance, and acceptance—all the things a person needs to be human and to be educated" (Love 2014, 302). Spirit murdering occurs when a person is injured as the result of being viewed as an "object." The consequence of spirit murder in academia includes Black women leaving opportunities out of survival, having to defend oneself against defenseless accusations, and gross mischaracterizations of one's persona even after leaving.

Since not a single person in a position of power and authority at my university stood up for me nor protected me from the WMA's visceral attacks on my personal and professional integrity, I decided to no longer subject myself to this psychological harm by opting to resign from all my professional responsibilities with CRES. Unfortunately, even after I removed myself, the spirit murdering continued when I was summoned to a meeting with the white leadership of my current position to provide a rationale for why these individuals were acting so hostile toward me. *As the victim, I was asked to defend and explain the misogynoir.* The efforts of misogynoir retaliation went as far as requests by the WMA and the interim chair (white woman) meeting with my chair to request my teaching contract as a lecturer not be renewed on the grounds that I was "unprofessional."

This spirit murdering continued further when the WMA submitted his end-of-year departmental report, which he shared with over fifty CRES-affiliated faculty and staff. In this report, the WMA included a section titled "Challenges Faced in 2018." In this section, while not mentioning me by name, he described me using racist tropes, referring to me as "disgruntled," while blaming me for his leadership failures. Other faculty and staff on campus, who were aware of the violent treatment directed at me, were complicit and did not interrupt these oppressive practices or intervene on my behalf. The silence of Black faculty, and Black women specifically, hurt my spirit most. Some even suggested that I must have done something to deserve this abuse.

I was never publicly defended. And I was punished for my unwillingness to remain silent, and through his abuse of power, when he sent a message to others in the academic community that this is what happens to Black women who do not understand their place in the academic hierarchy. We will become a victim of structural violence—via forcible removal from leadership roles and threats to one's contract—if we do not comply with the status quo. I include the section of the WMA's report below.

> Challenges Faced in 2018
>
> Our most visible challenge stemmed from discontent among a vocal minority of students that was, to some extent, fomented by a single disgruntled colleague. CRES leadership worked transparently to engage with the students, but the one faculty member undermined this work by misleading students she had taught in our introductory course. None of the concerns or critiques were presented directly or clearly to CRES leaders, nor did they come up in faculty meetings in which the colleague regularly participated. Attempts to remedy this situation with the faculty member led to renewed antagonism among students, including their blasting of outlandish charges on social media. By the end of 2018, a meeting with the colleague's Dean appeared to have resulted in an improved situation. On the other hand, students learned that they could take grievances directly to the Chancellor while simultaneously refusing to engage in transparent conversations with the elected CRES leaders. We have not received any formal notices or reports on the correspondence between the students and TCU administrators, nor have TCU administrators responded to our

requests to help facilitate renewed dialogue. This has made it much more difficult for us to ascertain what the students want, much less try to substantively address their concerns. We believe that there are both misperceptions among students and real areas in which we would like to improve, but the climate of distrust and a lack of support from the administration has made it challenging to move forward.

As we invite readers to witness through Lynn's powerful testimonio, we want to highlight how the violence in real time was significantly worse, while at the same time normalized within the institution. When Sylvia began her visiting position the following year, in the fall of 2018, students began to open up and share about their experiences on campus. New to the city and the institution, Sylvia decided to attend a women of color faculty luncheon early in the semester, in search of community and folks who could provide institutional knowledge. This is where we met.

At this luncheon, Sylvia asked other faculty about their experiences with the WMA, the interim chair (a white woman), the CRES department, and the university. Based on their responses, Sylvia would (or would not) ask follow-up questions. When Sylvia asked Lynn about the WMA and the department, Lynn extended an invitation for us to meet off campus at a local coffee shop, which is how our friendship/femtorship developed and flourished through our often weekly pláticas.

When we would meet, it was understood that we were going to be seen, affirmed, and validated. We saw in each other opportunities to discharge, heal, laugh, strategize, and chismiar[1] in ways that offered us protection on a campus where we felt isolated and where Lynn was subjected to misogynoir daily. Through our pláticas, we gave each other the support, mentorship, and healing that was not available at this institution—neither with human resources nor with the office of diversity, which both revealed their commitment to protecting the university. It was our pláticas where we cleared Lynn's name, where we named the white supremacist violence taking place, and where we strategized, leading Sylvia to produce and submit an eleven-page complaint to human resources and the chief inclusion officer of the Office of Diversity, Equity and Inclusion at the end of her appointment. We include an excerpt here:

> Within my one-year appointment, I have witnessed [interim chair], [staff] and [WMA] attempt to silence and/or punish specifically Black undergraduate students that openly criticized the CRES department, in particular one young Black male student. [Interim chair] requested updates about [this student] in meetings not about CRES students, and only about [this student] (no other students)—and not in regard to his academic career. This occurred via email on November 30th and during meetings on December

1st and December 10th of 2018. I felt like [interim chair] used meeting times during the Fall 2018 semester to retrieve intel from me—a lecturer who is trying to start her own professional career—about any staged protests or criticisms circulating amongst the students, rather than her as CRES interim chair addressing these students directly via a town hall meeting, which I suggested to [interim chair] and [staff] on multiple occasions (week of September 24, December 1st and December 10th, meetings). As a result, as a lecturer I felt denied opportunities for professional mentorship that would help advance my career during these meetings with [interim chair], and instead witnessed the use of these meeting times as a way for [interim chair] to surveil [student], which created a hostile work environment.

Through pláticas we developed tangible skills, including the documentation of the violence that we experienced. It was through our pláticas where we practiced vulnerability, reciprocity, and self-reflection that helped Sylvia to witness the ways Black women are subjected to misogynoir in higher education, and how non-Black faculty of color can be complicit in this. Through the act of witnessing, as an intentional praxis of solidarity, Sylvia reflected on the following, which we hope is useful for other non-Black contingent faculty of color:

- Most of the universities in which we are trying to become permanent employees are anti-Black and anti-Indigenous. As non-Black faculty of color, are our organizing, forms of resistance, and leadership within these institutions centering Black and Indigenous colleagues?
- How frequently are non-Black people of color engaging in self-care and protecting ourselves? Is it all the time, to the point that we are not intervening or disrupting frequently or at all within our institutions?
- If we are in a moment when we are choosing self-care, is it during an instance when anti-Blackness is being addressed?
- If we feel that we have figured out a strategy to "play the game" within the institution, how much of this strategy is actually just proximity to whiteness? How might reflecting on this question change our choices in advancement opportunities, the ways we lead and/or resist, and whom we choose to work with and bring along with us as we advance?

Our pláticas made evident the options and opportunities to engage in solidarity in intentional ways, where we do not have to engage in racial opportunity costs just because we are working within the confines of white supremacist institutions. In our praxis of solidarity, we made the choice to see, choose, and support each other. Drawing from women of color feminisms and from what we learned through our pláticas, we conclude here with practices we found healing, insightful, and supportive in our developing praxis of solidarity:

- Reading, listening to, believing, and organizing with Black women and students.
- Committing to regular plática sessions and actively engaging in witnessing, followed by discussions on what to do collaboratively, moving forward from our specific positionalities (factoring in the ways we are racialized/sexualized and the bodies we occupy and the positions we are in, to gauge who can act in particular ways).
- Documenting everything as evidence.
- Having access to templates (legal documents, formal complaints) as well as a list of resources of whom to share formal complaints with (Lynn had the institutional knowledge of which office/administrator to email for what, and we sent our complaints through the proper chain of command as designated by the institution, but we made sure to also include other administrators outside of the chain of command to apply pressure).
- Creating opportunities for senior faculty/folks with institutional knowledge to provide background information for entering contingent/tenure-track junior faculty in candid ways (off campus).
- Engaging in self-reflection and checking in on what we actually believe (do we believe in playing the game, and what does playing the game look like in a way that does not perpetuate or condone misogynoir?).
- Refusing labor, as evidenced by Lynn resigning from her duties to CRES, as well as Sylvia's refusal to apply for permanent employment with this institution.
- Acknowledging fear and stress and how this makes us feel sick and paralyzed, and sitting through that fear to recognize that we have more choices in our collaboration with each other than the institution wants us to believe.
- Inviting each other to discharge not just through pláticas, but also through body movement, reminding each other of the importance of physical, emotional, and mental health.
- Building from our pláticas to shift how we mentor students: Are we repeating things we heard and do not actually believe? Are we engaging in behaviors that show our students there are other ways to engage in solidarity in academia?
- Making room in pláticas for joy, laughter, celebration, and opportunities to treat ourselves as a reminder that we will see our way out of these situations, and that we are always deserving of joy, rest, and goodness.

We hope that sharing the ways testimonio and pláticas have helped us through the violence imbedded within a PWI in historically white supremacist north Texas offers insight and strategies of support for other Black women and faculty of color. Further, we hope our discussion around pláticas as inviting witnessing contributes to existing discussions around what is involved in a praxis of solidarity with and through difference.

Note

1. Chismiar translates from Spanish to English as "gossip" and is a feminist praxis.

Bibliography

Brown, Nadia E. and Lisa Young. 2015. "Ratchet Politics: Moving Beyond Black Women's Bodies to Indict Institutions and Structures." *National Political Science Review* 17(2): 45–56.

Chabram-Dernersesian, Angie and Adele de la Torre. 2008. *Speaking from the Body: Latinas on Health and Culture*. Tucson: The University of Arizona Press.

Davis, Shardé M. Black. n.d. In *The Ivory*. Accessed May 4, 2021. https://blackintheivory.net/.

Delgado Bernal, Dolores, Rebeca Burciaga, and Judith Flores Carmona. 2012. "Chicana/Latina testimonios: Mapping the Methodological, Pedagogical, and Political." *Equity & Excellence in Education* 45(3): 363–372.

DiAngelo, Robin. 2018. *White Fragility: Why It's So Hard for White People to Talk About Racism*. Boston: Beacon Press.

Edwards, Kirsten T. 2018. "Stories of Migration: Passing through, Crossing over, and Decolonial Transgressing in Academyland." In *Black Women's Liberatory Pedagogies*, edited by O. N. Perlow, 85–100. Gewerbestrasse, Switzerland: Palgrave.

Fierros, Cindy Ochoa and Dolores Delgado Bernal. 2016. "Vamos a pláticar: The Contours of Pláticas as Chicana/Latina Feminist Methodology." *Journal of Chicana/Latina Studies* 15(2): 98–121.

Figueroa-Vásquez, Yomaira C. 2020. *Decolonizing Diasporas: Radical Mappings of Afro-Atlantic Literature*. Evanston, IL: Northwestern University Press.

Finkelstein, Martin J., Valerie M. Conley, and Jack H. Schuster. 2016. "Taking the Measure of Faculty Diversity." TIAA Institute. https://www.tiaainstitute.org/publication/taking-measure-faculty-diversity.

Gutiérrez y Muhs, Gabriella, Yolanda Flores Niemann, Carmen G. González, and Angela P. Harris. 2012. *Presumed Incompetent: The Intersections of Race and Class for Women in Academia*. Boulder: The University Press of Colorado.

Hampton, Lynn, and Sylvia Mendoza Aviña. 2023. "Chicana/Latina Feminista Plática Methodology as a Praxis of Solidarity for Black Women and Women of Color Contingent Faculty at a Predominantly White Institution (PWI)." *International Journal of Qualitative Studies in Education* 36(9): 1769–1980.

Hamzeh, Manal, and Judith Flores Carmona. 2022. "Critical reflexión and plática-testimonio/hak-shahadat: Enacting Decolonial Praxis of Solidarity from the Mexico-US Borders to Palestine." *Curriculum Inquiry* 52(3): 266–274.

Harris, Jake. 2020. "2 More Women Added to Racial Discrimination Lawsuit against

Texas Christian University." wfaa.com. WFAA, https://www.wfaa.com/article/news/local/2-women-added-texas-christian-universitydiscrimination-lawsuit/287-b464f389-8d58-4e23-828c-feda426ca8d0.

Haynes, Chayla, Nicole M. Joseph, Lori D. Patton, Saran Stewart, and Evette E. Allen. 2020. "Toward an Understanding of Intersectionality Methodology: A 30-Year Literature Synthesis of Black Women's Experiences in Higher Education." *Review of Educational Research* 90(6): 757–787.

Hernández, Tanya Katerí. 2022. *Racial Innocence: Unmasking Latino Anti-Black Bias and the Struggle for Equality.* Boston: Beacon Press.

Higginbotham, Evelyn Brooks. 1993. *Righteous Discontent: The Women's Movement in the Black Baptist Church, 1880–1920.* Cambridge: Harvard University Press.

Hoff, Pamela Twyman. 2020. "Picked to Pieces: The Cost of Opportunity." In *Presumed Incompetent II: Race, Class, Power, and Resistance of Women in Academia,* edited by Yolanda Flores-Niemann, Gabriella Gutiérrez y Muhs, and Carmen M. González, 39–48. Denver: Utah State University Press.

Johnson, Kaley. 2020, January 23. "TCU Student's Lawsuit Says Faculty 'Dehumanized' Her, School Ignored Reports of Racism." Fort Worth Star-Telegram. https://www.star-telegram.com/news/local/education/article239541988.html.

Latina Feminist Group. 2001. *Telling to Live: Latina Feminist Testimonios.* Durham: Duke University Press.

Love, Bettina L. 2014. "'I See Trayvon Martin': What Teachers Can Learn from the Tragic Death of a Young Black Male." *Urban Review* 46: 292–306.

Mohanty, Chandra Talpade. 2013. "Transnational Feminist Crossings: On Neoliberalism and Radical Critique." *Signs* 38(4): 967–991.

Mohanty, Chandra, and Linda Carty. 2018. *Feminist Freedom Warriors: Genealogies, Justice, Politics, and Hope.* Chicago: Haymarket Books.

Molina, Natalia. 2013. *How Race Is Made in America: Immigration, Citizenship, and the Historical Power of Racial Scripts.* Berkeley: University of California Press.

Moraga, Cherrie, and Gloria Anzaldúa. 1983. *This Bridge Called My Back: Writings by Radical Women of Color.* Latham: Kitchen Table: Women of Color Press.

Nzinga, Sekile M. 2020. *Lean Semesters: How Higher Education Reproduces Inequity.* Baltimore: John Hopkins University Press.

Pérez Huber, Lindsay. 2009. "Disrupting Apartheid of Knowledge: Testimonio as Methodology in Latina/o Critical Race Research in Education." *International Journal of Qualitative Studies in Education* 22(6): 639–654. https://doi.org.libweb.lib.utsa.edu/10.1080/09518390903333863.

Rose, Tricia. 2003. *Longing to Tell: Black Women Talk about Sexuality and Intimacy.* New York: Picador.

Saavedra, Cinthya, and Michelle Perez. 2012. "Chicana and Black Feminisms: Testimonios of Theory, Identity, and Multiculturalism." *Equity & Excellence in Education* 45(3): 430–443.

Trudy. 2013. "Misogyny, In General vs. Anti-Black Misogyny (Misogynoir), Specifically." *Gradient Lair,* September 11, 2013. https://www.gradientlair.com/post/60973580823/general-misogyny-versus-misogynoir.

Venzant Chambers, Terah T. 2011. "Mergers and Weavers: Using Racial Opportunity Cost to Frame High-Achieving African American and Latina/o Students' School Culture Navigation Styles." *Journal of Educational Administration and Foundations* 22: 3–26.

Venzant Chambers, Terah T., and Kristen S. Huggins. 2014. "School Factors and Racial Opportunity Cost for High Achieving Students of Color." *Journal of School Leadership* 24: 189–225.

Villenas, Sofia. 2019. "Pedagogies of Being with: Witnessing, *Testimonio*, and Critical Love in Everyday Social Movement." *International Journal of Qualitative Studies in Education* 32(2): 151–166.

Williams, Patricia. 1991. *The Alchemy of Race and Right*s. Cambridge: Harvard University Press.

3

Embodied Precarity
Feminist Politics, Laboring Bodies of Color, and the Neoliberal University

AZZA BASARUDIN and TINA BEYENE

Teaching through Turmoil: Political Upheaval and Global Pandemic

In March 2020, when the first California statewide lockdown to contain COVID-19 was declared, we were early-career and then-adjunct scholars of color teaching in Gender Studies, where the intersecting inequalities of the pandemic became instantly evident from the vantage of higher education. While juggling a flurry of online teaching workshops as a result of the "shelter-at-home" directive, we also had to re-envision the conceptual frameworks of our courses to respond to the realities of our mostly working-class, immigrant, and nonconventional students who were the faces of COVID-19's disparities. Panicked messages informed us of students who were essential workers in high-risk places or those who worked in community organizations and had to assist the elderly with their own money when social service agencies were unresponsive due to staff shortages. We learned of students who found themselves as the breadwinners overnight when parents lost jobs. Many students were the only English-speaking adults in their households and had to step in to educate younger siblings. LGBTQIA students reported sheltering in unsafe spaces. Many female students who had found freedom in college were suddenly back in deeply patriarchal family homes. The pandemic also turned privilege and disadvantage into a visual and audio field, which made us acutely aware of the disparity of space and the digital divide in our classes.

The crisis we saw dovetailed with the never-ending political turmoil of the Trump administration, which had intensified to such an extent that being Gender Studies professors now means teaching in, for, and through crisis. The pandemic, along with George Floyd's murder, which reignited the Black Lives

Matter (BLM) uprisings in May 2020, and scorching fires that turned the Los Angeles skies into an apocalyptic scene, served as a stark reminder that as feminist faculty of color, we are also responsible for our successes and failures in adjusting to the pandemic and for assuaging the distress students of color felt because of police violence and a racist, misogynist, homophobic, and transphobic election, as well as climate change and the onslaught of capitalism. In the meantime, during these crises, university administrators around the country were churning out "toothless statements and symbolic gestures" and empty affirmations that "we are in this together" (Walker 2020). As the steady stream of institutional emails to upgrade our online teaching, adjust our grading to accommodate students, and enroll students in our overfilled classes constantly reminded us, we, the marginalized faculty, are expected to serve as foot soldiers as universities try to stave off student discontent. While we have both been educators for over a decade, we have repeatedly reexamined this question: What does it mean to operationalize anti-racist and decolonial feminist pedagogy in times of crisis and precarity?

Feminist praxis has long highlighted the codirectional nature of learning, and intersectionality pedagogy does not merely theoretically map the multiple ways oppression and privilege coalesce. At its best, feminist praxis aims to decolonize a key site—the institution—where power is exercised through knowledge production by reimagining the classroom as continuity of social justice movements. As decolonizing pedagogy, feminist praxis then refuses "to get over histories that are not over" (Ahmed 2017, 262). In this collaborative essay, we reflect on our instructional approaches and maneuvering to decolonize our classrooms with a focus on the pandemic and the BLM movement, two events that reminded us of histories of power that are not over. The project emerges out of our own feminist strategy of survival as committed social justice faculty in the neoliberal academy. Since meeting in our UCLA Gender Studies doctoral program in 2005, we had maintained, along with a community of other feminists of color, an enduring friendship that anchors our personal and professional lives. This feminist space of friendship had seen us through romantic relationships, children's births, transnational family visits, quotidian challenges, job searches, book launches, and career moves. Our community was also crucial for our feminist rage at a diminishing world and for collectively imagining just alternatives. We seek ways to address the neoliberal administration's cruel onslaught in our classrooms through daily exchanges about unfolding crises, sharing pedagogical strategies, co-designing syllabi and lessons, collaborating on events, curating resources for students, and supporting each other in class when we get overwhelmed. Even more than our academic training in Gender Studies, our feminist community is indispensable to teaching in and through crisis. This community is the place from which we engage in decolonizing our world.

We conceptualize feminist pedagogy as home—not as a "comfortable, stable, inherited, and familiar space, but instead as an imaginative, politically changed space where the familiarity and sense of affection and commitment lay in shared collective analysis of social injustice, as well as a vision of radical transformation" (Mohanty 2003, 128). Our feminist pedagogy, in which Mohanty's concept of home is a decolonial project, seeks to provoke students to critique the production, acquisition, dissemination, and application of Eurocentric/colonizing/imperial epistemologies; and the privilege, power, and hierarchy in the classroom through intersectional, anti-racist, and transnational feminist approaches that center collaborative learning between students and instructors (Freire 1970). Under the neoliberal regime, only few spaces in academia, chief among them Gender and Ethnic Studies, remain the "most radical space of possibility in the academy" (hooks 1994, 12). Hence, we pivot our teaching so that students can think critically and capaciously about how moments of crisis are potent sites for radical rethinking of power and injustice. However, we also face challenges that muddy this work in a neoliberal setting that is extractive of the invisible labor of faculty of color. In the following sections, we discuss the vexed relationship of our radical feminist praxis and solidarity in times of political crisis and catastrophe, within a neoliberal education system that exploits invisible labor, undermines solidarity, and perpetuates structural violence.

Education-Industrial Complex: Neoliberal University and the Politics of Crises

For decades, neoliberalism has gutted public universities under the guise of efficiency, transparency, accessibility, and job preparedness. Corporate donors, neoconservative politicians, and corporatized administrators have justified massive budget cuts while aggressively promoting the development of degrees that supposedly lead to jobs (Giroux 2014; Prashad 2014; Lorenz 2012). And yet, higher education has become increasingly unaffordable, and students endure precarious job markets while deeply indebted. Meanwhile, college enrollment rises (Prashad 2014). The debt crisis falls hardest on Black and Latinx families (Scott-Clayton 2018). College dropout rates are highest for Black and Latinx students, while the gender gap for Black students is widest. Structural oppression, such as expulsions, incarceration, low wages, and unaffordable childcare, also fuels dropout rates (Ford and Triplett 2019).

Faculty conditions are also in crisis. Exploited adjunct labor is now the principal mode of organizing teaching. In times of crisis, adjunct faculty face added pressure to continue performing at a level beyond tenure-track faculty, since students' evaluations serve as either a gateway or a barrier to future employment. Tenure-track faculty also continue to lose autonomy via administrative attacks on unions, unilateral decisions over faculty governance, prioritization of donor-driven research agendas, budget cuts that limit critical research, the difficulty of acquiring course release, teaching upgrades, increasing course loads, increasing class sizes, elimination of tenure lines, and the denial of tenure to social justice–oriented scholars (Campbell et al. 2019; Chatterjee and Maira 2014). Meanwhile, senior university administrative compensation soars and top administrative positions remain predominantly white (86 percent) (Seltzer 2017), with grave implications for junior faculty of color who have fewer opportunities and face hostile tenure review committees and requirements, especially if their work is decolonial and feminist (Osei-Kofi 2012).

The convergence of neoliberalism and neoconservatism—the logic of "so-called individual responsibility in place of the public good, social Darwinism, the acceptance of social inequities as 'common sense' and conservative control of curricula, pedagogy, and knowledge production"—further determines what is taught and what counts as valid research (Osei-Kofi 2012, 230). In this environment, social justice–oriented programs such as Gender and Ethnic Studies are frequently targeted via rhetoric such as simplifying graduation requirements and cost-cutting unprofitable majors in the humanities, where many such programs are housed (Campbell et al. 2019). Moreover, neoconservatives decry these fields as "victim studies" and not "real" scholarship (Guy-Sheftall 2008, 159). Meanwhile, faculty labor in these fields is appropriated by the university as a form of institutional polishing: when labor is successful, the image is shiny and serves as "a technique for not addressing inequalities by allowing institutions to appear happy" (Ahmed 2017, 102).

Thus, it is not surprising that within the neoliberal university, anti-racist feminist pedagogy is a double-edged sword; how we extend ourselves to our craft and our students often leads to the erasure of our laboring bodies. As Reena Goldthree and Aimee Bahng (2016, 25–26) note of their effort to implement a BLM course, what are the prospects of carrying out decolonizing efforts like the Ferguson Teaching Collective "when 'Black and Brown scholarly bodies' are 'churned up' by Dartmouth and other elite spaces?" After all, despite the power of their course to create sites of meaningful change, the faculty, who labored to create the class, were also denied tenure while Dartmouth usurped their work and appeared as a forward-thinking space. In the spirit of Goldthree and Bahng, we ask: What does it mean for faculty of color to be the invisible labor behind radical feminist praxis within the neoliberal university?

The Politics of Refusal:
Feminism and Transformative Communality

As Gender Studies professors, we view our teaching responsibility in the pandemic to include the provision of care and compassion to students. This is non-negotiable. We follow in the footsteps of Audre Lorde (1988) and Sara Ahmed (2014) to enact communal and collaborative practices that designate "selfcare as warfare." Hence, for us, our classrooms, and by extension, the university, must become spaces where we initiate the creation of a learning community built on meaningful relational existence, where we care for each other, where emotional and experiential epistemologies are contextualized, and where the personal is indeed political. We aim to remake learning spaces not only as resistance to neoliberal ethos, but more actively, as spaces that value historically invisible, devalued, and excluded laboring bodies.

Furthermore, while we had long been committed to teaching about police brutality, after George Floyd's murder, we both also felt that our classrooms have to be not only spaces for a national conversation but also extensions of the movement itself. As adjunct faculty and early-career faculty, the normative academic success trajectory would have us automate our classes to streamline course preparation in the coming year. Instead, we spent the summer months updating and/or redesigning all our courses to centralize the 400-plus-year history that foregrounds the BLM movement and to draw deeper connections between the historical and contemporary solidarity efforts of Black, Indigenous, and people of color (BIPOC). We also re-envisioned our large classroom sizes—the result of neoliberalism—as an opportunity for numerous students to partake in the movement by offering them a space to deeply engage the politics of white supremacy.

In the following sections, we use autoethnography and draw on sample narratives from student assignments and classroom discussions to narrate our radical feminist praxis and connect our experiences to wider sociopolitical meanings and institutional configurations during the pandemic and the BLM uprisings.

Beyene: Anti-Racist Feminist Pedagogy
and Feminist Networks

The injustice of the pandemic on my students' lives was immediately clear the day the lockdown took effect, necessitating that I revamp my remaining classes to help students articulate and address the unfolding inequities. For instance, one class that I retooled was my feminist theories course. From the outset, the course was guided by bell hooks's (1991, 12) call to "create a feminist theory, a feminist practice, a revolutionary feminist movement that can speak directly to the pain that is within folks, and offer them healing words, healing strategies, healing theory." As the pandemic hit, I aimed to illuminate the power and relevance of feminist theories in making sense of the moment in real time. For instance, as then-President Trump escalated racist assaults on China during the pandemic, I decided to link our ongoing study of empire, orientalism, and colonialism to the pandemic. Like many Gender Studies professors, I am in the habit of cultivating a network of like-minded feminist scholars and activists, so I invited a feminist science studies scholar to share her work on race, gender, and empire in the politics of germs. The lecture was structured to help students develop a genealogical understanding of infectious disease by grounding it in the history of anti-Asian immigration and public health policies, and imperialist US foreign policies in China and the Middle East. After discussing other recent racialized and gendered disease crises such as the 2003 SARS scare and the war on terror, students had to apply feminist theoretical concepts from class, such as colonialism, empire, neoliberalism, and intersectionality and generate a feminist analysis of COVID-19. Many Asian American students shared their encounters of anti-Asian racism since the start of the pandemic and Trump's racist dubbing of the coronavirus as the "Wuhan Virus," while other students discussed the anti-Asian racism unfolding in their communities. Collectively, they strategized ways to intervene in such discourse.

I reimagined the remaining assignments in a way that built on these in-class insights and turned their final paper into an intersectional feminist theory essay on the pandemic where students had to map inequalities of the lockdown entirely within their own homes, communities, or jobs. The goals of this assignment were to respond to the time and space constraints they were facing by building on existing in-class activities and to demonstrate how anti-racist feminist theory can draw on our own worlds to produce legitimate knowledge. The resulting student essays, selective and anonymous excerpts of which I share here, demonstrate the astute standpoint of working-class students, students of color, and gender nonbinary students who easily saw the racial, capitalist, and gender injustice of the pandemic. For instance, a Latinx student who was let go from her job of many years at the start of the pandemic while her boss retained a male employee of only six months, recalls confronting her boss, whose response was: "'Well he's a guy and he come all the way from Texas and he's very hard-working. Plus, I'm pretty sure it will be easy for you to find a job. After all, girls just need to look pretty and smile and boom they are hired.'" When she realized that reasoning with him was useless, she snapped. "I finally went off . . . [And] when he realized that I got bothered, he apologized immediately and said that he didn't realize that what he had said was as bad as it sounded. The best part of this is that he still tries to call me for help, and for the first time he did this, I responded with 'Scott from Texas couldn't handle it? Why would you ask me if I was just sitting pretty at the office?'" Her story demonstrates a diagnosis of power and feminist agency. As she notes, "Although I said it in a joking manner, I meant it and he knew it!"

Another student of Guatemalan descent reflected on the pandemic's economic impact on her and her single mom, who were laid off simultaneously at the start of the pandemic lockdown. Like many of her peers who also came from working-class and immigrant families, her theorizing demonstrates her ability to connect, through her intimate awareness, how class, race, gender, and citizenship were inextricably linked in the pandemic:

> This quarantine has made me realize how unfair the system is for those who are undocumented or a part of the informal labor force. My mom is a nanny and housekeeper, and ... [she] was furloughed from all three of her jobs. The reason my mom and I did not worry about money as much at the moment was because luckily enough, we have a sizable savings account and one of the families my mother works for was going to give her paid time off. What I started to realize through this pandemic is that my mom is probably one of the lucky ones.... Most nannies within the world are usually undocumented minorities paid in cash.

The pandemic's unique impact on the immigrant community in other sectors, especially the education system, was also a common theme. A Chicana student from a farming town north of Los Angeles theorized her experience as teacher's aide during the lockdown, noting:

> The city I work for is primarily Spanish-speaking, low-income individuals and the students that are in my program, their parents work late.... Homework assistance is super helpful for the non-English-speaking parents because they cannot help their kids at home on these assignments, and also because the kids get picked up late.... I have parents emailing me and asking if I can come to their houses and help their child complete classes ... and I even have parents that refuse to take computers from the school because they cannot afford damages if anything were to happen. I think it is also important to note that the moms are the ones emailing me regarding their children.

By the end of her paper, this student circled back to the course: "I feel like this class really assisted in helping me view everything around me with a new lens.... I am able to apply theories to this pandemic and even come up with my own, which I would not have been fully able to prior. I am even able to question the ignorance of it all so much more clearly!"

Students also highlighted the precarity of marginalized lives as gender-based violence, white supremacy, and capitalism converged during the pandemic. For instance, a student from a predominantly working-class Latinx neighborhood, Pacoima, recalls how predatory businesses started targeting young women there:

> Two days ago, I was at the store and this man approached me and he [complimented] my hair and my nails. As I walked away uncomfortably, he kept following me, and he whipped out his business card . . . he [also] made sure to show me the huge stack of $100 bills that he had in his pocket. He then told me, 'I know that right now because of the coronavirus, and you're female, you probably aren't working, so here, take my card.' I walked away, and I didn't see the card until I got to my car, just to find out that it was a gig for adult movies.

A white trans woman also wrote about navigating the terror of white supremacy and transphobia as she was forced to shelter with her Christian evangelical family in one of Southern California's alt-right stronghold towns. Her teenage brother, who was involved with the white supremacist groups, often harassed her and hurled misogynistic attacks at their mother in response to any housework demand, mirroring the national trends of white supremacist, misogynist violence:

> I have been stuck at home with a bigoted family member, which has been a problem for my friends and the wider LGBTQ plus community as well. Surgeries for trans people have been labeled nonessential, which has been similarly harmful. Overall, while my privilege shields me from the worst effects of the coronavirus lockdown, I can see several of the societal problems this difficult time reflected in my life.

As these excerpts from the final assignment demonstrate, radical feminist pedagogy fosters a space in which students can understand feminist theory as a collective project that is responsive to lived realities. And most urgently, their voices illustrate how the Gender Studies classroom is a crucial site of social transformation and agency.

Basarudin: Spaces of Dissent and Feminist Insurrections

When news of the pandemic broke, I was teaching an upper-division feminist course that explores the relationship between knowledge and power. My main concern as we transitioned to online learning was how to retool my pedagogy to create a collaborative space to foster a sense of community. I allocated a portion of student grades to this endeavor: the three methods were Intake Sheet (IS), Personal Biography (PB), and Radical Feminist Care Sessions (RFCS). These methods helped me to know each student as a human, not just a body enrolled in my course. For the PB section, students had to post a short write-up on the course's message board about their sense of self, passion, and interests, and include an image/self-portrait. Each student also had to read and comment on at least two of their peers' PB. For the RFCS, I allocated at least two sessions per student. RFCS allowed me to enact care in the tradition of a radical feminist praxis for collective warfare, as there is an increasing need to recognize that we are interconnected and interdependent with one another to survive and thrive. I follow Angela Davis's explanation of radical as "grasping things by the root" to address oppression and injustice; radicalism, then, is about agency and self-determination in practicing social justice. Through my RFCS sessions, I, thus, channel Mohanty's articulation of home as an "imaginative, politically charged space" (2003, 18) by extending self-care to collective care and by building solidarity and compassion in moments of crisis.

By devoting significant time and energy to the methods, I was able to intimately connect with my students, which allowed me to gauge their living situations and well-being, as well as their preparedness to receive online instruction. Through casual conversations during RFCS, I gleaned intricate details about how the pandemic wreaked havoc in their lives, from deepening patriarchy in the home, gender violence, homophobia, and houselessness to white supremacy. These conversations often circled back to the power of intersectional and transnational feminist theories to anchor their troubles and boost their confidence in their ability to be competent learners online. I practiced email check-ins every two weeks with each student, to ensure that they grasped the material and that they did not lag. The following quotes from the course evaluations reflect students' thoughts on the effectiveness of this feminist praxis.

> The professor was incredibly understanding given all of the different and unpredictable circumstances presented to students with online learning. I appreciated the professor's openness to extensions, to office-hours whenever we needed them, and consistently checking with students to make sure the lectures not only made sense but were helpful in understanding the required texts. I also appreciated that part of the class was to have Radical Feminist Care Sessions as it made the connection much more personal and authentic. It really shows how much the professor cares about us as students and how much she cares that we understand the material, which is the kind of knowledge that does not just stay in the class, but beyond.

> This class has been a light in my life in all aspects. Professor Basarudin was extremely considerate during this whole quarter with the pandemic and extremely attentive towards all her students and our needs. She made it part of our grade to participate in "Radical Feminist Care Sessions" with her in order to facilitate space and divert time out of the quarter for her to personally check in on the well-being of every student in her class TWICE.

Professor Basarudin and her class are the reason why I managed the quarter the best that I possibly could.

I share these quotes not to self-aggrandize but to illustrate how radical feminist praxis, that is, the creation of "home" within a classroom context, allows students to be seen and heard. In turn, it instills in students the courage to grapple with contentious course topics in a manner that will sustain them beyond the course. Because of the pedagogic investment in their embodied experiences outside the classroom, students are more than willing to actively participate in decolonizing the classroom. As agents of change, they see the centrality of collaborative knowledge and the possibilities in imparting knowledge to their own respective communities.

Toward the end of the course in May 2020, we were again reminded of the implications of systemic racism and dehumanization of Black bodies. The senseless murder of Floyd coincided with the final topic of the course I was teaching on feminist anger and BLM. Los Angeles, like other cities, was in various states of unrest; uprisings erupted, police brutality escalated, and curfews were imposed. I immediately reached out to students to reinforce that, considering Floyd's murder, it is imperative that we flood our class space with discussions of how we feel and what to do with our emotions, and more important, how to sharpen and harness the spectrum of emotions flooding us, in service of insurgent knowledge. To teach about BLM is to teach about the legacy of slavery; the inherited systems of racism, oppression, and exclusion in this country that have expunged humanity from Black bodies and reconstituted them as disposable; and the lack of accountability for racist behavior and utterances. To teach about BLM is to teach about interconnected struggles of racialized minorities and to expose the various surveillance strategies of empire, such as the "Counterintelligence Program" (COINTELPRO) and the "Countering Violent Extremism" (CVE) that legitimize and unleash state intrusion and violence on these communities. To teach about BLM is to teach about how Black women, two of them queer, demanded the centering of their voices and those who have long been marginalized in the heteropatriarchal organizing of resistance movements, by making *all* Black lives matter. To teach about BLM is to teach about key strands of Black feminist thought, including historical experiences with enslavement, anti-lynching organizing, segregation, and Civil Rights and Black Power movements, as well as sexual politics, patriarchy, and capitalism. To teach about BLM is to teach about harnessing the power of anger by rejecting its normative deployment to denigrate Black women. To teach about BLM is to truly practice feminist pedagogy of home, where the classroom is not a comfortable or stable space but one where we are committed to a radical collective analysis of social injustice despite our differences.

In that vein, our final class sessions were spent not merely theorizing BIPOC anger and its historical roots, but also meditating on anger in conjunction with topics of criminalization of Blackness, prison abolition, defunding the police, allyship, performative activism, and more. We had a contentious yet generative discussion about how demands for justice can be made and realized in relation to how Black humanity can be embedded in the consciousness of the nation—law enforcement, elected officials, institutions, media, businesses, neighbors, and families. It was immensely rewarding to witness the students' level of engagement, respect, and care despite their differing or conflicting strategies of putting boots on the ground in mobilizing resistance. There was anger, rage, tears, regret, passion, hope, and for some, redemption, all of which I deeply believe resulted from creating a learning condition that affirms students' embodied experience, which in turn allowed them to step out of their own protective zones to participate in making the classroom a space that is truly liberatory and transformative. The following narratives are from students' Reflection Papers.

A queer Salvadorean-American student whose parents escaped the Central American crisis in the 1980s wrote:

> My learning of systemic racism and unlearning of anti-Blackness does not revolve around my personal journey as that would be counterproductive to the goal of uplifting Black voices. . . . All non-Black communities have engaged in some form of anti-Blackness. Now the division between true supporters of Black Liberation and performative activists lies within the ability to either disrupt or perpetuate systems of oppression generated by imperial and colonial influences. This is why I have such an issue with the Blackout Tuesday trend due to the fact that by simply showing solidarity with a singular post that has no weight attached to it and makes no lasting impact on the progress towards equity. What the post essentially is all but an acknowledgment that racism exists and offers not one contribution towards aiding that fight. Even if COVID-19 prevents some people from engaging in protests, no petitions were signed nor shared, no donations to bailout organizations or underrepresented Black subcommunities, no advocacy prior nor after the Blackout Tuesday post. This negligent behavior is equally damaging to the Black Liberation movement as people do not understand the importance of making genuine contributions that might take not even ten minutes of their day, which is essentially why non-Black folks cannot centralize themselves in a discussion about Black lives.

A student of African and Pacific Islander heritage shared his reflection:

> When I think about Black anger, I think about my mother. Her rare instances of anger left a lasting mark on me. I have been thinking about how, when I was a kid, I used to openly shame my mother during periods when she was

angry, which happened to be in public, and how I would feel embarrassed by her in those moments. I have been thinking about how I, a child with 40-odd years less experience in this world than her, found it befitting to assume authority over her, call her out, and side against her even though my mother operated such circumstances in defensive positions. I see an aspect of my relationship to my mother, my valuing of "reason" over emotion, is an extension of support for the western patriarchal system, which historically subjugated and oppressed people of color and especially women. I basically existed as an indoctrinated person, positioning logics as a condition of idealized civility, specifically recreating discourses around political power, which are gendered and racialized hierarchies that African-Americans are forced to deal with and acknowledge daily.

Suppressing anger was ultimately more dangerous, depriving [a] Black woman of the community [that] anger could/should have otherwise bonded her to. When she is told her feelings are unjust, she is invalidated in her anger and, as such, told that the feelings of others also are invalid. And, the anger, the nature of being fed up, the disgust for systems of oppression which have led people to protest for what has existed for centuries now, become diminished. There is no such thing as light anger. Light anger is agitation; it is an annoyance that can quickly be forgotten and shifted to other matters of the association. Anger sticks, impressing itself upon the holder's mind until they have to unpack it, and that is why it is crucial.

The following are thoughts articulated during class discussions by Black students, the first a returning student and the second, a first-generation college senior:

> I have two teenage Black sons and every time they leave the house I fear for their safety. I wonder if I will get the dreaded "call" that someone has hurt them. They are boys, not men but because of their size (over 6 feet) and skin color, they are seen as threatening. The system vilifies my sons and yet if they get angry, they are deemed violent. How are these young Black men supposed to externalize their anger in a system and society that is ready to criminalize, maim, and kill them because of their appearance?

> I am tired of being the angry Black woman. I am tired of anger. In fact, I feel nothing when George [Floyd] was killed. I was numb. Is that strange? I feel strange saying this because it might seem like I don't care. But as a Black person, this is just another day, another instance of violence, another death. So many of us have died. None cared. Even if they did, it is always temporary. It doesn't translate into concrete action. I am tired. Numbness is my company these days. I am sorry if I cannot feel.

Antithetical to neoliberal ethos, I *deliberately created space and time* for students to explore, contemplate, and engage as humans in the process of knowledge production, instead of "customers" who respond to standardized assignments and expectations. The students' eloquent voices, courageous spirits, and communality reinvigorated our conception of justice and collective knowledge-building in the tradition of home as a politically charged space of dissent.

Decolonizing the Neoliberal University: The Cost of Radical Feminist Praxis

Crises such as COVID-19 bring into focus the structural violence that existed long before the pandemic and the precarious conditions that BIPOC faculty experience to sustain radical feminist praxis. As we respond to, and teach against, the stream of crises, we also must contend with a capitalist entity that extracts uncompensated labor to manage crises and treats the laboring BIPOC bodies as disposable. We find ourselves grappling with administrations that manufacture meaningless solidarity statements while refusing to address the structural production of inequality. On both our campuses, the tremendous organizing to address BLM, anti-Asian violence, and the crisis of care during the pandemic has been led primarily by women of color faculty. Despite the meticulously curated list of burdens endured by students, staff, and faculty of color, administrators have not met the crucial workplace equity demands for the new reality of academic work in COVID-19, reduced teaching load, class-size debate, invisible labor (mentorships and emotional support), adequate mental health services, and more.

With our heavy teaching load, crisis teaching has meant managing the disaster faced by 150-plus students, fielding hundreds of student messages a week that involve constant adjustment of pedagogy, and securing resources for struggling students, from solutions to evictions, domestic violence, hunger, joblessness, and homelessness to deportation threats and mental health breakdowns. This invisible labor requires an inordinate amount of care, time, and energy, which consistently leaves us feeling hopeless about not doing enough for students and saddles us with Secondary Stress Trauma (SST). While SST is apparent to our fellow feminist comrades and families, it is indiscernible within the workings of neoliberalism. While we understand that our invisible labor is necessary to decolonize knowledge, it also muddies our career focus and diminishes our well-being, as well as that of many women faculty of color in a neoliberal university, especially those in fields like Gender Studies and Ethnic Studies.

There is a cost to living and sustaining radical feminist praxis. In collectively remaking the university and reimagining our existence, SST will continue to be our companion as we labor within yet another class and another academic year. Radical praxis that is unapologetically feminist is risky and messy, but what is the alternative for making the classroom a more democratic, political, and dynamic feminist space? At the heart of a liberatory education are the laboring bodies of women of color who instill in students the need to question authority and power and generate oppositional consciousness, particularly in moments of crisis, so that we can all "imagine another world. And [be] ready to fight for it" (Roy 2020). Fighting for a just and democratic future requires not only deep and courageous communalism but also sustainable and healing feminist praxis to continue producing and disseminating revolutionary knowledge. As feminist scholar-activists, we are committed to not only imagining but also attaining a new horizon that uplifts justice and equity through the connectivity of struggle in intellectual and political works.

Bibliography

Ahmed, Sara. 2017. *Living a Feminist Life*. Durham: Duke University Press.

Ahmed, Sara. 2014. "Selfcare as Warfare." Feministkilljoys. https://feministkilljoys.com/2014/08/25/selfcare-as-warfare/.

Campbell, Malik, Kelly De Leon, Martha Escobar, González González, Guadalupe Granados, Carla Martínez, Diego Paniagua, Rocio Rivera-Murillo, and Tracy Sadek. 2019. "Ethnic Studies as Praxis." *Ethnic Studies Review* 42(2): 131–50.

Chatterjee, Piya and Sunaina Maira, eds. 2014. *The Imperial University: Academic Repression and Scholarly Dissent*. Minneapolis: University of Minnesota Press.

Coscarelli, Joe. 2020, June 4. "#BlackoutTuesday: A Music Industry Protest Becomes a Social Media Moment." *The New York Times*. https://www.nytimes.com/2020/06/02/arts/music/what-blackout-tuesday.html.

Ford, James, and Nicholas Triplett. 2019, August 16. "E(race)ing Inequities: Does Race Influence Who Drops Out of School? It's Complicated." Education NC (EdNC). https://www.ednc.org/eraceing-inequities-how-does-race-influence-dropping-out-of-school/.

Freire, Paulo. 1970. *Pedagogy of the Oppressed* (translated by Myra Bergman Ramos). New York: Seabury Press.

Friedman, Zack. 2020, February 3. "Student Loan Debt Statistics in 2020: A Record $1.6 Trillion." *Forbes*.

Giroux, Henry. 2014. *Neoliberalism's War on Higher Education*. Chicago: Haymarket Books.

Goldthree, Reena N., and Aimee Bahng. 2016. "#BlackLivesMatter and Feminist Pedagogy: Teaching a Movement Unfolding." *Radical Teacher* 106: 20–28. https://radicalteacher.library.pitt.edu/ojs/radicalteacher/article/view/338/237.

Guy-Sheftall, Beverly (with Evelynn Hammonds). 2008. "Whither Black Women's Studies: Interview." In *Women's Studies on the Edge*, edited by Joan Wallach Scott, 155–168. Durham: Duke University Press.

HigherEd Jobs. 2018–2019. "Administrators in Higher Education Salaries." https://www.higheredjobs.com/salary/salaryDisplay.cfm?SurveyID=22.

hooks, bell. 1994. *Teaching to Transgress: Education as the Practice of Freedom*. New York: Routledge.

hooks, bell. 1991. "Theory as Liberatory Practice." *Yale Journal of Law and Feminism* 4:1 (1–12). https://digitalcommons.law.yale.edu/cgi/viewcontent.cgi?article=1044&context=yjlf.

Lorde, Audre. 1988. *A Burst of Light: Essays*. Ithaca: Firebrand Books.

Lorenz, Chris. 2012. "If You're So Smart, Why Are You Under Surveillance? Universities, Neoliberalism, and New Public Management." *Critical Inquiry* 38(3): 599–629.

McKee, Kimberly, and Denise Delgado. 2020. *Degrees of Difference: Reflections of Women of Color on Graduate School*. Champaign: University of Illinois Press.

Mohanty, Chandra Talpade. 2003. *Feminism Without Borders: Decolonizing Theory, Practicing Solidarity*. Durham: Duke University Press.

NACE Staff. 2018, October 10. "Class of 2018's Preliminary Starting Salary Shows Slight Drop." National Association of Colleges and Employers. https://www.naceweb.org/uploadedFiles/files/2018/publication/executive-summary/2018-nace-salary-survey-fall-executive-summary.pdf.

Osei-Kofi, Nana. 2012. "Junior Faculty of Color in the Corporate University: Implications of Neoliberalism and Neoconservatism on Research, Teaching and Service." *Critical Studies in Education* 53(2): 229–44.

Prashad, Vijay. 2014. "Teaching by Candlelight," in *The Imperial University: Academic Repression and Scholarly Dissent*, edited by Piya Chatterjee and Sunaina Maira, 329–342. Minneapolis: University of Minnesota Press.

Roy, Arundhati. 2020, April 3. "The Pandemic Is a Portal." *Financial Times*. https://www.ft.com/content/10d8f5e8-74eb-11ea-95fe-fcd274e920ca.

Scott-Clayton, Judith. 2018, June 21. "What Accounts for Gaps in Student Loan Default, and What Happens After." Brookings Institution. https://www.brookings.edu/research/what-accounts-for-gaps-in-student-loan-default-and-what-happens-after/.

Seltzer, Rick. 2017, March 2. "Failing to Keep Up." *Inside Higher Ed*. https://www.insidehighered.com/news/2017/03/02/racial-gap-among-senior-administrators-widens.

Walker, Rafael. 2020, June 23. "The Emptiness of Administrative Statements." *The Chronicle of Higher Education*.https://www.chronicle.com/article/the-emptiness-of-administrative-statements.

Yakoboski, Paul. 2018. "Adjunct Faculty: Who They Are and What Is Their Experience? Teachers Insurance and Annuity Association of America (TIIA Institute). 2018, November. https://www.tiaa.org/public/institute/publication/2018/adjunct-faculty-survey-2018.

4

The Emotional Labor of Reconciliation and Indigenization
Indigenous Women Creating Decolonial Feminist Praxis within the Academy

TRICIA MCGUIRE-ADAMS and
JANICE CINDY GAUDET

> We begin this chapter with a dedication. We dedicate this work to the late decolonial self-lover Dr. Jennifer Ward, who passed away in the spring of 2022. Even though she left this world before our collaborative book chapter was published, we know that she is still with us. She is alive in the resonance of her words, our hearts, and our ongoing labor for reconciliation. Jennifer's deep unconditional love for her daughter, husband, family, and community are perfect examples of why creating kind spaces is needed for our kinship to prosper.
>
> Caring for myself is not self-indulgence, it is self-preservation, and that is an act of political warfare.
> —Audre Lorde, A Burst of Light

Being Bold and Living Boldly

Weaving our way through the body politic is exasperating
The interruption of all that is political in putting ourselves first
These uncommon wellness codes set us apart from our colleagues and even our allies, but
    they want in, to be inside our un-patriarchal bundles
A demonstrable act of taking care of ourselves is discerning when to say no and when to say yes
Healing and connection is found in our humour and laughter

A counternarrative to the constant patriarchy is to honour and flourish our herstories
Reclamation of our spirits and bodies happens through our political act of self-care
Our ceremony is enacted by coming together with a purpose, Wiisokotaatiwin
Self-care IS community
It is a practice rooted in love, in dreaming
It is spirit work
Receiving is giving
Giving is receiving
Self-care, being in good relationship with yourself, is the law of the land

Considering Reconciliation in the Academy

With the uptake of the rhetoric of reconciliation within Canada and a parallel movement to address the underrepresentation of Indigenous peoples in academic institutions, universities are becoming more inclusive of Indigenous peoples. Indeed, among Canadian universities, there is a desire to engage in reconciliation work between Indigenous and non-Indigenous peoples to address the institutional erasure of Indigenous peoples (Gaudry and Lorenz 2018; Treleaven 2018). As such, universities are seeking to hire Indigenous scholars to address the severe shortage of Indigenous professors in the Canadian professoriat, where Indigenous professors make up a mere 1.4 percent of all professors across Canada (Academic Women's Association 2018). Because of the longstanding absence of Indigenous faculty in universities, many professors have been hired across Canada recently. From anti-racist work to Indigenizing academic spaces to efforts to challenge settler colonialism, many Indigenous faculty are compelled to bring their Indigenous ways of being into universities. As three Indigenous women scholars in academia, we are bringing more attention to our personal experiences with navigating the era of reconciliation and the Indigenization processes of our university, and we pivot the discussion toward enacting wellness as an act of resistance. While we amplify our voices in discussing these tensions, we recognize there are others who came before us (Archibald 2009; LaRocque 1996; Monture and McGuire 2009), and we are adding to the ongoing conversations among Indigenous women academics.

Some Indigenous women scholar experiences speak to the reconciliation overwork that is often placed on the few Indigenous women across the Canadian professoriat (Bedard 2018; Gabel 2019). Yet, for those Indigenous women scholars who are in academic spaces, there is little attention to how they navigate the complexities that arise. Further, narratives of the inner workings of how Indigenous women thrive in such spaces are scarce. While our Indigenous women academic aunties and ancestors carved pathways for the current cohort of Indigenous women scholars, we recognize that there is not a broader conversation occurring where newly arrived scholars may learn the practices of navigating the often exclusionary and dominant settler-colonial spaces, where we seek to thrive.

Thus, in this chapter, through narratives and poetry, we explore this reconciliation work and the challenges to creating *decolonial care* among ourselves. Through our narratives and poetry, we demonstrate the expectations of this reconciliation labor, the emotional labor associated with it, and how we create kind, loving spaces from which to generate support; in so doing, we craft our Indigenous feminist praxis, which we call Codes of Wellness. Our aim in this chapter is to not promote a deficit-view of our professions but to bring much-needed awareness to the emotional and physical labor that reconciliation and Indigenization work demands of us. By drawing on our narratives and poetry, we seek to add to the ways Indigenous women are creating Indigenous feminist and decolonial practices in the academy by engaging in truth-telling and enacting deep care among each other. In this chapter, we first provide an overview of Indigenous feminisms as our conceptual framework to engage in our narratives. Second, we share three narratives that are interwoven with poetry to show the complexities of reconciliation labor, and the decolonial praxis that emerged from our work together. To this end, some of our poems were created individually, while some were created collaboratively in the spirit of our decolonial self-care. We hope that bringing awareness to the (extra) emotional labor of our work may help create a broader community of support across decolonial alliances.

Conceptual Framework: Indigenous Feminisms

Indigenous women are often the first ones to name the issues in our spheres of work, family, or wherever we may find ourselves. This ability to name that something is wrong to find solutions is a fundamental aspect of Indigenous feminist praxis. For decades, strong-willed Indigenous women have bravely named the issues in academia to usher in much-needed change in the academic realm (Acoose 1995; Anderson 2016; Arvin, Tuck, and Morrill 2013; Battiste 2013; Fredericks 2011; Green 2007; Maracle 1996; Mihesuah and Wilson 2005; Monture-Angus 1995; Suzack et al. 2010; Tuhiwai Smith 2013). Some of the overarching issues Indigenous women contend with while working within the academy include the ongoing proliferation of colonialism, heteropatriarchy, and whiteness (Arvin et al. 2013); sexism, racism, and other disempowerments (Nickel 2020); universities seeking Indigenization without first understanding what Indigenization demands (Gaudry and Lorenz

2018); and the metaphorization of decolonization (Tuck and Yang 2012), among others. It is important to critically examine the issues and complexities of the academy as a means to change it for the betterment of Indigenous students and professors now and into the future. One way to continue to draw attention to the complexities is using our voices to share our experiences, which is a hallmark of Indigenous feminist scholarship and praxis.

Indigenous feminist scholarship and praxis are often deeply personal and strengthened by narratives (Anderson 2020; Suzack et al. 2010). As Emma LaRoque, who is Cree/Métis, clarified:

> My use of voice is a textual resistant technique. It should not be assumed, as it so often is, that using voice means "making a personal statement," which is then dichotomized from academic studies. Native scholars and writers are demonstrating that voice can be, must be, used within academic studies not only as an expression of cultural integrity but also as an attempt to begin to balance the legacy of dehumanization and bias entrenched in Canadian studies about native peoples . . . [and is understood as] Native resistance scholarship (LaRoque 2009, 13).

Indeed, Indigenous feminist decolonial praxis is necessarily "messy" (Anderson 2020, 209), and it is deeply personal. As much as it draws attention to the issues and complexities often experienced within the academy, Indigenous feminist praxis also regenerates our ancestral teachings (McGuire-Adams 2020).

Indigenous feminisms create a space for Indigenous women to bring their ancestral traits, coupled with our collective decolonial praxis, into the spaces where we work, to better support our thriving. The definition of thrive is to grow or develop vigorously, to flourish. In the academy, a key element for Indigenous women to thrive is to enliven our ancestral traits and teachings. Child (2012), who is Ojibwe, describes how contemporary Indigenous women do not leave behind their ancestral traits but reinvigorate them into their everyday lives and careers. For instance, among the Ojibwe it was women who had authority over *manoomin*, or wild rice, from production to distribution and trade. And it was women who drove the *manoomin* economy. This drive to lead, which supports families and communities, is ongoing, but it has shape-shifted into other leadership roles. Among the Métis, women uphold the visiting way (keeoukaywin), which operationalizes the ways of governing ourselves in the ways that kinship, well-being, and cultural values intersect with one another. This practice is ongoing (Flaminio et al. 2020; Gaudet 2019).

Monture-Angus (1995), who was a Mohawk scholar (and is now in the spirit world) imagined the creation of an Indigenous Women's Network, representing many Indigenous women and our identities, to address the oppression and exclusion Indigenous women often experience. More recently, Anderson

(2020), who is Métis/Cree, considered how the university can be a space where she animates her role as an academic auntie, which brings responsibility, acknowledges her authority, and bridges her Indigenous community roles to her academic roles. In doing so, Anderson creates a community praxis within academia that is deeply informed by Indigenous feminisms; she brings other Indigenous women together in the academy to build a network of Indigenous women-led initiatives, which fosters connection and community where Indigenous women thrive. Indeed, as Indigenous women, when we come together to see, hear, and support each other, we enact our roles as catalysts of change. As three Indigenous women who seek to disrupt the challenges we encounter and thrive within the academy, we take up our decolonial feminist praxis by offering our narratives that are braided together with our poems. The poems were written in the moments when we embodied deep care for each other and felt the most exhaustion from carrying the weight of the emotional labor. Through our poems and narratives, we add to the growing crescendo of Indigenous women's voices, across the academy, that speaks back to the often-troublesome spaces we encounter that disrupt our well-being. Rather than face these tensions in isolation, we offer our voices and experiences, which we came together to share. Through our sharing with one another and other Indigenous women scholars, we offer our Codes of Wellness, which are acts of caring among each other and for oneself. It is the Codes of Wellness that demonstrate our collective resistance to the heaviness we often carry as Indigenous women in the academy.

First Narrative: Reflecting on "Giving Voice," Our Broader Research Project

The broader relationship-building this chapter is drawing from is driven by the conversations we had when we saw one another for brief moments at campus meetings or events. We would meet intentionally to catch up, or catching up would be an unintended result of another campus-wide event that had reconciliation as a broad outcome. We were always stealing time, because there is never enough time in the academy with competing priorities. The overarching question of these campus and faculty reconciliation events and meetings was often "What do Indigenous peoples want?" While we spurred a separate research project titled "Giving Voice" that described what Indigenous women in the academy want to see regarding reconciliation (Ward et al. 2021), we can tell you what we do not want: more promises with little action, epistemic violence and racialization, disrespect, fuller plates of things to accomplish because we are the only one in our department or faculty carrying the heavy and ominous banner of reconciliation and Indigenization, to be in isolation anymore, and to be tokens or ignored when we ask critical questions.

Consequently, we seek to evoke our grandmothers' resistance and resilience through gathering and not isolating ourselves, as the Western worldviews dictate. We gathered Indigenous women scholars together to talk about reconciliation and how reconciliation manifests itself in the work we do. This was the impetus of the gatherings we hosted in 2018 and 2019. We hosted a sharing circle, a collaborative workshop, and a kitchen table conversation (Ward et al. 2021). We asked the following questions:

1. How do you define reconciliation?
2. What is the role(s) of women in the work of reconciliation?
3. What issues arise, personally or professionally, when doing reconciliation work?

As one can imagine, these questions were not easy to answer without defining reconciliation, as there are different understandings of the word. Some women felt that reconciliation is dead and should be called "wreckonciliation," while some remained optimistic about what it offered. Some women felt beholden to reconciliation because they were hired because of reconciliation efforts. Some women even felt that a return to our ways of treaty-making and working together would bring true reconciliation. But one comment hung in the air: "What do Indigenous people have to reconcile?"

Throughout the gatherings we had with Indigenous women, we did not settle on one definition of reconciliation, but we deeply considered themes, complexities, experiences, and tensions of reconciliation. The three main findings from our initial research project are: 1) returning to our grandmothers' ways: relational accountability and responsibility, 2) settler responsibilities and accountabilities, and 3) working together to build a new way: giving space for the hardships of reconciliation (Ward et al. 2021). While the results of our coming together are published elsewhere, in this chapter we want to write about our process of becoming decolonial sister scholars through this research, and to discuss creating our Codes of Wellness.

Some of our gatherings' outcomes were building community and returning to our lifeways as women. Although our overarching purpose was to unpack reconciliation, to find out what was happening with our women-kin in the academy, and to hold space for one another, something really beautiful manifested, something unintended—the creation of our deep connection as decolonial sister scholars and the envisioning of our Codes of Wellness.

We recognize the complexity of speaking about reconciliation in the academy and the power dynamics at play, including the creation of jobs stemming from the Truth and Reconciliation Commission of Canada's Call to Action

(2015). And yet we must maintain a critical eye on the systems of power within the academy, given the lack of institutional accountability toward Indigenous scholars. Bringing our Indigenous ethics with us wherever we go entails enacting them in even the hardest of situations. It makes us think about how settlers need to take up the language of and implement the values of consent, accessibility, and inclusion in their reconciliation work. When we start to turn the sword inward and blame ourselves for being complicit in colonial ideologies, that is when the trickster's medicine is doing its job. We cannot be complacent or forget that we need to disrupt settler colonialism in all that we do, which is exhausting. This trickster's medicine demands that we must be mindful of the colonial dynamics implicated in academia, or we may begin to turn on ourselves and one another.

NICENESS IS NOT KIND
By Tricia

I'm too kind for academia
In an act of niceness, White people invite me for coffee, not to form a relationship with me
But to take from me
Use my knowledge
Without giving back
Taking
But offering nothing in return
Are there any genuine relationships between us and White people in these academic spaces?
If people showed genuine kindness
Genuine care
Then they would give of their time
Willingly
No preconceived asks
No favours
No teach-me moments
I'm too kind for academia
That is why I am asked for coffee

Second Narrative: Creating Sister Scholar Relationships and Reflecting on the Risks and Emotional Labor

These situations, of sitting in the discomfort of having to perform our Indigeneity for people who wish to navel gaze, gave rise for us to flesh out what it means for us as Indigenous women to work together and to create our Codes of Wellness.

NÎCI-ISKWÊWAK[1] (MY FELLOW SISTERS)

By Jennifer

Starting from a place of self-love and self-care is not easy,
When we've been taught to feel shame and feel less than.
When we've been told we will never make it in this place,
So we embody that; we feel it; it's our felt theory,
Within the academy.
But then we come together,
To riff off one another,
To sit at the kitchen table together,
To be in the same space as one another.
To build our knowledge bundles together,
To work in concert with one another,
Be in wahkohtowin[2] with one another,
Not in competition, but in collaboration.
Building each other up.
When I hurt, you hurt,
Because we are in this together.
Letting one another know that if they fall,
We will be there,
To say:
You're amazing.
Now get up.
Âpahkawihisok[3]
Don't allow colonial beliefs to seep in,
To your bones,
To the marrow and the sinew,
Of who you are.
You are F*CKING brilliant decolonial sister scholar.
Your ideas are going to change the world.
Iskwewak[4]
Sâkihitowin[5]
Pimâtisiwin[6]

Coming together as decolonial sister scholars can be compared to seeking a (metaphorical) life raft. We felt isolated performing the work of the newly hired Indigenous scholars with all the self-doubt and complexities that came with it. We often say yes to all the invitations and requests that come our way and have to put our goals and visions on hold to serve others. We came to one another breathless, swimming in the ocean of academia with no bottom, and climbing onto the life raft that is a space to catch our breath, to check in with one another, and to hold space for one another.

The purpose of this work was to gather and to write about what is meaningful to us as Indigenous women in the academy, especially as we had just been hired as part of the university's reconciliation strategy. The isolation we felt within our respective faculties was the first driving force to come together. As Indigenous women, we carry and honor our responsibilities to ourselves, our families, and our communities. We each are choosing to be within colonial academia for the betterment of ourselves and the next generation of students and scholars, and we have a right to be here. And we are here because of the previous Indigenous women scholars who came before us; we stand on the shoulders of and draw strength from the women who came before us from our communities and other decolonial sister scholars. But this work is crushing at times.

POETIC INTERLUDE

By Cindy and Jennifer

Is anyone else complaining about feeling reconciliation burn-out?
Hitting the wall?
> Wanting to re-frame our complaints to concerns in an effort to shift the downward spiral of the reconciliation gaze cloaked in compliments, threats, justifications, manipulation, and even the perception that "reconciliation is the new sexy" within the academy.

You feeling sexy yet???
In some ways, we wanted to interrupt the sexiness of reconciliation given we had not yet even Flirted
Courted
> Dated or perhaps even consented to what felt like an arranged marriage, imposed.

In our conversations, we began to identify the pitfalls of reconciliation such as the false empowerment resulting in losing sight of our power in its isolation.
Is there a trickster in the room?
Or maybe the trickster is inside of us tickling our funny bones or urging us to gather in solidarity with one another.

We became aware that our isolation was distancing us from our bodies, our teachings, our land, and each other. Georges Erasmus's strong statement: "we are sick and tired of being your conscience," from his speech titled "What do we have to celebrate?" (Fiery Speech on Native Rights 2010) that was given during the 125th Anniversary of Canada, struck a chord in our heart storm, which includes ideas generated from thinking with open hearts and not just our minds. See Photograph A. We could see ourselves getting physically sick as we felt the mental and emotional burden of our presence being perceived as the "inconvenient scholar," as if we didn't fulfill the checkbox of reconciliation or behave accordingly.

The Emotional Labor of Reconciliation and Indigenization 73

Reconciliation work often feels like performativity, performing our Indigeneity through playing the part of the tokenized Indian (Bedard 2018). As Bedard (2018) unapologetically states, "Universities like to hire us to be their token Indians, like cigar store Indians standing quietly inside their institution, but we are not welcome to have a voice, opinion, or thought that articulates our worldviews" (p. 82).

As Indigenous women, we came to realize that we need each other to be well. We need to visit, to engage in deep dialogues and conversations, to laugh, to cry, and to help one another. Given that our women's kinship ways were interrupted with colonization and Christian ideologies, coming together is a decolonial method of re-linking ourselves to shared responsibilities, as ancestrally, Indigenous women were always together. We were the catalysts of our communities and our homes, and we depended on each other. However, in the colonial spaces of the academy, with the perpetual busy-ness, competing for funding and evaluations, and the continuous requests, we are kept apart. How often do we pass each other in the hall or at a meeting and ask, "How are you?" and reply "I am so busy, but let's make time to visit." In these moments we can sense a deep yearning to continue our connections;

FIGURE 4.1. Photograph: A Heart Storm. Photograph by Cindy Gaudet.

it is ancestral, and it is in our blood memory. Becoming mindful of how the academy will work us to exhaustion and how we need our connections to help us thrive was a critical moment for us as decolonial sister scholars.

When we first came together, we could feel the energy of good medicine as our spirits felt uplifted. The warmth of space and feeling welcomed and not judged was vital to feeling safe enough to share our burdens. There was no interference, such as attempts to fix or save one another, or to compare stories. Listening deeply and empathetically to the experiences of each other, our voices were and are interwoven throughout, not separate. We hope that in writing this chapter, the light will shine on our experience. We recognize that there is a long history of Indigenous women in the academy that remains untold and unknown. The invisibility of Indigenous women's struggles and leadership within the academy is reinforced by the assumption that, through showing our vulnerabilities, we will be assumed to be incapable or incompetent of succeeding in these spaces. So we started each meeting by sharing our vulnerabilities. We are expected to perform the labor, to take on all the requests, but we are not allowed to express the emotional labor and the risk of saying no.

We acknowledge the risk we are taking in sharing our truths of being decolonial sister scholars and dealing with the reconciliation labor we face. Often these sorts of vulnerabilities are hidden, tucked away from colleagues. But nothing will change for us, as decolonial sister scholars now and in the future, if we do not start to speak about the isolation, the burnout, the self-doubt. We became each other's life rafts, and in the space where we caught our breath together, we built a strong connection from which to thrive. Don't all sister scholars need this? We believe we do, and we offer our vision for coming together.

Third Narrative: Enacting Codes of Wellness

KEEOUYKAYWIN: INTERRUPTING COLONIALITY

By Cindy

I have learned to psychologically coerce myself. Doubt. Shame. Oppression. Guilt.
Yet there is power in the beaded earrings I adorn my body with.

I have learned to imprison myself. Dignity. Integrity. Pride. At stake.
Yet there is power in my mother's way of visiting me out of darkness.

I have learned to hate myself. Love. Respect. Truth. Gone missing.
Yet there is power in my grandmother's life story.

I have learned to submit and to aggress. Kindness. Wisdom. At the margins.
Yet there's power when I sit with my sisters.

I have learned to be uptight. Costing laughter. Play. Pleasure.
Yet there is power in the children I belong to.

I have learned to ignore the invisible. Spirit longing.
Yet there is power in our songs and dances.

I have learned to alter my voice. Creativity gone stagnant.
Yet there is power in my drum and chant.

I have learned to isolate myself. Gossip winning.
Yet there is power in gathering around old women's teachings.

I have learned to believe in lies. Questioning my value and my people's resistance.
Yet there is power in putting my feet and hands into the river.

I have learned to clothe myself with toxins. Creating new forms of dis-ease.
Yet there is power in my sister made clothing.

I have learned to trust false prophets. Masking the truth.
Yet there is power when I breathe into the belly of my respond-ability.

I have learned that psychological coercion is normalized. Unspoken violence.
Yet there is beauty and love in each bead of truth we sisters regenerate together.

    We practiced and felt our Codes of Wellness before we knew them as such. We gathered in Edmonton to finalize the research methodology and article preparation for our Giving Voice project with Cindy and Jennifer. Cindy offered her home for our work and invited Tricia to stay with her. When the three of us came together, Cindy was sick, Tricia was becoming sick, and we were all dealing with many exhausting and trying issues at work. Through our visit, though, which occurred over three days in October 2019, we engaged in debriefing, visiting, caring for one another, laughing, and crying. The debriefing was a letting go of the stressors by talking about them in safety with each other, while being met with love, honesty, and validation. There was no judgment, no harsh words, just love. Through this, we visited. We talked about our project, our lives, our families, our hardships, and our successes. We laughed big belly laughs, as Indigenous women do, and we cried, too. As we visited, we cooked for each other, we drank wine and tea, we took care of one another. We smudged and prayed. We remembered our grandmothers' ways of visiting that produced wellness. We held space for one another to be vulnerable. We were not aware of it as it was happening. It was only after, when we reflected on our visit together and the overall research project, that we began to articulate that the process we just enacted was our Codes of Wellness.

A key theme running throughout our narratives is how we, as Indigenous women, embody our ethics and values when we do this work: following our teachings, listening to our ancestors, and connecting to future generations. Part of our creation of Codes of Wellness is developing Indigenous processes of reconciliation in the academy based on our deep connections, rather than relying solely on Western/colonial frameworks. This approach challenges the all-encompassing, male-centered, patriarchal, sexist, and productivity-capitalist labor the academy demands of us. We are creating a different way of operating in academia to actualize wellness in our careers and our relationships, amid the service, teaching, and research.

We offer our examples of the Codes of Wellness we heart-stormed after our three-day visit (see Photograph B), and since that time, we have invited more sisters and grandmothers to enliven and expand our Codes of Wellness. By inviting women to help expand our Codes of Wellness, we aim to continue building our decolonial praxis into the future. Thus, the Codes of Wellness are in flux and will be carved, shaped, and envisioned for years to come. For now, our Codes of Wellness include a variety of actions that hold space and reflect truth for one another. They include:

- Checking in with each other if we are unsure about an issue, a commitment, or anything that comes up in our academic careers. We often do not have formalized mentors, and even if we do, we may not have a deep level of trust built, as we do in our decolonial sister scholar relationships.
- Through this checking in, we are also helped to see what we cannot necessarily see. Often, when we are deeply connected to an issue, etc., we may need someone who understands the ecosystem of academia to offer their trusted advice.
- We help each other shift or recalibrate the harmful messages and actions we often experience in academia by naming them. We hold each other up, to help one another see our strengths and value.
- We keep one another accountable to what is meaningful research for our respective visions within the academy and value our contributions, despite the invisible and visible forces of settler colonialism.
- When we visit, we unburden our backpacks to let go of our pain and harms, which creates honesty and authenticity within ourselves and each other.
- We create mindfulness about the toxicity of lateral violence (e.g., microaggressions, gossip), and we actively engage in decolonization

processes. Throughout these processes, we acknowledge we make mistakes, but we practice kindness when we do.
- We have practice conversations with one another when we need to challenge or confront a toxic situation. Often, when we encounter such harmful or toxic comments or situations, we become quiet or paralyzed in shock. Through practicing conversations with one another, we gain confidence, through preparation, for challenging these harmful comments in the moment.
- We encourage each other to flex our creative expression within the academy.

FIGURE 4.2. Photograph: Heart Storming Codes of Wellness. Photograph by Tricia McGuire-Adams.

- We collectively agree to be discerning on the research projects we take part in as collaborators and co-principal investigators. Whose bus are you getting on? And why?
- We enact ceremonies with one another. An outcome of the broader research project is the creation of an Indigenous Women's Wellness Society in which a pipe ceremony was held to start our society off in a good way. We hope that the society will flourish with the initial members but also extend to create supportive ecosystems for other Indigenous and decolonial sister scholars across what is currently known as Canada.

Centering Indigenous women's experiences cannot happen in isolation, as it risks reproducing siloed successes, failures, and detachment. Creating Codes of Wellness and enacting them is essential for fostering our collective wellness in academia. By creating and enacting our codes, we challenge the isolation and the self-doubt we often experience in academia. By following the Codes of Wellness, we demonstrate a loving kindness with one another, as we navigate the tensions of being an Indigenous woman scholar. Through these actions, we are regenerating our authority as Indigenous women. We are re-envisioning our grandmothers' ways of taking care of one another to fit into our current lives and contemporary contexts. With this in heart and mind, we close this chapter with reflections on what lines our wellness bundles and invite other sister scholars to add to our narrative.

Final Reflections

THE LINING OF OUR WELLNESS BUNDLE

By Cindy, Jennifer, and Tricia

Sister-made beaded earrings adorn my body
Maamaa's love calls my spirit home
Gramma's courage dwells in my bones
Children invite me to their circle

Old women's teachings wake my senses
Sister-made and designed clothe my flesh.
Auntie stories regenerate my mind
Lullabies soothe my lingering ache
River medicine releases my burdens
Grandmother Moon binds me to the feminine mind

Sister scholars regenerate my spirit
Laughter and light invigorate
Ancestral knowledge bundles
Regenerated through our relationships

Ensuring our collective wellness
What lines your wellness bundle?

Through our narratives and poems, we created a decolonial praxis with each other, as we navigate the tensions of being decolonial feminist scholars within the academy. Through our narratives, we aim to assist in the broad dialogue among engaged Indigenous feminist scholars in the academy, and to reach out to build coalitions among Black, Indigenous, and people of color (BIPOC) feminist scholars. It is important to cultivate such practices as we build resistance to the erasures that often occur with BIPOC scholars in the academy. But this work is not complete. As cisgender Indigenous women, we cannot speak for 2SLGBTQIA scholars' experiences and tensions as they also navigate these settler colonial institutions and imposed erasures. Thus, we hope that future works will also speak to their experiences as we seek to build a collective of resistance.

Notes

1. The work Nîci-iskwêwak was learned from https://creeliteracy.org/2019/02/23/wake-up-my-sisters/.
2. Wahkohtowin: Kinship/relationality
3. Âpahkawihisok: Bring yourselves to consciousness
4. Iskwewak: Women
5. Sâkihitowin: Love
6. Pimâtisiwin: The good life

Bibliography

Acoose, Janice. 1995. *Iskwewakkah'ki YAW ni wahkomakenak: Neither Indian Princesses Nor Easy Squaws*. Toronto: Women's Press.

Academic Women's Association. 2018. The diversity gap in 2018: Where Are the Indigenous Peoples at Canadian Universities [Infographic]. https://uofaawa.wordpress.com/awa-diversity-gap-campaign/equity-at-canadian-universities-national-disaggregated-and-intersectional-data/.

Anderson, Kim. 2016. *A Recognition of Being: Reconstructing Native Womanhood*. Second Edition. Canadian Scholars Women's Press.

Anderson, Kim. 2020. "On Seasons of an Indigenous Feminism, Kinship, and the Program of Home Management." *Hypatia* 35: 204–213.

Archibald, Jo-Ann. 2009. "Creating an Indigenous Intellectual Movement at Canadian Universities: The Stories of Five First Nations Female Academics." In *Restoring the Balance: First Nations Women, Community, and Culture*, edited by Gail Guthrie Valaskakis, Madeline Dion Stout, and Eric Guimond, 125–48. Winnipeg: University of Manitoba Press.

Arvin, Maile, Eve Tuck, and Angie Morrill. 2013. "Decolonizing Feminism:

Challenging Connections Between Settler Colonialism and Heteropatriarchy." *Feminist Formations* 25(1): 8–34.
Battiste, Marie. 2013. *Decolonizing Education: Nourishing the Learning Spirit*. Saskatoon: Purich Publishing Ltd.
Bedard, Renee. 2018. "'Indian in the Cupboard': Lateral Violence and Indigenization of The Academy." In *Exploring the Toxicity of Lateral Violence and Microaggressions: Poison in the Water Cooler*, edited by Christine Cho, Julie Corkett, and Astrid Steele, 75–102. Cham: Palgrave MacMillian.
Child, Brenda. 2012. *Holding Our World Together: Ojibwe Women and the Survival of Community*. New York: Viking.
Erasmus, Georges. 2010, February 3. Fiery Speech on Native Rights, solidarity. Retrieved from https://www.youtube.com/watch?reload=9&v=ipxq8sR0_Lc.
Flaminio, Anna, Janice Cindy Gaudet, and Leah Dorion. 2020. "Métis Women Gathering: Visiting Together and Voicing Wellness for Ourselves." *AlterNative: An Indigenous Peoples Journal*. https://doi.org/10.1177/1177180120903499.
Fredericks, Bronwyn. 2011. "'Universities Are Not the Safe Places We Would Like To Think They Are, But They Are Getting Safer': Indigenous Women Academics in Higher Education." *Journal of Australian Indigenous Issues* 14(1): 41–53. https://eprints.qut.edu.au/38492/.
Gabel, Chelsea. 2019. "Being an Indigenous CRC in the Era of the TRC #Notallits crackeduptobe." *Aboriginal Policy Studies* 7(1): 88–98. https://doi.org/10.5663/aps.v7i2.29356.
Gaudet, Janice Cindy. 2019. "Keeoukaywin: The Visiting Way—Fostering an Indigenous Research Methodology." *Aboriginal Policy Studies* 7(2): 47–64. https://doi.org/10.5663/aps.v7i2.29336.
Gaudry, Adam, and Danielle Lorenz. 2018. "Indigenization As Inclusion, Reconciliation, and Decolonization: Navigating the Different Versions for Indigenizing the Canadian Academy." *AlterNative* 14(3): 218–227.
Green, Joyce. 2007. *Making Space for Indigenous Feminism*. Halifax: Fernwood Publishing Ltd.
LaRocque, Emma. 1996. "The Colonization of a Native Woman Scholar." In *Women of the First Nations: Power, Wisdom, and Strength*, edited by Christine Miller and Patricia Chuchryk, 11–18. Winnipeg: University of Manitoba Press.
Maracle, Lee. 1996. *I Am Woman: A Native Perspective on Sociology and Feminism*. Vancouver, B.C.: Press Gang Publishers.
McGuire-Adams, Tricia. 2020. *Indigenous Feminist Gikendaasowin (Knowledge): Decolonization Through Physical Activity*. Cham: Palgrave MacMillian.
Mihesuah, Devon, and Angela Wilson. 2005. *Indigenizing the Academy: Transforming Scholarship and Empowering Communities*. Lincoln: University of Nebraska Press.
Monture-Angus, Patricia. 1995. *Thunder in My Soul: A Mohawk Woman Speaks*. Halifax: Fernwood Publishing.
Monture, Patricia, and Patricia D. McGuire, eds. 2009. *First Voices: An Aboriginal Women's Reader*. Toronto: Inanna Publications and Education Inc.
Nickel, Sarah. 2020. "Introduction." In *In Good Relation: History, Gender, and

Kinship in Indigenous Feminisms, edited by Sarah Nickel and Amanda Fehr, 1–19. Winnipeg: University of Manitoba Press.

Suzack, Cheryl, Shari Huhdorf, Jeanne M. Perreault, and Jean Barman, eds. 2010. *Indigenous Women and Feminism: Politics, Activism, Culture.* Vancouver: UBC Press.

Treleaven, Sarah. 2018, December 7. "How Canadian Universities Are Responding to the TRC's Calls to Action. Universities Wrestle with How To Begin Their Transformation—and What They're Willing to Change." *Maclean's.* https://www.macleans.ca/education/how-canadian-universities-are-responding-to-the-trcs-calls-to-action/.

Tuck, Eve, and K. Wayne Yang. 2012. "Decolonization Is Not a Metaphor." *Decolonization: Indigeneity, Education & Society* 1(1): 1–40.

Tuhiwai Smith, Linda. 2013. *Decolonizing Methodologies: Research and Indigenous Peoples.* London: Zed Books.

Truth and Reconciliation Commission of Canada. 2015. Truth and Reconciliation Commission of Canada: Calls to Action. https://nctr.ca/about/history-of-the-trc/truth-and-reconciliation-commission-of-canada/.

Ward, Jennifer, Cindy Gaudet, and Tricia McGuire-Adams. 2021. "The Privilege of Not Walking Away: Indigenous Women's Perspectives of Reconciliation in the Academy." *Aboriginal Policy Studies (APS) Journal* 9(2): 3–24.

PART II
Spatialities and Temporalities

5

Methods, Modes, and Mapping
The (Re)Construction of Palestinian Sites as an Act of Return

LYDIA ZAKEL

Maps, geography, and cartography as historical media (Wilson and Stephens 2015, 209) have created borders and caused violence, from the "scramble for Africa" to Sykes-Picot (Wood and Fels 1992). As white explorers "mapped" the world, they organized and structured borders across spaces that had previously existed without them. These mapped borders have enabled conflicts for centuries, leading to dispossession, displacement, and genocide, among other issues. I, along with other decolonial geographers, call for geography and its maps to begin alleviating some of their past effects. The work of creating and alleviating conflict does not fall upon the objects of the maps themselves, but rather, it falls upon the mapmakers and cartographers that create the maps as material objects that represent their positionalities and ideologies. The map itself is a complex object involving multiple actors whose own positionality end up influencing the final product of the map and the problems that they often create. So, while people draw these maps, and governments recognize and honor the borders of the maps, the maps exist as material representations of both the actors of the people and the governments that they are mapping for.

Mapping, cartography, and other geographical methods have been harmful to communities. New methods and modes were developed that addressed these damages, including participatory action research (PAR), counter-mapping, and decolonial praxis, by trying to undo them. Just as maps once codified one vision of the world, they can now be repurposed to reduce and ease local and global tensions. In this chapter, I show how these new methods not only undo past damages and harms to communities but also highlight the ways that they provide possible futures through decolonial acts, specifically the right of return. I show how three villages (Sataf, Miska, and Al-Nada) were mapped and planned for reconstruction, allowing for an imagined and physical right of return for Palestinians to these places. As each place is (re)constructed and planned by different organizations or individuals, they contain specific imaginations and representations of return for Palestinians. Through these examples, I analyze how different village (re)construction projects allow Palestinians to practice the right of return through different modes of mapping. Here I use Matthew Edney's "modes" rather than "methods" of mapping, as each practice of creating a map is distinct to its time, space, and cultural, social, and political context (Edney 1993). Modes of mapping allow the material product of the map to become an intimate and distinct artifact that accounts for the situated context of its creators, thereby merging the creator's life and experience with the space on the map. As each planning process has unique and different objectives, I argue that by using decolonial spatial practices and modes, the planning and construction of Palestinian villages is an act of return for Palestinians to that (re)constructed place. Each place has its own modes and objectives of planned futures, and each of those modes and objectives demonstrates the multiplicity of futures existing among the Palestinian diasporic imagination.

State governments create maps to legitimize themselves and receive recognition from the world, thereby validating their territorial claims. Simultaneously, though, the map-making process provides recognition to the state as well. The maps are then a mode of recognition by and for the state. Therefore, under Israeli occupation and settler-colonization, the maps that Israel produces give Israeli villages and spaces legitimacy while erasing Palestinian villages, names, and spaces. Land is integral to the fight for Palestinian freedom, from the moment of ethnic cleansing from the Nakba in 1948 to the settler outposts and occupation today. The key to a Palestinian future is the reclamation and maintenance of their land, and these decolonial mappings can play a small role in the much larger struggle. Noga Kadman (2019) establishes the groundwork on counter-mapping in Palestine, where she works toward undoing Israel's history of erasing Palestinian land and history. But even when Palestinians themselves name their own places and sites, an elitist politics of remembering and place-naming controls the linguistic landscape from Rawabi to Ramallah (Brocket 2019). As second-class citizens in Israel, Palestinian spaces and place names become lost, and as citizens under Israeli occupation in the West Bank, their place names are hidden or altered. Through this normalization of maps that creates "spatial facts," (Edney 1993, 4) new theories and modes of mapping and cartography have come out of geography. To try to counter state-centric mapping, geographers have turned toward decolonial praxis through counter-mapping, PAR, and decolonial architectural work as techniques to actively give land back to Indigenous peoples (Townsend 2022; Campbell 2024). Briefly, counter-mapping is mapping that challenges dominant structures, such as bus riders or potential bus riders mapping potential bus lines that would remove the need for cars in a city or would improve public transit for people who need and use it most. PAR is project-based research that is done by and for the benefit of a community, like a development project planned and carried out by a community that increases their use of solar technology in the community. And finally, decolonial architecture is architecture that is designed and built with the communities' needs in mind, such as architecture that supports daily activities and living, like a garden built in the center of a building, so all the building's inhabitants can care for and share that garden space.

There is enough space in Israel and Palestine for all Palestinian refugees to return, but who then has the right to create the roadmap to return? There is no correct answer, as no one individual or body can represent the multiplicity of Palestinian voices and opinions on return and what it will look like for each of them. This tension is why creating a map of return and a map of the future for Palestinians has been so difficult. Each of the village examples described below shows a different design of Palestinian future towns and different conceptions of what return to that village means to the individual planners.

Maps are constantly changing, as they are objects that are never fixed (Edney 2019, 234). Feminist geographer Doreen Massey argues that space is always being constructed as an ongoing process (Massey 2005). Similar to Massey's argument on space, maps are physical objects that are constantly being constructed. Maps project a moment of space in time that is outdated from the moment of its production, as space's constant changes cannot be visualized on the map. Specifically, in Palestine, maps are inaccurate because of the "chaos" of everyday life encompassing Palestinian experiences. Maps are out of date immediately after (and even while) being drawn, because space is constantly changing through pop-up checkpoints, settler outposts, road closures and blockages, walls, and home demolitions. This constant flux in landscapes makes it nearly impossible for geographers to link spatial theory to map-making and create future maps of return. Instead, the patterns of changes in the present and past can be recognized, and a map for the future that reflects those patterns can be created. This can be seen in the example of the village of Sataf, where a part of the project for village reconstruction is including the changes from the occupation in the planning process. Another example is Al-Nada, where planners looked at past Palestinian traditions of spatial belonging to create a future space that reflected their presence in the past.

While under Israeli occupation, the most feasible act of return for Palestinians is mapping. Since return is seen as unattainable for Palestinians because of law, policy, demolitions, and violence, mapping becomes an active practice of return that works toward return through recognizing space through a material object. With a multiplicity of tools (software that includes ArcGIS, AutoCAD, Esri, Revit, and Forma), techniques, modes, and media that exist for positive village mapping and reconstruction, Palestinians can create places that can help build their futures.

In this chapter I will "map" through three villages in Palestine and three distinct mapping processes that Palestinians are using to map out return. The first village is Sataf. It is located in the Jerusalem district in Israel, which means that Palestinians in the West Bank and Gaza Strip cannot access or visit the village without a permit. By using Sataf, I show how the mode of countermapping can be used for village reconstruction for Palestinian return. Then, moving eighty-four kilometers northwest up highway 6, a segregated highway that does not allow those with Palestinian IDs to drive on it, we will come to our second case and example, the village of Miska. This mixed Palestinian and Israeli village is located within Israel's borders, meaning that the Palestinians who live there do so with Israeli residency and IDs. Miska's mapping can show how PAR is used to show a multiplicity of options for Palestinian return. Then finally, by going ninety-five kilometers down the Mediterranean coast, and across the checkpoint and border into Gaza, we will arrive at the last example village, Al-Nada. This village is not located on most maps but has plenty of mapping documentation by Palestinians. I will discuss how the mapping of architecture in Al-Nada creates a process of return for a group of Palestinian refugees that are often left out of policy and international law. Together, these villages and decolonial mapping modes show the intricate and nuanced possibilities for return that exist for and were created by Palestinians.

Before I continue any further, I would like to discuss my own positionality. As a non-Palestinian, non-Israeli, and non-Jew, my own identity has no stakes in this project. But as a member of a diaspora, I contemplate and experience life away from "home," but not to the same extent that Palestinians do. While many of them are not able to return to Palestine, I am able to return to the places of my parents and grandparents. As a woman who was privileged enough to travel to Palestine on multiple occasions with my American passport, I acknowledge the ways my own experiences shape my research and writing. One example is that many diasporic Palestinians are refused entry into Palestine or Israel by Israel and therefore are not able to conduct research using the same or similar methodologies. So my research has always been done in abiding by Palestinians and alongside Palestinians. I also want to make it clear that the Palestinians I spoke with during my research do not represent the voices and opinions of all Palestinians throughout the diaspora.

Counter-Mapping

Geography's disciplinary history is one of violence, produced through the process of map-making. Map-making and cartography as processes show a set place in time that can describe both the past and the present. As people are constantly changing their environments around them, maps are almost immediately outdated as they are being drawn, therefore showing a past space. This is especially true in Palestine, as life under occupation continues to change Palestinian environments and spaces at each minute, with either demolitions, road closures, or pop-up checkpoints happening at each moment. As local populations have historically and presently experienced violence and conflicts caused by maps, geographers have slowly begun to realize the ways maps have become objects created by and representative of governments and state actors that are central to creating this violence. Since realizing these dangers, some geographers have worked to shift map-making's purpose and methodologies to assist communities, rather than governments or corporations, in using maps for their own ends.

Bill Bunge is a historic example of this shift; he used maps in his community of Fitzgerald, Michigan, to make changes in space that benefited the community members, rather than ordering, structuring, counting, and disciplining them (Bunge 1971). Two examples of his most well-known maps are: "Where Commuters Run Over Black Children" and "Region of Rat-Bitten Babies." In addition to his mapping projects, he created free and accessible classes for community members to participate in and learn the process of counter-mapping and how to identify issues and use maps to create solutions in their communities.

By mapping out the problems to create solutions to fix them, counter-mapping was born. Here I look to the case study of Sataf in Israel (historic Palestine) as an example of counter-mapping and a decolonial spatial practice. Through Sataf, I explore counter-mapping by redesigning a destroyed village, allowing Palestinian student participants to understand the possibilities of return.

Counter-mapping as a decolonial spatial practice tells stories of the past, present, and future by linking together the past and the future to tell a story of the present. As a method and medium, counter-mapping originated in critical cartography and is a term coined by Nancy Peluso in 1995; she used mapping methods to support Indigenous interests in forest policies in Indonesia to challenge state and colonial powers (Peluso 1995). Counter-mapping has been used by geographers, critical cartographers, Indigenous peoples, allies, activists, and accomplices to change current maps and hegemonic views of space to work alongside and with Indigenous people so that they regain a right to their land. While many counter-mappers are Indigenous themselves, the mode of counter-mapping by non-Indigenous people cannot be done correctly without Indigenous consent and input. Indigenous work should be included in the process if the counter-mapping is being done in Indigenous spaces.

Counter-Mapping Sataf

As Palestine has been divided by empires throughout history, the maps of the land have changed, showing the rule and order of the land that is holy and sacred not only to multiple religions but also to many ethnic groups. (For example, these include Ottoman maps of Palestine during the Ottoman Empire, Ayyubid and Mamluk period maps, and maps during the Crusader period. Some of the ethnic groups included in these maps are Arabs, Kurds, Druze, Phoenicians, Bedouins, Roma, and Armenians.)

Despite the pretensions of objectivity by mapmakers and governments, these maps are arbitrary, as spatial belonging has always existed, no matter the political borders (Trudeau 2006). Beginning with the end of the British rule, Palestine has seen an increase of maps, borders, and control over the land from outside forces, including the United States, the United Kingdom, the United Nations, and the new state of Israel. By examining colonial maps with colonial and Anglicized place names, counter-mapping is a medium for resisting imperial histories of borders, place-naming, and violence created by geography's entanglement with the state. Also, counter-mapping can aid in visualizing return and its possibilities spatially on a map.

Salman Abu-Sitta, a Palestinian refugee and researcher who created the first Palestinian atlas of return, is the father of Palestinian counter-mapping. As his publications included extensive research on villages lost during the *Nakba* (the "catastrophe" of 1948) and the plight of refugees, he also includes maps on spatial futures in his projects (Abu-Sitta 2016; for example, see https://www.plands.org/en/maps-atlases). Abu-Sitta maps out the places that Palestinians can return to as well as the places that could be reconstructed for potential return in the future. He shows how Palestinians are reclaiming space through maps to tell a new future, including one of return. He founded the Palestinian Land Society (PLS), which has created a competition on mapping return. The PLS competition, "Reconstruction," allows university students in the Levant to spend a semester preparing a counter-mapping project of a destroyed village from 1948. With a semester to put together their reconstruction plans, students work toward creating a possible village that could exist both today and in the future.

Each village has its own unique history that holds specific stories of people, land, history, culture, and space. But during the *Nakba*, entire villages were

Methods, Modes, and Mapping   91

destroyed along with their "intricate social networks and cultural achievements" (Pappe 2007, 154). For the Reconstruction competition, students can select one out of one hundred villages that are listed (Competition History and Operation—Year 3 2019) and work to reconstruct the village and its stories from before its erasure. One of these villages is Sataf, located in Israel proper, to the west of Jerusalem. What was once a lively Palestinian village sits ruined and desolate among the Moshe Dayan Forest that was planted by the Jewish National Fund (JNF) after the *Nakba*. Today the village has remnants of bricked walls that remain, as tourists visiting the forest pass by and ignore the history that was once there. After Sataf's destruction, the village never repopulated, leaving the histories, people, and stories of Sataf to be forgotten or dispersed among the refugees in the diaspora.

Yasmina Salman was the winner of last year's Reconstruction project with her reconstruction of the village of Sataf. Salman, a university student and Palestinian of the West Bank, chose Sataf not because she had a personal or familial connection to the village, but because she was interested in learning about its history and the history of a Palestinian space outside the West Bank. She was given Google satellite imagery, British mandate maps, data, surveys, demographic information for the residents and their descendants, and hand-drawn maps of the village by its survivors. Through this data, Salman was able to show the new and possible future of Sataf through her careful

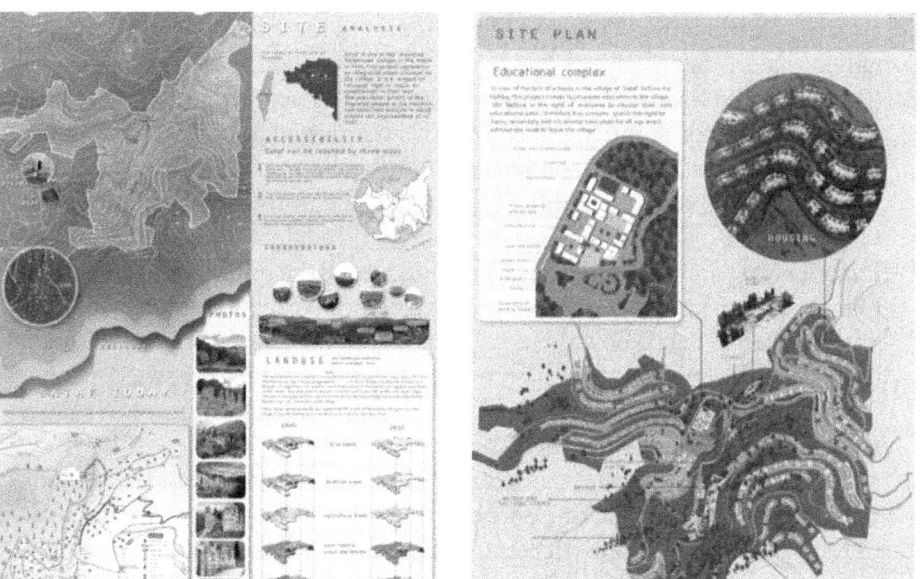

FIGURE 5.1. A small part of Salman's reconstruction project of Sataf. Created by Yasmina Salman (2019).

reconstruction, as well as prove that there is space for return (Competition History and Operation—Year 3 2019).

Colonial influence often lasts on maps through renamed or reconstructed places, while previous Palestinian spaces are lost or forgotten. To claim a space of return on a map for Palestinians, many students in Reconstruction start by removing Israeli influence and remnants on the land. The last land survey of Sataf while Palestinians were living in the village was conducted in 1945, three years before the *Nakba*. By using this final land survey in comparison to surveys and satellite imagery of today, Salman stated that her first task for the village's reconstruction was to remove anything "alien" that was added to the scene, such as a park built by the JNF after Sataf was destroyed during the *Nakba*. In her plan, Salman reconstructed this park as agricultural terraces for natural vegetation. Salman also decided to remove JNF-planted forests and replace them with Palestinian traditional housing. Through this removal of Israeli spaces on the land, I observe from Salman's competition statement (Competition History and Operation—Year 3 2019) that she is imagining and claiming a future Palestinian space on her maps by first erasing the colonial influence.

Although Salman's Sataf was carefully planned and executed, she faced multiple obstacles along the way to her reconstruction. One such obstacle was accessing quality aerial photographs of the village. Because Salman is a resident of the West Bank, she cannot access high-quality aerial data online, which made it difficult for her to construct or view the present-day land clearly. Additionally, 97 percent of the homes in the village were destroyed, which, according to Salman, "had made the village without a clear identity" (Competition History and Operation—Year 3 2019). As homes and dwelling spaces display the identity and culture of a family and a community, Salman said that she was left without knowing how dwelling space was used prior to the *Nakba*. Without an identity, it becomes difficult to reconstruct a village for a future that is recognizable to the displaced and their descendants. While historical maps show geographical imaginations of the future, Palestinians are often excluded from historical maps of their land. Through counter-mapping, villages such as Sataf show those Palestinians on the map again, on their own terms. This mapping mode can become an imaginative practice where people from Sataf (and their descendants) can begin to imagine a future of return to their village and see themselves reflected on future maps.

Many of the maps that came out of Reconstruction included temporary housing or hostels for people in the Palestinian diaspora who want to temporarily visit their ancestral villages. By including these, the urban plans allow for multiple options of return, rather than just one. As feminist geography shows us a multiplicity and fluidity of identities and belongings regarding space (Valentine 2007), counter-mapping, as shown through

Reconstruction, shows how that same belonging to space can also apply to a multiplicity of returns.

These counter-mapping projects, through Abu-Sitta's collection and PLS Reconstruction competitions, show Palestinians various possibilities of a future to which they can return. By mapping these possibilities of return on Palestinian land, Salman and other participants in Reconstruction make a claim to the land through the materiality of the map. These various possibilities of return bring together decolonial praxis and feminist geography to demonstrate that there is no single way of gaining access to land, but rather a multiplicity of returns that depend on the unique identities and experiences of each individual Palestinian refugee. In addition to counter-mapping, more modes have resulted in village reconstruction and the practice of return through the materiality of mapping.

Participatory Action Research

While counter-mapping is a useful mode of creating Palestinian space on maps, Zochrot takes it a step further by combining counter-mapping with PAR to map out Palestinian spaces of return. Zochrot is an Israeli nonprofit organization that aims to promote awareness of the *Nakba*. Its slogan, "To commemorate, witness, acknowledge, and repair," speaks directly to its research projects, including those using counter-mapping and those aimed at geography that embody decolonial praxis. Zochrot has projects that link counter-mapping with PAR methodologies, while conducting research and work *alongside* Palestinians rather than *for* them.

Since Palestinians know what is best for them and for return, PAR is a useful method for Zochrot "to abide by" Palestinians. Qadri Ismail argues that scholars should be "abiding by" rather than "abiding for" the places and people they are researching (Ismail 2005). PAR does this by creating research that is a collective effort between the scholars and participants, while at the same time trying to remove any hierarchies that exist between the scholars and participants. Rather than the researcher deciding what is best for people, the people themselves make that decision and then use the researcher as a tool, or a part of the process, to create change for themselves and/or the community. Previously, Zochrot has used PAR to document Palestinian needs and resources and used that documentation to create both theoretical and empirical solutions to solve problems that Palestinians face (Maoz 2000). Using PAR, Zochrot created a co-collaboration process where team members worked with historical data and maps of the village of Miska, located west of Nablus and north of Tel-Aviv, in Israel proper. PAR and counter-mapping are not mutually exclusive, and counter-mapping can be a mode within a PAR-constructed methodology, as Zochrot's project on Miska is.

Miska's PAR Project

Miska's location is known today, but its history before 1948 is often left untold. The village of Miska before the *Nakba* was rather small and obscure. The Palestinians living in Miska were predominantly Muslim, and their homes formed a square with two streets that intersected at the center of the village. Its population was small, but the village constructed a mosque and a school, as faith and education were important to the local community. Located in fertile land in the valley, Miska was a prime spot for agriculture, including the misk apple, thought to be named after the town.

During the *Nakba,* the people of Miska were wiped out. By the spring of 1948, the village became depopulated through forced removal and death. According to Zochrot, today the village:

> is covered with citrus groves, enclosed by cactuses growing along the perimeter. In the agricultural fields that once surrounded the village there exists Israeli villages.... The two-room school was still present up till 2006 when activists would hold memorial services to commemorate the lives that were lost at Miska and the [Israeli Occupation Forces] destroyed it on the grounds of trespassing. The mosque now serves as a storehouse for hay bales and agricultural tools. Fragments of the village well and surrounding enclosure can be seen today among the surrounding Israeli citrus trees throughout the land. ("Miska" 2014)

While parts of the village are still present, the people are gone, leaving the village uninhabited. The violence and destruction of the past and the scars that it left were covered by the planted groves and woods of the JNF. This has left the village unrecognizable, as the history of the people and the massacre they faced are concealed by non-native nature.

Zochrot's PAR project, Counter-Mapping Return, attempted to show the barriers that existed for Palestinian return to Miska. Fourteen Israelis and Palestinians worked together to show the details of return to a specific place rather than return as an abstract concept discussed in politics and policy. One of the project's first steps was autobiographical. Each participant brought an object, placed it on the map of Miska, and shared a story of the connection between the object, Miska, and themselves. This activity showed participants that each person had a personal connection to the village of Miska. The stories that were shared showed displacements and political awakenings around Miska (Segalo, Manoff, and Fine 2015, 352). While Israeli participants brought seeds or other agriculture products that represented the fertility of the land, Palestinians brought keys, representing the homes that used to exist in the village, to which they could no longer return. This divide between perishable objects of the present (agriculture) and the material objects of the past (keys) shows the divisions between who has access to the land presently, in the past, and in the future.

The second part of the PAR project was to design a future Miska. The group was divided into two groups, one of Israeli participants and another of Palestinian participants. Each group worked together to collaboratively create a map of Miska that could host Israelis, Palestinians, and returnees. Like the Reconstruction project through PLS, the maps needed to be comprehensive and show the plans for not only housing but also agriculture, schools, businesses, and transportation.

When finished, the Israeli group presented their map that attempted to restore Miska to its pre-*Nakba* roots. Although their map was made with complete sincerity, the Palestinian group was annoyed with it and commented on how it tried to keep Palestinian dwelling space in the past rather than moving forward toward a new future of reconciliation. While recreating a place to represent its existence in the past was thoughtful, space is constantly changing; therefore, a representation of the past would not reflect the landscape and lifestyle changes of Palestinians today. Returning to a reconstruction of a place in the past would be unrecognizable for Palestinians in Israel, Palestine, and throughout the diaspora. When reconstructing a village such as Miska, it is important to consider the ways Palestinians presently live and conduct their lives, rather than tying their whole existence and belonging to a place of the past. The Israeli group's map in this case subtly assumed that Palestinians were a people of the past, and their culture, landscapes, and identity stopped growing or changing at the point of the *Nakba*, while in reality, Palestinian identity grew, expanded, and challenged the ways we think about diasporic identity and belonging today (Mavroudi 2007). The final part of the project was to construct a map and a policy paper that everyone could agree on by incorporating criticisms of previous maps. This led to a map of Miska that included Palestinian spaces that were designated for Palestinian use as well as cohabitating spaces, so returnees could have multiple dwelling options.

Of course, problems arose during the PAR project, including around the issue of segregation. Participants spent a great deal of time zoning the dwelling spaces for Israelis, Palestinians, and returnees; the debate of segregating the returnees into their own zone was contested. Would it have been more useful to keep Palestinians in one space, where they are comfortable with each other? Or would it be more productive toward reconciliation to live all together? While these questions were debated during discussions on housing, the participants decided that the solution was to create multiple spaces for returnees. This would allow returnees to feel comfortable to choose where they would like to live in the new Miska.

Another problem that participants had with developing Miska was that each development plan, in some way, mirrored Zionist planning ("Miska" 2014). From the ways that villages were structured for Jewish refugees in 1948 to outposts that were set up and eventually turned into settlements, plans created by the PAR project participants tended to mirror Zionist planning initiatives. Although it was completely unintentional, people were adamantly against having their Miska, in any way or form, carry a part of Zionist planning. So the participants continued until they found the perfect way to build the village without any Zionist influence.

As PAR allows for a multiplicity of voices in the work of constructing a village for returnees, the unique history of the land and its people come together to create a city that is a space for returnees without displacing the current population. PAR as a mode shows how intricate networks and histories can be used for a specific place where all actors involved can come together and agree as a team. Also, through the planning process for returnees, Palestinians and Israelis can see the materiality of what return would look like in their present spaces and maps. But whether the future plan for Miska will be constructed and accepted by the Israeli state and relevant departments is completely out of the PAR team's hands.

Hidden Villages

Al-Nada is a village in Gaza that has been hit with waves of destruction. Close to the Gaza–Israel border, with the Eretz checkpoint just meters away causing friction with the patterns of immobility in Gaza, Al-Nada suffers from Israeli violence by the Israeli Occupation Forces (IOF) and other actors that enforce the border and blockade. Located in the North Gaza governorate of Palestine, between Beit Hanoun and Beit Lahia, a simple internet search for Al-Nada shows the remaining bones of architecture that lie where a once lively neighborhood stood.

Beginning this project, I found it nearly impossible to locate Al-Nada on a map. By using aerial images provided by Decolonizing Architecture Art Residency (DAAR), Google Maps, and written descriptions from village stories, I was able to pinpoint the location of Al-Nada before its most recent destruction in 2014 ("Al Nada Neighbourhood Community Based Reconstruction Plan" 2016). The destruction of a village from space that cannot be found online is a key tactic that the corporate leaders of Google Maps and other technologies use to erase the history, narratives, and futures of Palestinian people. Zena Agha shows us:

> Moreover, as a direct consequence of US government policy, Google Earth is legally required to restrict access to images of Palestine-Israel. Bipartisan

legislation passed by the US House of Representatives in 1997 limits the quality of satellite imagery of Palestine-Israel available to the public through US-based platforms like Google Earth and Bing Maps. The Kyl-Bingaman Amendment (KBA) to the US National Defense Authorization Act restricts the availability of high-resolution satellite imagery by preventing satellite operators and retailers in the US from selling or disseminating images of Palestine-Israel at a resolution higher than that available on the non-US market. (Agha 2020)

These legal restrictions of aerial imagery of Palestine are intentionally made by corporate leaders of Google Maps and other mapping technologies and by state governments. Only low-quality imagery is available, and since it is not being updated at the same rates as other places around the world, laws and technologies are complicit in erasing Palestinian space, people, histories, and presence. Google Maps and other online maps are used for political ends and reflect modern geopolitical power relations (Soeller et al. 2016). Also, present human rights violations are being obfuscated by the never-updating imagery that does not show home demolitions, settlements, the blockade, the Apartheid Wall, or the everyday tear gas that Palestinians face. Because people are not able to view these violations of international law and human rights online, Palestinian lives are left invisible to the outside world. The insistence on low-quality resolutions for aerial views of Palestine does not reveal the intricate detail of the land that shows people's spaces, agriculture, villages, and ways of life, making it nearly impossible to recreate or build return. Even though online maps are erasing Palestinians and the reality of the land, Palestinian refugees are using these same media through decolonial methodologies to refuse their erasure and map themselves onto the land in a justice-centered approach (Quiquivix 2014). Palestinians are showing how decolonial work and mapping are important for refugees, to keep ties between themselves and the land of Palestine.

Decolonial Architecture in Al-Nada

The materials (maps, projects, and architecture) in these examples are more than a metaphor for decolonization. Rather, they are physical representations of decolonial acts (Tuck and Yang 2012). Through patterns of destruction and occupation, Al-Nada has a unique tie to decolonial acts through the materiality of architecture. This piece was written and submitted before the Gaza genocide that began in October 2023. Therefore, much of the destruction that was already done to the places that were being reconstructed are further destroyed, which has further affected the decolonial mapping projects, including that of Al-Nada. However, as Palestinians have shown and demonstrated their resilience in the past, they are doing so again by already starting development and reconstruction plans for homes and places that were lost due to the genocide.

In 2005, Israel withdrew its military and citizens from Gaza and then proceeded to implement a harsh and destructive blockade on Gaza that allows Israel to continue to implement waves of violence that destroy villages and agricultural land. Al-Nada, being close to the border, has experienced the patterns of this violence, most recently in 2014 when an "Israeli military operation between July and August 2014 caused the destruction of approximately 18,000 housing units throughout Gaza" (Petti 2016). In Al-Nada, during this period, 192 homes were destroyed, and seventy-two families were displaced, creating new patterns of refugees that go unrecognized as legal refugees through the UN Relief and Works Agency (UNRWA) and international law. From this, Al-Nada became a project to create a Palestinian space of return for those who were internally displaced.

To recreate Al-Nada and repatriate the refugees who were internally displaced, DAAR partnered with the Ministry of Public Works and Housing in Gaza to reconstruct the village and allow Palestinians to return ("Al Nada Neighbourhood Community Based Reconstruction Plan" 2016). DAAR centers a decolonial architectural approach in its work, with goals of Palestinians regaining access to land and returning to their villages. DAAR's focus on decolonial architecture attempts to recreate buildings and infrastructure on Palestinian land that build up Palestinian social and community structures, rather than copying Israeli architectural practices that ignore Palestinian contexts. As these architects in Palestinian space remove their infrastructure and architecture from Western-centric ideas of space, therefore decolonizing Palestinian architecture by allowing Indigenous Palestinian architecture and design to enter, the architectures also serve as spaces that build Palestinian embodied autonomy and organizing (Naylor 2017). DAAR's material constructions allow for its projects to implement the right of return.

Al-Nada's patterns of construction, destruction, and reconstruction show the cycle of Palestinian displacement and return to Gaza in relation to Israel's violence. Al-Nada was originally constructed as a village to host Palestinian returnees to Beit Hanoun, displaced since 1948. Its location was selected as a place on Palestinian land that would hopefully stop the encroaching Israeli settlement on the other side of the Eretz checkpoint. DAAR's reconstruction project for Al-Nada "forces us to see things from the ground and from the perspective of the community, rather than from a distance or above . . . and forces us to consider longer temporalities of transformations, rather than short-lived events cultivated by the media" (Petti 2016). These architectural outputs through reconstruction create something much larger than new homes and a village; they create new imaginations of a future, new views of people and their lives, and concrete visions of Palestinian claims to land.

FIGURE 5.2. A part of the construction plans of Al-Nada that show the communal hosh. Created by DAAR (2016).

Communal space is fundamental to Palestinian resistance and return. As Palestinians gathered in schools, hospitals, mosques, and churches during the First Intifada to strategize, plan, and mobilize their communities, Israel made it illegal for groups of five or more people to gather in public. These public events moved to private locations in people's homes to continue their strategies. As collective space is planned through each of these projects, Al-Nada's planned communal space in the center of the neighborhood is different from those observed and controlled by state actors and the IOF, since it would not be mediated or cared for by the state or any governing agency. Designed like a *hosh*, or private courtyard shared by families, these spaces would be maintained by neighborhood families, while still preserving the social structures of the Palestinian family (Petti 2016). These would then allow Palestinian returnees a space of familiarity and a structure of communal and familial support.

As the other village reconstruction projects focused on the return of legally recognized Palestinian refugees from between 1948 and 1967 (and their descendants), Al-Nada's reconstruction prioritized the return of refugees who were displaced from their homes by the patterns of violence from the past few decades. Many reconstruction projects forget about displaced Palestinians who are not recognized through international law; their right of return is not recognized. Al-Nada's project is different in that it includes those Palestinians who are often invisible from everyday violence and displacement;

it makes their right of return visible through their maps and to their place. This mapping of return is metaphorically returning Palestinians to their land. It is the first planning step of many toward the visionary return to land. By recognizing the multiplicity of identities that exist among Palestinian refugees, DAAR's architecture of return is working toward physically allowing return for those refugees who are internally displaced in Gaza and are often overlooked by international agencies and states.

Conclusion

From the *Nakba* until today, Palestinians have held on to memories of their spaces in Palestine through their stories, hand-drawn maps, atlases, artwork, memoirs, books, and other media. As Palestinians continue to recreate their villages, they are not only holding on to memories of the past, but they are also constructing visions of the future. Memories of the past and the experiences of the present are mapped out to allow future maps that envision return to a specific space.

Through each of these village construction projects, return is imagined differently by each person, allowing for multiple possibilities and conditions of return. While Sataf can hold returnees for a lifetime through permanent housing, temporary housing also has been planned for returnees who wish to stay periodically, or for smaller periods of time. Miska has prepared for housing Palestinian returnees alongside Israeli and Palestinian populations, in a way that allows them to live where they feel most comfortable. And Al-Nada prepares for the return of internally displaced Palestinians in Gaza, while maintaining social structures through the village's architecture. A multitude of projects similar to the ones I have described allow Palestinians to envision possible futures of their villages, camps, and cities, and the different possibilities of return. (See Palestine Open Maps, https://palopenmaps.org/en#/, and Forensic Architecture https://forensic-architecture.org/.)

Each of these intimate imaginations of return relates to Palestinian identity, experience, and space. This shows us how, through reconstruction or construction projects, a multitude of Palestinian opinions on return exists, and Palestinians know the possibilities of return and are preparing for a Palestinian return to Palestine. Mapping these returns through each of their unique modes and techniques allows for that first step of return: physically envisioning the places of return on the land and showing Palestinian claims to land through the materiality of maps.

These three modes of mapping—counter-mapping, PAR, and decolonial architecture—are very radical, as they are done by Palestinians. While living under harsh occupation, settler-colonial violence, and an uncertainty of everyday life about whether they will be imprisoned, detained, or have their home demolished, these modes show the ways that Palestinians are actively creating a new future that exists outside of their harsh reality. Palestinian decolonial mapping is not only radical and important for those reasons, but it also counters the erasure of Palestinian space that Israeli lawmakers, governments, and IOF members are mapping. It gives the world a new and better way to see Indigenous land and Palestinian return that includes Palestinians on the physical space of the map.

Matthew Edney argues that mapping should be descriptivist and not prescriptivist (Edney 2019). Taking a descriptivist view of mapping is exactly what each of these cases did. There is not a set of rules for preparing a village for return; rather, the individuals who were working on the village (re)construction projects used the history of the space, the people who would be returning and their identities, and the existing social and familial structures to craft the village specifically to the people, place, and their needs. By taking a descriptivist approach, one that recognizes the multiple experiences, identities, and types of Palestinian refugees, village reconstruction allows for a multitude of returns that function properly for the descendants of those villages. The next step is for state actors to physically allow Palestinians to return to these places.

Bibliography

Abu-Sitta, Salman H. 2016. *Mapping My Return: A Palestinian Memoir*. Oxford University Press.

Agha, Zena. 2020, January 14. "Maps, Technology, and Decolonial Spatial Practices in Palestine." *Al-Shabaka*. https://al-shabaka.org/briefs/maps-technology-and-decolonial-spatial-practices-in-palestine/.

"Al Nada Neighbourhood Community Based Reconstruction Plan." 2016, January 23. *Studioauze: Informal Urbanism and Bioecology*. http://www.studioazue.eu/strengthening-the-national-early-recovery-and-reconstruction-of-gaza-detailed-development-plan-of-al-nada-neighborhood-gaza-2016/.

Brocket, Tom. 2019. "Governmentality, Counter-Memory and the Politics of Street Naming in Ramallah, Palestine." *Geopolitics*: 1–23.

Bunge, William. 1971. *Fitzgerald: Geography of a Revolution*. University of Georgia Press.

Campbell, Laura. 2024. Land Back: A Case Study of the Saugeen Ojibway Nation and One County's Attempt at Reconciliation. Diss. Toronto Metropolitan University.

"Competition History and Operation—Year 3." 2019, September 6. *Palestine Land Society*. https://www.plands.org/en/competition-news/competition-history-and-operation-year-3.

Edney, Matthew. 1993. "'Cartography without Progress': Reinterpreting the Nature and Historical Development of Mapmaking." *Cartographica: The International Journal for Geographic Information and Geovisualization* 30(2–3): 54–68.

Edney, Matthew. 2019. *Cartography: The Ideal and Its History*. University of Chicago Press.

Ismail, Qadri. 2005. *Abiding by Sri Lanka: On Peace, Place, and Postcoloniality*. University of Minnesota Press.

Kadman, Noga. 2015. *Erased from Space and Consciousness: Israel and the Depopulated Palestinian Villages of 1948*. Indiana University Press.

Maoz, Ifat. 2000. "An Experiment in Peace: Reconciliation-Aimed Workshops of Jewish-Israeli and Palestinian Youth." *Journal of Peace Research* 37(6): 721–736.

Massey, Doreen. 2005. *For Space*. Sage.

Mavroudi, Elizabeth. 2007. "Learning to Be Palestinian in Athens: Constructing National Identities in Diaspora." *Global Networks* 7(4): 392–411.

"Miska." 2014. *Zochrot*. https://www.zochrot.org/publication_articles/view/51436/en?CounterMapping_Return.

Naylor, Lindsay. 2017. "Reframing Autonomy in Political Geography: A Feminist Geopolitics of Autonomous Resistance." *Political Geography* 58: 24–35.

Pappe, Ilan. 2007. *The Ethnic Cleansing of Palestine*. Simon and Schuster.

Peluso, Nancy. 1995. "Whose Woods Are These? Counter-Mapping Forest Territories in Kalimantan, Indonesia." *Antipode* 27(4): 383–406.

Petti, Alessandro. 2016, June. "Destruction and Reconstruction." *Decolonizing Architecture Art Residency*. http://www.decolonizing.ps/site/cycles-of-destruction-and-reconstruction/.

Quiquivix, Linda. 2014. "Art of War, Art of Resistance: Palestinian Counter-Cartography on Google Earth." *Annals of the Association of American Geographers* 104(3): 444–459.

Segalo, Puleng, Einat Manoff, and Michelle Fine. 2015. "Working with Embroideries and Counter-Maps: Engaging Memory and Imagination within Decolonizing Frameworks." *Journal of Social and Political Psychology* 3(1): 342–364.

Soeller, Gary, Karrie Karahalios, Christian Sandvig, and Christo Wilson. 2016. "Mapwatch: Detecting and Monitoring International Border Personalization on Online Maps." In *Proceedings of the 25th International Conference on World Wide Web*: 867–878.

Townsend, Justine. 2022. Indigenous and Decolonial Futurities: Indigenous Protected and Conserved Areas As Potential Pathways of Reconciliation. Diss. University of Guelph.

Trudeau, Daniel. 2006. "Politics of Belonging in the Construction of Landscapes: Place-Making, Boundary-Drawing and Exclusion." *Cultural Geographies* 13(3): 421–443.

Tuck, Eve, and K. Wayne Yang. 2012. "Decolonization Is Not a Metaphor." *Decolonization: Indigeneity, Education & Society* 1(1): 1–40.

Valentine, Gill. 2007. "Theorizing and Researching Intersectionality: A Challenge for Feminist Geography." *The Professional Geographer* 59(1): 10–21.

Wilson, Matthew, and Monica Stephens. 2015. "GIS As Media?" In *Mediated Geographies and Geographies of Media*, edited by Chris Lukinbeal, Julie Cupples, and Susan Mains. 209–221. Dordrecht: Springer.

Wood, Denis, and John Fels. 1992. *The Power of Maps*. Guilford Press.

6

Subaltern Ways of Knowing
A Critical Spatial Analysis of Migrant Worker Knowledge Production in Beirut, Lebanon

SHIREEN KEYL

The Migrant Center is in the ethnically diverse and low-income eastern Beirut suburb of Naba'a. Naba'a is a complex place, home to Sunni and Shi'i Muslims, Armenian Christians, and other religious, ethnic, and political groups. This suburb is densely populated, with an estimated population of 12,000 in an area of three square kilometers. Naba'a is situated within meters of a highway that runs over the top of the interconnecting neighborhoods. Several lanes of traffic run directly under this stretch of highway; on one side is Naba'a, and the other is the suburb of Borj Hammoud, the Armenian Christian district. Along this centralized thoroughfare of commerce, street vendors, and heavy traffic, one finds the busy-ness and chaos of urban life. The narrow side street to the Migrant Center is lined with two- and three-story buildings that function as commercial and residential spaces.

On weekday mornings, coffee and friendly conversation are available from the Armenian Christian metal shopkeeper whose shop is steps from the Migrant Center. Nighttime brings the scent of *shisha* (flavored tobacco) bubbling from the *nargile* (water pipe), as friends and family gather to sit around the pipe while the business day winds down. The narrow alleys off the busy side streets are wide enough for one car to slowly creep through, although motorcycles commonly use these narrow passageways to avoid traffic. A zigzag pattern of miniature flags hanging from top-story balconies spot the blue sky, conveying the flag-owner's political or religious affiliation. The Migrant Center's alleyway is home to Shi'i Muslims and Armenian Christians. Along the maze of intertwining back alleyways and ubiquitous residential entrances, the shiny red door of the Migrant Center, with its red metal shutters, stands out among the faded brick.

Naba'a can be an unsafe place for migrant workers. Several of the domestic workers described being sexually and/or verbally harassed near the Migrant Center. Suba, the center's coordinator, reports: "Every single day, I go five meters from here to there, there is someone who teases you, who asks you, 'What's your price?' Very stupid, you feel so angry. This is very, very nonhuman." I too have witnessed many occasions of the harassment described by the migrant domestic workers. On one day at the center, someone had lit fireworks and had thrown them up against the window, and we heard an extremely loud blast. According to Dakshi, Suba's husband, these were not isolated incidents, and they occurred often. The Migrant Center had also been vandalized as well.

The decolonizing feminist praxis of the Migrant Center is apparent in that it recognizes how Western intervention in the Southwest Asia and North Africa (SWANA) region promulgates foreign agendas, namely U.S. interests, in the name of development and assistance.[1] Also, the center was created at the request of migrant domestic workers themselves. The role of Lebanese women and women migrant workers—both in their leadership and in the day-to-day operations of the Migrant Center—demonstrates how Lebanese activists honor the knowledge production of historically marginalized groups and actively resist the epistemic violence[2] forwarded by the Western-backed development industry.

An exploration of physical space is important because the Migrant Center, the site of this research, represents a powerful use of space for two main reasons. The first reason is the juxtaposition of the contentious space of the neighborhood of Naba'a, where the Migrant Center is located, against the empowering and oppositional nature of the Migrant Center itself. The neighborhood of Naba'a is at times perilous for the migrant workers and other patrons who attend the Migrant Center. Second, it is worthy to note how the center space is appropriated as a decolonial feminist space—that the Migrant Center exists independently of any funding originating from a Western entity (even though many of these institutions have offered monies) is in and of itself a reification of resistance to colonial powers offered under the guise of "development." The center is an activist space filled with overt human rights and anti-racist messaging, in addition to imagery that invokes feminist ideology. It is wholly relevant to bring a discussion about spatial analysis to this study, to demonstrate the ways that use of space acts as a conduit for power for migrant domestic workers, which I will present in the following pages.

Human migration has increased due to an influx of natural disasters,[3] armed conflict, economic hardship, and social and religious persecution.[4] Trends of women's international migration to work in the domestic labor market from the Global South to the Arab League States has been referred

6

Subaltern Ways of Knowing
A Critical Spatial Analysis of Migrant Worker Knowledge Production in Beirut, Lebanon

SHIREEN KEYL

The Migrant Center is in the ethnically diverse and low-income eastern Beirut suburb of Naba'a. Naba'a is a complex place, home to Sunni and Shi'i Muslims, Armenian Christians, and other religious, ethnic, and political groups. This suburb is densely populated, with an estimated population of 12,000 in an area of three square kilometers. Naba'a is situated within meters of a highway that runs over the top of the interconnecting neighborhoods. Several lanes of traffic run directly under this stretch of highway; on one side is Naba'a, and the other is the suburb of Borj Hammoud, the Armenian Christian district. Along this centralized thoroughfare of commerce, street vendors, and heavy traffic, one finds the busy-ness and chaos of urban life. The narrow side street to the Migrant Center is lined with two- and three-story buildings that function as commercial and residential spaces.

On weekday mornings, coffee and friendly conversation are available from the Armenian Christian metal shopkeeper whose shop is steps from the Migrant Center. Nighttime brings the scent of *shisha* (flavored tobacco) bubbling from the *nargile* (water pipe), as friends and family gather to sit around the pipe while the business day winds down. The narrow alleys off the busy side streets are wide enough for one car to slowly creep through, although motorcycles commonly use these narrow passageways to avoid traffic. A zigzag pattern of miniature flags hanging from top-story balconies spot the blue sky, conveying the flag-owner's political or religious affiliation. The Migrant Center's alleyway is home to Shi'i Muslims and Armenian Christians. Along the maze of intertwining back alleyways and ubiquitous residential entrances, the shiny red door of the Migrant Center, with its red metal shutters, stands out among the faded brick.

Naba'a can be an unsafe place for migrant workers. Several of the domestic workers described being sexually and/or verbally harassed near the Migrant Center. Suba, the center's coordinator, reports: "Every single day, I go five meters from here to there, there is someone who teases you, who asks you, 'What's your price?' Very stupid, you feel so angry. This is very, very nonhuman." I too have witnessed many occasions of the harassment described by the migrant domestic workers. On one day at the center, someone had lit fireworks and had thrown them up against the window, and we heard an extremely loud blast. According to Dakshi, Suba's husband, these were not isolated incidents, and they occurred often. The Migrant Center had also been vandalized as well.

The decolonizing feminist praxis of the Migrant Center is apparent in that it recognizes how Western intervention in the Southwest Asia and North Africa (SWANA) region promulgates foreign agendas, namely U.S. interests, in the name of development and assistance.[1] Also, the center was created at the request of migrant domestic workers themselves. The role of Lebanese women and women migrant workers—both in their leadership and in the day-to-day operations of the Migrant Center—demonstrates how Lebanese activists honor the knowledge production of historically marginalized groups and actively resist the epistemic violence[2] forwarded by the Western-backed development industry.

An exploration of physical space is important because the Migrant Center, the site of this research, represents a powerful use of space for two main reasons. The first reason is the juxtaposition of the contentious space of the neighborhood of Naba'a, where the Migrant Center is located, against the empowering and oppositional nature of the Migrant Center itself. The neighborhood of Naba'a is at times perilous for the migrant workers and other patrons who attend the Migrant Center. Second, it is worthy to note how the center space is appropriated as a decolonial feminist space—that the Migrant Center exists independently of any funding originating from a Western entity (even though many of these institutions have offered monies) is in and of itself a reification of resistance to colonial powers offered under the guise of "development." The center is an activist space filled with overt human rights and anti-racist messaging, in addition to imagery that invokes feminist ideology. It is wholly relevant to bring a discussion about spatial analysis to this study, to demonstrate the ways that use of space acts as a conduit for power for migrant domestic workers, which I will present in the following pages.

Human migration has increased due to an influx of natural disasters,[3] armed conflict, economic hardship, and social and religious persecution.[4] Trends of women's international migration to work in the domestic labor market from the Global South to the Arab League States has been referred to as the feminization of labor migration. The act of migration for women, especially when brought about by the above conditions, makes an already vulnerable population even more so in the receiving country, as they are viewed as a liability.[5] Central to this population are issues of social justice and social welfare, and access to health care, economic opportunities, and educational parity. Structural racism, xenophobia, and human rights abuses, especially sexual violence against women, are a significant problem for migrant domestic workers in the SWANA region.[6]

It is necessary to question these uneven systems of power for the purposes of seeking justice relating to the spaces marginalized women inhabit, the knowledge they claim, and the abuses of power they resist. A third world feminist framework endeavors to address these issues of power, space, and knowledge production.[7] This chapter contributes to the scholarship of decolonizing feminism in a critical analysis of the use of space. This writing also desires to bring to the forefront stories of hope, resilience, and determination. The purpose of this chapter is to examine acts of empowerment and resistance of African and Southeast Asian migrant domestic workers in Beirut, Lebanon. Even within the corrupt *kafala* (sponsorship) system under abject conditions, migrant women have not just persevered but created powerful lived experiences, which encourage and empower each other to foster and participate in community spaces.[8]

Critical Spatial Analysis

Theories of spatialization in human geography encompass discussions regarding the use and appropriation of space, and spatial analysis satisfies the "need to link experience, practice, and structure."[9] Early theoretical discussions that surround the use and appropriation of space detail how space acts as a mode for replicating, in various ways, the hegemony of a culture and society in which that space is located; according to Edward Soja, "[H]uman activities are not only shaped by geographical inequalities but also play a role in producing and reproducing them."[10] There are many ways to discuss, categorize, and analyze notions of space, including gendered spaces,[11] third space,[12] and embodied spaces/proxemics.[13]

For this chapter, I look at Soja's spatial theory of (in)justice, which incorporates a critical frame in its ontological analysis of the "triple dialectic": the social/societal, the temporal/historical, and the spatial/geographical "for understanding the nature of a critical spatial perspective and the new spatial consciousness that has been emerging in recent years."[14] This ontological triad for spatial analysis suggested by Soja is a necessary component when discussing use and appropriation of space for groups whose livelihoods are precipitated by movement and migration, sometimes as a result of human trafficking, and for some groups who, by way of human agency, assistance from social and nongovernmental organization (NGO) networks, and grassroots activism, have created authentic counter-cultural communities of practice. In the following, I will describe my research design; the participants of this study; the macro, meso, and micro sites; and my data collection tools.

The Study

This Institutional Review Board—approved qualitative study is informed by grounded theory, which does not aim to make generalizable claims "abstracted from empirical realities"; rather, the strength of grounded theory situates "grounded theories in their social, historical, local and interactional contexts," which strengthens theorizing claims that emerge and allows for "making nuanced comparisons between studies."[15] This study aims to contribute an emergent theory and practice of subaltern, transnational groups to explain how knowledge production, spatial analysis, and power are intertwined and create liberatory and resistance frameworks that function in educational and community spaces.

Participants

The main participants in this study were migrant domestic workers, NGO coordinators, and volunteer teachers. For this chapter, I draw from five interviews with Suba, the Nepali coordinator of the Migrant Center and former domestic worker; Dakshi, Suba's husband and a Nepali community organizer; Fakira, a Lebanese activist and coordinator of Tamkin, a feminist organization; Laurencia, a domestic worker from Madagascar and student at the Migrant Center; Irene, also a domestic worker from Madagascar taking classes at the center; and Thomas, a migrant worker.

Research Site

The physical location at which I conducted my fieldwork was the Migrant Center, located in Naba'a, a suburb of Beirut. The center is a cultural space specifically provided for migrant workers and their families. It came about because Lebanese activists sought the input of migrant workers, asking them what they wanted in terms of material resources. They said they wanted their own space and educational opportunities; as a result, the Migrant Center was created. I will elaborate in more detail on the space of the research site in the following pages.

Data Collection Tools
In-Depth Interviews

The in-depth interviews took place throughout the three months I conducted fieldwork. Research participants were the migrant domestic workers who patronized the Migrant Center, volunteer teachers, and NGO coordinators. Teachers, coordinators, and migrant students were interviewed at a place of their choosing, such as at a restaurant, on the campus of Lebanese American University, at the Migrant Center, or at their own homes; the migrant workers were interviewed at the center. As a starting point, I used a list of questions to begin the interview, but the in-depth interview does not work from a script of questions. On the contrary, the interview process is an organic process, one in which the interview becomes a dialogue, a space where the participant feels safe to share their lived experiences and their reflections on those experiences. I use the in-depth interview as a tool to allow for a reciprocal and dialogic discussion to take place and to allow space for agency, so the participant could speak freely, asking me questions as well during the course of our conversation. Participants were invited to discuss with the researcher their lived experiences in Lebanon, how the community center fostered connection, and educational experiences through the center. The following are examples of questions I asked: "Why do you come to the Migrant Center, and how do you feel when you come here?," "What have you learned since coming to the Migrant Center?," "What kind of friendships have you made at the Migrant Center?," and "In what ways have you changed since you started coming to the Migrant Center?"

Participant Observation

I am a dual Iranian American citizen and have lived and worked in Iran. I taught English as a Foreign Language at several schools and, as a graduate student, conducted fieldwork at a women's center in Tehran, Iran. Being a woman educated in the United States and holding an Iranian passport has helped to grant access to women's populations in educational contexts—it also shaped my interests in girls' and women's education in the Middle East/SWANA region. When the opportunity to conduct fieldwork in Lebanon with Tamkin came about, I told the organization's co-founder, Fakira, that I was Iranian American with Shi'i Muslim heritage ties. I also shared that I was a single mother familiar with living below the poverty line in the United States and acquainted with the subjugation and alienation that an unmarried woman with a child experiences as a cultural Muslim in the SWANA/Middle East region and the United States. Because Tamkin is an organization founded on feminist, anti-racist, and anti-classist principles, Fakira viewed my positionality as a practitioner-researcher and single mother from a Shi'i Islamic background as an asset. In summer 2012, Fakira invited me to conduct fieldwork at the Migrant Center, where I spent time every day for three months.

It is within the space of the Migrant Center that I used the ethnographic method of participant observation. Ethnography, according to Brice-Heath and Street, "forces us to think consciously about ways to enter the life of the individual, group, or institutional life of the 'other.'"[16] By applying an ethnographic lens as a researcher at the center, my aim was to become aware of the attitudes, opinions, and ideas of the patrons and migrant students. Participant observation helped me understand how the participants drew conclusions about knowledge and what informs their knowledge base. Now I will relay the physical descriptions of the spaces of the neighborhood, the center, and the words of the NGO coordinators and students.

Photos, Listservs, and Social Media

In addition to the in-depth interviews and participant observation, I collected photos and documents for data purposes as well. For example, the teacher group had a listserv, to which I subscribed, so I frequently received emails that discussed teaching issues, testing and assessment issues, ideas about curriculum, and teacher meetings. I also have used social media as a source of data, specifically photos, which serve as a visual tool for documentation purposes.[17] Such data is significant to this study because it reflects several key issues, such as access to technology, enactment of agency, and evidence of activism and empowerment for migrant communities.

The Space, the People, and Their Words

The Migrant Center as a Space of Refuge, Activism, and Women's Empowerment

The Migrant Center was established in the summer of 2011 as a social, cultural, and activist space for the diverse Asian and African migrant worker communities in Lebanon. Naba'a is a poverty-stricken suburb of Beirut, and the residential and commercial buildings of this area were constructed between the 1930s and the 1970s, and with age, the buildings are somewhat run-down and not properly maintained. However, the interior of the Migrant Center tells a different story: its brightly painted blue, green, and red walls and inviting rooms run contrary to Naba'a's abject poverty. Inside the front door hangs the address of the center in both Arabic and English. The entranceway leads to a small kitchenette with a refrigerator, stove, sink, and small cabinets. According to Suba, the center's coordinator, the migrant workers are encouraged to cook the food of their homeland at the center, because most Lebanese employers forbid domestic workers from cooking their native foods. Near the kitchenette is a hallway, which also acts as a study area; along the wall of the hallway runs a desk-like countertop with colorful ottomans for sitting and doing homework or eating a meal. There are also photographs hanging on the wall in the hallway: Suba appears in a large, professionally styled photograph. The photo was taken when she was pregnant with her firstborn. In the photo, Suba is tenderly cradling her belly. Next to this photo are several smaller pictures of migrant domestic workers participating in workers' rights rallies and protests (see figure 6.1).

The hallway leads to a large community room. It contains a wall-mounted TV, a table, a desk, and several chairs facing the TV. There is also a free-standing closet for storing donated items, such as women's and children's clothes, diapers, baby items, and bathroom items. On the wall in this room hang whiteboards for teaching and bulletin boards. A window with large, red metal shutters lets in natural light when opened, but it is often closed because of the prolonged harassment by neighborhood bullies, as mentioned previously. A partial wall and a door separate the community room from the

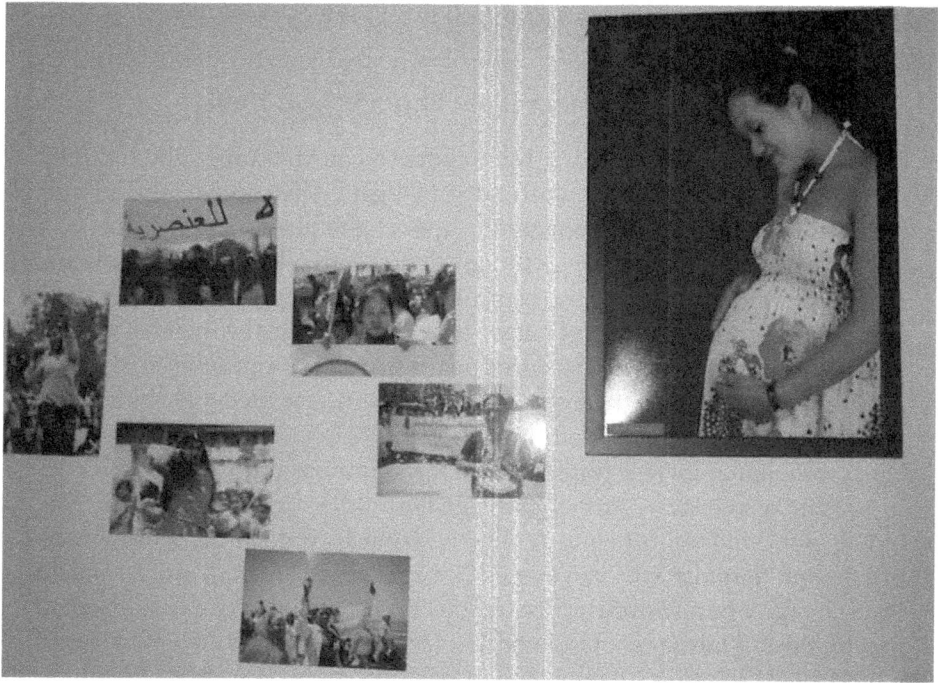

FIGURE 6.1. "Migrant domestic workers participating in worker's rights rallies and protests." Source: Unknown author.

large office room where Suba and her husband, Dakshi, conduct their work and hold meetings. Above the door to the office is a clay wall hanging that reads "Namaste," the common greeting in Nepal. Colorful wooden African masks hang next to this door.

Inside the office, several shelves filled with educational books line the walls, such as French and English dictionaries, and other Teaching English as a Foreign Language materials. There are also works from the Brazilian novelist Paulo Coelho, and the African American civil rights activists Malcolm X and Martin Luther King Jr. Children's paintings of the Nepal flag also adorn the wall. Some of these children's drawings include Nepali writing. One can surmise that Suba's own cultural background influences the center's décor. In front of the shuttered window in the office runs a string with t-shirts hung up by clothespins; these t-shirts contain anti-racism and anti-sexual harassment messages such as "Stop Sexual Harassment" in bold, black letters, "Fight for Human Rights" in bright neon, psychedelic font, and "I am not racist anymore."

The second floor of the center is located above the community room and can be reached by metal stairs painted to match the red door and shutters. Computers sit on long tables that line the perimeter of the room so that the middle of the room is still spacious enough for desks and a teaching space. On the wall hangs a long whiteboard for teachers to use.

Horizontal Help Instead of Vertical Help

Several times a month, Fakira, the Lebanese coordinator of the feminist organization Tamkin, meets with Suba to ensure she receives the administrative, emotional, and managerial support she needs. Tamkin acts as a scaffold for the center so it can function interdependently. Fakira told me that Suba was chosen to be the coordinator of the Migrant Center because she was a migrant worker and knows best how to serve the migrant worker population. Our conversation focused on the notion of local knowledge versus outsider, or colloquially perceived of as Western, knowledge. Fakira states that Westerners' voluntourism or attempts to "help" as interns or volunteers can be problematic: "One time I was corresponding with someone who lives in Toronto who has no roots whatsoever, nothing to do with the Middle East or Lebanon, who wants to join a collective from Toronto. If you're that much of a fervent feminist, why can't you join a collective there in Toronto and do local change wherever you are? What position are you to want to even email us with this?" These are not isolated incidents—she receives dozens of emails a day from Westerners, namely U.S. Americans, who desire to volunteer at Tamkin. Fakira, herself a third world feminist and activist, recognizes how the international development sector and its volunteers often tout Western centrism, the antithesis of a decolonizing mindset. Fakira desires local, grassroots, horizontal, and collective help over outsider/Western, "charity," or vertical help and actively resists outside interventions, as this would negatively affect the decolonizing and holistic nature of the Migrant Center.

Several of the migrant workers relay that the Migrant Center for them was a space of refuge, safety, and acceptance. Here, Laurencia and Irene, domestic workers from Madagascar, describe their feelings about the Migrant Center as a safe space:

> LAURENCIA: Ici [Migrant Center] c'est ma deuxième maison à moi . . .
> SK: Quand t'es venue et que t'as commencé à prendre les cours d'anglais toi estce que t'as senti comme une sensation de communauté, de famille ici?
> LAURENCIA: Oui! Et tu sais, rapidement j'ai trouvé une autre amie avec qui j'ai appliqué l'anglais. Par exemple elle parle anglais.
>
> LAURENCIA: The Migrant Center is like a second house to me . . .
> SK: When you came and you started taking English classes here, did you feel a sense of community here? Did it feel like family?
> LAURENCIA: Yes, I did! And I quickly made a friend with whom I could practice English. She speaks English [she is referring to Suba, the Migrant Center coordinator].

Irene, who has a high school diploma, also expressed her feelings about the Migrant Center:

> Moi je ne pensais pas du tout qu'il y aurait ce centre parce que lorsque j'ai appris j'ai dit : "Non, mais dis donc, quoi? Un centre au Liban, ici? Mais c'est impossible!" Parce que dans tous les pays à peu près des environ il y a des centres comme ça qui aident et j'ai de la famille qui voyage en Europe et quand même ils étudient ce n'est pas seulement ils font le ménage. Mais ici quand tu fais le ménage ici, tu fais le ménage jusqu'à la fin de ta vie.
>
> I would have never thought that there would be this center because when I found out about it, I said, "Wait a minute, what? A center here, in Lebanon? That's impossible!" In almost every country around us there were centers that helped migrants and I have relatives who went to Europe and they could study, not only do the cleaning. Whereas here if you do the cleaning, you do it until you die.

The Migrant Center as Space of Learning and Knowledge Production

The Migrant Center came to be known as a learning space with its language and computer classes. The migrant workers very much welcomed the classes. Here, Laurencia comments on how it feels to be back in a classroom after many years:

SK: Après toutes ces années passes au Liban, ces années de malheur, d'esclavage. Avant t'étais à l'école, t'es allée à la fac pendant un an, comment tu t'es sentie quand, après toutes ces années de malheur, après toutes ces [douze] années de Malheur que tu as passes au Liban, comment tu t'es sentie quand tu t'es assise au cours d'anglais?

LAURENCIA: Comme si je sortais d'une prison, je voyais la liberté. Je suis très intéressée, j'ai envie tout le temps d'apprendre.

SK: Before, you were in school and then you went to college for a year. After all those years in Lebanon, those unhappy years, slaving away, how did you feel when you sat down and you attended the English class the first time?

LAURENCIA: It was as if I was getting out of jail, I could see freedom. I am so interested; I want to learn all the time.

Thomas, a migrant worker and Christian pastor from Nigeria, discusses here the importance of informal education for migrant workers:

SK: There are some Lebanese activists who think that allocation of resources for migrant workers should be spent on immediate needs like food, shelter, or medicine, instead of educational opportunities. What are your thoughts on that?

THOMAS: We need something to go back home with.

SK: Go back home with . . .

THOMAS: Knowledge, it is power. Knowledge is power. Whatever someone takes back home [to the African continent], you can use it to establish yourself. If you have the money . . . maybe you work here, get some money, go back home, and don't know how to use it, you waste it. So when you give them this education, this knowledge, they will know how to manage their resources. So it's not a waste of resources. For example, if I love graphic design. If I now take that knowledge in graphic design, and when I go back to Africa, I can use it. . . . I can use PowerPoint in educating people . . . so, education is power. If you can learn PowerPoint, you can do something. If you learn graphic design, you can do something. Whatever you learn in the computer classes, is not a waste. For someone, somewhere back home, it will help. Ya, we need clothing, we need medical help. Yes, we need that. But what if you give someone medicine, give someone a drug, but they don't know how to take it? I might get overdosed. What if I cannot read the letters on the side [of the bottle]? So, knowledge is power. And I prefer that they can use that knowledge. It will help them run their life. If they want to open up a small business, education, it will help them. So, most Africans, Nigerians you see, they want to run their own life. They need to be educated to know how to do it. We need this.

In the following, Suba describes the need for language courses at the Migrant Center:

> SK: So in your experiences, in your work and professional experiences, you see learning English as serving a practical purpose, in the center. And you have seen a migrant worker kind of change as they learn English?
>
> SUBA: Definitely.
>
> SK: Can you give me an example?
>
> SUBA: Do you know Laurencia? From Madagascar? She takes English classes here.
>
> SK: Yes, I know her.
>
> SUBA: When I met her first, she did not know English at all. It was very hard to communicate. She has a child, she's four years old. Last year, I was going to give birth to my baby. Laurencia wanted to tell me many things about the delivery, about breastfeeding, about many things. She wanted to tell me what to expect. But we could not communicate. She knows French, I do not. She did not know English [yet]. Now, since she has been taking English classes, we can communicate. She tells me many things, everything how she feels. She is even teaching her daughter English. Now, when she comes here, she only speaks with her daughter in English. This feels very good. I told her once, "Now you can speak English with me." So, it's amazing. I feel very, well done, and successful about all that we are doing here at the Migrant Center. I feel successful. I am the witness of the changes here. And it feels great.

Knowledge Production, Intentionality of a Safe and Empowering Space, and Spatial Justice

Privileging Subaltern Insights, Knowledge, and Wisdom of Women

The resistance to outside intervention or assistance is evident in Fakira's ideas about outside "help"; recall her comments about Westerners desiring to come to Beirut to volunteer. She had relayed to me that some of the inquiries she receives are worded in such a way as to suggest that they are "doing Beirut a favor" by offering their volunteer services for a month, and they carry a sense of Western hubris and entitlement. What Fakira is referring to is called "voluntourism," or the combining of volunteerism with a vacation/tourism experience for the purpose of an internship or merely for volunteering. Most voluntourists who desire such an experience possess the expendable material resources for such an endeavor, often coming from a "first world" country. Her words are reminiscent of Mohanty's analysis of first world feminism's academic foray into the third; she exposes "[T]he power-knowledge nexus of feminist cross-cultural scholarship expressed through Eurocentric, falsely universalizing methodologies that serve the narrow self-interest of Western feminism" and highlights the "connection between feminist scholarship and feminist political organizing while drawing attention to the need to examine the political implications of our analytic strategies and principles."[18] Fakira's positionality of resistance to Westerners' attempts of voluntourism/volunteerism is informed by a privileging of the local, or third world, feminist subaltern voice over the first world feminist foreign voice, which typically lacks an understanding of the complexities of the local's "micropolitics of context, subjectivity, and struggle."[19] This privileging of the feminist-subaltern voice is evident in Tamkin's establishment of the Migrant Center at the migrant population's request; the selection of Suba, a former migrant domestic worker, as the major leader of the Migrant Center; and support of migrant-proposed initiatives, such as language and computer classes. Because Fakira recognized the importance of situating women's subaltern, transnational knowledge at the forefront of this project, it allowed for the fruition of an empowering and decolonizing space.

Social Construction of an Empowering Space

As is evident in the description of the Migrant Center, this is an organization that seeks to provide a social, cultural, educational, and activist space while also providing a safe, welcoming, and empowering space for migrant domestic workers. This space reflects a feminist ideology that encourages a critical consciousness[20] within those who manage, interact with, attend, and use the Migrant Center, as evidenced by several indicators. First, recall Fakira's criticism of Western charity and volunteerism. With intentionality, she set out to establish a feminist collective, Tamkin, that eschews foreign charity and volunteerism, opting instead to center local knowledge in the creation of the Migrant Center. This third-world feminist project is a reification of resistance to Western intervention.

Another indicator that the center is a decolonizing feminist space is the photos that adorn the walls: the large portrait displayed in the foyer of Suba in the later stages of her pregnancy lovingly looking down and caressing her belly suggests that the Migrant Center is a gendered space, one that privileges the voices of women, especially migrant domestic workers. Childbearing and motherhood are held in high regard in Lebanese, Southeast Asian, and African societies; still, to publicly privilege the pregnancy of a former domestic worker rather than a Lebanese woman's pregnancy implies not only that is this a space for migrant domestic workers, but also that this group takes precedence over others, be they Lebanese, expats, or foreigners. Also note the photos of women migrant workers participating in workers' rights protests—such prominent display of an oppressed group's outright activism speaks to the idea that migrant women are not passive but rather, with the support of local activists, can engage in direct action by way of protests. The ideologies and pedagogies that support the Migrant Center's mission and function are evident in its existence, hang on its walls, sit on its bookshelves, and inhabit its spaces on Sundays in the form of educational opportunities.

This is a space not for just anyone but specifically designated for migrant workers—there is purposeful intent in making this a sacred space for migrant workers, especially women domestic workers, to escape the oppressive space of their employers. The t-shirts with anti-racism and anti-sexual harassment slogans suggest a direct affront to the required uniform some migrant workers must wear; the ascribed meanings of social justice etched on the shirts potentially act as a shield of sorts to combat the maid uniform's confinement and control. The social and employment conditions in Beirut for most migrant workers are deplorable—the *kafala* (sponsorship) system is tantamount to human trafficking; labor laws are nonexistent for migrant workers; health care for migrants is subpar; racism, sexism, and xenophobia aimed at migrant populations, especially women, are rampant. And educational parity for migrant workers does not exist. The Migrant Center was created, chiefly, as a reaction to a multitude of social ills existing in Beirut that necessitated a space specifically for migrant domestic workers. A group of people, namely Fakira and other Lebanese activists, are deeply vested and knowledgeable about the structural problems affecting migrant workers. These committed individuals valued the input of the very population they sought to assist, thereby privileging migrant voices over the opinions of other stakeholders, including Westerners, expats, and people who hold degrees or positions of power.

According to Lawrence-Zúñiga and Low, spaces "are socially constructed by the people who live in them and know them."[21] The Migrant Center's creation is a case in point of how local, situated knowledges are exchanged and shared in a reciprocal fashion between local stakeholders and the marginalized group. Fakira and Suba meet frequently—Fakira assists from the periphery, with Suba managing the migrant space autonomously. Their camaraderie and mutual respect are evident as they drink their morning coffee and work together on administrative issues. A unity between these two women sends a clear message to the center patrons, volunteer teachers, and Lebanese activists that the building of relationships is central to an effective activist movement. That Suba was chosen to manage the center's everyday operations speaks to Tamkin's (and, as general coordinator of Tamkin, Fakira's) own beliefs: this feminist organization places more value on Suba as a coordinator for the center due to Suba's unique positionality, with an insider/outsider perspective, over the knowledge or vision of a foreigner, Westerner, or expat.

Spatial (In)Justice

Feminist geographer Doreen Massey relays that "spaces and places, and our senses of them ... are gendered through and through. Moreover, they are gendered in a myriad of ways, which vary between cultures and over time. And this gendering of space and place both reflects and has effects back on the ways in which gender is constructed and understood in the societies in which we live."[22] The intentionality in creating a gendered space, the Migrant Center, is a reaction to the myriad social ills, especially sexualized and racialized violence, committed against migrant domestic workers. While one objective of reifying a gendered, feminist space is to empower the women who frequent the center, it also serves as a kind of physical embodiment of feminist resistance to the public. As Massey notes, gendered spaces serve as a reaction to the space they inhabit, and the Migrant Center exemplifies this notion. This socio-spatial phenomenon, that is, the creation and reification of a physical space as a reaction to social injustices, is rooted in notions of what Edward Soja refers to as "spatial justice," which is a spatial theory of justice that endorses "foregrounding a critical spatial perspective and seeing the search for social justice as a struggle over geography [which] can open up new ways of thinking about the subject [spatial justice] as well as enriching existing ideas and practices."[23] A theory of spatial justice takes into account three ontological assumptions: the societal/social, the temporal/historical, and the spatial/geographical. It is from these three assumptions that all human knowledge arises,[24] and this theory is a way to understand the organization of space where justices and injustices play out in the physical realm. The Migrant Center helps facilitate the exchange of knowledge to create new epistemologies, new funds of knowledge, in this in-between, liminal space, which results in a community of practice that empowers its community.

Conclusion

This chapter has examined how the women of the Migrant Center have navigated an unjust society by facilitating a space of resistance and opportunities for learning. By unpacking epistemologies of learning within an extremely oppressive social system, community leaders, authentic educators, and critical scholar-practitioners have a more nuanced understanding of how community education can appropriate space for empowerment and activism. The women and other social actors were able to harness agency and power of their own making to access NGOs, social networks, governmental agencies, and other peripheral assistance to not only survive within the oppressive system but also flourish. The decolonizing feminist praxis presented here offers a blueprint for how community education can function successfully and independently of Western funding and other outside intervention.

Notes

1. A. Sumner and M. Tribe, *International Development Studies: Theories and Methods in Research and Practice* (Thousand Oaks: SAGE Publications, 2008); A. Escobar, *Encountering Development: The Making and Unmaking of the Third World* (Princeton: Princeton University Press, 2011).

2. G. C. Spivak, "Can the Subaltern Speak?" C. Nelson and L. Grossberg (Eds.), *Marxism and the Interpretation of Culture* (pp. 271–314). Urbana: University of Illinois Press; W. Mignolo, "Geopolitics of Sensing and Knowing: On (de) Coloniality, Border Thinking, and Epistemic Disobedience," *Confero: Essays on Education, Philosophy and Politics* 1, no. 1 (2013): 129–150.

3. John Podesta, "The Climate Crisis, Migration, and Refugees," *The Brookings Institution*, July 25, 2019, https://www.brookings.edu/research/the-climate-crisis-migration-and-refugees/.

4. Marie McAuliffe and Binod Khadria, "World Migration Report 2020," November 2019, United Nations International Organization for Migration.

5. Pat Cox, "Issues in Safeguarding Refugee and Asylum-Seeking Children and Young People: Research and Practice," *Child Abuse Review* 20 (2011): 341–360.

6. Ray Jureidini, "Trafficking and Contract Migrant Workers in the Middle East," *International Migration Special Issue: Special Issue on Human Trafficking* 48, no. 4 (2010): 142–163.

7. C.T. Mohanty, *Feminism without Borders: Decolonizing Theory, Practicing Solidarity* (Durham: Duke University Press, 2003).

8. I want to emphasize that this discussion is not meant to fetishize the neoliberal doctrine of "pulling oneself up by the bootstraps" that is prevalent in the U.S. discourse regarding the overcoming of structural inequalities that have been built into its legal systems, educational systems, and public discourse. Rather, it is meant to demonstrate how feminist-oppositional knowledge production manifests when fomented by powerful messages of solidarity and unity in explicitly feminist spaces.

9. Setha M. Low, "Spatializing Culture: The Social Production and Social Construction of Public Space in Costa Rica," *American Ethnologist* 23, no. 4 (1996): 863.

10. Edward W. Soja, *Seeking Spatial Justice* (Minneapolis: University of Minnesota Press, 2010), 72.

11. Lila Abu-Lughod, *Remaking Women: Feminism and Modernity in the Middle East* (Princeton: Princeton University Press, 1998).

12. Edward W. Soja, *Thirdspace: Journeys to Los Angeles and Other Real-and-Imagined Places* (Malden: Blackwell Publishers, 1996).

13. Edward T. Hall, *The Hidden Dimension* (Rockland: Anchor Press, 1966).

14. Soja 2010, 71.

15. Kathy Charmaz, *Constructing Grounded Theory: A Practical Guide through Qualitative Analysis* (London: Sage Publishers, 2006), 180.

16. Shirley Brice Heath and Brian V. Street, *On Ethnography: Approaches to Language and Literacy Research* (New York: Teachers College Press, 2008), 31.

17. John W. Creswell, *Research Design: Qualitative, Quantitative, and Mixed Methods Approaches* (Thousand Oaks: SAGE Publications, 2014), 193.

18. Chandra Talpade Mohanty, "'Under Western Eyes' Revisited: Feminist Solidarity through Anticapitalist Struggles," *Signs: Journal of Women in Culture and Society* 28, no. 2 (2003): 501.

19. Mohanty, "'Under Western Eyes,'" 501.

20. Paulo Freire, *Education for Critical Consciousness* (London: Bloomsbury Publishing, 2021).

21. Denise Lawrence-Zúñiga and Setha M. Low, *The Anthropology of Space and Place: Locating Culture* (Oxford: Blackwell, 2012), 15.

22. Doreen Massey, *Space, Place, and Gender* (Minneapolis: University of Minnesota Press, 2001), 186.

23. F. Dufaux, P. Gervais-Lambony, C. Buire, H. Desbois, "Spatial Justice and the Right to the City: An Interview with Edward Soja," Jssj.org, 2010, 8. Retrieved from: http://www.jssj.org/wp-content/uploads/2012/12/JSSJ3-11en.pdf.

24. Soja 2010, 70.

Bibliography

Abu-Lughod, Lila. 1998. *Remaking Women: Feminism and Modernity in the Middle East*. Princeton, NJ: Princeton University Press.

Abu-Lughod, L. 2002. "Do Muslim Women Really Need Saving? Anthropological Reflections on Cultural Relativism and Its Others." *American Anthropologist* 104(3): 783–790.

Charmaz, Kathy. 2006. *Constructing Grounded Theory: A Practical Guide through Qualitative Analysis*. London: Sage Publishers.

Cox, Pat. 2011. "Issues in Safeguarding Refugee and Asylum-Seeking Children and Young People: Research and Practice." *Child Abuse Review* 20: 341–360.

Creswell, John W. 2014. *Research Design: Qualitative, Quantitative, and Mixed Methods Approaches*. Thousand Oaks: SAGE Publications.

de Certeau, Michel. 1984. *The Practice of Everyday Life*. Los Angeles: University of California Press.

Dufaux, F., Gervais-Lambony, P., Buire, C., Desbois, H. 2010. "Spatial Justice and the Right to the City: An Interview with Edward Soja." Jssj.org. Retrieved from: http://www.jssj.org/wp-content/uploads/2012/12/JSSJ3-11en.pdf.

Escobar, Arturo. 2011. *Encountering Development: The Making and Unmaking of the Third World*. Princeton: Princeton University Press.

Foucault, Michel. 1984. *The Foucault Reader*. New York: Pantheon.

Freire, Paulo. 2021. *Education for Critical Consciousness*. London: Bloomsbury Publishing.

Hall, Edward T. 1966. *The Hidden Dimension*. Rockland: Anchor Press.

Heath, Shirley Brice, and Brian V. Street. 2008. *On Ethnography: Approaches to Language and Literacy Research*. New York: Teachers College Press.

Hughes, Jason, Nick Jewson, and Lorna Unwin. 2013. *Communities of Practice: Critical Perspectives*. New York: Routledge.

Jureidini, Ray. 2010. "Trafficking and Contract Migrant Workers in the Middle East." *International Migration Special Issue: Special Issue on Human Trafficking* 48(4): 142–163.

Lawrence-Zúñiga, Denise, and Setha M. Low. 2012. *The Anthropology of Space and Place: Locating Culture*. Oxford: Blackwell.

Low, Setha M. 1996. "Spatializing Culture: The Social Production and Social Construction of Public Space in Costa Rica." *American Ethnologist* 23(4): 861–879.

Low, Setha M. 2009. "Towards an Anthropological Theory of Space and Place." *Semiotica* (175). https://doi.org/10.1515/semi.2009.041.

Massey, Doreen. 2001. *Space, Place, and Gender*. Minneapolis: University of Minnesota Press.

McAuliffe, Marie, and Binod Khadria. 2019, November. "World Migration Report 2020." United Nations International Organization for Migration.

Mignolo, Walter. 2013. "Geopolitics of Sensing and Knowing: On (de) Coloniality, Border Thinking, and Epistemic Disobedience." *Confero: Essays on Education, Philosophy and Politics* 1(1): 129–150.

Mohanty, Chandra Talpade. 2003. "'Under Western Eyes' Revisited: Feminist Solidarity through Anticapitalist Struggles." *Signs: Journal of Women in Culture and Society* 28(2): 499–535. https://doi.org/10.1086/342914.

Podesta, John. 2019, July 25. "The Climate Crisis, Migration, and Refugees." *The Brookings Institution*. https://www.brookings.edu/research/the-climate-crisis-migration-and-refugees/.

Sharma, Aradhana. 2008. *Logics of Empowerment: Development, Gender, and Governance in Neoliberal India*. Minneapolis: University of Minnesota Press.

Soja, Edward W. 1996. *Thirdspace: Journeys to Los Angeles and Other Real-and-Imagined Places*. Malden: Blackwell Publishers.

Soja, Edward W. 2010. *Seeking Spatial Justice*. Minneapolis: University of Minnesota Press.

Spivak, Gayatri Chakravarty. 1988. "Can the Subaltern Speak?" C. Nelson and L. Grossberg (Eds.), *Marxism and the Interpretation of Culture* (pp. 271–314). Urbana: University of Illinois Press.

Sumner, A., and Tribe, M. 2008. *International Development Studies: Theories and Methods in Research and Practice*. Thousand Oaks: SAGE Publications.

7

Say, Who's Online?
Building Feminist Futures through South Asian Collectivity in Texas

RACHEL AFI QUINN

South Asian Youth in the South

One weekend in April 2021, South Asian Youth in Houston Unite (SAYHU) hosted two successful virtual events that were exemplary of the kind of connectivity the community had built online and assembled via Zoom during the COVID-19 pandemic. That Saturday, community members facilitated a workshop on "letter writing to incarcerated people" and educated their peers about the carceral system; they acknowledged who was disproportionately affected by the prison industrial complex and encouraged critical dialogue about the ways that SAYHU members might respond. Sunday was "Brown Bodies Bold Stories," an annual sharing circle in collaboration with Daya Houston, an organization that supports South Asian survivors of domestic violence; the year's theme was "trauma." Through the Zoom window of each event, one could see South Asian participants finding their voices, claiming space, working collaboratively, and sharing writing, music, and personal testimonies. They were inviting others into an imagined community, cheering for one another, and bearing witness with a remarkable openness and vulnerability.

The following essay documents SAYHU's work organizing feminist community among South Asians in Houston (and Texas more broadly), within and beyond Zoom's digital frame, and names some of the strengths and weaknesses of youth organizing in this way. Outside the frame of the Zoom window, SAYHU worked for years to foster community engagement among a diverse group of South Asians in Houston, work that we were able to sustain and grow during the global pandemic through the use of digital tools.

SAYHU was created in April 2017 by group of seven women of color—six of them South Asian—who came to the project as graduate students and junior faculty at the University of Houston, along with other members of our Houston community.[1] We established a feminist collective to design and implement an annual summer institute for South Asian youth. Inspired by social justice summer institutes for South Asian youth in other parts of the country, our programming explored issues of race, gender, sexual orientation, class, religion, caste, and ethnicity, and other intersecting aspects of identity. We found that Texas youth were rarely receiving the tools necessary to name their own experiences, and our project soon involved gathering and publishing online knowledge and testimonies produced by and specific to the experiences of these South Asian Houstonians. As a transnational feminist project, we created SAYHU in part to practice collaborative learning and provide year-round popular education in social justice to eighteen- to twenty-four-year-olds in Houston, who were seeking to connect with one another around cultural affinities and local social issues. In our first year, we expanded to include thirty-something South Asian Houstonians who were equally hungry for such a space in which to connect. Across numerous collective and collaborative leadership iterations—culminating with just two women of color at the helm in our final year—we worked in creative ways to support a periodically engaged community of about fifty people.

Because SAYHU is not faith-based or volunteer-oriented or fundraising for nongovernmental organizations (NGOs) abroad, like many of the South Asian–led groups in Texas, often it was hard for people to conceive of what we were, how we did our work as a collective, or how to engage with it. Unlike other comparable summer institutes or social justice organizations, such as South Asian Americans Leading Together (SAALT) or the South Asian American Digital Archive (SAADA), SAYHU took a decidedly feminist approach to our work.[2] In an effort to keep women of color feminist values at the fore, our guiding principles highlighted collectivity and resisted hierarchy and caste-ist and patriarchal values that were so familiar to our community members; we likewise critiqued and resisted the traditional power dynamics of nonprofits at every turn. We valued intergenerational exchange and opportunities for connecting with South Asian role models and mentors across our diverse network, doing so with a transnational feminist vision for SAYHU rooted in the globalized city of Houston. Eventually, we also named within SAYHU the many ways that we valued scholarly research as a critical component of our community-engaged efforts.

When we started SAYHU, "South Asian" was common enough language that it could coalesce the community we hoped to connect with, even though individual participants said they did not necessarily label themselves as such. The category "South Asian" is temporally and spatially defined, and SAYHU's use of the term differs from the way past waves of migrants to Texas had claimed it. It was being taken up by organizations in the region and student groups, and it fit SAYHU better than the term "Desi," which our cofounders of Indian and Pakistani descent understood as used specifically for Indian Americans in Texas. Instead, "South Asian" helped us to bring together Houstonians whose families have roots in Bangladesh, Bhutan, India, Nepal, the Maldives, Pakistan, Sri Lanka, and their diasporas, as well as Indo-Caribbean South Asians and those with ties to central Africa. The concerns of SAYHU's youth were different from the youth that Sunaina Marr Maira identified in the early 2000s as the "9/11 generation," who were organizing in resistance to state repression in the northeastern United States.[3] SAYHU youth likewise struggle to navigate life choices under "neoliberal capitalism, racial violence and imperial democracy," but as "Gen Z" South Asians in the U.S. South, they face the pressures of being seen as a model minority with limited understanding of their social position. We witnessed among them lots of "code-switching," a word that many learned for the first time at our summer institute; not only were they speaking English with a Southern accent and then speaking other languages when with family members, but they were often performing gender differently when at home.

SAYHU's approach to producing a coalitional politic among South Asian Texans was inherently decolonial. As community activists and scholars, we led SAYHU as a decolonial practice in the way that media studies scholars Pavitra Sundar and Debashree Mukherjee suggest: in an effort to "reckon with the ongoing epistemic and material harms wrought through the nexus of coloniality, racial capitalism, heteropatriarchy and the academy."[4] However, we never articulated a decolonial approach to participants, yet students and scholars among us conveyed a decolonial feminist praxis in reading groups, mentoring conversations, and writings by SAYHU youth published online. It was black feminist theory that was our model for feminist collectivity and that inspired our everyday resistance to systemic oppression in our South Asian community, including anti-blackness, Brahminical supremacy, gendered labor divisions, patriarchy, and which people were seen as knowledge producers within our community. We consistently led with black feminist theories of intersectionality and collaboration that we understood as viable models and built into our curriculum. We found these theories to be, as Emma D. Velez argues, "necessary for the coalitional praxis of decolonization that is the goal of decolonial feminism."[5] Feminist theory more broadly had also trained us to question "the assumption that knowledge can only be produced in academic circles."[6] We aimed to democratize knowledge in SAYHU—for ourselves and for the benefit of our broader community—by publishing South Asian stories on our website, archiving South Asian Houstonian oral histories, cultivating vast social networks, and sharing resources. As a scholar, my own interests in transnational feminist world-building and knowledge production led me to write about feminist praxis, and after five years of experimenting with strategies for community-building in SAYHU, I have many insights to share.

With this essay, I capture some of the strategies that SAYHU used to organize South Asian youth in Texas during the COVID-19 pandemic lockdown, particularly our use of technology. SAYHU existed as a social experiment through which we could ask: How do we advance collective work on social justice in this contemporary moment in Texas? How do we teach SAYHU's decolonial vision for feminist collectivity in the South Asian social justice spaces that we create online? What are the unexpected connectivities that emerge in this context?[7] By 2021 we had four cohorts of SAYHU summer institute alumni to connect to one another but were unable to safely host in-person events. A feminist vision for democratizing knowledge shaped our approach when we brought our community network and summer program online. As with other communities engaged in youth organizing in the last decades, digital networks offered us capacities for community building that we otherwise might not have had. In what follows, I detail SAYHU's efforts to embrace digital humanities "in pandemic times" for the purpose of coordinating a Virtual Summer Institute (VSI) and building solidarity. I draw on Roopika Risam's postcolonial theories of pedagogy and information sharing in the digital age and point to the evolving locations of knowledge production that emerge as we construct new digital worlds. Although there is much more to say about the numerous lessons learned through feminist organizing with SAYHU, here I focus on how digital tools—from Asana to Zoom—made our coalitional work possible.

Black and South Asian Connectivities

As a queer Black Southerner and feminist scholar-activist, I sought to build feminist collectivity with and among a network of South Asians in Houston because they were my immediate community, my mentees, friends, and extended family. As a SAYHU cofounder, my steadfast commitment was to building South Asian social justice networks and archiving South Asian Texans' experiences online, specifically helping SAYHU participants create and publish a blog, resource pages, and an oral history archive, to contribute to making this community more visible. While it is often assumed that as a Black person I would not be or should not be equally invested in the goals of a South Asian–centered feminist project, I served as a driving force in this work in part because of my commitment to educating young people of color in my own community.[8] I invested in the success of each of my South Asian mentees, exploring our capacity for feminist collaboration. At the same time, cofounder Eesha Pandit, who was my partner at the time and collaborator in leading the final year of SAYHU, had long been an active member of the

Crunk Feminist Collective (CFC). As a Southern Black feminist collective that included a diversity of feminist activists and scholars, CFC was a model for our efforts to center South Asian and Black feminist Southern knowledges and publish them online. By nature of SAYHU's location in the South, a Black and South Asian politics of solidarity was essential for those of us wanting to build coalitions for social justice.[9]

Before 2020's global uprisings against anti-black violence, SAYHU had been teaching about colorism, caste, and anti-blackness to youth participants in our summer institute, and we were eager to expand this to our broader community. We deliberately drew on the insights of members of Black feminist collectives to sustain a vision of possibility. For example, Combahee River Collective (CRC) cofounder Demita Frazier, in an interview with SAYHU community member and University of Houston-Clear Lake professor Shreerekha Subramanian for our archive, advised that a unifying vision is necessary to sustain a collective project.[10] We regularly returned to and expanded our unifying vision to be inclusive of those who wanted to be a part of SAYHU. Taking the CRC and the CFC as models of Black feminist praxis, SAYHU created a space for "defining and clarifying our politics," in which "we see Black feminism as the local political movement to combat the manifold and simultaneous oppressions that all women of color face."[11]

Like many grassroots organizing efforts today, we looked to African American histories and knowledge in our social justice work.[12] As in most such movements and communities, SAYHU navigated its fair share of interpersonal conflicts, through which we learned about the work of coalition-building. Black feminist theory and decolonial theory remained central to SAYHU's notions of community building because, as Velez makes clear, "decolonial feminism reorients our practice of resistance toward the possibility of generating decolonizing coalitions among women of color that affirm what Audre Lorde has called our nondominant differences."[13] Furthermore, as CRC cofounder Margo Okazawa-Rey teaches us, the work of "connectivity" in community has meant "not just a commitment but a practice to work together to understand and dig deeper, to work together to engage conflicts in very generative and creative ways, and to not give up on each other unless it is the absolute last resort."[14] Nevertheless, like many before us, SAYHU experienced numerous feminist failures in community-building during this process: more than once we abandoned relationships that we could not recover after trust was broken, or for which no clear path emerged, or when collective members ran out of emotional energy to continue to mend ruptures and do care work; sometimes these intimacies unearthed too much trauma and required time and space for recovery.[15]

Understanding ourselves to be part of a legacy, we sought to "commit and practice" through the most difficult and essential work of solidarity across difference. Okazawa-Rey had done the same, inspired by Civil Rights Movement organizer Septima Clark's notion of "wonderful thinking" as an essential component of community organizing, which also requires

> popular education gatherings—intergenerational, multi-identities, cross-issue, cross-sector—wherever we are located, whenever possible, across geographies. To share local knowledges and personal experiences; to look deeply into and through differences and identities that consistently divide; apply various critical theoretical perspectives, including socially lived theories; and to generate collective identities, shared structural analyses, and comparable visions of justice, sustainability, and genuine security are radical, potentially transformative acts.[16]

Likewise, SAYHU came together to teach our community about issues of social justice, community leadership, and organizing around political ideology across our online network and via multiple social media platforms (Twitter, Facebook, and Instagram), circulating theoretical concepts in small bites to reach a diffuse community and sustain an ongoing dialogue. Our efforts to engage in popular education necessarily located youth whom we hoped to connect with in online spaces. We would add them to SAYHU's online networks, but often they would safely "lurk" rather than engage with the community, reading the posts but only responding if "tagged" by others. As we explored what it would take to create coalitional movements among South Asian youth in Texas, I also had to ask, as Robin D. G. Kelley does, "How can social movements actually reshape the desires and dreams of the participants?"[17] Ultimately, our success at this endeavor was measured by having numerous young people describe the friendships they had cultivated within SAYHU as "life-saving."

Organizing South Asian Youth in Texas

For many South Asian youth, their dreams are not yet individuated from those that their parents impose on them. They are often seeking economic success so that they can serve as a social safety net for their immigrant families and yet do so in a different economy (and educational system) than their parents imagined they would join. Following the 1965 Immigration Act, South Asian immigrants to Houston enjoyed particular success because, as Usma Quraishi has shown, they "built on existing historical formations of modernity, cosmopolitanism, and middle classness in South Asia."[18] Cold War–era Indian and Pakistani immigrants were already positioned as upwardly mobile before migrating to the United States, through professions such as engineering, medicine, and education, and due to social locations of caste, religion, and gender that reinforced their middle-class status.[19] However, it is all too common to overlook the many other South Asian immigrants to Houston. Young people seeking out SAYHU also had to confront class differences and the segregation of our city: working-class Gujarati youth found one another at our social gatherings, as did the many Ismaili Muslims who were not affiliated with their well-resourced religious community. Many members of SAYHU were the children of immigrants who came to Texas without the benefits of education; their parents and grandparents rely on them heavily to speak English and help their whole families navigate life in a new country. These working-class South Asian youth often grow up in neighborhoods and apartment complexes alongside Black and Latinx Houstonians. Yet because of class (and caste), these particular immigrant histories get erased or ignored in larger narratives of who South Asian Texans might be. SAYHU digital humanities projects therefore worked to publish more nuanced personal histories that represented the diversity of our community.

At the same time, wealthier South Asian Houstonians—often organized around their religious communities—are part of an influential donor class that had until quite recently been ignored. They became more visible in September 2019 with the success of the "Howdy Modi!" event that took place at Houston's NRG Stadium.[20] Texas India Forum, an NGO that was created for the purpose of organizing donors and volunteers to orchestrate this "community summit," hosted Indian Prime Minister Narendra Modi and then-U.S. President Donald Trump.[21] Hindu Americans in Houston, we learned, are funding right-wing conservative movements in South Asia and in the United States. Fifty thousand people attended the sold-out program while thousands of protesters rallied outside. The publicity for the event focused on a "new" conservative voting bloc of Hindu Americans and obscured the political diversity of the South Asian population. SAYHU's community was made up of youth who critiqued these values—many were forced to grapple with the fact that their parents attended the rally. On our SAYHU Slack channel, they were able to connect and make plans to attend protests at the event together.

As students and early-career educators who are developing facilitation skills and research methodologies, the SAYHU leadership was deliberate about building in readings and discussions that would help us come to some agreement about SAYHU's praxis. Yet many among us found it challenging to commit the time and labor to coalition-building and feminist community solidarity because of obligations to family or religious communities that they had been taught since childhood should always come first.[22] This sense of obligation overwhelmed some of our members who enthusiastically joined us but then did not stay involved. I spent a significant amount of time communicating, meeting, planning, facilitating, and co-facilitating in SAYHU spaces in an effort to expand community members' thinking around what it means to be in meaningful relationship with one another, online and off. Phone calls and chats with interns about responsibilities to community were a regular part of this work. I also tried to impress on SAYHU youth the importance of holding the space that they valued by getting involved and contributing, so that it would also be there for others in the future.

Some people found SAYHU and stayed long enough to begin to build community with us, to produce digital archives on Black and South Asian solidarity, to help with outreach, to expand our networks on social media, and to promote the summer institute, but in the role of paid interns. Others, who were already organizing through student groups and political campaigns, struggled to make time for learning our feminist methodology for coalition-building, and they seemed satisfied with mainstream political organizing approaches (such as phone-banking, mass emails, and one-sided communication). We found that those most comfortable joining us were not already working in social justice movements elsewhere and wanted to learn how to organize around issues and find others to organize with; for many, it was the first time they had encountered other South Asians in social justice spaces. At the same time, in many conversations with participants and collective members, we heard about how difficult it was for them to enter into a South Asian space like SAYHU because they had been traumatized by the patriarchal values, homophobia, and bodily policing that so frequently occur within the tight-knit social networks of South Asian immigrants. These and other unique challenges of community-building in SAYHU required deliberate approaches to creating a safe space and empowering youth to participate.

Community members often needed to experience the type of space we created firsthand to understand for themselves what SAYHU had to offer and how it made them feel. Many times, they required a personal invitation to join us, attend a community hangout, get involved in a book group, or initiate conversations with peers online, and I found that I was more willing than many of my collaborators to do that work. Community-building for SAYHU included crossing generational divides and bridging differing understandings of what it might mean to build a feminist collective and praxis critical of racism and anti-blackness. SAYHU made space for the self-reflection required to undo these logics and the logics of insularity for South Asian immigrants and their children. Unsurprisingly, all of these cultural shifts take time.

Through the VSI and our broader community network online, youth connected with peers who could relate to their experiences: nonbinary South Asian youth found one another on our Slack, as did the writers, organizers, artists, lawyers, and law students among us. Yet many youth came with limited skills in building lasting relationships, or they were not naturally curious about others' experiences. In *Asian American Feminisms and Women of Color Politics*, Lynn Fujiwara and Shireen Roshanravan assert that "political projects of knowledge generation are liberators only if they are informed by on-the-ground struggle. The terrain of struggle can and should vary to maximize and sharpen the production of multiple tools for liberation."[23] Although it is often the most common way for social justice communities to connect, we found it to be too simple to rely on adversity to bind us together. For sustainability, we recognized that we must also connect around joy and friendship, which might foster an accountability to one another that proved otherwise difficult to learn.

Building community among strangers during a pandemic was a priority for SAYHU because we knew from experience that feminist friendship was life-sustaining. Those who joined us generally found SAYHU to be a welcoming community, though some left without explanation: a young person admitted to the in-person summer institute showed up for the opening gathering but left right away and never returned for the week-long program; a collective member collaborated with us for years but when life became overwhelming, they dropped SAYHU responsibilities first and opted to leave not just the collective but the community entirely.[24] Some were unaccustomed to being accountable to non-relatives for their actions (or inactions). Some youth were dissuaded or forbidden to keep in contact with SAYHU, because of the queerness of our community, while others said they found it overwhelming to have a South Asian space where it was actually safe to be themselves. Because our community looked so different from their families and South Asian cultural communities, being a part of SAYHU forced them to reimagine being South Asian in Texas in this contemporary moment.

The intellectual and political work of engaging South Asian youth in Texas also may have been more challenging because we struggled to connect with members of Generation Z, who know the world differently from the way we do. They have many online options for "community" that look different from what Gen X and Millennial colleagues understand as meaningful relationships. Plus, "ghosting" or disappearing from friendships and romantic relationships that were sustained primarily online—to avoid difficult dialogues—is commonplace for youth we work with. Similar to lurking in online spaces while choosing not to engage, ghosting reflects how youth reserve the option to leave virtual spaces, as an escape hatch, and thus protect themselves from overcommitment, vulnerability and accountability to others. More than once, SAYHU youth chose "digital disappearance" over conflict resolution or speaking their truth to a collaborator. One tried to resolve minor conflict, they said, only after realizing there was no other South Asian social justice organization in the region that they could move on to. Other community members held tight to a model in which they knew how to do social justice work only from the front, in a role that was often performative—precisely because of the nature of social media—and they were unable to share that space.

It is hard to support youth leaders and teach them about feminist collectivity and Black feminist knowledge when they are certain they already know. SAYHU seemed to best serve youth seeking community around issues of social justice who were eager to learn, pause, and engage. And often, this was youth with limited social privilege. Like classroom educators, we were not always aware of our impact, but our program participants also did not immediately recognize that one of the primary things that we sought to teach them was what it felt like to invest in feminist community-building and life-sustaining relationships. We wanted them to experience in SAYHU feelings of support, engagement, and accountability that they are often not getting elsewhere—that might then compel them to return. We soon recognized that the obstacles that we would face in building our imagined community went well beyond the heterogeneity of our community to include unexamined anti-blackness, lack of exposure to political organizing, lack of exposure to gender studies, and a vast urban geography. We came to accept that it takes a long time to unpack existing knowledges, build sustainable community projects, archive our work cumulatively online, reach our desired audience, and motivate people to sustain the work.

All along the way, community engagement ebbed and flowed. As we state on our website, "our aim is for SAYHU to be a self-sustaining community network in which all members feel inspired and emboldened to contribute, collaborate and steer the direction of our South Asian-centered transnational feminist community programming in Houston." However, what was initially a volunteer-run community project was soon well-funded by a local foundation that saw our grassroots social justice education work aligning with their mission. Community members who were oriented toward hierarchy sought out and sometimes became reliant on the leadership of core collective members to facilitate programming that aligned with SAYHU's feminist project. Participants often stayed passively involved, hesitant to run their own programs for their peers. Yet we were regularly surprised by the various waves of momentum in SAYHU, after many periods in which we had considered calling it quits, when the burden of sustaining community engagement was overwhelming. Eventually, however, we learned that our metrics for success were often wrong: the number of attendees or regular attendance didn't necessarily translate into impact. Each time we felt like we were dragging youth participants into engagement with one another, we would get an offhand comment about connections made or opportunities explored only because of SAYHU's existence, which affirmed the value of our work. For example, a recent college graduate was able to have flexible and meaningful work with SAYHU for a semester before heading to law school, and a grad student was able to find many volunteers for her dissertation research while also serving as a role model for curious undergraduates. Along with the life-changing friendships that emerged within SAYHU, youth interns got paid for their labor while learning new job skills, and community members could access culturally relevant health practitioners, books, classes, and jobs listed on SAYHU's website.

@sayhutx

SAYHU's website, blog, and digital archive became tools of dissemination but, more important, sites of knowledge production that were specific to the experience of South Asian youth in Texas. Drawing on transnational feminist theory as a framework of understanding for our work within and beyond the academy, and a digital humanities methodology, I invited SAYHU community members to think in broader ways about information sharing and gathering. As supervisor to the students developing SAYHU's digital archive projects (the Preservation Project and blog described below) and as the driver of our community-building efforts on Slack and Twitter, I supported youth on research, writing, and self-publishing, as well as developing a feminist methodology for SAYHU's approach to collecting oral histories.

In March of 2020, we were just beginning outreach for the annual summer institute when the pandemic was getting under way. Looking at a summer in lockdown, we realized that the institute was more necessary than ever for so many South Asian young people living at home with their parents. We decided to lean into the digital tools we had available for organizing as an experiment and hoped that community members would come along. By that time, we had only four active collective members, and one of them decided to leave the project, so as a leadership team of three, we called on other community members to help us produce, refine, streamline, and teach the SAYHU VSI curriculum. This effort, amid learning new technology for teaching university classes online, allowed us to practice these new tools as we expanded our networks, and to build community across our largest cohort ever—twenty-two participants ages eighteen to twenty-four.

SAYHU embraced being able to reach South Asian youth from across Texas via our multiple social media accounts (Instagram, Facebook, and Twitter). We streamlined our core curriculum, publishing it all on the website for easy access by participants as well as our broader community. We also held ourselves accountable for making the space accessible to South Asian youth with disabilities and working-class youth, asking in our application about technical, logistical, or financial obstacles to participation, and not assuming participants had access to a working computer, stable internet, or a private space where they could get online. Our low overhead costs meant we had additional resources to respond to these concerns, including stipends if they were missing work to attend, though none called on us for that support.

SAYHU's monthly events on Zoom overlapped with VSI programming, as we brought community members and local organizations into conversation with SAYHU summer institute youth, empowering the youth to lead these online events themselves. We soon opted to use the messaging app Slack for organizing the collective and coordinating the VSI to connect youth to one another, because it is easy to use on a smartphone or computer for instant messaging, sharing links, and making video calls. On Slack one can respond with enthusiasm to others' messages with a range of emojis, and can carry on multiple group or individual conversation threads, in both public and private; all conversations stay archived and searchable in one workspace.[25] While Slack provided SAYHU a subscription at no cost, we were responsible for driving all of our community online to use it. Targeted discussion channels on Slack encouraged individual engagement and resource sharing—a mental health channel, for example, allowed many to share their experiences and have conversations they would not have had elsewhere. For VSI, we made unique chat threads related to topics that we were initiating dialogue around with youth; we asked them to share and respond in those spaces. We imagined that SAYHU VSI could counteract the growing isolation for Houston's South Asian youth that was already so mediated by the internet; we could see, however, that although they were often immediately connected to one another, they were not necessarily effectively or affectively connected in this way.

While young people may be familiar with the newest social media and digital tools, they have less experience with outreach and communication, let alone recruitment and how to teach others to use online tools. For example, SAYHU interns introduced SAYHU to project management on Notion (with more features than Google Docs and Asana), but as with Slack and other new technology, individuals needed time to learn how to use it—and had to be motivated to do so. Many expressed hesitancy to adopt Slack for communication, and some were no longer using Facebook or Twitter but kept up with us on Instagram, but they did not have an alternative approach. If they decided they didn't want to use a digital app, or felt overwhelmed by the thought of learning another, then they did not get the benefits of our virtual community and resource sharing about vision and values. For SAYHU, the terrain of struggle was still taking form, and although youth participants were very comfortable with digital tools in their hands for "following," "Tweeting," and "reposting," few already carried a methodology for online organizing. Moreover, they sometimes failed to understand or embody feminist concepts central to SAYHU's work, which they had access to but we did not have time to teach regularly. We had used a Google Survey for our summer institute application that asked questions like: What do you know about intersectional feminism, and what does it mean to you? Have you participated in social justice work here in Houston or elsewhere, such as organizing or taking part in community-related projects for social change? What are you hoping to learn?

VSI made space for youth who might have otherwise struggled to connect with us because of barriers to participation, including but not limited to social anxiety and transportation limitations—some participants were located in Dallas or Austin, and others in the distant Houston suburbs. Houston's diffuse urban geography and unreliable infrastructure for transportation in the Global South often inhibit the mobilization of social movements, but new digital tools and new habits of connectivity helped us address that challenge. Digital infrastructure for SAYHU—from community networks on Slack to the website and the digital archive for oral history, to audiences on our different social media platforms—allowed us to expand our social network, be recognized by national South Asian organizations, share about the specificities of the diverse experiences of South Asian youth in Texas, and circulate new knowledges we had developed in community with one another. I worked with one intern to conduct our first SAYHU community survey via Google Survey and then report the data about SAYHU members' needs and interests to our community. Our research revealed that many SAYHU community members—nearly half of those actively participating—identified as queer or questioning. For some, a desire for queer brown immigrant community kept them returning. Our community-engaged research ultimately led us to focus more on mental health concerns and LGBTQIA+ identities in SAYHU's final year.

Along with outlining our vision online and hosting a blog on our website to highlight the stories of community members, SAYHU produced the Preservation Project, a digital repository initiated by a public history graduate student, to house oral histories of a first generation of South Asian Texans and conversations about Black and South Asian feminist solidarities that inform our work. The Preservation Project led us to produce a SAYHU-specific feminist methodology for oral history in our community that we also shared with related resources on the website. Being able to publish accessible transnational feminist content on the SAYHU website allowed youth access and understanding; it relied on participants' willingness to share their personal narratives with a broader online audience. In these and other ways, we continued to grow into who we hoped to be, informed by those who joined our community: artists, parents, students, organizers, and scholars.

Organizing in a Pandemic

Shifting away from what had always been a weeklong in-person program, for VSI we organized four morning sessions online over two weekends in August and included one Wednesday evening online event that was open to the public, and one closing program on Sunday afternoon that youth would coordinate themselves for their friends and family to join online. As a college educator, I frequently guessed what could work best for optimum online instruction, drawing on recent intensive experience with online teaching. Still learning our way around Zoom, we experimented with what could work for making introductions online, actively using the chat, and directing focused learning in bursts and in breakout groups (which were a newer feature at the time), to cultivate relationships. We also grouped participants into deliberately curated "pods" of five or six youth for the duration of the institute, each with a community member as a facilitator. To get youth participants using Slack for the summer institute, I built in some incentives, like daily icebreaker questions, an "assignment" to reach out to one other participant, and a live survey on the app Kaaput, where they respond by text about different features they had tried out on Slack (thus reminding participants to use them). Trivia apps and word cloud tools were more engaging, and youth responded to other daily directives. In one activity, VSI participants posted to a dedicated Slack channel an image of one item that held significance for them, plus a few lines describing it. An activity that had previously been done in person now produced a digital visual archive in which they could respond to one another.

To set the tone for VSI, we also sent out a digital care package to participants, with Spotify playlists and some of our favorite music videos so that they could know our leadership team better. As SAYHU Summer Institute leads, we introduced ourselves through video recordings in advance, to save our time together for other things and to model ways that they might share about themselves in the online space. As with the university classroom, not all participants did the readings we shared or kept showing up. Only a fraction came to understand SAYHU's work in ways that they could articulate it well to others or were motivated to help us build the community.[26] We were sometimes united by the specificities of our location in the South, cultural familiarities among South Asians, histories of migration, experiences of generational trauma, and our care for one another, but differences abound. Like anywhere else in organizing, some people came to SAYHU with a desire to lead in that space, while others were frustrated to encounter a non-hierarchical model, often confounded in their attempts to reproduce hierarchy by habitually deferring to more senior folks or expecting younger collaborators to defer to us. But others were drawn to SAYHU precisely because we offered an alternative vision, very much the work of holding a decolonial imaginary. Regardless, talking through what feminist collectivity might look like and trying to apply that to SAYHU's community culture in the face of a youth culture of individualism was consistently a challenge for us and not always successful.

Creating spaces to talk about anti-blackness, caste, sexuality, reproductive justice, and mental health, for example, and repeatedly inviting hesitant but curious community members into multiple conversations and modes of communication as a method of organizing online has proved influential—even when the responses are not immediate. Our work required a kind of uncertain "relational ethic of radical vulnerability" that transnational feminist Richa Nagar theorizes as essential to the work of collectivity because it provides opportunities for unlearning and purposeful, if imperfect, knowledge-producing collaborations.[27] Youth participants are only just discovering that "Revolutionary dreams erupt out of political engagement; collective social movements are incubators of new knowledge."[28] With an attentiveness to power and hierarchy and a transnational feminist analysis, we increasingly moved to create a South Asian space that was queer, and a digital space safe for queer and questioning youth. The question of how to get people who join SAYHU to take ownership, to lead, and to hold on to the feminist lessons we learn together when doing so remained. They have to imagine it first.

Another World Is Possible

In *New Digital Worlds: Postcolonial Digital Humanities in Theory, Praxis and Pedagogy,* Risam argues for the necessity to imagine something different as we build new worlds online: "Avoiding reproducing existing inequalities in regimes of knowledge requires attending to postcolonial critiques of the archive. Through the convergence of postcolonial digital archiving practice and the role of social media activism in the public sphere, the emancipatory and expansive possibilities of resisting colonial world making in digital worlds are visible." Moreover, a postcolonial digital humanities approach "reshapes the hierarchies that determine what is knowledge and who can produce it, bringing public communities of the Global South into view as contributors to knowledge production."[29] Applying a feminist and postcolonial digital humanities practice to SAYHU's project development is inherently an iterative process. SAYHU was constantly evaluating what worked and what did not and adjusting accordingly. We were only just beginning to move toward strategies of resistance and social justice movement-building through political education, as we mentored youth whose most pressing concerns often were survival in a capitalist system. They vaguely identified with wanting to do more in the world than earn money to support their families. Because of age and experience, they had yet to develop a specific vision for their lives in the long term.

Just as youth came to SAYHU with many assumptions about who we were, we held many assumptions about them, including that they would know more than we did about building community networks online. Rather, the idea that young people today are "digital natives" employs problematic language that reinforces social hierarchies and, as Risam notes, "the fundamental fallacy . . . is the assumption that the increased consumption of digital media and technologies produces a deeper understanding of them."[30] In fact, through SAYHU we learned time and again that while young people presented as savvy on social media, they knew little about networking strategies that might expand the reach of a social justice network. We assumed that they understood the concepts *behind* online organizing work, including how outreach could build ideological community, yet they had never been trained on this kind of work. They might be regular users of social media, but they are not always comfortable receiving guidance on strategies for how to use it for community organizing. We also assumed that if they did not know how to do something, they would look it up on the internet or ask for help, which was not necessarily the case. Many high-achieving youth grappled with feeling they should already know how to do the tasks being asked of them as SAYHU interns, and our being friendly and approachable appeared to trigger guilt and shame when they were unable to solve problems on their own, let alone juggle SAYHU work projects with their many school and family responsibilities.

Most SAYHU youth were unprepared to organize others for even the most low-stakes events like book groups, art workshops, and casual conversations—even after we published guidelines on how to do outreach and host an event with this community. Building a feminist community meant we were often asking SAYHU participants for a radical vulnerability with one another that they were not prepared for, and they had few models for showing up in those ways. SAYHU's methodology truly approximated the kind of vulnerable feminist pedagogical approach that Anna Ríos-Rojas describes as requiring heartbreak, to unsettle traditional student/teacher dynamics and make decolonial moves.[31] Our individual limitations and obstacles in these community relationships were related to those we faced in our immediate families and communities around honesty and vulnerability, so we sought to model and practice ways of sharing and supporting one another, with a sense that there is transformative power in feminist collectivity. We did so around mental health, family dynamics, and other kinds of relationships, including experiences of coming out as LGBTQIA+.

Indeed, convening a South Asian space as one that we had initially deemed "queer-friendly" was important, and being radically vulnerable in our queerness was equally significant. Still, we were only able to do so as queer and gender nonbinary community members made themselves known and served as role models in SAYHU for other LGBTQIA+ South Asian youth. In *Lone Star Muslims*, a rare monograph on South Asians in Texas, Ahmed Afzal provides insights into the particularities of Pakistani immigrant subjectivities in Houston and necessarily confronts the "presumed heterosexuality in South

Asian and Muslim American population movements in the United States that renders invisible the experiences of gay and lesbian South Asian Muslim Americans."[32] Our normalization of gender diversity and queer sexualities in SAYHU was significant to them, SAYHU participants told us, even if they have no intention of ever coming out to their family and friends. At times, it was intimidating.

Zoom Fatigue

While bringing our work online offered more access for some, others are hesitant to connect via the internet because they are concerned about their digital footprint and being monitored or surveilled by family members and by the government. In repeatedly inviting, compelling, and cajoling participation in the digital realm, I sought to build a community of resource sharing, peer mentorship, and dialogue in our online networks where youth might find role models or co-conspirators in social justice work. At the time of this writing, we were years into a global pandemic, all of us having learned firsthand how sitting for hours in front of a screen zapped us of our energy. We would stare into our camera in an effort to "make eye contact" in the ways that humans know how to do when face to face, trying to demonstrate our engagement through facial expressions and nodding. Talking with groups of people on camera while attempting to intuit emotions and understand different registers of communication may have become commonplace, but it remains exhausting. Even our preoccupation with our own image on the screen distracts us from the conversation as we try to read the body language and facial expressions of others on the video call.[33] As we work toward a shared social justice vision in times of sustained duress, an entirely different kind of attentiveness and energy is required to facilitate meaningful dialogues in these digital worlds.

For those of us who are not only community weavers but also empaths, much was lost in this pandemic organizing moment. "Zoom fatigue" thus becomes a useful metaphor for this moment of community organizing toward connectivity that SAYHU engaged in during the final year of our summer institute. We were unable to be physically present with others or in ways where we "felt seen" and were motivated to respond, but we continued to use technologies in ways that allowed for this to be experienced differently. The exhaustion we felt was from being vulnerable, in order to feel connected in the digital realm; emotional labor was required of us to produce a decolonial digital space that was safe for community members to join and contribute to. Only in this way were they able to imagine—and sometimes unlearn—what it means to be South Asian in the South. Yet we also know how necessary it is to stay connected over time and space for movement-building and community sustainability. Although the collaborative labor felt exhausting at times, the amount of content we shared, and the immediacy with which we could circulate it, was powerful and meaningful to many who said so and others who will find our resources in the future.

Ultimately, SAYHU is able to draw the following key lessons from our experimental organizing of youth online that may be extremely useful to other social justice networks:

1. Online or off, building community requires patience, persistence, and consistent efforts at communication. Expect failures. Feelings of trust take time to solidify and sometimes, no matter how much effort you put in, it is not possible.
2. Social media is not inherently a lesser form of communication. It offers new types of "connectivity" that allow us to reach individuals we might otherwise not have connected with and share feminist knowledge, resources, and opportunities.
3. You can't want feminist community more than the other members of the community. But you *can* make space to help them imagine that it could exist, and sometimes connecting online is what is available to you. Find out what your community wants and needs and help them aim for it.
4. Accountability and transparency in community are uncomfortable for many people, and high-achieving South Asian youth who have succeeded within social hierarchies of their family and community by gaining approval from those in power and following all the rules may find navigating a non-hierarchical community organization overwhelming. Collaborative projects and iterative processes can be frustrating for task-oriented youth who might be seeking paid internships and leadership opportunities but not relationships for growth and learning.
5. Many in your orbit will be grateful to know that your queer immigrant community exists but may never choose to be more involved than reading the information you publish online, and that can be enough.
6. Much more is happening beyond the frame of the Zoom screen and well beyond the collaborative process. Naming those experiences and archiving them online produces important new knowledge for community organizing in a digital era.

For more inspiration and examples of lessons we have learned along the way, you can explore our website at www.sayhutx.org.

Notes

1. The other cofounders of SAYHU are Eesha Pandit, Saneea Sakhyani, Gayatri Joshi, Samira Ali, Rachna Khare, and Praveena Lakshmanan, with Noorulanne Jan joining in year three. For more details, see "SAYHU's Origin Story" on the website at www.sayhutx.org.
2. In the Northeast, social justice programming for South Asian youth includes East Coast Solidarity Summer and Desi Summer, and on the West Coast, the long-established Bay Area Solidarity Summer.
3. Maira 2016.
4. Sundar Mukherjee 2022.
5. Velez 2019.
6. Curiel 2016.
7. We first formally asked this question at the 2017 National Women's Studies Association conference, in a panel on "Black Feminisms and South Asian Feminisms: In Solidarity, In Collaboration" that included me, Eesha Pandit, Chandra Talpade Mohanty, Linda E. Carty, LeConte Dill, and Brittany Brathwaite. However, I leave the work of theorizing these solidarities for elsewhere, to focus here on concrete strategies for building feminist community online.
8. My scholarship on social media use among Dominican feminists informs my understanding of the value of digital networks for transnational feminist organizing.
9. For a brief overview of the many intersections of black and South Asian experience, see the preface to the *Feminist & Queer Afro-Asians* special issue of the *Scholar & Feminist Online*, by Nitasha Sharma. Sharma argues, "Afro-Asian studies, like the broader field of ethnic studies, remains tied to heteronormative and resistant narratives by male and Western scholars. As a result, we miss the vast archive of compelling intimacies and political engagements that can guide us to alternative futures. Racial formations cannot be adequately analyzed without insights from feminist and queer studies scholars."
10. Frazier 2020.
11. Taylor 2017, 15.
12. I am thinking of the organizing work of United We Dream and how its protests in Houston employed Civil Rights Movement strategies and song, for example.
13. Velez 2019.
14. Mohanty and Carty 2018.
15. Along the way, we came to understand the importance of having a trauma-informed approach to our collective work, particularly among South Asian immigrants and first-generation South Asian Texans.
16. Mohanty and Carty 2018.
17. Kelley 2002, 10.
18. Quraishi 2020, 21.
19. Quraishi 2020, 20.
20. Paul 2019.

21. Texas India Forum Inc. website at www.howdymodi.org.
22. Quinn 2020.
23. Fujiwara and Roshanravan 2018, 7.
24. People did circle back to us when they were ready, and this was made easier by our presence online, virtual events, and monthly emails.
25. SAYHU leadership had already been using the app for our work in the collective as an effective way to avoid email chains, in which collective members responded in thanks every time one of us announced a completed task or shared information.
26. Koshy and Patel 2021.
27. Nagar 2019, 29–30.
28. Kelley 2002, 8.
29. Risam 2019.
30. Risam 2019.
31. Ríos-Rojas 2020, 163.
32. Afzal 2014, 8.
33. This surely is even more distracting for adolescents who are experimenting with self-expression.

Bibliography

Afzal, Ahmed. *Lone Star Muslims: Transnational Lives and the South Asian Experience in Texas.* New York: New York University Press, 2014.

Curiel, Ochy. "Rethinking Radical Anti-Racist Feminist Politics in a Global Neoliberal Context," Transl. Manuela Borzone, Alexander Ponomareff. *Meridians* 14, no. 2 (2016): 46–55.

Frazier, Demita. "Interview: Black Feminist History," on *SAYHU Preservation Project* (www.sayhupreservation.org), 2020.

Fujiwara, Lynn, and Shireen Roshanravan, eds. *Asian American Feminisms and Women of Color Politics.* Seattle: University of Washington Press, 2018.

Koshy, Jennifer, and Saaj Patel. "Meet SAYHU's New Interns!" *SAYHU Blog*, January 17, 2021.

Kelley, Robin D. G. *Freedom Dreams: The Black Radical Imagination.* Boston: Beacon Press, 2002.

Maira, Sunaina Marr. *The 9/11 Generation: Youth, Rights and Solidarity in the War on Terror.* New York: New York University Press, 2016.

Mohanty, Chandra Talpade, and Linda E. Carty, eds. *Feminist Freedom Warriors.* Chicago: Haymarket Books, 2018.

Nagar, Richa. *Hungry Translations: Relearning the World through Radical Vulnerability.* Urbana: University of Illinois Press, 2019.

Okazawa-Rey, Margot. "No Freedom without Connection: Envisioning Sustainable Feminist Solidarities," in *Feminist Freedom Warriors: Genealogies, Justice, Politics, and Hope,* eds. Chandra Talpade Mohanty and Linda E. Carty. Chicago: Haymarket Books, 2018.

Paul, Sonia. "'Howdy, Modi!' Was a Display of Indian Americans' Political Power." *The Atlantic*, September 23, 2019.

Quinn, Rachel Afi. "SAYHU Feminist Community-Building in the Time of Covid-19." *SAYHU Blog*, April 24, 2020.

Quraishi, Usma. *Redefining the Immigrant South: Indian and Pakistani Immigration to Houston during the Cold War*. Chapel Hill: University of North Carolina Press, 2020.

Risam, Roopika. *New Digital Worlds: Postcolonial Digital Humanities in Theory, Praxis, and Pedagogy*. Evanston, IL: Northwestern University Press, 2019.

Ríos-Rojas, Anne (Anna). "'Pedagogies of the Broken-Hearted': Notes on a Pedagogy of Breakage, Women of Color Feminist Decolonial Movidas, and Armed Love in the Classroom/Academy." *Frontiers* 41, no. 1 (2020): 162–178.

Sharma, Nitasha. "Preface" to the *Feminist & Queer Afro-Asians Online* special issue of the *Scholar & Feminist Online*. 14.3 (2018).

Sundar, Pavitra, and Debashree Mukherjee. "Editors' Introduction: Decolonial Feminisms: *In Medias Res*." *Feminist Media Histories* 8, vol. 1 (2022): 1–15.

Taylor, Keeanga-Yamahtta. *How We Get Free: Black Feminism and the Combahee River Collective*. Chicago: Haymarket Books, 2017.

Velez, Emma. "Decolonial Feminism at the Intersection: A Critical Reflection on the Relationship between Decolonial Feminism and Intersectionality." *Journal of Speculative Philosophy* 33, no. 3 (2019): 309–406.

PART III

Resistance

8

"I Am Not Oppressed! Give It a Rest!"

The Hijab Project As Resistance to Western Narratives about Muslim Women

ANA CAROLINA ANTUNES

"Sometimes, I worry about what people at school think about Tabarek," Amina told me one day when I was driving her home after one of our weekly meetings. When I asked her why, she continued: "Tabarek [Amina's best friend] and I weren't really friends in junior high, we really became friends in high school and one year after I started hanging out with her, I decided to wear the scarf. I think people are going to get mad at her thinking she made me [wear a hijab]." Amina summarized how Muslim girls who veil are perceived in the West: as voiceless victims who are oppressed by their community and families. Amina knew that peers and teachers would see her not as somebody who thought deeply about her choices, but as a victim and not an agent of her own life. Due to her experiences as a Muslim girl in the United States, she knew people would come up with several justifications for why she had decided to cover, and none of them would include "because she chose to do it."

Besides being best friends, Amina and Tabarek were members of the *Al Ahad* research collective, the group behind *The Hijab Project,* an art exhibit developed as the action portion of a Critical Participatory Action Research (CPAR) (Torre et al. 2012) project that sought to understand how Islamophobia manifests in the lives of Muslim teenage girls in a suburban high school in Utah. This chapter will draw on the intersection of a decolonial approach to transnational feminist theory (Mikkonen 2020) and girlhood studies to explore the ways a group of Muslim girls living in Salt Lake City, Utah, spoke back against colonial mainstream discourse of victimhood through the praxis of transgressive solidarity.

The Study

Data for this study was collected during the 2016–2017 academic year at Mt. Top High School, a high school in Salt Lake City, Utah. The location of this study is important because Salt Lake City is the headquarters of the Church of Jesus Christ of Latter-Day Saints (commonly known as the LDS church or Mormon church). Although religiosity is encouraged and perceived to be a positive characteristic in this community—the Pew Research Institute affirms that 83 percent of Mormons in Utah attend religious service regularly, and 81 percent of them consider religion to be a very important aspect of their lives (Pew Research Center 2019)—our larger study demonstrated that at Mt. Top High, Muslim religiosity was understood as a negative thing. Everyday examples such as white students using a religious phrase, "Allahu Akbar," (Arabic phrase for "God is most great"), followed by "I am a terrorist" in the classroom demonstrated that at Mt. Top, Muslim religiosity is associated with racialized stereotypes of Muslims as terrorist (Antunes 2023; Khoja-Moolji 2016). I foreground this information because it is through the lens of a conservative religious community that the girls constructed their subjectivities.

The data presented here is part of a larger CPAR project that sought to understand how Islamophobia framed the educational experiences of Muslim girls who veil. The research group, *Al Ahad,* was constituted of five high-school-aged girls, all of whom were first-generation Americans, and me, a Latina woman with a large number of body modifications (tattoos, piercings) in my early thirties. Any written description of the young members of *Al Ahad* will not do justice to the beauty and complexity of their individualities, but, for the purpose of brevity, in this section, I will list their ages and ethnic backgrounds with the hopes that, as I share more of their work and our experiences together, you will get to know them a little bit more:

- Amina, seventeen, was born in Salt Lake City from Bosnian parents.
- Iqra, sixteen, was born in Kenya from Somali parents.
- Kadi, fifteen, was born in the Ivory Coast from Malian parents.
- Tabarek and Shams, both seventeen, were born in Iraq.

Last, it is important that I disclose that I was born and raised in Brazil, making our research collective truly transnational. I met the girls while working at a junior high after-school program and, at the time this project was developed, I had known all but one of them (Shams, who was invited by Tabarek to join) for at least two years.

Mainstream Narratives about Muslims Who Veil

The literature surrounding the understanding of Muslim young women identity in U.S. society recognizes that these girls often are perceived "as pathological victims of their familial cultural and religious practices" (Mirza 2015, 40). Muslim families are blamed for not instilling in their daughters the desire to learn and succeed, as well as educating them to be submissive and passive (Macey 1999; Osler 2009; Timmerman and Vanderwaeren 2003). Amireh (2005, 231) uses the term "death by culture" to describe people's misguided ideas that Muslim girls are inescapably trapped in their culture and can free themselves from it only through death. The perception that Muslim women and girls are oppressed by their religion is not new, and it has its roots in European colonial endeavors in North Africa and the Middle East (Scott 2009).

In the opening vignette, Amina expertly recognizes how these colonial readings are expressed in the way the non-Muslim world sees her. She recognizes that non-Muslims around her see her religion as a prison, something forced on her. The narrative of the veil as a tool of oppression is a manifestation of a larger systemic barrier that makes Muslims into "the other"; this narrative feeds into the systemic discrimination of those who are visibly Muslim or perceived to be Muslim and is also known as Islamophobia. Islamophobia came into prominence in the United States after September 11, 2001, (Mirza 2015) and encompasses anti-Muslim ideas, feelings, and behaviors in the West (Kundnani 2014; Love 2017). Although Islamophobia prominence in the national discourse is recent, Joan W. Scott (2009, 45) argues that since the late 1700s, "the veil has long been a symbol of the irreducible difference and thus the unassimilability of Islam." Scott further argues that particularly in French colonies in the Maghreb, the veil was seen as barbaric and symbolized the incongruence between European perceptions of progress and the "oppressive" way of life of majority Islamic societies. The hijab, then, seen through the colonizers' lens, came to represent women's lack of freedom and internalized oppression. The colonial perspective of the veil has continued to inform the West's relationship to Islam in a postcolonial context, furthering what Gayatri Chakravorty Spivak (1988) describes as the desire of white people to save brown women from brown men. In the United States, the veil remains a symbol of the impossibility of assimilation, because it marks Muslim women's refusal to adhere to "traditional" (read: white) US culture (Cainkar 2009; Mirza 2013). That is, women who reject the possibility of uncovering are seen as rejecting American values such as freedom and individualism.

The veil's politicization in the US context has been furthered by colonial endeavors in the Middle East and Asia, where US military occupation in

Iraq and Afghanistan is discursively circulated as the rationale for the "War on Terror" (Feldman 2011; Abu-Lughod 2013; Ahmed 1982; Bullock 2010; Bush 2001; Mohanty 1988; Scott 2009). "War on Terror" is the name given to a set of federal policies and programs that, under the guise of antiterrorism, has curtailed several citizen rights, including the right to privacy in America (Lee 2003; Osher 2002; Rackow 2002). The Patriot Act, the most important piece of legislation that supports the War on Terror, effectively allowed for law enforcement to racially profile Muslims or those perceived to be Muslim (Ashar 2002; Johnson 2004; Pitt 2011). To justify these invasions and policies, the U.S. government created a narrative of fear of the enemy within: Muslim terrorists who infiltrated our country to destroy it (Thorne and Kouzmin 2010).

Discussions about the understanding of the veil in a national American context are important. Although the young women in this study have spent most of their lives in the United States, their subjectivities are influenced by colonial narratives and are transnationally constructed. That is, the construction of their identity is framed not only by local understandings of gender and race, but also by historical contexts and transnational networks of family, friends, and media consumption (Grewal and Kaplan 1994). In fact, transnational feminism makes the connection between international power imbalances on a macro level and its everyday manifestation in people's lives. The way Islamophobia is experienced in their lives is both part of a much larger colonial narrative and a map that helps us trace a political project of occupation and domination in the Middle East (Alexander and Mohanty 2010). While narratives of citizenship and nation building exist on a macro level, it is their materialization in everyday life that maintains and perpetuates such narratives (Thayer 2009). These are the narratives that the young women in this project sought to push back against.

Transnational Girlhood Studies

Transnational feminist theory was developed by Third World women to explore the complex intersections between gender, race, place, and citizenship. Despite the fact that scholars such as Chandra Mohanty, Trinh Minh Ha, and Jacqui Alexander were doing transnational work long ago, the term and its concrete definition can be traced to Grewal and Kaplan's anthology *Scattered Hegemonies* (Grewal and Kaplan 1994, 3), in which the authors argue that "if the world is currently structured by transnational economic links and cultural asymmetries, locating feminist practices within these structures becomes imperative." Grewal and Kaplan argued that since the lives of third world women are influenced by events that expanded beyond the nation-state's borders, feminist theory that sought to understand oppression in these contexts had to do the same. For that reason, the term "transnational [is used] to refer to a critical mode of thinking across borders and thus thinking across multiple intersections, forms and sites of difference at once" (Dosekun 2015, 11). To build a feminist praxis that is transformative, we need to take politics, economics, policy, histories of occupation, pillage, and trade into consideration. Though transnational feminist theories at their origin sought to move units of analysis of gender, race, and power relations away from Western understanding of these issues, in recent years some of the theorizing has been co-opted by liberalism to talk about economic and social development in the Global South (Mikkonen 2020). Therefore, I approach transnational feminism in this project through its original decolonial roots, seeking to emphasize the agency of the girls involved in this project.

Transnational feminism and girlhood studies are rarely thought of as intersecting fields, but a growing number of scholars are recognizing that, like womanhood, girlhood is not a "global sisterhood" (Marshall 2012, 211), and that to understand the realities of girls, it is necessary to historicize them. The field of girlhood studies traditionally places girls in an "ideal-victim subjects or empowered/rescued subjects" (Khoja-Moolji 2017, 380) dichotomy and recognizes the only possibility of moving from the first to the second is a one-way linear "chain of vulnerability-suffering-empowerment" (Khoja-Moolji 2017, 383). Furthermore, in much of the literature, the girl-child is characterized as "white, middle-class, heterosexual females in an English-speaking Western country" (Vanner 2019, 120). However, scholars in the emerging subfield of transnational girlhood argue that this simplistic understanding of girlhood "leaves little room for girls' intersectional complexities" (Bent and Switzer 2016, 127). Lisa Weems argues that (2009, 179) non-Western and Third World girls embody transnational relations among economic, political, and colonial powers and that transnational girlhood studies seeks to understand the ways they "create, inhabit, and transgress the discursive positions to which they are subject." It is through this interaction with each other and with the reality around them that that girls with transnational experiences build their subjectivity.

This process of developing an understanding of oneself in relation to others and to the environment is often called relationality (Bent and Switzer 2016; Khoja-Moolji 2017). More than self-reflexivity, relationality is about the comprehension that one's experience exists in parallel to multiple and different experiences. Arturo Escobar (2009, 5) corroborates this understanding of the term by defining it as one's ability to imagine life differently, that is, to recognize that there is not one correct way to live. In that manner, relationality becomes the focus of transnational girlhood analysis, as transnational experiences of girls "emphasiz[e] a heightened sense of complementarity and interdependency" (Khoja-Moolji 2017, 379). Relationality recognizes the other as the agent, as someone who crafts their subjectivities in connection to, but not dependent on, outside readings of them. Relationality asks us to consider oppression and the tools used to fight against it not as a "one size fits all" approach, but rather as realities embedded in specific national, religious, and cultural contexts (among others) that can only be fully understood by those within. Escobar's perspective directly connects with a decolonial approach to transnational feminist theory in that it moves away from global feminism perspectives and recognizes the importance of historicizing ideas such as freedom and agency (Vanner 2019). Sylvanna Falcón (2016, 176) extends the concept by demonstrating that when we examine women's and girls' issues through a relational lens, it allows us to move away from simplistic binary understandings of reality toward a more nuanced perspective, based on co-construction and connectivity. As such, relationality becomes crucial to the decolonial project of transnational girlhood studies because it recognizes girls not only as full humans capable of critically interrogating their own selves, but also as holders of knowledge that is often excluded from the mainstream and academic discourses.

Transgressive Solidarity

It is the centrality of relationality in transnational girlhood that allows for the development of transgressive solidarities. I use the word transgressive here to define relationships that defy social expectations and create new decolonial possibilities for the future, in which racialized communities build an antiracist world. Defining solidarity in the context of transnational feminism is not new; the field has emphasized the importance of the tension between power and solidarity among women working within and across borders (Thayer 2009). In fact, scholars have used terms like cross-cultural solidarity and coalition building to define relationships developed across nation-states and cultural differences (Campt and Thomas 2008; Falcón and Nash 2015; Mohanty 1988; Moosa-Mitha and Ross-Sheriff 2010; Rankin 2011; Thayer 2009; Wang 2016). I follow a long history of thinking and theorizing about transnational relationships to think about how the relationships developed among the members of *Al Ahad* became a form of resistance against race- and gender-based assumptions placed on women and girls of color's bodies.

Transgressive solidarity becomes a form of resistance because, particularly in the American context, one of the roles of racial hierarchy is to "divide and conquer" groups deemed as minorities, to pit racialized groups against each other (Song 2004). As a matter of fact, Grewal argues that "racial and gender formation enable the disciplinary and governmental technologies that support neoliberal policies" (Grewal 2005, 15). When minoritized groups perceive each other as rivals instead of supporters, white supremacy wins.

Therefore, alliances between and among minoritized women challenge the imperial/colonial expectations that we would fight each other for the proverbial breadcrumbs. Maria Lugones (2003, 219) writes about the power of "hanging out" in defying social fragmentation and in challenging white spaces in society. Minoritized communities are expected to exist in silos, away from each other and away from white spaces.

It is important to highlight that, in talking about relationships based on transgressive solidarity, they "have not transcended the disparity of power and privilege.... Rather that genuine affection and love is possible in spite of it" (Basarudin and Bhattacharya 2016, 46). Basarudin and Bhattacharya's (2016) statement is so powerful because it serves as a reminder that all relationships are embedded in asymmetrical power relations. It highlights how alliances should be analyzed as the asymmetric power relationships that they are (Desai et al. 2012). However, while some may see power asymmetry as problematic, in this context it is seen as powerful because it "den[ies] the stories that structural power tells and demonstrate[s] that the imperial imagination does not control our horizon of possibilities" (Chowdhury and Philipose 2016, 3). Yes, research collectives formed by adults and young people are fraught, but so are all the other relationships we have. The success of transgressive solidarities lies not in trying to even out this asymmetry (which is impossible) but in learning to love and respect each other through it.

Troubling Expectations

The first obvious instance in which transgressive transnational solidarity played a big role was the formation of our research group, *Al Ahad*, an intergenerational, multinational, and multilingual collective. While the members of *Al Ahad* had previous relationships with each other, being a member of the group transformed these relationships in ways that are best put into words by Kadi: "I'm never going to forget this until the day I die. I'm gonna tell my kids, and they are going to tell their grandkids [about the project]." While the relationships that we strengthened through our work together were transformative for us, for some, the existence of the friendships formed among the members of the research collective was unimaginable, and for that reason, they were transgressive. Just the fact that we were together was enough to cause confusion and disturb assumptions.

Amina wrote in her journal about our outing to a local mall that her "favorite part was when a man asked Ana if she was Muslim without a headscarf." It was clear that the man was trying to figure out what we were doing together; for him, the girls and I did not belong together. After that day, Amina kept wondering what people saw when they saw me, a tattooed and heavily pierced Latina woman, entering spaces such as fast-food restaurants, Wal-marts, libraries, and coffee shops with five (or four, or three, depending on the day) *hijabis*. "Do you think they think you adopted all of us?" she asked. Finally, Amina's curiosity was addressed by a cashier when we went to a dollar store to buy supplies for our hijab workshop. The teller could not fathom why we were together. Even before it was our turn to check out, she had already mumbled a surprised comment about us. In my field notes for the day, I wrote:

> We got to Dollar Tree and looked for our stuff when we were ready to pay we got in line. The cashier was an older White lady.... She was ringing the person in front of me, she looked up and said "Wait, the four of you are Muslims but she isn't?" The person in front of me finished paying and the cashier asked me (this time it seems like she was looking at me/ talking to me) "are you with them?" and I said, "yes we are together." She seemed uncomfortable and tried to make small talk asking me if we were planning on having a party. On the way out, the girls were like "What the hell." (Field Notes, 3/18/17)

Although the analysis of how people perceive me was not part of this project, it is possible to link individual surprise at my association with the girls to assumptions about Muslim womanhood. Tattoos are still linked with ideas of criminality and social deviance, especially when body modification (tattoos, piercings, and other forms of body art) are on women's bodies. When we consider mainstream ideas of Muslim womanhood, including piety (Abu-Lughod 2013), conservatism (Hatem 2011), backwardness (Read and Bartkowski 2000), and subjugation (Bilge 2010), the idea of Muslim girls "hanging out" with someone who looks like me seems contradictory, to say the least. However, despite people's assumptions, we do not need to occupy the same social identity to share meaningful bonds (Chowdhury 2016). "Hanging out" is transgressive because it allows oppressed subjects to challenge the colonial geographies and because it does not legitimize "oppressive arrangement and logics" (Lugones 2003, 219). Hangouts as forms of resistance are fluid and flexible, and they occur on the "street-level" (Lugones 2003, 208). Hangouts approach resistance not through a distant theoretical perspective but through intimate connections.

The instances I used above to describe our interactions with white folks exemplifies Lugones's (2003) understanding of hanging out as a challenge to fragmented locations. In urban environments designed to uphold white supremacy, racialized communities are allowed to inhabit spaces marked as such: the Black neighborhoods, the Latino markets, the mosque—each of us is to stay contained in our allotted area. However, as "streetwalkers" (Lugones 2003, 208), the members of *Al Ahad* transgressed these demarcations and forced people interacting with us to rethink who we are and where we belong. As demonstrated by the example above, our encounters were met with confusion, which, for white folks, created a need to come up with a reasonable explanation (she must be a Muslim without a hijab!) to the situation.

That was not the only way folks involved in the project developed transgressive solidarity: the development of the hijab workshop is another example. The project's objective was to take up what Sylvanna Falcón (2016) argues is the task of transnational feminist researchers, which is more than just highlighting and analyzing injustice, but rather conjuring "a confluence of imagination and action, of creativity and resolution, of feminist analysis and forming coalition" (Falcón 2016, 187). Through the hijab-making workshop and the exhibition of its product at the Utah Museum of Contemporary Art, *Al Ahad* used the research results to engage other Muslim young people in the fight against Islamophobia as well as to educate museum visitors about the significance of the veil for different Muslim women. The girls of *Al Ahad* used the space they were given in the museum to raise up the voices of other women in their community. In doing that, they also allowed for voices different from theirs to come out; for example, they invited Muslim women who do not veil to share their thoughts on the hijab. Sahar, a sixteen-year-old young woman who does not veil, wrote: "I love the hijab and one day I will definitely wear it . . . I am so proud to be a Muslim and one day, I will wear a hijab." Sahar's write-up complemented the exhibit because it brought to light the weight of deciding to wear the veil. While the young women leading the project felt they were ready to take on a deep commitment to their faith, others still chose not to wear it. Opening spaces for a dialogue around the hijab, the pieces in the exhibit functioned as *"social mirrors*, scientific instruments designed to reflect back lived realities that were being denied by dominant ideologies and 'official definitions'" (Torre et al. 2012, 174). While "official" definitions of the hijab link the veil with oppression and victimhood, the project proved that these definitions are not accurate. In these instances, transgressive solidarity extends the decolonial feminist project because it makes space for Muslim women and girls to display their individuality, agency, and a subjectivity that is constructed outside the bounds of the colonial imaginary. The young women invited to participate wrote, for example: "I am not oppressed! . . . Give it a rest! The hijab is my identity!"; "[The hijab] is my crown and my decision. When I wear it, I feel confident and I stand out." The exhibit provided space for the artists to take charge of the narrative surrounding Muslim womanhood, telling their stories on their own terms. Furthermore, including Muslim young women who do not veil in the exhibit served to dispel the idea that there is a chasm between "secular" Muslims (those who relegate religious practice to private spaces) and the "pious" ones (those who make their faith public). Again, in this instance, the peaceful coexistence of voices of *hijabis* and non-*hijabis* in the same space challenges the fragmentation discourse that creates the image of animosity and separation among groups of people. In including young women who may have different understandings of their shared religion, the young women showed that solidarity and friendship do not have to be bounded by the colonial imaginary and its rules.

Conclusion

In this chapter, I introduced the concept of transgressive solidarity. Based on decolonial and transnational approaches to alliances among minoritized groups, transgressive solidarity builds on concepts such as "hanging out" (Lugones 2003) and coalition building (Falcón and Nash 2015) to describe how cross-group relationships can be a form of resistance. Using the observations of one of the youth members of our research group, *Al Ahad,* as the departure point of analysis, I described how the simple fact that I, a thirty-something tattooed Latina, was walking around with a group of *hijabi* girls disturbed people's understandings of colonial racial and social hierarchies. While the act of hanging out (Lugones 2003, 219) may seem like a small act, it presents to those around us a decolonial possibility in which minoritized groups do not have to exist only in isolated and fragmented silos. Together, our presence as a group in majority-white spaces challenged assumptions about Muslim girlhood, the veil, and what kinds of alliances are possible in a decolonial future.

Similarly, I used the concept of transgressive solidarity to explain the art exhibit that was created as a result of *Al Ahad*'s research project. Through a collection of interpretations of the *hijab* created by both *hijabis* and non-*hijabi* women and girls, the exhibit also subverted traditional and colonial expectations about the kinds of relationships that Muslim women and girls who veil have with those who do not. The importance of this form of transgressive solidarity lies in breaking the boundaries created by colonial powers that divide communities to weaken them. The fact that conversations about the *hijab* and its meaning and importance happened outside of the colonial framework, through collective art making, is also transgressive.

Bibliography

Abu-Lughod, Lila. 2013. *Do Muslim women need saving?* Harvard University Press, 2013.

Ahmed, Leila. 1982. "Western ethnocentrism and perceptions of the harem." *Feminist studies* 8(3): 521–534.

Al-Saji, Alia. 2010. "The racialization of Muslim veils: A philosophical analysis." *Philosophy & Social Criticism* 36(8): 875–902.

Alexander, Jacqui, and Chandra Mohanty. 2010. "Cartographies of knowledge and power: Transnational feminism as radical praxis." In Amanda Lock Swarr and Richa Nagar, eds., *Critical transnational feminist praxis*: 23–45. State University of New York Press.

Amireh, Amal. 2011. "Palestinian women's disappearing act: The suicide bomber through western feminist eyes." *Arab and Arab American feminisms: Gender, violence, and belonging*: 29–45.

Antunes, Ana Carolina. 2023. "Why does everybody want to know if I shower with my hijab?": Understanding the process of gendered racialization of Muslim girls in a suburban majority white high school." *Girlhood Studies Journal* 16 (3): 35–51.

Ashar, Sameer M. 2002. "Immigration enforcement and subordination: The consequences of racial profiling after September 11." *Immigration & Nationality Law Review* 23: 545.

Basarudin, Azza, and Himika Bhattacharya. 2016. "Meditations on friendship: Politics of feminist solidarity in ethnography." In Elora Halim Chowdhury and Liz Philipose, eds., *Dissident friendships: Feminism, imperialism, and transnational solidarity*, 43–70. University of Illinois Press.

Bent, E., and H. Switzer. 2016. "Oppositional Girlhoods and the Challenge of Relational Politics." *Gender Issues* 33, 122–147.

Bilge, Sirma. 2010. "Beyond subordination vs. resistance: An intersectional approach to the agency of veiled Muslim women." *Journal of intercultural studies* 31(1): 9–28.

Bullock, Katherine. 2002. *Rethinking Muslim women and the veil: Challenging historical & modern stereotypes*. International Institute of Islamic Thought.

Bush, Laura. 2001. *The weekly address delivered by the First Lady*. The American Presidency Project. Retrieved from: https://georgewbush-whitehouse.archives.gov/news/releases/2001/11/20011117.html.

Cainkar, Louis A. 2009. *Homeland insecurity: The Arab American and Muslim American experience after 9/11*. Russell Sage Foundation.

Campt, Tina, and Deborah A. Thomas. 2008. "Gendering diaspora: Transnational feminism, diaspora and its hegemonies." *Feminist Review* 90(1): 1–8.

Chowdhury, Elora. 2016. "The space between us: Reading Umrigar and Sangari in the quest for female friendship." In Elora Halim Chowdhury and Liz Philipose, eds., *Dissident friendships: Feminism, imperialism, and transnational solidarity*, 131–144. University of Illinois Press.

Chowdhury, Elora Halim, and Liz Philipose, eds. 2016. *Dissident friendships: Feminism, imperialism, and transnational solidarity*. University of Illinois Press.

Desai, Jigna, Danielle Bouchard, and Diane Detournay. 2012. "Disavowed thievery: The work of the 'transnational' in feminists and LGBTQ Studies." In Elora Halim Chowdhury and Liz Philipose, eds., *Dissident friendships: Feminism, imperialism, and transnational solidarity*, 46–64. University of Illinois Press.

Dosekun, Simidele. 2015. "For western girls only? Post-feminism as transnational culture." *Feminist Media Studies* 15(6): 960–975.

Driscoll, Catherine. 2008. "Girls today—Girls, girl culture and girl studies." *Girlhood Studies* 1(1): 13–32.

Escobar, Arturo. 2010. "Latin America at a crossroads: Alternative modernizations, post-liberalism, or post-development?" *Cultural studies* 24(1): 1–65.

Falcón, Sylvanna M. 2016. "Transnational feminism as a paradigm for decolonizing the practice of research: Identifying feminist principles and methodology criteria for US-based scholars." *Frontiers: A Journal of Women Studies* 37(1): 174–194.

Falcón, Sylvanna M., and Jennifer C. Nash. 2015. "Shifting analytics and linking theories: A conversation about the 'meaning-making' of intersectionality and transnational feminism." *Studies International Forum* 50: 1–10.

Feldman, Keith P. 2011. "Empire's verticality: The Af/Pak frontier, visual culture, and racialization from above." *Comparative American Studies An International Journal* 9, 4: 325–341.

Grewal, Inderpal. 2005. *Transnational America: Feminisms, diasporas, neoliberalisms*. Duke University Press.

Grewal, Inderpal, and Caren Kaplan, eds. 1994. *Scattered hegemonies: Postmodernity and transnational feminist practices*. University of Minnesota Press.

Hatem, Mervat F. 2005. "Arab Americans and Arab American feminism after September 11, 2001: Meeting the external and internal challenges facing our communities." *MIT Electronic Journal of Middle East Studies* 5: 37–49.

Jiwani, Yasmin. 2014. "Posthumous rescue: The Shafia young women as worthy victims." *Girlhood Studies* 7(1): 27–45.

Johnson, K. R. 2004. "Racial Profiling after September 11: The Department of Justice's 2003 Guidelines." *Loyola Law Review* 50: 67–87.

Khoja-Moolji, Shenila. 2016. "The sounds of racialized masculinities: Examining the affective pedagogies of Allahu Akbar." *Feminist Media Studies* 16(6): 1110–1113.

Khoja-Moolji, Shenila S. 2017. "The making of humans and their others in and through transnational human rights advocacy: Exploring the cases of Mukhtar Mai and Malala Yousafzai." *Signs: Journal of Women in Culture and Society* 42(2): 377–402.

Koegeler-Abdi, Martina. 2017. "Muslim feminist agency and Arab American literature: A case study of Mohja Kahf's the girl in the tangerine scarf." *Gender Forum* 65.

Kundnani, Arun. 2014. *The Muslims are coming! Islamophobia, extremism, and the domestic war on terror*. Verso Trade.

Lee, Laurie Thomas. 2003. "The USA PATRIOT Act and telecommunications: Privacy under attack." *Rutgers Computer & Tech. LJ* 29: 371.

Lorde, Audre. 2012. *Sister outsider: Essays and speeches*. Penguin Classics.

Love, Erik. 2017. *Islamophobia and racism in America*. New York University Press.

Lugones, María. 2003. *Pilgrimages/peregrinajes: Theorizing coalition against multiple oppressions*. Rowman & Littlefield Publishers.

Macey, Marie. 1999. "Religion, male violence, and the control of women: Pakistani Muslim men in Bradford, UK." *Gender & Development* 7(1): 48–55.

Mahmood, Saba. 2011. *Politics of piety: The Islamic revival and the feminist subject*. Princeton University Press.

Marshall, Paul A. 2002. *God and the Constitution: Christianity and American politics*. Rowman & Littlefield.

Mikkonen, Enni. 2020. "Decolonial and transnational feminist solidarity: Promoting ethically sustainable social change with women in rural Nepalese communities." *International Journal of Community and Social Development* 2(1): 10–28.

Mirza, Heidi Safia. 2013. "'A second skin': Embodied intersectionality, transnationalism and narratives of identity and belonging among Muslim women in Britain." *Women's Studies International Forum* 36: 5–15.

Mirza, Heidi Safia. 2015. "Dangerous Muslim girls? Race, gender and Islamophobia in British schools." *The Runnymede School Report: Race, Education and Inequality in Contemporary Britain*: 40–43.

Mohanty, Chandra. 1988. "Under Western eyes: Feminist scholarship and colonial discourses." *Feminist review* 30(1): 61–88.

Moosa-Mitha, Mehmoona, and Fariyal Ross-Sheriff. 2010. "Transnational social work and lessons learned from transnational feminism." *Affilia* 25(2): 105–109.

Nijdam, Elizabeth. 2020. "Transnational girlhood and the politics of style in German Manga." *Journal of Graphic Novels and Comics* 11(1): 31–51.

Osher, Steven A. 2002. "Privacy, computers and the Patriot Act: The Fourth Amendment isn't dead, but no one will insure it." *Florida Law REview* 54: 521.

Osler, Audrey. 2009. "Patriotism, multiculturalism and belonging: Political discourse and the teaching of history." *Educational Review* 61(1): 85–100.

Pew Research Center. 2019, April 1. "The countries with the 10 largest Christian populations and the 10 largest Muslim populations." https://www.pewresearch.org/fact-tank/2019/04/01/the-countries-with-the-10-largest-christian-populations-and-the-10-largest-muslim-populations.

Pitt, Cassady. 2011. "US Patriot Act and racial profiling: Are there consequences of discrimination?" *Michigan Sociological Review*: 53–69.

Rackow, S. H. 2002. "How the USA Patriot Act Will Permit Governmental Infringement upon the Privacy of Americans in the Name of 'Intelligence' Investigations." *University of Pennsylvania Law Review* 150(5): 1651–1696.

Rankin, Katharine N. 2011. "Assemblage and the politics of thick description." *City* 15(5): 563–569.

Read, Jen'nan Ghazal, and John P. Bartkowski. 2000. "To veil or not to veil? A case study of identity negotiation among Muslim women in Austin, Texas." *Gender & society* 14(3): 395–417.

Rinaldo, Rachel. 2014. "Pious and critical: Muslim women activists and the question of agency." *Gender & Society* 28(6): 824–846.

Scott, Joan Wallach. 2009. *The politics of the veil*. Vol. 7. Princeton University Press.

Song, M. 2004. "Introduction: Who's at the Bottom? Examining Claims about Racial Hierarchy." *Ethnic and Racial Studies* 27(6), 859–877.

Spivak, Gayatri Chakravorty. 2003. "Can the subaltern speak?" *Die Philosophin* 14(27): 42–58.

Switzer, Heather, Emily Bent, and Crystal Leigh Endsley. 2016. "Precarious politics and girl effects: Exploring the limits of the girl gone global." *Feminist Formations* 28(1): 33–59.

Thayer, Millie. 2009. *Making transnational feminism: Rural women, NGO activists, and northern donors in Brazil*. Routledge.

Thorne, Kym, and Alexander Kouzmin. 2010. "The USA PATRIOT Acts (et al.): Convergent legislation and oligarchic isomorphism in the 'politics of fear' and state crime(s) against democracy (SCADs)." *American behavioral scientist* 53(6): 885–920.

Timmerman, Christiane, Els Vanderwaeren, and Maurice Crul. 2003. "The second generation in Belgium." *International migration review* 37(4): 1065–1090.

Torre, María Elena, Michelle Fine, Brett G. Stoudt, and Madeline Fox. 2012. "Critical participatory action research as public science." In H. Cooper, ed., *APA Handbook of Research Methods in Psychology*.

Vanner, Catherine. 2019. "Toward a definition of transnational girlhood." *Girlhood Studies* 12(2): 115–132.

Wang, Bo. 2016. "The global turn and the question of 'speaking from.'" *Composition Studies* 44(1): 134–137.

Weems, Lisa. 2009. "CHAPTER 11: Border crossing with MIA and transnational girlhood studies." *Counterpoints* 369: 178–194.

9

Children's Bodies and the Sensual Disruptions of Schooling in India and Turkey

AKANKSHA MISRA

I am sitting all the way at the back of a grade five class section in Istanbul's premier Alliance middle school for a one-class-period (forty-minute) *mahremiyet dersi* (privacy lesson) run by the school counselor, Alara.[1] Alara is conducting this lesson as a follow-up to the comprehensive sexuality education[2] (henceforth CSEd) lesson just a few weeks ago that focused overwhelmingly on bodily changes during puberty. This *mahremiyet* lesson, on the other hand, engages children with their feelings and teaches them to respect and maintain their and their peers' feelings. This class that is normally very well behaved is unusually disruptive today. Trying her best to keep them calm, Alara pushes on with her agenda for the day. She asks the students a set of ten questions related to emotional changes during puberty, on topics such as "problems I experience in my family" and "name of one person that I fancy." In the course of the conversation, a question arises about who the children should speak to regarding problems in their lives. The children predictably insist on their best friends, but Alara interrupts them. "You should always go to your parents or teachers and not to your friends." Merve's hand shoots up. "But why?" Merve, blonde, blue-eyed, and extremely precocious, has been quiet until this moment. "Because your friends are going through the same things as you, but your parents and teachers are older and they have already lived these things. So, you should go to them," Alara says. "But I am experiencing them now," mutters Merve under her breath, insistently, unconvinced by Alara's conviction.

Her fleeting comment that goes unacknowledged makes two strong points. First, by emphasizing her experiences "now," Merve implicitly challenges the teleological narrative of future time-as-progress and developmental modernity[3] that continues to weigh heavily on postcolonial[4] nations like India and

Turkey. She offers a stinging critique of "fantasies of futurity" (Dyer 2020), or the idea that the future is necessarily a "better" version of our past and present lived experiences. The horrors of environmental destruction, growing national and global economic inequalities, and ever-increasing crises, such as COVID-19, that are constantly securing absolutely abysmal (non-) futures for a large section of the global population amply demonstrate that this might not be the case (Alvaredo et al. 2018; Roy 2020). Secondly, by doing so, Merve also demonstrates how this civilizational teleology is embodied by the biological figure of the child who is not yet a complete "being" like an adult but supposedly "becoming" (James and Prout 1990) a better version of itself and what we were as children. Instead, she urges us to pause in the present and validate the role of children as thinking, feeling "beings" in the present moment instead of future investments in becoming adult citizens.

In this chapter, by centering children's sensual (comprising all five senses) experiences, desires that they voice, and visceral responses in and out of CSEd and other lessons in schools in Istanbul, Turkey, and Hyderabad, India,[5] I demonstrate how children expose and resist colonial and nationalist civilizational and biological teleologies of progress and childhood development in contemporary schooling that seeks to create (hetero)normative, sexually moral middle-class citizens. Schools in Istanbul and Hyderabad, two cosmopolitan urban centers in rapidly neoliberalizing authoritarian regimes, with a rising new middle class (Ergenç 2018), which export the largest number of school graduates from their respective countries to universities in the United States, are especially invested in creating global, market-oriented, gendered and "sexual citizens" (Evans 1993). However, in doing so, they build on the historical project of contemporary schooling that has emerged from violent suppressions of the voices of the non-privileged, national "others" and scientific biological models of childhood development. They also continue to drive the same exclusions and teleologies of childhood and national development by invisibilizing the embodied historical privilege that constitutes the normative middle-class citizen and continuing to treat children as incomplete embodiments of adulthood, disregarding their developing sexual bodies, desires, and the very sensual ways—touching, feeling, smelling, tasting, seeing—through which they engage with the world. Employing a transnational feminist methodological praxis that follows children's strikingly similar sensual and bodily disruptions of mundane, sanitized, and "cerebral" school spaces and lessons across two countries, I argue that children expose the paradoxical project of contemporary schooling—one that promises education for all children but continues to demarcate the social, sexual, and gendered contours of national citizenship.

A Note about Fieldwork and the Perils of Focusing on Children's Bodies

This chapter is based on two years of extensive participant observation notes of school life and recorded interviews with school administrators, teachers, civil society workers, activists, and education-based governmental and nonprofit organizations in Istanbul and Hyderabad. I specifically observed two highly popular private schools in Istanbul and Hyderabad each, which cater to middle- to upper-middle-class populations and have been around since the late 1990s, when deep market capitalism and privatization of school regimes in both countries took off in earnest. Between 2016 and 2017, I worked as a fifth-grade English teacher at Alliance middle school in Istanbul and observed students and teachers in and out of classrooms, including CSEd lessons provided by an organization called the Family Planning Vakfı (Foundation) (henceforth FPV). For the 2017 to 2018 academic year, I regularly visited and worked as a substitute teacher at the middle school section of Global Schools in Hyderabad, the capital of the southern Indian state of Telangana. I also observed several government schools in both cities during this period. I wish to acknowledge here my eternal debt to the wonderful students and teachers who opened up their hearts and lives to accommodate me, and my critique of schooling in the following pages is only my attempt to rethink education and feminist activism through the lives and bodies of children who get completely lost in our unquestioned zeal for "progress."

There is a tension between academic theorization of children's sensual desires—including acknowledging their bodies as a means of critiquing colonial and racist notions of progress—and activist work against sexualization and abuse of children's bodies. During the same period I was in Hyderabad, I also volunteered as a child sexual abuse (CSA) prevention trainer in schools as a part of a citizens' initiative. This experience made me acutely aware of the fine line between honoring children as beings in their own right (rather than as "incomplete" adults), along with the role their sensuality plays in education—and the violation of a child's body in sexual abuse. In the following pages, while I center children's viscerality, I also hold on to the reality of CSA and have elsewhere (Misra 2022) argued that viewing the body as embodiment of historical privilege and engaging with children's mundane, sensory responses to situations can in fact help us reimagine more effective forms of CSA prevention work.

Schooling and Ongoing Colonial and National Histories of Race, Progress, and Childhood Development

Excellent scholarship in education has repeatedly and convincingly shown (Somel 2001; Fortna 2011; Ghosh 2013; Kumar 2015) how schooling plays a central role in both the Turkish and Indian colonial and nationalist projects, and how the republic of Turkey post-establishment in 1923 and India post-independence in 1947 have actively imagined and promoted an exclusionary vision of national citizenship in schools. In Turkey's case, this has been based on the erasure of Armenians, Kurds, and a multilingual Ottoman past. The contours of national schooling in India as well are dominated by Hindu, dominant-caste, Hindi-speaking imaginaries. In more recent years in both countries, schools have been the battleground for promoting nationalist visions of right-wing populist religious parties in power, namely the Bhartiya Janata Party (BJP) in India and Adalet ve Kalkınma Partisi (AKP) in Turkey, which are based on strict ideologies of gender, race, ethnicity, and religion. It is especially these dominant Brahmanical Hindu[6] and Sunni Turkish ideologies' articulations of sexual morality that form the core of creating citizens in schools. One only has to read the debates around opposition to non-abstinence-based CSEd in schools (Mukherjee 2020) or the bullying and even public shaming of queer students (Menon 2019).

Additionally, the rise of the new, consumptive middle class in both nations since the 1990s has gone hand in hand with the rise of pious, religious, ethnonational political values. This is evident in the rise of all levels of private schools across both countries promising quality education in exchange for money, especially in cities like Istanbul and Hyderabad. Contemporary schooling is thus a medium central to reinforcing middle-class aspirations of national and global citizenship, which, as we have seen, is already premised on all kinds of exclusions. Therefore, any transnational feminist intervention interested in looking beyond colonial nation-state borders must take the school-going child's body in countries of the South experiencing right-wing populism as a serious site for studying narrow nationalism, unfettered capitalist modernity, and how children's bodies and desires resist these, transcending national borders. Childhood and education studies scholarship drawing on feminist theories has repeatedly demonstrated the discourse of developmental time in institutions like schools as a linear narrative of progress that not only aims to move individual (racialized) bodies (Krishnaswamy 1993) from primitive to civilized but also really unfolds through the biological body of the child, especially the marginalized child (Castañeda 2002; Burman 2008; Balagopalan et al. 2010; Veiga 2018). However, while education reports have accurately documented the humiliating discrimination against children in schools, especially Dalit ("lowest" caste) children in India and Kurdish children in Turkey (Human Rights Watch 2014; Kaya 2015), very few transnational feminist studies have demonstrated how ethnic markers of "difference" directly play out through progress narratives of children's developing biological bodies. While feminist scholars have focused on how women embody discourses of nation through performances of strength and "womanhood" (Sarkar 2001; White 2002), very little attention has been paid to schools where national and colonial discourses work through children's biological bodies that are marked by backwardness, incomplete adult embodiment, and "not normal" sexual behaviors, which the postcolonial nation aims to uplift through national schooling.

For instance, in the following anecdote, one clearly sees how the flesh of the school-going child is the site where discourses of colonial modernity, class, nation, and child development unfold. One fine morning, in a renowned central school in Hyderabad (henceforth KVP), I sit listening to the primary school principal, Meena's, firsthand experiences of children's bodies and behaviors. Central schools follow the uniform countrywide CBSE curriculum and are required to execute the Adolescence Education Program (AEP), one of the Indian government's first systematic attempts that started in the late 1990s to teach children about gender, health, and the body (Das 2014). Meena, a well-dressed and elegant woman, is an embodiment of a "modern" woman—she speaks English fluently, has tons of family in the United States, and is all about gender equality. However, as the clock ticks and we get more comfortable and deeper into her many years of experience as a principal and teacher, she suddenly starts talking about the challenges that certain kids' bodies pose in schools. As a government entity, central schools are supposed to strictly adhere to the Right To Education (RTE) Act,[7] which means increasing the number of seats for historically underprivileged Indigenous and caste-oppressed students at school. She asks me, "Do you know how these children are and how they behave? These SC/ST[8] children ... the way they behave ... have we seen their background? There are still people in this country, tribes in Odisha [an Indian state], where women don't wear blouse, where pre-marital sex is ok ... I mean whatever ... but look ... this kind of modern even we aren't here. ... " As her voice trails off, I realize that her "we" is accompanied by a gesture toward me. My tall, light-skinned, dominant-caste, English-speaking "modern," "female" body is for her modern but not immoral and fulfills the criteria of "proper" citizenship—of matrimony, (assumed) heterosexuality and monogamy, unlike the premarital sex practices of the "uncivilized" Indigenous folks. Also, I am wearing a *sari* that day. It is an extremely revealing garment, but I wore it "normally" with a blouse, thereby covering my Hindu-woman-modesty, instead of immodest displays of the flesh by the tribal women and their children who are sent to KVP. My

Hindu dominant-caste privilege that enables my position as an educated scholar in a "modern" world—being able to speak English and travel to the United States for higher education, and that in fact defines the normative ideas of modernity and progress in the postcolonial Indian nation-state—remains invisible. For Meena, my body is desirable and is a stark contrast to the promiscuous bodies of these children, especially girls whose "immoral" behaviors and "not normal" practices and lifestyles pose a threat and need to be veered, sometimes forcibly, through schooling,[9] into the linear narrative of time-as-progress and modernity.

The discourse of contemporary schooling that sees "education for all" as a means of upliftment goes unquestioned unless we confront the ways adult educators re-create the very colonial, nationalist, racist, and gendered embodiments of modern citizenship through the body of the child. Even though in every single school I visited in both countries, teachers knew very well about all children getting fascinated by sex and many even masturbating against classroom desks all the time, it is remarkable how the sexual bodies of some children embody unwanted, uncivilized excesses that can be fixed through schooling and, these days especially, through modern lessons like CSEd. This urges us to pause and engage with our tactile experiences and children's desiring bodies in the present instead of imagining "future" citizens, for the present—a time that weaves our violent histories, privileges, and future hopes together—is the time to create our bodies and the way we think of ourselves, others, and the world (Casey 2000). As evident from the anecdote above, the past is not a chunk of time we leave behind, but it informs the present in the form of historical privileges of race and nation, reminiscences, trauma, and nostalgia, and it is always present and looming large in our imaginations of schooling. During all my fieldwork, both schoolteachers and education policy makers typically were drawing on their own childhood experiences and social biases or dreams in designing school curricula, pedagogy, and imagining futures of schooling.

In the following section we encounter children with all their unruliness, curiosities, "improper" desires, and sensualities in the present, as they challenge these ongoing civilizational and biological teleologies of development and force us to reckon with the project of schooling and imagine a form of feminist knowledge production centered around sensual bodies.

Unruly Desires and Sensual Entanglements: Children Disrupting Teleologies of the Adult National Body

I am taken back to the numerous CSEd lessons offered by FPV at Alliance in Istanbul, Global in Hyderabad, and freelancers/nonprofits in both cities that

I sat through, observing children and their very viscerally engaged, sensual reactions to this new form of knowledge that they were being exposed to. Even as the trainers invited to conduct these sessions explained the scientific terms of body parts and puberty processes such as "wet dreams" and "ovulation" with the aid of life-size pictures of the male and female anatomy, the children's senses were always buzzing with all kinds of questions unrelated to these explanations, titillated often by the pictures on the board, across these different spaces.

Alliance in Istanbul prides itself on being one of the first Turkish schools offering high-quality English education and CSEd to middle- and upper-class children. In one grade five section at Alliance, Ela, a chatty ten-year-old, is convinced that women's eggs are like pizza in shape and texture. When the trainer talks about menstruation, she also complains about the stench of her elder sister's sanitary napkins in the bathroom. "When my sister leaves the bathroom after changing her sanitary napkin when she has periods, you can't even enter it after. It stinks!" This elicits a lot of "ooo"s and "aaa"s and "ewwwww"s (sounds of disgust) from other students. While on the topic of menstruation, Semih, who has been quiet so far, has to mention that his sister's friend started her period at the age of eight! There is surprise and momentary silence in the classroom as students digest this information. However, before the FPV trainer, Tayfun, can capitalize on this silence and push forward with the lesson that is repeatedly being interrupted, one of the girls punctuates the silence with her shrill voice: "ama vajinadan bebek nasıl çıkıyor [but how does a baby come out of the vagina]?" Everybody starts giggling; an embarrassed few hide their faces under their desks or in their hands, and one or two even try escaping the class to wash their faces or use the restroom, only to be gently reprimanded by the counselor, Alara, who is in the classroom, to go back to their seats and calm down. Tayfun, clearly an experienced trainer, who has been very open with the children right from the beginning about his own sex and gender identity and has patiently endured the children's reactions, just laughs off the comment and carries on.

In yet another grade five section, Levent, like most students I have observed across all grade five sections, is thoroughly confused about sex, gender, and sexuality. He asks, "are intersex people gay and lesbian?" Tayfun attempts once again to clarify concepts, even as most students remain confused and more interested in the physical, material realities of bodies marked by various sex/gender/sexuality identities. Merve, the same precocious girl we met in our introductory anecdote, asks, "If a [transgender] person doesn't have money for surgery, what happens?" In Hyderabad, a completely different group of children, this time all girls belonging to a poor Dalit community, are also all giggles when the sexuality trainer talks of sex and periods. "Why don't our periods come after the board exams? Why does everything come together?"

asks one of the girls, referring to the pains and social stigma of starting menstruation that often coincides with the most stressful written exams that many students in India have to take to determine their future careers.

In the examples above, children's visceral and sensual engagement with CSEd lessons reveals some pertinent realities. For starters, they reveal the larger historical inequalities that are invisibilized even in radically progressive forms of CSEd, such as the one offered by FPV and by trainers like Tayfun who do a fantastic job of honoring children's bodies and sensual responses. For instance, it is great to teach children about sex, gender, and sexuality, and what transgender means, but Merve's question about money, about what kind of transgender person can really afford surgery, forces sexuality trainers to really integrate ideas of gender expression and belonging with race, class, and other historically continuing forms of socioeconomic privileges and oppressions. Similarly, the Dalit girl's comment in Hyderabad highlights the disconnect between routine school exams and gendered realities of children's bodies (the actual physical pain and process of bleeding) and the absence of the gendered, sexual body in schooling imaginaries.

Also, by instinctively and sensually not following the sex/gender/sexuality distinctions, which are very much driven by Western, Euro-American ideas of history and human embodiment,[10] these children indicate to us the ongoing hegemony of Western forms of knowledge production and the invisibilization of more local, Indigenous attitudes to the body and sexuality that histories of colonization and nationalism, which privileged European whiteness but also sexual mores of ethnically "white" and dominant peoples within each nation, have changed. After all, most of these CSEd programs in the South have emerged from Northern, donor-driven sexual health initiatives. For instance, same-sex desire and multifarious notions of what is sexual and bodily desire abounded in pre-colonial Indian and Ottoman Turkish times. Courtesans in India or the beloved beardless youth (emred) and their besotted male lovers in Ottoman Istanbul were considered a major "turn on," to use modern parlance, if they had mastered the art of seducing through words, socializing, flirting, and of course writing beautifully lyrical Gazel poetry (Vanita and Kidwai 2000; Andrews and Kalpaklı 2005). However, these histories disappear in the modern Indian and Turkish republic, established very much as we have seen on Brahmanical and Sunni Muslim ideologies of gender and sex, which were also very deliberately juxtaposed with British/European identity but also with unique markers of "Indian" and "Turkish" national cultures. For example, in colonial India, it was the anti-colonial male imperative (Chatterjee 1989) and dominant-caste Hindu feminist movement that used the liberal, Western discourse of feminism to define the contours of normative Indian womanhood that was based on caste and class hierarchies and sexual assumptions (Sinha 2000). Similarly in late Ottoman and early republican Turkey, the founding father Mustafa Kemal Atatürk's vision of the "modern" woman in the public sphere was in alignment with Europe—in the way the new Turkish woman was expected to dress and conduct herself. But the "Turkish" woman still very much remained the possession of her patriarchal family in the private sphere—thereby making her the ultimate symbol of modern Turkey (Kandiyoti 1991). Children's visceral reactions in the present and the persistent questions that they ask instinctively force us as adults to reckon with these colonial and national erasures of histories and historical privileges.

Although children's sensual responses highlight these problematic historical, racial, and civilizational narratives, they also point to the similarities in human embodiment across multiple socioeconomic differences and national borders. Even from the two brief anecdotes above, children—irrespective of their national and social locations—are very similarly performing their fascination with sex and sexuality by talking about the texture of things, giggling, hiding their faces, and so on, frustrating both trainers' serious attempts to explain the working of the biological body, child development, and the "scientific" terms of body organs and processes. They indicate to us the inarticulable desire that is immanent in all of us, that is beyond social, economic, and political systems of power, beyond national borders and the civilizing march of time. It is this desire in the Deleuzian sense, one that always escapes national and colonial configurations of gender and sexuality and that we should pause and take seriously. What is it about children's fascination with the texture of women's eggs or the motility of the sperm? Perhaps pausing at these moments can help us imagine a more de-colonial, de-nationally embodied future where it is such simple and tactile pleasures that can help determine our notions of society, self, and belonging.[11]

In other words, schooling is in essence a project of disembodying the ideas, beings, and sensualities of children that fundamentally threaten the normative articulations of class, caste, religion, gender, and ethnicity of the national body. This was very evident to me in one particular state school visit in Istanbul. Located in a poor neighborhood not far from the busy center of the European part of Istanbul, *Taksim*, Hasan Yücel *Ortaokulu* (middle school) (henceforth HYO) caters to neighborhood children who hail from working-class Kurdish, Turkish, and Laz (Black Sea region) families. The school is severely underfunded, as are many other state schools (*devlet okulları*) in the city's poorer neighborhoods. One of the school's Turkish language teachers, Fırat, who is Kurdish and from the city of Mardin in southeast Turkey, invites me to visit his classes one afternoon. Fırat wants me to say hello to his sixth graders as they are a "fun bunch" and would love to have me in their class.

Even before we enter the class, the students' senses are buzzing with excitement. They have seen me walking around the school corridors earlier with Fırat and have many questions—Who am I? Where am I from? What am I doing here? One of the girls screams out in joy when we enter the class, "*Ay! Çok güzel!* [Wow! So beautiful!]," most likely referring to my colorful Indian skirt and jewelry. It's the end of the school year, and with the entire syllabus covered, Fırat has decided to develop his students' critical thinking skills. He is asking them questions about the novels they have read during the year, and the children are responding very creatively, using poetic vocabulary to describe their books and using their imaginations to describe parts of the world that remain unknown to them. As they speak, I realize they are staring at me, as I probably represent the unknown. Sure enough, very soon one of them asks me, "*hocam* [teacher], where are you from?" Thus begins the guessing game as I give them clues and challenge them to show me their knowledge of the world. It is interesting to observe how sensually children form ideas about places and peoples unknown: "you could be Spanish *hocam*, because of your [curly] hair," "*hocam* did you have to walk or drive a car or take a flight to get here? How far is your country?" "your Turkish has an accent, are you German?" and so on. Finally, when I tell them I am Indian, their excitement reaches a crescendo. Funnily enough, compared to the upper-middle-class children at Alliance, these working-class urban Istanbul kids know much more about Indian geography, festivals, and of course, Bollywood movies. Some of them are fascinated by *Ganpathi Visarjan* festivities, where a giant statue of Lord Ganesha is carried through a mighty street procession and submerged into a water body. But most of the questions and comments are about more sensual pleasures of food and Bollywood dance. A couple of students insist on giving me a demo of a popular Bollywood actor's dance routine and I oblige, so they start twirling their hips and moving their arms and legs frantically while babbling incoherent Hindi lyrics. The show is a huge success. Some other students keep on punctuating the show by asking me if they can touch my dress or what kind of food I like—"have you tried *Adana kebap hocam*?" and many, many more questions and comments follow.

Just when the children's performances and sensual displays are at their peak, Fırat, probably embarrassed by their volley of questions and probably also mindful of my time, interrupts them: "Akanksha *hoca* has come all the way from the United States, where she is working at a university. Ask her how she got there … wouldn't you all like to go to the United States of America?" There is a palpable energy shift in the room. The students are suddenly serious, and those who were dancing and jumping and waving their arms to ask questions go back to their desks and sit down demurely. Yes, this is what they are supposed to be doing, asking an Indian teacher, a woman, who made it all the way to the United States about how she did that, so that they could also make their (assumed) dreams and aspirations of going abroad, going to the United States come true. As for my part, I instantly know that I am supposed to be drilling the value of schooling and higher education so that they too have a chance of winning the golden ticket that can help them achieve the "American dream." "Yes *hocam*," one of them who had just been describing the flavor of *karadeniz pidesi* (Black Sea Turkish pizza) to me moments ago asks me, "how did you end up going from India to the United States?" Before I can say anything, another child interrupts, *"para lazım dimi* (you need money, isn't it)?" Again, before I can say anything else, another student adds, *"ama para herşey değil ki* . . . (but money isn't everything right)?" looking at Fırat for approval. Smart kid. I then go on to tell them about how hard I worked at school and indicate my socioeconomic and caste privilege that enabled me to go to English-medium schools in India. I finally end by saying, "work hard children, but yes, you also need money."

Fırat's intentions are noble, and as a Kurdish man from a poor family, he is only too aware of the struggle that these children, much like him, will face in the world if they didn't figure out a way of accessing "traditional" middle-class jobs and lifestyles, such as moving to the United States. As an aspiring filmmaker himself, forced to teach Turkish at a state school to make ends meet, Fırat's concern is very real. And the children's sensual displays and entertaining mood and revelry that betray any serious concern for the future automatically threatens the future, adult national body that these children should be aspiring toward, and Fırat gently tries to nudge them back in line. However, this whole scenario—the children's sensual worlds and the teacher's reaction—also reveals glaring class distinctions in our society despite contemporary schooling's promise of equal opportunity and access for all children to become global citizens. As the one student immediately points out—"you need money, isn't it?"—yes, money is important. For these children who are so systemically failed by the Turkish state into getting quality education (Kaya 2015) and are born into families that are not only financially poor but also embody ethnicities that have been brutally violated by the Turkish nation in the past and that continue to negotiate their ethnic articulations of Turkish-ness through inter-ethnic violence (Ceyhan and Çayır 2012; Öz 2018; Serdar 2019), how is going to America just a question of attending school and working hard? Feminist analyses of economics and development have long spoken of structural constraints that situate different (historical) bodies differently in the new world economic order.[12] Fırat's response, then, in some ways typical of a schoolteacher's response, that indirectly asks children to snap out of their fantasy world and dancing and tomfoolery to look for inspiration from an American-dream success story, really reveals both the threat of non-normative articulations of the (child's) body and the violent (racist) histories that comprise visions of national citizenship that keep on subduing the ethnic, religious "other" in national discourse and institutions such as schools. Soon after the conversation above, the children start jumping up and down again, eager to change the topic back to India and my travels to the many countries I have just told them about.

Conclusion: Children's Sensual Resistances and Decolonizing Knowledge and Feminist Praxes

While their voices are often ignored in policy making and discussions of schooling access and equity, children perform a much-needed queering of our school spaces and our assumptions of time, belonging, and nation through their bodies, desires, and sensual entanglements. In doing so, they offer a stinging critique of both colonial temples of knowledge production, such as schools, and transnational feminist methodological interventions. Much of the latter continues to be wedded to nation-state borders, despite criticism of their colonial/nationalist conceptualizations since the 1990s (Alexander and Mohanty 1997; Nagar and Swarr 2010), continues to prioritize discursive and material flows of identities and capital over connected human embodiment,[13] and continues to dismiss the child's sensual body (Balagopalan, Burman, and Stacey 2010). In this chapter, by centering children's everyday bodily practices and disruptions of schooling spatio-temporalities that are based on European/colonial legacies of time-as-progress and separation of bodies and spaces (Lefebvre 2014) in two cities in the Global South, I have attempted to employ a form of decolonial transnational feminist methodological praxis to achieve a twofold purpose. One, it doesn't discursively (re)-colonize (Mohanty 1991) the "developing" nation's "poor child" (Hopkins and Sriprakash 2015). Two, it decolonizes our racialized, gendered, and sexual assumptions of nation and modern schooling (Lugones 2010) and their teleological legacies of childhood by shifting feminist focus to children's sensual bodies as disruptive, decolonial sites of knowledge production. By listening to the everyday cacophony of all kinds of children's voices between two bustling urban cities, I have revealed the diverse ways in which children expose and resist colonial essentialisms of culture and nation in the ways their desiring bodies relate to each other and the world, and they help us as feminists imagine transnational alliances, activism, and knowledge production that are not only "South-South" (Roy 2016) but also centered around bodies and unruly excesses.

Notes

1. All names have been changed to respect privacy, and all translations are mine unless otherwise noted.

2. I use the term "comprehensive sexuality education" (CSEd) instead of "sex education" since all the lessons I observed went beyond just talking about

sexual organs and safe sex to encompass teachings about sexual identities, gender roles, human rights, and several other topics that fall under the larger ambit of "sexuality." In contrast to abstinence-based approaches, these programs were comprehensive since they promoted positive messages about sex and sexuality. Also, since these programs in the global "South" have explicitly emerged from population control, sexual health, and other national or international development-driven initiatives, I use the language of comprehensive sexuality education widely used in global development (U. N. Women et al. 2018).

3. Throughout the chapter, I use "modernity" to refer to the ongoing legacy of a historical epoch that goes back to the start of European enlightenment, mercantilist capitalism, and European colonization of the world and continues in the form of Western hegemony and American imperialism in the New World Order (Israel 2001; McMichael 2017). Specifically in the case of postcolonial nations, the idea of the "modern" is also an aspiration that has buried itself in quotidian practices, such as schooling, which are meant to move us one step closer to becoming industrialized, scientific, rational, like our "Western" counterparts; in other words, "developed," even though the core of the "modern" citizen or institution maintains a culturally essentialist notion of the nation. This notion, as we'll subsequently see in the chapter, is once again problematic as it privileges dominant race, class, religion, gender, and sexual normatives within nations and is expressed through the bodies of children and women (Chatterjee 1989; Kandiyoti 1991). The teleological discourse of development and progress from becoming "savage" to "civilized," which overwhelmingly focuses on education, has been central to becoming "modern" or participating in "modernity" since colonial times. However, development will always be a failed process because it is intrinsically premised on its own legacies of social Darwinism and scientific racism that will always keep certain bodies at the bottom of the racial hierarchy (Cowen and Shenton 1996).

4. Whether Ottoman Turkey can be called colonized by European powers is a highly contested question in Ottoman history. However, one can safely claim that from the beginning of the nineteenth century, the Ottomans were increasingly subjected to European economic domination and political interference in their administrative affairs and that European influences were subsequently central to the shaping of Turkish nationalism and formation of the Turkish republic (Kasaba 2006; Hanıoğlu 2008).

5. This chapter derives from my dissertation project based on more than two years of fieldwork in Istanbul, Hyderabad, and Delhi. My own positionality as an Indian researcher and former middle school teacher in Turkey, by embodying shifting roles and privileges across the gendered borders of these two nation-states, has deeply informed the decolonial transnational feminist praxis in this piece that attempts to challenge our inherited meanings of nation, modern schooling, and the sexual body. Both nations share very long and connected histories of gendered nation-state formation and Islam (Adıvar 1938, Aydın 2007, Bose 2018), specifically the cities of Istanbul and Hyderabad. Even though both nations have embarked on different modernization trajectories, these deeply

shared histories of people and events across time and borders—Hyderabad's last king or Nizam was married to a Turkish princess of course(!)—still haunt public spaces and leave traces in popular imagination. The fact that those histories and embodied connections have to be invoked itself is a sign of how our bodies and knowledges have been colonized. For a more detailed explanation, please refer to Misra 2022. The aim of a decolonial transnational feminist praxis is precisely to reconnect us beyond national borders through new knowledges and desires that modern systems of national schooling continue to prevent through their colonially inherited meanings of childhood, knowledge, and citizenship.

6. Brahmanical Hinduism is the hegemonic understanding and practice of Hinduism in India that is enshrined in the vedic scriptures, the maintenance of the hierarchical caste system, and control of women. For more details on how this form of Hinduism emerged as the dominant form historically and through the national independence struggle and how it continues to be upheld by the BJP, please refer to: Mani 2015; Wankhede 2019.

7. For debates and critiques about RTE implementation and how it is affecting the most marginalized children, please refer to: Joshi 2010; Saxena 2012.

8. Indigenous or Tribal populations in India are referred to as Scheduled Tribes (ST) and Dalit populations are categorized under Scheduled Castes (SC). According to the 2011 census data (the 2021 census is currently being conducted as of the writing of this chapter), 16.6 percent of the Indian population is SC and 8.6 percent is ST: https://censusindia.gov.in/census.website/data/population-finder.

9. International organizations working on universal education across the world and country-specific studies of universalizing primary education have shown the multiple levels of violence against poor children, especially girls, that occurs in bringing them to school, separating them from their families and domestic work, and keeping them at school as well. For example: İlköğretime Zamanında Kaydolmama 2011; Aikman and Rao 2012; Balagopalan, Burman and Stacey 2010.

10. See for example: Najmabadi 2006. Najmabadi here explicitly talks about the perils of assuming what gender and sexuality mean without acknowledging the histories and social, geographical contexts they emerge in as she tries to read these Eurocentric notions into her own research on gendered and sexual performances in Qajar Iran.

11. I draw here on Dorothea Olkowski's feminist phenomenological reading of Deleuze and Guattari's Anti-Oedipus. According to Olkowski, Deleuze and Guattari see "desire" as an "explosive" machine, connected to other machines, that produces us—what we call bodies—but what can be better understood as a series of becomings—flows, molecules, energies, and so on. Whilst there is no guarantee where desire can take us and what gets produced over time, for Olkowski (drawing on Deleuze and Guattari), it is desire that produces social, political systems and what forms these will take is "unpredictable" precisely because desire is "unpredictable.": Olkowski 1999.

12. For a more general feminist analysis of how macroeconomic policies act as a structure of constraint for gender and other inequalities, please read: Berik, Rodgers and Seguino 2009. For a more nuanced understanding of debates within

development economics that fails to account for people's histories and social contexts/constraints, please read Kabeer's critique of "Randomista" economics: Kabeer 2020.

13. Here I am not referring to any particular study but rather to the plethora of rich transnational feminist scholarship that has undoubtedly increased our knowledge of how gendered and sexual subjectivities across nations are shaped by histories and ongoing political economic inequalities of capital and development. However, very few of these studies start from the human body and go beyond our discursive understandings of gender and sexuality to see how people in their everyday lives desire, feel, and understand what it means to belong to a society, a nation and how meanings of gender, nation, self are created through sensual bodies as products of historical privilege and discrimination that transgress national borders. Some notable exceptions include: Weinbaum et al. 2008; Mehta 2019.

Bibliography

Adıvar, Halide Edib. 1938. *Inside India*. New York: Macmillan.

Aikman, Sheila and Nitya Rao. 2012. "Gender Equality and Girls' Education: Investigating Frameworks, Disjunctures and Meanings of Quality Education." *Theory and Research in Education* 10(3): 211–28.

Alexander, M. Jacqui and Chandra Talpade Mohanty. 1997. "Introduction: Genealogies, Legacies, Movements." In *Feminist Genealogies, Colonial Legacies, Democratic Futures*, edited by M. Jacqui Alexander and Chandra Talpade Mohanty, xiii–xlii. New York: Routledge.

Alvaredo, Facundo, Lucas Chancel, Thomas Piketty, Emmanuel Saez and Gabriel Zucman. 2018. *World Inequality Report 2018*. Cambridge, MA: Belknap Press of Harvard University Press.

Andrews, Walter G. and Mehmet Kalpaklı. 2005. *The Age of Beloveds: Love and the Beloved in Early-Modern Ottoman and European Culture and Society*. Durham, NC: Duke University Press.

Aydın, Cemil. 2007. *The Politics of Anti-Westernism in Asia: Visions of World Order in Pan-Islamic and Pan-Asian Thought*. New York: Columbia University Press.

Balagopalan, Sarada, Erica Burman and Jackie Stacey. 2010. "Rationalizing Seclusion: A Preliminary Analysis of a Residential Schooling Scheme for Poor Girls in India." *Feminist Theory* 11(3): 295–308.

Berik, Günseli, Yana Van Der Meulen Rodgers and Stephanie Seguino. 2009. "Feminist Economics of Inequality, Development, and Growth." *Feminist Economics: Inequality, Development, and Growth* 15(3): 1–33.

Bose, Sumantra. 2018. *Secular States, Religious Politics: India, Turkey, and the Future of Secularism*. New York: Cambridge University Press.

Burman, Erica. 2008. *Developments: Child, Image, Nation*. London: Routledge.

Casey, Edward S. 2000. *Remembering: A Phenomenological Study*. Bloomington: Indiana University Press.

Castañeda, Claudia. 2002. *Figurations: Child, Bodies, Worlds*. Durham, NC: Duke University Press.

Ceyhan, Müge Ayan and Kenan Çayır. 2012. Ayrımcılık: *çok boyutlu* yaklaşımlar [Multidimensional approaches to Discrimination]. Istanbul Bilgi Üniversitesi Yayınları.

Chatterjee, Partha. 1989. "The Nationalist Resolution of the Women's Question." In *Recasting Women: Essays in Indian Colonial History*, edited by Kumkum Sangari and Sudesh Vaid, 233–53. New Delhi: Kali for Women.

Cowen, Michael and Robert W. Shenton. 1996. *Doctrines of Development*. London: Routledge.

Das, Arpita. 2014. "Sexuality Education in India: Examining the Rhetoric, Rethinking the Future." *Sex Education* 14(2): 210–24.

Dyer, Hannah. 2020. *The Queer Aesthetics of Childhood: Asymmetries of Innocence and the Cultural Politics of Child Development*. New Brunswick, NJ: Rutgers University Press.

Ergenç, Ceren. 2018. "A Political Analysis of Middle-Class Based Social Movements: India and Turkey Compared." In *New Perspectives on India and Turkey: Connections and Debates*, edited by Smita Jassal Tewari and Halil Turan, 219–33. Abingdon, Oxon: Routledge.

Evans, David T. 1993. *Sexual Citizenship: The Material Construction of Sexualities*. London and New York: Routledge.

Fortna, Benjamin C. 2011. *Learning to Read in the Late Ottoman Empire and the Early Turkish Republic*. Houndmills, Basingstoke, Hampshire, New York: Palgrave Macmillan.

Ghosh, Suresh Chandra. 2013. *The History of Education in Modern India, 1757–2012*. New Delhi: Orient Blackswan.

Hanıoğlu, Şükrü M. 2008. *A Brief History of the Late Ottoman Empire*. Princeton: Princeton University Press.

Hopkins, Lucy and Arathi Sriprakash. 2015. *The 'Poor Child': The Cultural Politics of Education, Development and Childhood*. Milton Park, Abingdon, Oxon: Routledge.

Human Rights Watch. 2014, April 22. "They Say We're Dirty." Denying an Education to India's Marginalized. https://www.hrw.org/report/2014/04/22/they-say-were-dirty/denying-education-indias-marginalized.

İlköğretime Zamanında Kaydolmama: Nedenleri ve Önlenmesi için Öneriler [Not Entering Primary School on Time: Reasons and Preventive Recommendations]. Ankara: UNICEF-MEB, 2011.

Israel, Jonathan. 2001. *Radical Enlightenment: Philosophy and the Making of Modernity, 1650–1750*. Oxford and New York: Oxford University Press.

James, Allison and Alan Prout. 1990. *Constructing and Reconstructing Childhood: Contemporary Issues in the Sociological Study of Childhood*. London: Falmer Press.

Joshi, K. M. 2010. "Indigenous Children of India: Enrolment, Gender Parity and Drop-Out in School Education." *International Journal of Sociology and Social Policy* 30(9/10): 545–58.

Kabeer, Naila. 2020. "Women's Empowerment and Economic Development: A Feminist Critique of Storytelling Practices in 'Randomista' Economics." *Feminist Economics* 26 (2): 1–26.

Kandiyoti, Deniz. 1991. "End of Empire: Islam, Nationalism and Women in Turkey." In *Women, Islam, and the State*, 22–47. Philadelphia: Temple University Press.

Kasaba, Reşat. 2006. "Dreams of Empire, Dreams of Nation." In *Empire to Nation: Historical Perspectives on the Making of the Modern World*, edited by Joseph W. Esherick, Hasan Kayalı and Eric Van Young, 198–225. Oxford, UK: Rowman and Littlefield Publishers.

Kaya, Nurcan. 2015. *Türkiye'de Eğitim Sisteminde* Ayrımcılık: *Renk, Etnik Köken, Dil, Din ve inanç temelli* [Discrimination in Turkey's Education System on the Basis of Color, Ethnicity, Language, Religion and Faith]. Istanbul: Tarih Vakfı, Minority Rights Group. https://www.egitimreformugirisimi.org/turkiyede-egitim-sisteminde-ayrimcilik/ (accessed April 2, 2020).

Krishnaswamy, Revathi. 1993. "Evangels of Empire." *Race & Class* 34(4): 47–62.

Kumar, Krishna. 2015. *Politics of Education in Colonial India*. London: Routledge.

Lefebvre, Henri. 2014. "The Production of Space" (1991). In *The People, Place, and Space Reader*, 289–93. Routledge.

Lugones, María. 2010. "Toward a Decolonial Feminism." *Hypatia* 25(4): 742–59. https://doi.org/10.1111/j.1527-2001.2010.01137.x.

Mani, Braj Ranjan. 2015. *Debrahmanising History: Dominance and Resistance in Indian Society rev. ed.* New Delhi: Manohar Publishers & Distributors.

McMichael, Philip. 2017. *Development and Social Change: A Global Perspective*. Sixth edition. Los Angeles: SAGE.

Mehta, Purvi. 2019. "Dalit Feminism in Tokyo: Analogy and Affiliation in Transnational Dalit Activism." *Feminist Review* 121(1): 24–36.

Menon, Priya. 2019, June 10. "LGBT Bullying in Schools Takes Heavy Toll, Reveals UNESCO Report." *Times of India*, https://timesofindia.indiatimes.com/india/lgbt-bullying-in-schools-takes-heavy-toll-reveals-unesco-report/articleshow/69718451.cms.

Misra, Akanksha. 2022. "Embodied Histories, Erotic Disruptions, and Sexuality Education in India and Turkey," *Feminist Studies* 48(2): 395–422.

Mohanty, Chandra Talpade. 1991. "Under Western Eyes: Feminist Scholarship and Colonial Discourses." In *Third World Women and the Politics of Feminism*, edited by Chandra T. Mohanty, Ann Russo, and Lourdes Torres, 51–80. Bloomington: Indiana University Press.

Mukherjee, Jashodhara. 2020, September 1. "'They Think We'll Teach Them How to Have Sex': NEP 2020 Misses the Point of Sex Education." *News18*. https://www.news18.com/news/buzz/they-think-well-teach-them-how-to-have-sex-nep-2020-misses-the-point-of-sex-education-2817981.html.

Nagar, Richa and Amanda Lock Swarr, eds. 2010. *Critical Transnational Feminist Praxis*. Albany: State University of New York Press.

Najmabadi, Afsaneh. 2006. "Beyond the Americas: Are Gender and Sexuality Useful Categories of Analysis?" *Journal of Women's History* 18(1): 11–21.

Olkowski, Dorothea. 1999. "Flows of Desire and the Body-Becoming." In *Becomings: Explorations in Time, Memory, and Futures*, edited by Elizabeth Grosz, 98–116. Ithaca, NY, and London: Cornell University Press.

Öz, Mine Eder Özlem. 2018. "'Problem Spaces' and Struggles Over the Right to the City: Challenges of Living Differentially in a Gentrifying Istanbul Neighborhood." *International Journal of Urban and Regional Research* 42(6): 1030–47.

Roy, Arundhati. 2020, April 3. "The Pandemic is a Portal." *Financial Times*. https://www.ft.com/content/10d8f5e8-74eb-11ea-95fe-fcd274e920ca.

Roy, Srila. 2016. "Women's Movements in the Global South: Towards a Scalar Analysis." *International Journal of Politics, Culture, and Society* 29 (3): 289–306. doi:10.1007/s10767-016-9226-6.

Sarkar, Tanika. 2001. *Hindu Wife, Hindu Nation: Community, Religion, and Cultural Nationalism*. Bloomington: Indiana University Press.

Saxena, Sadhna. 2012. "Is Equality an Outdated Concern in Education?" *Economic & Political Weekly* 47(49): 61–68.

Serdar, Ayşe. 2019. "Strategies of Making and Unmaking Ethnic Boundaries: Evidence on the Laz of Turkey." *Ethnicities* 19(2): 335–69.

Sinha, Mrinalini. 2000. "Refashioning Mother India: Feminism and Nationalism in Late-Colonial India." *Feminist Studies* 26(3): 623–44.

Somel, Selçuk Akşin. 2001. *The Modernization of Public Education in the Ottoman Empire, 1839–1908: Islamization, Autocracy, and Discipline*. Leiden and Boston: Brill.

U. N. Women, UN AIDS, UNFPA, WHO and UNICEF. 2018. *International Technical Guidance on Sexuality Education: An Evidence-Informed Approach*. UNESCO Publishing.

Vanita, Ruth and Saleem Kidwai. 2000. *Same-Sex Love in India: Readings from Literature and History*. New York: St. Martin's Press.

Veiga, Cynthia. 2018. "The Body's Civilisation/Decivilisation: Emotional, Social, and Historical Tensions." *Paedagogica Historica: Special Issue: Education and the Body* 54(1–2): 20–31.

Wankhede, Harish S. 2019, August 5. "As Long as Caste Bears Dividends, Hindutva Politics Will Do Little To Bring Social Reforms." *The Wire*. https://thewire.in/caste/caste-discrimination-bjp-dalit-manipulation.

Weinbaum, Alys Eve, Lynn M. Thomas, Priti Ramamurthy, Uta G. Poiger, Madeleine Yue Dong and Tani E. Barlow, eds. 2008. *The Modern Girl around the World: Consumption, Modernity, and Globalization*. Durham, NC: Duke University Press.

White, Jenny B. 2002. *Islamist Mobilization in Turkey: A Study in Vernacular Politics*. Seattle: University of Washington Press.

10

Decolonial Pedagogy
Resisting through Transnational WGS Introductory Courses

ESTHER OLUWASHINA AJAYI-LOWO

Resisting social injustices through Women's and Gender Studies (WGS)[1] pedagogy is a significant tool for engaging a decolonial social justice discourse and praxis capable of laying solid foundations for future generations of feminist scholar-activists. For a decolonial discourse in WGS, pedagogical approaches should be transnational and transcend the imperialist tendencies of the tokenizing global/international teaching framework. By transnational WGS pedagogy, I mean the teaching philosophy, approach, and strategy that take the nation as one of the critical intersections in addressing social justice issues. Transnational WGS pedagogy entails teachers working with students to acknowledge the commonalities and differences between and among social justice issues across geographical boundaries. At the same time, it helps interrogate the fundamental oppressive systems of capitalism, imperialism, orientalism, colonialism, neocolonialism, and other globalized "isms" that repress, suppress, and oppress marginalized peoples. In essence, transnational WGS pedagogy should not only be in the name or the uncritical engagement with social justice issues from multiple geographical locations. It is in the teaching praxis that is decolonial in prioritizing marginalized identities while decentering privileged places, thoughts, and epistemologies that silence and reinforce the invisibility of others. Transnational WGS pedagogy should consciously engage the impacts of not only race, gender, and class, among other vectors of identities, but also the nation while deliberately grappling with the cultural, historical, and other significant contexts.

Transnational WGS pedagogy aligns with the established scholarly articulation of transnationalism in WGS. The concept of transnationalism is a process by which WGS, as a field of study, takes nationality and geographical location as critical features of intersectionality while retaining the significance of other intersectional identities such as race, gender, class, and sexuality. As M. Jacqui Alexander and Chandra Talpade Mohanty (2013) argue, it is a process of using WGS knowledge production and pedagogy to analyze social justice issues beyond a specific location or national border and simultaneously pay attention to how different categories of people are affected differently. It entails using WGS research and pedagogy to interrogate the fundamentally common trends of the systems and power of oppression that operate globally, which bell hooks (2013, 4) succinctly describes as "imperialist white supremacist capitalist patriarchy." In the same breath, the transnational in WGS engages the different impacts of interlocking systems of oppression across geographical boundaries on groups of people with differences in historical, social, cultural, economic, and political dynamics. Hence, simultaneously interrogating the commonalities and differences across borders is fundamental and essential for transnational WGS research and pedagogy. This interrogation is critical given WGS's aim for holistic social justice that is not location-bound but pays attention to specific contexts of location, histories, cultures, and the nuances of local advocacy efforts. It is that which transcends geographical borders with intentional attention to cultural, historical, economic, and political contexts. This concept of the transnational in WGS should guide WGS pedagogy.

While scholars have laid transnational feminist theoretical groundings, the challenge of transforming those contexts into teaching persists, particularly in teaching the WGS introductory courses. Given the greater prominence of WGS in the Global North than in the Global South, salient questions usually arise on how WGS pedagogy can become effectively transnational, and consequently decolonial. As Laura Parisi (2012, 325) asks, "Who is understood as having 'expertise'" for transnational WGS curriculum? How might WGS professors situated in Global North institutions teach about the social justice issues in the Global South without reinforcing what Chandra Talpade Mohanty (1988, 81) calls Western feminists' "re-presentation" of "universal images of the 'third-world woman'"? Also, how might WGS professors from the Global South who teach WGS in the Global North adopt a transnational pedagogy without promoting what Uma Narayan (2000) describes as the danger of a "package picture" of cultures? How might WGS instructors adopt a transnational pedagogy that traverses geographical borders, even when the course is focused on or located in a specific place or group of people? Drawing on my teaching experience as a Nigerian graduate teaching fellow of WGS in the United States, this chapter discusses my pedagogical tactics for transnational WGS introductory classes. It presents transnational pedagogical strategies in WGS as subversive tools for resisting colonial epistemologies and democratizing knowledge.

By acknowledging and critically connecting social justice issues across geographical borders and decentering the Western iteration of the "others," especially in the Global South, transnational WGS pedagogy is decolonial. Decoloniality in feminist thought is a critique of the colonial exaltation of the Western system of knowledge and the marginalization, distortion, or demonization of traditional and indigenous epistemologies. As Maria Lugones (2010) argues, feminist decoloniality is a theory of reclaiming colonized thoughts and identities. Building on Lugones's (2010, 1987) decolonial pedagogy, some feminist teachers emphasize the significance of inviting students into the world of "others" who are often marginalized in racist and colonial teaching (Fukushima and Vei 2022; Verhaeghe et al. 2018). Hence, by inviting students to engage the critical connections between and among social justice issues in the United States and the rest of the world through course readings, class discussions, and assignments, the transnational WGS pedagogical approach is decolonial. It allows students to rethink the colonial reductionist perception of the "other."

Methodology

This chapter echoes my pedagogical strategies between 2015 and 2021, which I continue to find beneficial for teaching WGS in the United States in ways that challenge Western colonial epistemological notions of "others" in the Global South. It entails a conceptual analysis of the transnational from the WGS perspective. In this chapter, I discuss the need for transnational pedagogy in WGS, using the intro classes as a case study and hoping to answer the following questions: "Why transnational WGS pedagogy?" and "Why transnational WGS intro courses?" In responding to Parisi's (2002) concerns and fears about the possibility of a transnational WGS pedagogy, I answer the question: "How does one teach WGS intro from a transnational viewpoint?" My response includes a discussion of my challenges with adopting transnational pedagogy and how I am overcoming them through the continuous journey of learning, unlearning, and relearning the "what" and "how" of transnational WGS pedagogy. I also share the specific strategies that have worked well for transnationalizing my WGS intro classes. As a graduate instructor from the Global South, I believe my teaching strategies will benefit similarly positioned instructors attempting transnational pedagogy. That said, transnationalizing WGS pedagogy is not only possible for instructors from the Global South but also for instructors with Western identities in the Global North. Hence, the strategies in this chapter will be handy for all instructors teaching WGS intro courses in the Global North, regardless of their identity and positionality. While a few instructors may have been attempting transnational WGS pedagogy, some have pending questions about transnational WGS pedagogy. I hope that sharing my personal WGS teaching experience aids WGS instructors in their quest for effective transnational pedagogy and curriculum, especially at the introductory level.

My Positionality

As a Nigerian international PhD student at Texas Woman's University (TWU),[2] I came to graduate school with an activist background. Among my several human rights and women's rights activist engagements, I had worked with nongovernmental organizations (NGOs), invoking the UN international human rights laws for women's rights issues through campaigns, workshops, seminars, lobbying, and community advocacy. I was trained at the United Nations University in Tokyo, Japan, in Human Rights and in the United Nations System. Moreover, I had the privilege of leading the writing of the shadow report on the Convention on the Elimination of Discrimination against Women (CEDAW), submitted by the Nigerian NGO CEDAW Coalition to the UN CEDAW Committee in 2008. Hence, I resumed graduate school in the United States in 2015 with prior scholarly and activist foundations in global women's rights. However, I was still seeking feminist and womanist theoretical groundings for addressing global women's issues, which I considered the byproducts of patriarchy. Inadvertently, my activist lens of women's rights before commencing graduate study in WGS was limited to seeing women's rights oppression—like child marriage, honor killing, femicide, female genital cutting (FGC), restricted girls' education, maternal mortality, widowhood rites/rituals/inheritance denial, and other repressive cultures—as only problems of and in the Global South and far removed from the Global North.

Through its several human rights campaigns in the Global South, I saw the United States as the epitome of women's rights. Therefore, one of my aspirations as a PhD student in the United States was to learn how to better engage and advocate for global women's rights. However, as I became grounded in the US women of color feminist and womanist theories, I found more commonalities among the social justice issues in the United States (Global North) and the Global South. It became clear to me that beyond patriarchy, women's experience of oppression in the Global South (just like all marginalized people's experience in every clime) are encumbered in other fundamental power structures, including capitalism, militarism, imperialism, and racism, to name a few. As I became immersed in transnational WGS scholar-activist theoretical approaches, I kept making connections among social justice issues in the United States and internationally. In making these connections, transnational analysis invariably occupies the core of my research and activist interests.

The principal motivation for writing this chapter is my position as a graduate teaching fellow for WGS introductory classes at TWU. At TWU, the intro to WGS, "Gender and Social Change: An Introduction to Multicultural Women's and Gender Studies" (WS 2013), is one of the courses that meet the "Global Perspectives" requirement for graduation. Hence, most TWU undergraduate students take the class as fresh students[3] or during their sophomore year. I saw this as an opportunity to make my teaching transnational. I was interested in working with my students to look simultaneously into and beyond their location, the United States, in understanding oppression and the need for social justice from a more in-depth viewpoint. For each discussion on a given social justice topic focused on the United States, I could see how the fundamentals of that topic transcend geographical borders. I see the need to work with the students to identify the commonalities and differences between and among social issues from local and global contexts—to become more open-minded to engaging the issues from a broader and more complex perspective not limited to their geographical location. Like most students, I had a prior understanding of oppression and social justice that divides the world into the Global North and Global South binary. I was interested in working with students to challenge this reductionist and location-bound understanding of the experiences of marginalized peoples.

Challenges with Teaching Transnational WGS

In my teaching experience and working with other graduate teaching instructors, I realized that Parisi's (2012) questions remain valid, and that adopting transnational pedagogy requires intentionality of purpose and strategy. I saw that as products of the US academy, which generally excludes critical discussion of the Global South, Western WGS instructors in the Global North[4] might genuinely be ill-equipped to adopt a transnational pedagogy, especially if they lack theoretical groundings in transnational WGS scholarship. Western instructors' genuine fear of inadvertently reinforcing imperialist ideals of a place or a people could limit their attempt to transnationalize their WGS pedagogy and syllabi. Yet, in some US institutions of higher learning, Western WGS instructors are responsible for teaching WGS intro courses. They are expected to promote curriculum requirements such as global, international, multicultural, and multiethnic perspectives. Even in higher institutions with no stated global or transnational curriculum requirements, WGS intro courses, by their very essence, are meant to introduce students to critical and decolonial approaches for critiquing power and privilege and interrogating the connection with social justice. As a graduate instructor, I witnessed how some white WGS graduate instructors grapple with the uphill task of ensuring that their WGS classes incorporate global perspectives while avoiding the tendency to essentialize "others" and collapse significant contexts. Faced with this challenge, some would avoid global or transnational discourse entirely. Others make unsuccessful attempts at transnational WGS pedagogy. The challenges Western instructors face in attempting transnational WGS pedagogy include locating course materials that engage global discourse from a critical viewpoint and finding the appropriate guest lecturers to teach the "global" aspect. These kinds of challenges, if not addressed, can hamper instructors' engagement with transnational WGS pedagogy. At best, instructors might merely introduce global topics but lack the strategy to make transnational connections.

As a graduate student with prior experience in international human rights education and advocacy experience in women's rights and development in Nigeria, I gladly accepted the offer to guest lecture in WS 2013 classes at my institution. Nevertheless, it was not long before I discovered that the challenge of teaching transnational WGS is not limited to the Western instructors of Global North descent, but it extended to all WGS instructors teaching in the Global North. Notwithstanding instructors' origins or national identity, teaching WGS in the United States, for example, entails working with students who mostly have a US-centered worldview that assumes the world to be divided into the blessed United States and the oppressed "others," especially the others on the continent of Africa and the Global South more broadly. As a Nigerian with global women's rights expertise, students expect me to represent my group by telling them all about the oppressed women in Africa. They were quick to express pity for "others" while expressing how blessed they are to be Americans. Students expect me to represent the whole group (of African women) in giving detailed explanations of issues as complex as the enormity of African cultures, histories, individual agency, and intra-group advocacy efforts. In fact, as only one country in the western region of the African continent, my country, Nigeria, has hundreds of cultures and languages that I am not qualified to represent authoritatively. I also found that international students are happy to have a professor who engages in social justice issues beyond the US context. They feel more welcome in the class and are genuinely eager to engage in discussions. Hence, there was no doubt that transnational WGS pedagogy is essential to address the assumption of "the blessed and the rest," deconstruct the privileged epistemological viewpoints, and demarginalize international students often pushed to the fringe in US-centric WGS pedagogy.

In one of my early semesters in the graduate program, working with a graduate instructor of Global North descent, I volunteered to teach a class module on sexual and reproductive health. I taught about FGC—using it as a specific example to problematize the label itself, highlight the NGO advocacy, discuss the complexities of legislation on FGC, and discuss the commonalities and differences among FGC and other bodily reconstructions, including intersex surgeries and designer vagina modifications, which are hardly talked about. Our reading included Virginia Braun's (2012) "Female Genital Cutting around The Globe" to enable conversation on FGC as a global phenomenon that requires transnational analysis. In addition, I used the documentary "The Perfect Vagina" (2008) to show predominantly white women undergoing plastic surgeries to reconstruct their genitalia. I anticipated that these course materials, put together, would show FGC as a transnational issue supported by the general culture of domination of female sexuality and bodily integrity—a form of domination capable of being internalized and considered the norm. However, most questions from students reflected a thirst for more information about the oppressive impact of FGC on women and girls in the Global South. Several students expressed pity, shock, desire to save others, and appraisal of themselves as more blessed than the rest. I explained the need for a broader, more open-minded approach that lets them see the connection among FGC and other kinds of bodily modifications over and over. I did not want students to leave the class with the pity party notion, which would be antithetical to my teaching objective. But it was a struggle. I realized that one class session was not enough to lay the required foundation for any transnational discussion. I continued to interject in most of the other topics in that class during the semester to let students see the fundamental connections between social justice issues across borders, even while stressing the diverse ways that people are affected, depending on their geographical location, nationality, and other critical identity markers. A one-off class within a semester is never enough to lay the desired foundation for transnational WGS teaching.

The Prospects of Teaching Transnational WGS

My teaching experience as an international graduate instructor confirms that not only white instructors struggle with transnational WGS pedagogy. I saw my colleagues, who are white graduate instructors, struggle with teaching transnational WGS. But I also experienced the same struggle (albeit differently) when I attempted to teach transnational WGS in a single class (module/week). Transnational WGS pedagogy is challenging for teachers of Global North descent and those of Global South descent. For instance, it is hard for students in the United States to imagine that marginalized people, irrespective of their geographical locations, might be oppressed by fundamentally oppressive forces of capitalism, imperialism, and white supremacy. Undoubtedly, instructors' positionality differs and would produce different teaching experiences on transnational WGS. But the common factor of attempting to teach WGS from a transnational perspective to students with a US-centered worldview shows that all instructors need to improve their strategies. Otherwise, an instructor of Global North descent might inadvertently essentialize and/or misrepresent others in the Global South. At the same time, a teacher of Global South descent might end up calling a pity party while becoming the center of such anormal ceremony. It became more apparent that Parisi's (2012) critical questions about the possibility of scholars in the Global North teaching about the Global South, given the ethical concerns, questions about expertise, and accessibility of scholarly publications in languages other than English, remain valid. At the same time, it was glaring that teachers of Global South descent also need to be prepared so they do not become the sole representation of diverse groups and cultures in attempting to transnationalize their pedagogy. Every instructor, regardless of their national identity, has to do the work of not propagating a "single story" of the groups outside of the United States.

Why Transnational WGS?

Before sharing my strategies, it might be beneficial to reiterate the significance of WGS transnational pedagogy. Transnational WGS pedagogy is a decolonial tool that helps to democratize knowledge. Avoiding the transnational in the WGS introductory course promotes essentialism and privileges Western thoughts, epistemology, and pedagogy. Limiting social justice discourse to the United States also tends to make any international student in such classes feel marginalized and unable to find relatable grounds with others. Their epistemologies and worldviews are sidelined or completely silenced in a supposedly multicultural country and a WGS class that should aim at a decolonized discourse. As an international student, I understand firsthand how invisible international students can become in a WGS that adopts only a US-centric lens in analyzing privilege and oppression.

Similarly, Native American students whose Indigenous identities and worldviews are marginalized by colonial settler powers also would not connect if our pedagogy and syllabi fail to include a critique of the Western colonial notions of power, borders, wealth, and knowledge. As Kaplan and Grewal (2002, 730) argue, the transnational must enable a critique of "the link among patriarchies, colonialisms, racisms, and feminisms." Because a shared link connects these oppressive powers, WGS courses, especially the introductory ones, need to incorporate transnational perspectives. Therefore, one of our goals as instructors of WGS introductory classes is not to let any students leave our classes believing the myths about what happens "out there" or be further marginalized in course readings and discussions.

WGS intro courses might be many students' only encounter with the field of WGS. If we let students walk out with a restrictive, US-centric view of oppression and social justice, our job is not done. Failure to provide a space that challenges these worldviews inhibits a holistic social justice discourse, a priority in WGS.

Over the years, WGS scholars and feminists have continued to expand on the concept of transnationalism. WGS pedagogy grounds women's issues in historical contexts and critiques the simple aggregation of international women's issues. Transnationalism in WGS is, therefore, not a mere appendix but a fundamental purpose of WGS. As Chandra Talpade Mohanty (1988, 81) argues in "Under Western Eyes," (re)presenting a global, international, or universal image of women in the Global South is oppressive. In going beyond the simplistic mention of global issues, transnational WGS pedagogy must pay intentional attention to social justice issues. While a global or international approach to WGS pedagogy can be significant and sometimes critical, it does not automatically transcend the interrogation of the several social justice issues in multiple countries—outside the specific teaching location. Hence, even though the knowledge of social justice issues from a global perspective is crucial, a transnational pedagogical approach must deliberately examine the commonalities and differences with attention to critical contexts across national borders. To interrogate commonalities and differences simultaneously, instructors require knowledge of local and global contexts to transnationalize WGS pedagogy, and such contexts must be put in critical conversation with each other. That is what I refer to as making the transnational connection. The intention to transnationalize WGS pedagogy enables the instructor to interrogate the hierarchical concentration of power in the hands of a privileged few and the resultant oppression of the marginalized. Any pedagogical approach that provides a generalized discourse about groups, cultures, and histories denies marginalized people justice and dismisses their existence, agency, and worldviews. Hence, transnationalizing WGS pedagogy adopts a critical lens to social justice issues, critiquing systems of power against the backdrop of acknowledged cultural, historical, and geographical differences.

The Transnational Is an Essential Part of the Intersectional

A crucial emphasis of transnationalism in WGS pedagogy is that it is a critical part of intersectionality. Our introduction of intersectionality to the students during the WGS introductory course can be holistic only with a deliberate effort to incorporate nationality and national orientation as important identity vectors that further complicate the oppression of people already marginalized. As Sylvanna Falcón and Jennifer Nash (2015, 5) argue, intersectionality and transnationalism have "similar institutional histories" in WGS and should not be "constructed as mutually exclusive." WGS introductory curricula should engage intersectional analysis that investigates the multiple systems of oppression that a group of people faces due to their intersecting identities, as articulated by Kimberlé Crenshaw (1989); nationality needs to be part of that. Identifying transnationalism as an essential aspect of intersectionality (in addition to race, sex, age, and class, among others) in WGS, Sally Kitch and Mary Fonow (2012, 107) opine that intersectionality and transnationalism are two key features in many WGS mission statements. A person's national identity and/or geographical location does not create oppression. But the forces of colonial, capitalist, white supremacist oppression of people of specific nationality intersect with other "isms" to produce unique forms of oppression. Intersectionality is not simply the interrogation of racism and sexism. Neocolonialism, imperialism, orientalism, and other globalized "isms" are equally important. When intersectionality incorporates these "isms," it engages the transnational. WGS curricula must integrate the analysis of all forms of oppression simultaneously. As a framework for analyzing the systems of oppression in WGS, intersectionality is not holistic if the oppression and inequality people experience due to their location are excluded from such analysis.

Also, intersectional WGS must engage transnationalism in theory, curricula, and pedagogy. When incorporating the transnational in the WGS introductory course, it is crucial that instructors and students refrain from what Vrushali Patil (2013, 863) calls "domestic intersectionality" and the "reification of the local"; this iteration of intersectionality limits WGS analysis to US perspectives while ignoring transnational implications. Hence, knowing that the intersectional is not complete without the transnational is my primary motivation for my WGS curriculum, especially at the intro level, where students need grounding in intersectionality and implications for marginalized identities. Transnational WGS pedagogy enables instructors to problematize the peculiar oppression of people within US borders who are not necessarily "documented" nationals, such as immigrants and refugees, and explores commonalities with other US citizens experiencing racism, sexism, classism, settler-colonialism, etc. Without ignoring one or the other, transnational WGS interrogates both the local and global forms of oppression. Unlike the widespread use of transnational in some fields of study to mean the movement of people, goods, or ideas across national borders, transnational in WGS allows us to incorporate an intersectional analysis that considers nationality a vital identity that complicates people's experience of oppression.

The Significance of Transnational WGS Intro Courses

Indeed, a transnational approach is essential and is what I adopt in all my WGS classes to decolonize epistemologies and social justice discourse. But it is undoubtedly of higher significance in WGS intro courses. As the name suggests, WGS introductory courses give students their first exposure to the field of WGS and its distinct epistemology and approaches for social change; these should incorporate the transnational. One of the crucial things that confronted me as a graduate instructor teaching in WGS introductory classes is that most of my students had prior sensationalized ideas of women's oppression in the Global South. The mainstream media's picture of women's rights in the Global South is that of oppression from patriarchy, complicated by poverty and reinforced by primitive cultures. The popular narrative of oppressive practices such as child (or early) marriage, femicide, polygamous marriage, acid baths, honor killings, poverty, sweatshops, and FGC usually shapes students' perceptions of the Global South.

On the other hand, most students have not yet been exposed to critical thought about the connections between the oppression of marginalized people regardless of their geographical location. I consider the introductory transnational WGS curriculum essential for providing the space to walk students through reflecting on and interrogating their prior views on the systems of power orchestrating global inequalities. Students who take the WGS intro classes need to leave with a critical understanding of the world and the structures of power that affect people's experience of oppression and the part they might play in working for social justice. WGS intro classes must then be transnational to live up to their aim.

Strategies for Transnational WGS Pedagogy

As a Nigerian graduate instructor teaching WGS intro in a US higher education institution, some specific teaching strategies that I have found helpful in guiding my WGS intro courses from a transnational perspective include the following.

Lay a solid foundation from the beginning of class by deconstructing the notion of the blessed and the oppressed: The first few weeks of class often have a significant impact on students and give them a glimpse of the course's trajectory. I, therefore, introduce the transnational as a critical aspect of the class, starting with Chimamanda Adichie's (2016) TED Talk "The Danger of a Single Story" and AnaLouise Keating's (2007, 125–26) "Dialogue: Some of My Presuppositions." Adichie explains the importance of open-mindedness to multiple perspectives from multiple groups and identities across borders.

With Adichie's video, international students and other marginalized identities know that their views are valid and do matter in the class. The fact that Adichie is a Nigerian woman like me and her "The Danger of a Single Story" challenges specific single stories about Nigeria helps me as an instructor to take off the burden of students' expectation that I will represent "the Nigerian culture" or explain the plight of "the oppressed Nigerian woman" or the "oppressed African woman." Keating calls students to reflect on prior worldviews and biases in their initial education—an invitation to a critical journey where the foundation of epistemology is social justice, self-accountability, and respect for diverse perspectives.

With these course materials, I set my students on a transnational WGS learning journey. I invite them to complete a free-write reflection on any reductionist perspective they have received about any group of people, and some of them cross borders in their analyses, even in the first assignment. This ground-laying challenges privileged perspectives up-front and will be helpful throughout the class for discussing social justice issues across borders with open-mindedness and self-reflection on previously held reductionist views of "others." As the course progresses, I groom students to view social justice issues from the Global South with a critical reflective lens. They are critical of the media portrayals of "the third world" as they think more of the power dynamics in the media and popular narratives of "others." To achieve this objective, instructors of transnational WGS must also be up-front about making students understand that the transnational entails making critical connections and not measuring who is more blessed or oppressed.

Build on that foundation by including transnational material for every class/module/theme/topic, starting from the first week of class: Rather than add the transnational perspective into just one or two weeks during the course, I am deliberate in incorporating readings with transnational perspectives for each weekly module, taking students beyond a US-centric discussion on important course themes, including race, gender, sexuality, religion, and class. Incorporating at least one source that discusses each course theme in a different Global South geographical location helps the students to keep making connections. It helps investigate the commonalities and differences between what they can relate to in their communities and the global impact of white supremacist, capitalist, imperialist, and patriarchal powers. Adopting this strategy ensures that students are not only introduced to a transnational framework of analyzing oppression and social justice but also have practical examples from various WGS topics. Students gain transnational perspectives on diverse social justice issues, and it becomes good practice so much that students can think beyond the United States in analyzing course themes and materials as the semester progresses.

Moreover, choosing resources that enable transnational class discussion reflects a strategic spread of course materials to cover multiple geographical regions. In addition to spreading readings that will allow transnational discussion weekly, assigning course materials on social justice issues across Africa, Asia, the Middle East, Europe, and the Americas throughout the semester gives the students an in-depth transnational worldview. I deliberately do not merely focus on Nigeria or the African continent alone in spreading my course materials for the WGS introductory course. I consciously try to include resources from major regions of the world and the social justice issues affecting such areas. Concentrating only on a specific location or only on the familiar parts of the Global South in comparison to the United States, for instance, leaves the United States at the center of analysis and reinforces a US–others binary, which is antithetical to transnational WGS pedagogy. For example, I have found pairing readings on body politics and FGC effective. A text on honor killing would also work in a module on gender and sexual violence. Instead of devoting one class to a module on global or transnational course materials and discussion, pairing course materials on social justice issues weekly and across geographical boundaries helps students engage with the fundamental global power systems that oppress people across borders. With these weekly border-crossing course materials, some social justice issues like FGC and honor killings do not stand out as things that happened to "oppressed" people over there but are examples of the interaction of power, privilege, and oppression of "others" globally.

Assign critical and intersectional course materials: It is crucial to find the right teaching resources that engage social justice issues from the Global South with a critical and intersectional perspective. I have found some WGS intro textbooks useful[5] and will be exploring some more in the future. Still, a single textbook might cover only some WGS topics from transnational perspectives. Including transnational course materials in each module can be daunting. Hence, instructors must creatively source teaching materials from elsewhere, including news reports, social media, blogs, short open-source videos, and interactive e-learning modules, to augment any major textbook. For my WGS introductory classes, I found some op-ed sources useful for offering critical transnational analysis. News media reports from trusted sources, including the *Washington Post, New York Times, BBC News, CNN,* and *Al Jazeera,* can sometimes help provide current global contexts. Finding specific news writers who write from transnational perspectives can also be beneficial.[6] Some short YouTube videos can also prompt transnational discourse on social justice issues while engaging students' audio-visual senses. Leyla Hussein's (2014) TedTalk on FGC is intersectional and transnational. One cannot overemphasize that WGS instructors must be creative in locating these critical reports and op-eds for transnational WGS. While the primary textbooks would provide the theoretical base, supporting each module with at least one course material not focused on the United States is beneficial for transnational pedagogy.

However, it is equally critical to note ab initio that the course materials do not in themselves do the transnational work. It might be challenging to find the "perfect" course materials that entail discourse beyond the Global North, which do not reinforce the Western savior, capitalist, racist, orientalist oppressive paradigms or essentialize the women/groups from a single cultural perspective. Instructors indeed may not find the "perfect" teaching resources that make engaging critical and intersectional analysis on every topic because they sometimes do not exist. For example, Adichie's (2013) "We Should All Be Feminist" offers a critical gender analysis beyond the United States and has great potential to aid students' understanding of transnational feminism. However, it is limited in its binary notion of gender as only male and female. Adichie has also openly marginalized transgender women in her "transnational" feminist discourse. This sort of marginalization of some minority groups is an example of how instructors of transnational WGS might keep facing the challenge of finding the perfect critical and intersectional teaching materials. Writers sometimes have oversights, write from a limited perspective, or inadvertently promote a generalized representation of "others." They could get caught in the politics of inclusion and exclusion, complicated by the divide-and-conquer scheme of white supremacy. In general, if we continue to wait for the perfect transnational readings for the WGS introductory courses, we might not begin to teach or end up with no materials to assign. The struggle to find the best resources is real, but are there perfectly intersectional resources that do not exclude some intersections? Maybe or maybe not. If it makes transnational connections, that's great! If it doesn't, pair the reading with one that allows students to see the transnational link.

When considering resources and materials for teaching WGS transnationally, WGS instructors need to broaden their horizons beyond scholarly sources. Teachable materials and resources abound in the work and research of individual women and organizations throughout the Global South. While university feminists or researchers may not have published such, they contain rich information, data, statistics, and documented strategies being used to promote the cause of women's liberation. As Lila Abu-Lughod (2002) argues, using reports and resources from local nonprofits or women's/feminist/activist organizations allows us to bring in the voices of those affected by the social issues discussed in our classes. The works of grassroots activists and advocates from the Global South have the potential to highlight complex voices, perspectives, and experiences of marginalized peoples in class, rather than them being represented as the subaltern[7] without a voice. It highlights their agency, acknowledging not only their challenges but also how they continue to resist and survive. The resources presented by stakeholders, including government officials and NGOs, can be suitable raw materials that scholars can use to gather helpful information for rigorous academic analysis. These primary sources about groups in the Global South may not be "scholarly." Still, they can provide the background information needed to make transnational connections across a spectrum of communities in the Global South.

But some NGO resources might reinforce international perspectives that lack intersectional and critical connections that enable transnational discussion, even if students find them helpful in understanding the topic of discussion. Instructors' ability to understand the difference between international and transnational is the primary expertise needed for transnational WGS teaching. Part of transnational pedagogy is training students to be critical in identifying the reductionist views in course materials and, by extension, whatever they read or encounter. The instructor must walk students through critical engagement with any assigned course materials, analyzing them from an intersectional and transnational perspective, identifying any reductionist thinking, and what Adichie (2016) identified as "single stories." That is why instructors and students need to understand the principle of transnational WGS and use that transnational lens to analyze course materials.

Have an assignment that assesses students' understanding of transnational analysis: An excellent strategy for assessing the effectiveness of transnational WGS pedagogy is evaluating students' understanding of and engagement with the transnational. It is best to assess students on primary course objectives. Since I prioritize transnational perspectives in the course, I adopt an assignment that measures students' understanding, which helps me improve my transnational WGS approach semester after semester. I assign what I call the *Global Current Event Assignment (GCEA)* (see sidebar) in my WGS intro classes, both online and face to face. For this assignment, I invite students to choose a current news article focusing on social justice issues in the Global South. I ask them to analyze the news article from a social justice viewpoint, using the learned transnational lens as they pose critical questions about any missing or reductionist views or perspectives that misrepresent a group of people. I ask questions like: Who wrote this piece, and from what perspectives? What are the missing perspectives and stories that could complicate the report further? How similarly or differently would such stories be told if they occurred in the Global North as opposed to the Global South, and vice versa? Because the media are a significant platform where students learn about "others" in the Global South, I point them to find articles in major news outlets that can provoke their transnational thinking. I have found this transnational teaching approach effective in making students shift their perspective of the world, promoting a change of thought that sets the stage for global change.

Global Current Event Assignment*

Created by Esther O. Ajayi-Lowo for WS 2013 Gender and Social Change: An Introduction to Multicultural Women's Studies, Texas Woman's University

Synopsis:

You are required to find a current news article on women (or any other group) outside the US reported/published within the last year in an international/global news outlet or a media source in the Global North region. You will write a 500-word analysis of your chosen news article and connect it to at least three of our class materials. You must include both readings and videos. While you are free to choose the source of your news article, I recommend international news sources such as *BBC News World, CNN International, Globe and Mail, Al Jazeera, New York Times/World, Washington Post, International Herald Tribune, All Africa, Reuters, Real Clear World, Reddit World News, Global Issues*, etc.

Objectives:

This assignment will enable you to

1. critically review how women (or other groups) outside the U.S. are presented in the media
2. reflect on stereotypes and the dangers of a single story
3. problematize the representation of women (or any other group) from the Global South within the paradigms of social justice
4. reflect on the transnational approach to social justice

Respond to the following prompts in your analysis:

1. What is the source of the news?
2. What "single story" is being told, if at all?
3. What are the missing perspectives that are under/unreported?
4. What is the power relation between the reporter (or source of news) and the subject (the people presented/represented) in the news?
5. How are the subject's voices/views/perspectives treated, presented, represented, or missing?

6. How similarly or differently would this story be reported if the subjects were in the U.S./Global North?
7. How would you rewrite the story to reflect multiple or missing perspectives?
8. How would you rewrite the story to enhance social justice?

Here are some possible topics that you can search for news articles on:

1. COVID-19
2. Female Genital Cutting
3. Human Trafficking
4. Child Marriage/Early Marriage
5. Polygamy
6. Menstruation
7. Immigration
8. Patriarchy
9. Veiling/Dressing
10. Femicide
11. Honor Killing
12. Acid bath
13. Maternal/Infant Mortality
14. Women's seclusion/restrictions
15. Empowerment
16. Education
17. Development
18. Motherhood/Parenting
19. Family Planning/Contraception
20. Population
21. Poverty
22. Health

This is just a guide. Feel free to choose news articles on other issues not listed here. If you are unsure about the relevance or appropriateness of your news event, please check with me.

* While crafted specifically for WS 2013: "Gender and Social Change: An Introduction to Multicultural Women's Studies," this assignment can be adapted for any writing course with objectives relating (but not limited to) conceptual analysis, and critical thinking, and transnational approaches to social justice.

Each semester I have been amazed at how effectively students critically analyze social justice issues, including veiling, honor killing, and FGC. They pay close attention to historical, political, and cultural contexts that are usually missing in popular texts and news reports. They identify the critical connections among social justice issues as the voices and agencies of marginalized peoples are made invisible. They recognize the privileged position of the writers of "single" stories about others. They discuss the fixation with some social justice issues in the Global South and the silence on the fundamental connection to such issues in the Global North, particularly the United States. They identify the desire to report others and act as their saviors and, in the process, reinforce the power binary of the blessed and the oppressed. I have had students use their GCEA to connect reproductive injustice in China to that in the United States, for instance, noting the different contexts and the fundamental commonality while engaging the reproductive justice framework and intersectionality theory. I have had a student connect honor killing to the killing of Black transgender people to protect the "heterosexual honor" in the United States. Students can see how marginalized people's oppression can be complicated by their nationality and geographical location. Students' response to the GCEA differs from the reactions I initially got when teaching social justice issues in the Global South. Laying the foundation at the start of class and building on it weekly was helpful for students' learning and mine.

Transnationalizing WGS is a continuous process: Most students' excellent essays meet and exceed my expectations of transnational analysis. But I am also mindful that some students' understanding of the transnational might need improvement, even at the end of the semester. Students might repeat cultural imperialist narratives and regurgitate white savior narratives. Some students might struggle to see connections between their "blessed" situations and the "oppressed others." Even if some essays prick my bones, I can intervene through grading feedback. Every observation of what a student understands or resists enables me, as the instructor, to improve from semester to semester. I aim to ensure that no students leave my class without understanding transnational perspectives through my teaching, assignment, or feedback that interrogates their thoughts and prompts them to think further. At the end of each semester, I believe that I have sown seeds with the potential to germinate into more transnational social justice. However challenging, teaching and guest-lecturing WGS intro and sharpening my pedagogy for transnational WGS has nonetheless been productive. I have gained valuable insights from teaching and guest-lecturing and keep evolving at transnational WGS pedagogy. Even though it all remains a work in progress, I have seen improvements in students' understanding, responses, and assignments over the years.

The strategies discussed above also benefit Western professors who desire to teach their WGS introductory courses from a transnational perspective. As mentioned earlier, Parisi (2002) raises concerns about the possibility that, in transnationalizing knowledge production, syllabi, and analysis, scholars in the Global North might lack the ethical ground or expertise to access teaching materials that incorporate critical perspectives on social issues occurring in the Global South. How exactly does one overcome Parisi's very valid concerns? How might Western instructors in the Global North gain the expertise to teach transnational WGS introduction ethically, with adequate course materials and effective strategies? More so, postcolonial and anti-imperialist scholars have questioned whether scholars in the Global North possess sufficient knowledge and ethical sensibilities to theorize on social justice issues in the Global South. This question remains a justifiable source of reservation for instructors in engaging transnational WGS, especially given the antecedent of the various ways that Western scholars have been critiqued for essentializing all women without attention to historical, cultural, national, and class differences (Sandoval 1991, 1–3; Mohanty 2003). Power dynamics favor women in the Global North, and this raises questions about addressing issues such as FGC and honor killing in the Global South when scholars in the Global South do not have the "luxury" of researching or teaching about the social issues in the Global North (Mendoza 2002, 299–300). I have experienced Western graduate instructors wondering how they might teach about cultures and groups outside of their location without collapsing the differences between and within groups. Hence, without glossing over it, the question of ethics requires more profound reflections by any WGS instructor engaging in transnational pedagogy.

Although teaching transnational WGS calls for attention to the risks of essentialism, it does not make teaching transnational WGS impossible. A deeper understanding of transnational WGS entails preparing instructors in the Global North with critical tools to self-reflect with the students, avoid collapsing differences, and refrain from generalizing about the Global South. Transnational pedagogy, therefore, entails a both/and intersectional approach where the instructors work with students not to focus on what goes on "out there" but instead to critically analyze what goes on both "out there" and "in here." It shows how joint oppressive powers connect to adversely affect marginalized peoples in fundamentally common ways, albeit differently. In practical terms, Inderpal Grewal (2013), in "Outsourcing Patriarchy," describes how a transnational WGS discourse should address the oppression of women who suffer honor killings in the Global South by making connections with issues related to honor that manifest in patriarchal structures in the Global North. Hence, instructors' understanding of the transnational must start with knowing that honor killings are not what happens "out there" when oppressive systems sacrifice women or girls for the "honor" of culture. It must progress to consider honor killings across borders in situations where oppressive systems mortgage individuals' (gender, race, sexual, or other) identities for the "honor" of colonial white supremacist hetero-patriarchal power.

Similarly, a transnational pedagogical approach to FGC would include a both/and intersectional analysis that refrains from engaging with FGC as solely a barbaric cultural practice in the Global South. Braun (2012) and Hussein (2014) argue that a nuanced transnational discussion of FGC must entail a discussion of FGC manifesting in the Global North in the forms of designer vaginas and other vagina surgeries. By knowing these essential ingredients of the transnational, instructors can avoid essentialism and discussions of FGC as a barbaric cultural practice in African and Asian countries. Rather than simply maintaining WGS pedagogical disengagement with FGC, veiling, honor killing, and other issues, WGS instructors can make transnational connections as they engage the commonalities and differences among systems of power and how they produce different forms of oppression.

Another concern an instructor in the Global North might have about teaching transnational WGS is expertise. But this is also surmountable. Instructors might feel like they do not have the expertise to teach about issues going on outside the United States in an effective transnational way, especially if their prior education and experience haven't prepared them well. The question of power and privilege of WGS scholars in the Global North being considered the "experts" who research, speak for, and represent the marginalized others in the Global South continues to be problematic. However, the question of expertise in transnational WGS research is a different conversation than the expertise needed for transnational WGS pedagogy, especially at the introductory level. As Parisi (2002) raises the question of expertise, she is also quick to acknowledge that the transnational WGS curriculum should be the "shared responsibility" of all WGS instructors (180). While we can continue to discuss the question of expertise in transnational WGS topics as a research focus, transnational WGS introductory pedagogy should be adopted by all WGS instructors rather than a particular course taught by a specific "expert" in transnational WGS. Transnationality is an approach that would then become a tool that every WGS professor, regardless of their areas of expertise, would be able to teach. Given the importance of the transnational in WGS, instructors of introductory classes need expertise in transnational pedagogy.

One way to overcome the challenge of expertise for transnational WGS teaching is for instructors to make the extra effort to educate themselves on how WGS practitioners and scholars continue to stress and engage the transnational as a critical component of WGS. The National Women's Studies

Association (NWSA), as the professional body of WGS, made transnationalism the theme of its 2019 and 2020 annual conferences. While the 2020 conference was canceled due to the COVID-19 pandemic, the 2019 conference had scholars, keynote speakers, and panelists discuss the significance of transnational WGS. Before that, NWSA also devoted the 2017 annual conference to celebrating transnationalism by having keynote speakers such as Chandra Talpade Mohanty stress the need for a transnational WGS lens for critiquing capitalism and imperialism.[8] More and more WGS departments seek to adapt to the institutional requirement to become more international or multicultural in research and pedagogy (Kitch and Fonow 2012; Kaplan and Grewal 2002, 71). WGS scholars with a research focus on the transnational have also produced relevant publications and maintain open forums and discussions[9] that instructors might find helpful. Therefore, WGS instructors' commitment to transnationality must reflect how we teach introductory courses. Indeed, WGS instructors can overcome the question of expertise by prioritizing the transnational and being willing to learn and do the work it requires.

Conclusion

Regardless of the teacher's positionality and identity, one challenge is the fear of feeding students' already sensationalized worldviews about the oppressive cultures in the Global South. Having taught the WGS introductory class for many semesters, my experience is that there is a thin line between working with students to obtain a transnational view of social justice and inadvertently inviting them to a pity party of the sorry situations of the oppressed groups in the Global South. Given students' prior exposure to the Global South/Global North hierarchical binary of inequality, with the South representing the inferior, underdeveloped third world and the North representing the developed first world, transnationalizing the WGS introductory course is tricky; it requires not only theoretical knowledge of the transnational but also intentional pedagogical strategies. Otherwise, an instructor could inadvertently invite students to compare the developed to the developing/underdeveloped in trying to be transnational. WGS instructors of the Global South teaching in the Global North would need to continue to avoid the danger of collapsing the representation of a group into a single analytical frame, as what Narayan (2000, 1084) calls the "package picture of gender/culture" in which scholars generalize about a group based on their embodied experience or scholarly orientation. Instructors need to work with students to pay closer attention to the dynamics of differences within and among groups, avoid seeing any group as a monolith, and avoid relying on a reductionist view of social justice issues from one's familiar national territory or multi-national territories. Similarly, Western instructors need to keep paying attention to avoid essentialism and, most important, understand that avoiding transnational perspectives in their teaching of WGS is not a desirable option, as it is tantamount to complicity with the reification of and centering of Western epistemology that marginalizes non-Western worldviews.

While the strategies for teaching transnational WGS in this chapter focus on WGS introductory classes, they can serve as guidelines for instructors in other WGS courses. Regardless of the instructors' identities, research interests, and locations, the transnational approach and perspectives can be entrenched in all WGS pedagogy. While these strategies are not exhaustive, they can serve as guidelines for instructors committed to decolonizing their pedagogy, syllabi, and teaching approaches. In higher education, in the United States and the Global North, teaching WGS from a transnational worldview can decenter Western epistemology for a decolonial approach to pedagogy. It allows us to acknowledge our interconnected world with its interwoven web of simultaneously relational differences. Our classes as a microcosm of the larger society and our pedagogy have the power to reinforce oppression, albeit inadvertently. In having a holistic teaching approach to social justice, transnational WGS teaching makes international students in our classes feel connected to the class materials and discussion. In entailing a critique of the uneven power relations in the world, transnational WGS gives students the critical tools needed to escape the bubble of limited situated knowledge of their worlds, where they continue to encounter capitalist and imperialist rhetoric. In general, silence about students' ideas of what happens "out there" cannot be permitted in WGS classes. Although most WGS programs in the Global North continue to challenge how our curriculum and pedagogy are effectively transnational, we cannot lose sight of the importance of adopting a transnational teaching approach. The refusal to adopt a pedagogy that digs deeper into the broader global power structural hierarchy of the Global North over the Global South is colonial. Transnational WGS teaching should be a continuous journey that requires fine-tuning our strategies. Let us all keep learning, reflecting, and adapting our pedagogy with holistic social justice in mind.

Notes

1. Women's and Gender Studies (WGS) as an academic field of study exists in different institutions under different names, including Women's Studies, Feminist Studies, Gender Studies, and Women's Gender and Sexuality Studies (Orr and Braithwaite 2012, 8).

2. I started writing the chapter as a doctoral candidate and graduate teaching fellow at TWU. Even though I had started working as an Assistant Professor of Comparative Women's Studies at Spelman College and completed the final

revisions of this chapter as an Assistant Professor of Women and Gender Studies at Texas Christian University (TCU), the chapter only captures my pedagogical experiences at TWU.

3. I use fresh students in place of the popular cliche "freshmen," a language that conceptually excludes fresh students who are not "men."

4. By western WGS instructors of the Global North, I mean the instructors who have had all their education in the United States and have no prior personal or education connection or experience with the Global South, except predominantly through the media or other public platforms that already promote the Global North versus Global South rhetoric.

5. The WGS intro textbooks that I have used in my courses are (i) Susan M. Shaw and Janet Lee. *Women's Voices, Feminist Visions: Classic and Contemporary Readings*. 5th ed. New York: McGraw-Hill, 2012, and (ii), Bonnie Kime Scott, Susan E. Cayleff. Anne Donadey, and Irena Lara, editors. *Women in Culture: An Intersectional Anthology for Gender and Women's Studies*. Second ed. 2017. I plan to explore other recommended textbooks with transnational perspectives, including i) *Gendered Perspectives: Intersectional Perspectives*, edited by Gwyn Kirk and Margo Okazawa-Rey, and ii) Janet Lee and Susan Maxine Shaw. *Women Worldwide: Transnational Feminist Perspectives on Women*. McGraw-Hill, 2021.

6. A graduate colleague of mine and I found a Washington Post reporter, Karen Attiah, who incorporates critical and transnational perspectives.

7. In Gayatri Chakravorty Spivak's "Can the Subaltern Speak?," the subaltern refers to the "oppressed" (78), especially women who act and struggle (70) but remain mute in discourse concerning them because they are unable to have necessarily unmitigated representation by an "intermediate group" (80), including the imperialists, patriarchy, the state, or the intellectuals.

8. In the plenary "Global Context and National Connections," Chandra Mohanty discussed the prospects and challenges of transnational solidarity. *2017 NWSA Annual Conference, November 16–19, 2017*. Baltimore, MD. https://www.nwsa.org/news/512938/NWSA-A-History-2017-38th-National-Conference.htm.

9. Platforms that provide intergenerational, transnational discussion include the Feminist Freedom Warriors Conversation online video archives available at http://feministfreedomwarriors.org/.

Bibliography

Abu-Lughod, Lila. "Do Muslim Women Really Need Saving? Anthropological Reflections on Cultural Relativism and Its Others." *American Anthropologist* 104, no. 3 (2002): 783–90. https://doi.org/10.1525/aa.2002.104.3.783.

Adichie, Chimamanda Ngozi. "The Danger of a Single Story." October 7, 2009. YouTube video. https://www.youtube.com/watch?v=D9Ihs241zeg.

Adichie, Chimamanda Ngozi. "We Should All be Feminists." April 12, 2013. YouTube video. https://www.youtube.com/watch?v=hg3umXU_qWc.

Alexander, M. Jacqui, and Chandra Talpade Mohanty. Introduction to *Feminist*

Genealogies, Colonial Legacies, Democratic Futures, edited by M. Jacqui Alexander and Chandra Talpade Mohanty, xiii–lii. New York: Routledge, 2013.

Braun, Virginia. "Female Genital Cutting Around the Globe: A Matter of Reproductive Justice." In *Reproductive Justice: A Global Concern*, edited by Joan C. Chrisler, 29–55. Santa Barbara, CA: Praeger, 2012.

Crenshaw, Kimberlé. "Demarginalizing the Intersection of Race and Sex: A Black Feminist Critique of Antidiscrimination Doctrine, Feminist Theory and Antiracist Politics." *University of Chicago Legal Forum* (1989): 139–67.

Falcón, Sylvanna M., and Jennifer C. Nash. "Shifting Analytics and Linking Theories: A Conversation about the 'Meaning-Making' of Intersectionality and Transnational Feminism." *Women's Studies International Forum* 50 (2015): 1–10. https://doi.org/10.1016/j.wsif.2015.02.010.

Fernandes, Leela. *Transnational Feminism in the United States: Knowledge, Ethics, and Power*. New York University Press, 2013.

Fukushima, Annie Isabel, and Tanjerine Vei. "Decolonial Feminist Pedagogies: Entering into the 'World' of the Zombie as Praxis." *International Journal of Qualitative Studies in Education* (2022): 1–16.

Grewal, Inderpal. "Outsourcing Patriarchy: Feminist Encounters, Transnational Mediations and the Crime of 'Honour Killings.'" *International Feminist Journal of Politics* 15, no. 1 (2013): 1–19. https://doi.org/10.1080/14616742.2012.755352.

Holloway, Karla FC. "'Cruel Enough to Stop the Blood': Global Feminisms and the US Body Politic, or: 'They Done Taken My Blues and Gone.'" *Meridians* 7, no. 1 (2006): 1–18. https://doi.org/10.2979/MER.2006.7.1.1.

hooks, bell. *Writing Beyond Race: Living Theory and Practice*. New York: Routledge, 2013.

Hussein, Leyla. "Breaking Cycles: Leyla Hussein at TEDxCoventGardenWomen." Jan 17, 2014. YouTube video, 17:58. https://www.youtube.com/watch?v=uiTaA0o-7gY.

Kaplan, Caren, and Inderpal Grewal. "Transnational Practices and Interdisciplinary Feminist Scholarship: Reconfiguring Women's and Gender Studies." In *Women's Studies on Its Own: A Next Wave Reader in Institutional Change*, edited by Robyn Wiegman, 66–81. Durham, NC: Duke University Press, 2002.

Keating, AnaLouise. "Dialogue: Some of My Presuppositions." In *Teaching Transformation: Transcultural Classroom Dialogues*, 125–26. New York: Palgrave Macmillan, 2007.

Kitch, Sally L., and Mary Margaret Fonow. "Analyzing Women's Studies Dissertations: Methodologies, Epistemologies, and Field Formation." *Signs: Journal of Women in Culture and Society* 38, no. 1 (2012): 99–126. https://doi.org/10.1086/665801.

Leach, Heather, director. The Perfect Vagina. North One Television, 2008.

Lugones, Maria. "Playfulness, 'World'-Travelling, and Loving Perception." *Hypatia* 2, no. 2 (1987): 3–19.

Lugones, María. "Toward a Decolonial Feminism." *Hypatia* 25, no. 4 (2010): 742–59.

Mama, Amina. "Is It Ethical to Study Africa? Preliminary Thoughts on Scholarship and Freedom." *African Studies Review* 50, no. 1 (2007): 1–26. https://doi.org/10.1353/arw.2005.0122.

May, Vivian M. "'Disciplining Feminist Futures?': Undisciplined Reflections about the Women's Studies PhD." In *Women's Studies for the Future: Foundations, Interrogations, Politics*, edited by Elizabeth Lapovsky Kennedy and Agatha Beins, 185–206. New Brunswick, NJ: Rutgers University Press, 2005.

May, Vivian M. *Pursuing Intersectionality, Unsettling Dominant Imaginaries*. New York: Routledge, 2015.

Mendoza, Breny. "Transnational Feminisms in Question." *Feminist Theory* 3, no. 3 (2002): 295–314. https://doi.org/10.1177/146470002762492015.

Mohanty, Chandra Talpade. "Under Western Eyes: Feminist Scholarship and Colonial Discourses." *Feminist Review* 30, no. 1 (1998): 61–88. https://doi.org/10.1057/fr.1988.42.

Mohanty, Chandra Talpade. *Feminism Without Borders: Decolonizing Theory, Practicing Solidarity*. Durham, NC: Duke University Press, 2003.

Mohanty, Chandra Talpade. "Under Western Eyes Revisited: Feminist Solidarity through Anticapitalistic Struggles." In *Women's Studies for the Future: Foundations, Interrogations, Politics*, edited by Elizabeth Lapovsky Kennedy and Agatha Beins, 72–96. New Brunswick, NJ: Rutgers University Press, 2005.

Narayan, Uma. *Dislocating Cultures: Identities, Traditions, and Third-World Feminism*. Thinking Gender Series. New York: Routledge, 1997.

Narayan, Uma. "Undoing the 'Package Picture' of Cultures." *Signs: Journal of Women in Culture and Society* 25, no. 4 (2000): 1083–86. https://doi.org/10.1086/495524.

Orr, Catherine M., Ann Braithwaite, and Diane Lichtenstein. "Introduction," In *Rethinking Women and Gender Studies*, edited by Catherine M. Orr, Ann Braithwaite, and Diane Lichtenstein, 1–13. New York: Routledge, 2011.

Parisi, Laura. "Transnationalism." In *Rethinking Women and Gender Studies*, edited by Catherine M. Orr, Ann Braithwaite, and Diane Lichtenstein, 310–27. New York: Routledge, 2012.

Patil, Vrushali. "From Patriarchy to Intersectionality: A Transnational Feminist Assessment of How Far We've Really Come." *Signs: Journal of Women in Culture and Society* 38, no. 4 (2013): 847–67. https://doi.org/10.1086/669560.

Ríos-Rojas, Anne (Anna). "'Pedagogies of the Broken-Hearted': Notes on a Pedagogy of Breakage, Women of Color Feminist Decolonial Movidas, and Armed Love in the Classroom/Academy." *Frontiers* 41, no.1 (2020): 161–78.

Sandoval, Chela. "US Third World Feminism: The Theory and Method of Oppositional Consciousness in the Postmodern World." *Genders* 10 (1991): 1–24. https://www.utexaspressjournals.org/doi/abs/10.5555/gen.1991.10.1.

Soto, Sandra. "Where in the Transnational World are the U.S. Women of Color?" In *Women's Studies for the Future: Foundations, Interrogations, Politics*, edited by Elizabeth Lapovsky Kennedy and Agatha Beins, 111–24. New Brunswick, NJ: Rutgers University Press, 2005.

Spivak, Gayatri Chakravorty. "Can the Subaltern Speak?" In *Colonial Discourse and Postcolonial Theory: A Reader*, edited by P. Williman and L. Chrisman, 67–111. New York: Columbia University Press, 1999.

Trotz, D. Alissa. "Going Global? Transnationality, Women/Gender Studies and Lessons from the Caribbean." *Caribbean Review of Gender Studies* 1 (2007): 1–18. https://sta.uwi.edu/crgs/april2007/journals/AlissaTrotz_Going_Global_pm%20_2.pdf.

Verhaeghe, Amy, Ela Przybylo, and Sharifa Patel. 2018. "On the Im/Possibilities of Anti-Racist and Decolonial Publishing As Pedagogical Praxis." *Feminist Teacher* 28 (2): 79–90.

PART IV

Genealogies and Futures

11

[A] Migrant Vernacular

EUN-JIN KEISH KIM and ANGEL SUTJIPTO

> Glossary: for readers from elsewhere, who don't deal very well with unknown words or who want to understand everything. But, perhaps to establish for ourselves, ourselves as well, the long list of words within us whose sense escapes or, taking this farther, to fix the syntax of this language we are babbling. The readers of here are future.
> —Édouard Glissant, Malemort, 231

Invigorated by decolonial scholars Eve Tuck and C. Ree's "A Glossary of Haunting," we offer a collection of words that haunt our lives as bodies deemed "alien" in the part of Turtle Island called the United States. Haunting, as an adjective, is defined as "poignant and evocative; difficult to ignore or forget," carrying a lingering feeling or an affect. As a verb, haunt takes on a presence and a form, to "be persistently and disturbingly present in (something)." In its etymology, haunt is rooted in Old Norse *heimta*, which means to "bring home."

We asked each other, *"What are you haunted by?"* By people who died in government custody; people who took their own lives because the government and society have failed them; people whose lives have been uprooted by separation and deportation. By this, we mean: *habeas corpus*, bring them back alive, bring them home to their families. By this, we mean: we are haunted by fear of such possibilities happening to our own bodies and those dear to us. At its roots, hauntings are about loss and disconnections from place, people, and self.

Hunted by this white settler state and haunted by anticipatory grief, we learned to transform our ongoing displacement into an ability to speak and dream about home, about leaving and returning, expressing our desire for safety and protection (from whom and how?) that are not yet tangible. This essay emerged from a conversation between two migrant writers. Talking about our families and notions of belonging developed into a shared migrant vernacular. Continuing our conversation on the page, we discovered that we desire different outcomes for ourselves. Neither of us is proposing a singular solution, nor do we believe there is only one. We write this knowing that the dominant language on citizenship, on belonging, on nation, is unable to hold, contain, or recognize our tongues. As Gloria Anzaldúa wrote, it split our tongues (1987).

It is onto our "alien bodies" that the US government imposes spatial and temporal limitations according to the empire's needs and desires for labor and economic comfort. The empire projects its own fears, shame, and guilt by categorizing the exploited bodies as invaders and criminals. As two antiracist, feminist migrant writers, we redefine words such as "A-Number," "Borders," and "Camps" to expose wounds on im/migrant mind-bodies.

Our essay relies on the form of a glossary, perhaps in a crude attempt to will ourselves whole, or as Glissant writes, "perhaps to establish for ourselves, ourselves as well, the long list of words within us whose sense escapes, or taking this farther, to fix the syntax of this language we are babbling" (1990). Perhaps if we reject the current linguistic rule that compels us to think of another human being as "alien," we may begin to be in relations with each other and other worldly beings. From readers of *elsewhere* to the readers of *here*, racialized im/migrants define and redefine what home means, in the past, present, and future.

Our essay shifts tenses to reflect how hauntings defy linear time. We write in first- and third-person point-of-view (POV) when we agree with each other. When we write in second person POV, it is because we are tired and traumatized from exposing the vulnerabilities of "I." When we write "you," we are addressing readers who are deemed "alien" by centers of empires/nation-states: the undocumented, the sans-papiers, the stateless, and those who exist in a state of bureaucratic limbo. "You" makes the reader uncomfortable. Where are you, the reader, in relation to [A] Migrant Vernacular? The "you" haunts.

We offer these words. We hope they contribute to a radical and embodied listening practice around narratives of migration. We encourage readers to recognize the context of settler-colonialism and slavery and how it pathologizes ways of being, to acknowledge the lingering affect of words, and to contemplate silences and absences.

A:

Airports:

Your nightmares always involved airports: landing strips, arrival and departure gates, and lines to enter or exit always activated the sweat glands. You are climbing over parked airplanes, crawling between the aluminum ceiling and the hood of the plane, balancing across the wing of the parked flying vehicle, running from patrols who could force you into an unmarked vehicle and ship you off somewhere[1]; anywhere away from "here." Funny thing is, you can't tell from the environment where you are in the dream. No place markers hint to a map-able place.

In one variation of the nightmare, you are running while being separated from your parents. We got split while running across the jetway, hiding between bushes of dry scrub. The jetway reminds you of the Japanese military airfield built by kidnapped laborers from war-torn countries during WWII. Dominant history called them "volunteers," but local history tells you they were forced and kidnapped from the lands they grew up in, to expand imperial military power that oppresses their family back home with their own weary hands and muscles.

Last night, you woke up from a nightmare where you delayed purchasing plane tickets back to Korea for your family. The family had agreed on a departure date, but you realized no one had bought the tickets. While the rest of the family packed, you went to find the next flight out. As the time ticked closer to the gate closing hour, you couldn't bring yourself to go with them. You kept hesitating while your mom and your brother grew flustered about wasted money, and time running out. Always running out and depleted. What shocked you the most was your hesitation. You didn't want to leave. It made you realize you had something to lose. You had something to lose.

If your nightmares from years before were manifested through the fear of being identified (see: Deportation), this one made it clear for the first time that you didn't want to leave. That you had something else to lose other than your family. This realization scares you.

Alien bodies like atoms:

Invisible yet indispensable, and any attempt to split us apart from our chosen families and communities is akin to a declaration of war (both within Congress's purview). Alien bodies becoming ghosts: unable to rest, existing fitfully (how long until we become vengeful spirits?).

Delivering the unanimous decision in *Chae Chan Ping v. United States*, Justice Field declares: "Those laborers are not citizens of the United States; they are ▮▮. That the government of the United States, through the action of the legislative department, can exclude ▮▮ from its territory is a proposition which we do not think open to controversy" (1889).

Four years later, in *Fong Yue Ting v. United States*, Justice Gray writes: "'Deportation' is the removal of an ▮▮ out of the country simply because his presence is deemed inconsistent with the public welfare, and without any punishment being imposed or contemplated. . . . " (1893). Dissenting,

Justice Brewer states: "Deportation is punishment. It involves—First, an arrest, a deprival of liberty; and, second, a removal from home, from family, from business, from property" (1893).

A Number:

The A▮ number is necessary for the im/migrant's family and advocates to identify, track, and fight for their humanity amid an immigration system that dehumanizes and erases the im/migrant through systems of incarceration, detention, and deportation. While legal permanent residents, foreign nationals who are residing in the United States, also have A▮ number for various residency and employment purposes. For most undocumented migrants, the ascription of an A▮ number signals a shifted state of being hidden from white settler government to detection, at the discretion of the state.

The A▮ Number is a tool used by the white settler state to track and identify im/migrant subjects deemed unwanted and removable. In ascribing an A▮ number to the undocumented im/migrant, the deportation policy dictates an "invisible enemy," and the im/migrant is no longer "invisible" (Ngai 2004). Through the A▮ Number, the white settler state tracks the im/migrant, using the latest surveillance technology, recording fingerprints (FIN #) of migrants in the Department of Homeland Security (DHS) database (See: Deportation). Arranged in nine-digit numbers, similar to the nine-digit Social Security number undocumented im/migrants often hope to obtain, the A▮ number is counter to the possibility of staying in the settler nation as a protected resident.

Appear, Notice to:

If the migrant fails to appear, the judge may proceed to hear the case in absentia. The paper is signed off by a field officer director, sent to an address on file through the US Postal Service. If you move from place to place a lot, if the mail gets lost and the postal worker does not understand how important such documents can be, no amount of pleading will help you find it. The structure of the document and the implication of its process raises crucial questions around the individualization of defense and discretion: 1) migrants must prove their worth in front of an immigration judge, prove their "significant" ties in the United States, prove they have built a life here through family, church, civil society (access to legal representation is not considered); 2) constructed fear around im/migrants expedites removal and warps statutory laws; due process is a staged performance. Racialized people line up in rows, hands cuffed, all wearing thin orange uniforms, judge reads script, "do you understand the charge against you, the maximum punishment, and your individual rights?" Judge is not listening, judge follows script, "how do you plead? Guilty or not guilty?" Judge decides, *Culpable, Culpable, Culpable.*²

B:

Bed

quotas to fill	visionary
double, twin, queen	site of resistance³, site of organizing
from 2009 to 2017, at any given time, 34,000 im/migrants must fill the beds	Jennicet Gutiérrez of La Familia: Trans Queer Liberation Movement
	INTERRUPTING, DISRUPTING because she needed to be heard.
in detention centers	Why did no one hear her until then?

Boats; Or, the Ocean Is Another Border

How do we hold all the lives on boats and ships across colonial and imperial history?

Afro-Caribbean lesbian writer M. Jacqui Alexander tells us, "Ocean will reveal the secrets that lie at the bottom of its silted deep. She requires no name before her. Not Pacific, not Atlantic, not Arctic, not Southern, not Indian. She is simply her watery translucent self, reaching without need of compass for her sisters whomever and wherever they are. She will call you by your ancient name, and you will answer because you will not have forgotten. Water always remembers" (2005, 285).

Above water, President Carter deployed the labeled Laotian, Cambodians, and Vietnamese displaced by US imperialism as "boat people" in 1978.

Above water, the "Wet Foot, Dry Foot" policy of 1995 simplifies Caribbean histories, masking the Bush- and Clinton-era policy that held Haitians and Cubans in hostage at Guantánamo Naval Base, blurring puppeteer's strings between post–Cold War politics that defined humanitarian rescue and threatening migrants.

Above water, the International Organization for Migration notes that deaths of migrants in the Mediterranean Sea have soared in the first eight months of 2016.

Above water, the nation-states re-border, building border walls with electrified fences to keep the disenfranchised out, while the international corporations poison lands, rivers, oceans, and the sky.

And the water rises, while the Pacific and the Caribbean islands claimed by imperial powers are sinking. The empires building electric fences on their re-bordered lands hold zero accountability for the lives once again displaced, lost, and drowning.

"When you sing to this ocean, our ghosts will sing back."[4]

Border/Binaries

Borders are violence inscribed on the land[5] and its people. In upstate New York, Immigration and Customs Enforcement (ICE) and Customs and Border Protection (CBP) officials board Amtrak and Greyhound buses, racially profiling Black and non-Black people of color, demanding that they produce immigration papers. Just as the southern border splits the ancestral Tohono O'odham land into two, the US-Canada border straddles the Haudenosaunee Confederacy. In her memoir *A Mind Spread Out on the Ground,* Tuscarora author Alicia Elliot writes, "Indigenous people are almost always put in a position where they're displaced in their own land." Elliot reminds me that Indigenous peoples are the first group of people to be subjected to US immigration policies: deported from their own lands and forced to assimilate.

Border imperialism (Walia 2013) has split the world in two, but as a friend once taught me: all binaries offer false choices, whether they are border, gender, or linguistic binaries. A shift in worldview is needed to bridge the rupture, to suture the alien/nation caused by border imperialism. There is no "us," and there is no "them." There is not even a "we," because all pronouns center the human experience. Is there a word in the English language that manages to both de-center the human experience and capture our interconnectedness to the land and other living beings? Can we learn to make the world, and ourselves, whole again?

C:

Camps

How many camps should we name, list, map, to convince you that holding people in the confines of camps is inhumane?

Off the coast of Italy, there is a zone of immobilized migrants: Lampedusa (immigrant detention) Camp.

Chosen Family/Calderas That Hold

In the near future, your hands are holding the warm pita bread as you break it in half to dip into freshly made hummus. "The key is to peel the chickpea for a soft consistency," she will let us in on the secret as she spreads the hummus with the back of the spoon, creating calderas that hold olive oil.

Breaking bread is an idiom that means to eat a meal, especially in companionable association with others, to distribute or participate in communion. The term occurs often in the New Testament. So the room full of delinquent dykes will sit around the table breaking warm pita bread over hummus and the best shakshouka in all of Boston. They will roar in laughter, talking about labor distribution around the house, keeping a good home, errands, and bickering over the details of who said what during the proposal.

We
A were
B are
C will be
D all of the above

living life.

Citizenship[6]

The story of citizenship on this stolen land resides in the US Constitution, in its infamous description of enslaved people as "three fifths of all other Persons." Nikole Hannah-Jones, creator of the 1619 Project, writes about this in her Pulitzer-winning essay: "Our democracy's founding ideals were false when they were written. Black Americans have fought to make them true." She says:

> Through centuries of black resistance and protest, we have helped the country live up to its founding ideals. And not only for ourselves—black rights struggles paved the way for every other rights struggle, including women's and gay rights, immigrant and disability rights. (Hannah-Jones 2019)

As an im/migrant, I cannot think about citizenship without considering race and racism and settler-colonialism. Because the Civil Rights movement led to the passage of the 1965 Immigration Act, which removed race-based quotas (Hannah-Jones 2019). The landmark *Brown v. Board of Education* ruling was later cited in *Plyer v. Doe*, which "guarantees all children, regardless of immigration status, equal access to basic public education" (Romero 2012).

In the past few years, I've been thinking about whether or not I want to (or need to) obtain US citizenship. *If* I wanted to see my father back in Jakarta during his lifetime, *if* I wanted to be able to provide my mother with her own safe haven, and *if* I wanted to travel and see the world—then yes, I would need to obtain US citizenship.

But what if we expand our imagination beyond the singular answer? Professor Elizabeth Ellis (2018) reminds me that there are 573 nations whose claims to Turtle Island precede that of the United States. The words of Gustav Landauer come to mind: "The state is a social relationship" (Kuhn 2010, 214). I am reminded that queer folks have always built relationships and families outside of state definitions.

What if we begin by imagining a world where we've already won, when we break through concrete and prison bars, and we are reunited with our biological and chosen families? What would the world feel like when we tend our splintered hands and, finally, belong to the land and each other? Shall we begin there?

D:

Deportation, Order of:

Within migrant communities, when we speak of deportation orders in an alert tone with a desperate call for help, "I just got my deportation order in the mail," it signals the removal proceedings before an immigration judge, which are initiated by issuance of a Notice to Appear (NTA). And the fear creeps through the process of writing a coherent legal, theoretical, and historical document. Fear of looking at a document that may one day have your name, your A▇ number, your address, or your siblings' or your parent's personal information. (See: Notice to Appear.)

The US Citizenship and Immigration Services (USCIS) defines deportation as "the formal removal of an ▇ from the United States when the ▇ has been found removable for violating the immigration laws. Deportation is ordered by an immigration judge without any punishment being imposed or contemplated."[7] (Read: *Fong Yue Ting*.) A deportation order then signals that the migrant has been found and the removal proceedings have been initiated.

Deportation is one of those words that is both historically laden and exceedingly quotidian. The simultaneity denotes a normalized violence against im/migrants.

What would it mean to call out an act of the state as compulsory?

Nicholas De Genova emphasizes, "if there were no borders, there would be no migrants—only mobility" (De Genova 2013).

E:

Empires turning people into ghosts:

The US government deports people to countries they have no connection to, have never been to, without proper travel documents ("Smuggled Into Exile," 2016).

Empire State

Read: "Manhattan is a Lenape word," by Natalie Diaz.

F:

From Families Separated and Migrants Harmed by US Deportation Policy[8]

To the President of the United States
To the United States Congress
To the Department of Homeland Security
To the Bureau of Population, Refugees and Migration

To criminal defense attorneys who advised their non-US citizen clients to take plea deals without understanding how it would lead to their eventual deportations; to the unscrupulous members of our "community" who prey on the hopeful; to the well-intentioned but overworked nonprofit lawyers who failed to consider Special Immigrant Juvenile Status (SIJS) for those who did not qualify for DACA:

We hold you accountable—not for "failing us," but for playing the part you were assigned: a bureaucrat. Every person who has been deported must have recounted their stories and asked for relief countless times. Their case files must have been read by several people, yet none of you saw them as human beings, only as an A▮▮▮ Number. To be deported.

We hold you accountable.

G:

Georgia

The Georgia license plate on the wall carries the tag number associated with an arrest warrant: Fugitive.[9]

Your license tag has been renewed all these years because the renewal practice occurs through a mail order. Back when we used to move around often, your appa fretted that the mail forwarding system would lose the renewal paper. If you had lost it, you'd have to go to the office in person with an expired ID. Which would mean they would find out you shouldn't be driving anymore. No more registered vehicle means no means of life. Somehow, you managed. Although it all came to an abrupt halt after the 2016 election and the 2017 car collision.

Your appa is tired of this economic reality and institutional system in Korea and in the United States. Call it neoliberalism, call it capitalism, but he is tired of being pushed away, and around, between limited options. None of which are really livable options. "Protection" seems facetious. Protection from what, but a practice of claiming. Ownership.

Appa, if you don't like Korea or the United States, where would you go? Where do you belong? Where would you feel safe to make life?

The Oxford English Dictionary defines "fugitive" as a noun, a person who has escaped from a place, or is in hiding; especially to avoid arrest or persecution. Adjective: quick to disappear, fleeting.

To enact the ▮▮▮ Immigration Reform and Enforcement Act of 2011 in "relating to offenses against public order and safety," the Georgia House Bill detailed, "A person who is acting in violation of another criminal offense and who knowingly conceals, harbors, or shields an ▮▮▮ ▮▮▮ from detection in any place in this state, including any building or means of transportation, when such person knows that the person being concealed, harbored, or shielded is an ▮▮▮ ▮▮▮, shall be guilty of the offense concealing or harboring an ▮▮▮ ▮▮▮."[10]

Conceals, harbors, or shields—you are quick to disappear, you are fleeting.

The state civil court sets the bond for an undocumented immigrant at $25,000. The immigrant is held in detention for an indefinite time.

Guantánamo Bay

where even US citizenship won't protect you from torture.[11]

H:

Home

My dear feminist warriors & queer comrades,
we've learned that holding each other close is sometimes the only way not to feel so alone and isolated
we've learned that, in learning to hold each other, we too can, and often do, inflict violence (& cycles of trauma) normalized in this uncaring world.
Caring courageously in such a world is articulated as a risk.
Take these risks courageously,

such risks are worth taking.
we are the revolutionary power, and we cannot do this without each other.

J:

Joy

In a private conversation with Lauren Q. for the podcast "A Revolutionary Love Letter: To All Migrants, past, present, and future," we spoke about how we found organizing spaces because we felt a sense of lacking. Lacking community, lacking space to see ourselves mirrored back at us, lacking the language to name what we once had but now lost.

But out of that sense of lacking, we found/find/will continue to find

1. You
2. I
3. reflected in each other

Lauren Q. reminds us, "Joy is very much the thing that keeps people in organizing spaces [and] once that joy is gone, it's pretty much just as messed up as any other systems in place right now that we're trying to dismantle."[12]

Organizing has taught me that, together, we can weather any storm. Mutual aid groups have always existed. My chosen families have taught me that perhaps home isn't a physical location, but in the ways that we feel rooted to, and responsible for, each other. In the ways that I allow my life to become inevitably tangled with yours. In the ways that I am a witness to your life, as you are to mine.

M:

"Migrate to me,"[13] Poet Kemi Bello reminds you.

P:

Papers

Colloquial for money, or immigration papers, legalization process. Read: *Bone* by Fae Myenne Ng.

What does it mean when you must carry papers to prove yourself, to validate your existence, that you have the right to exist here? "US forms of documentation, from the slave pass, to sailors' passports, to free papers, were a means of furthering the surveillance of people of color within the US" (Fukushima 2019).

Why does paper carry so much weight? Anti-racist poet Minnie Bruce Pratt reminds you how important it is to sustain queer archives.

Palimpsests

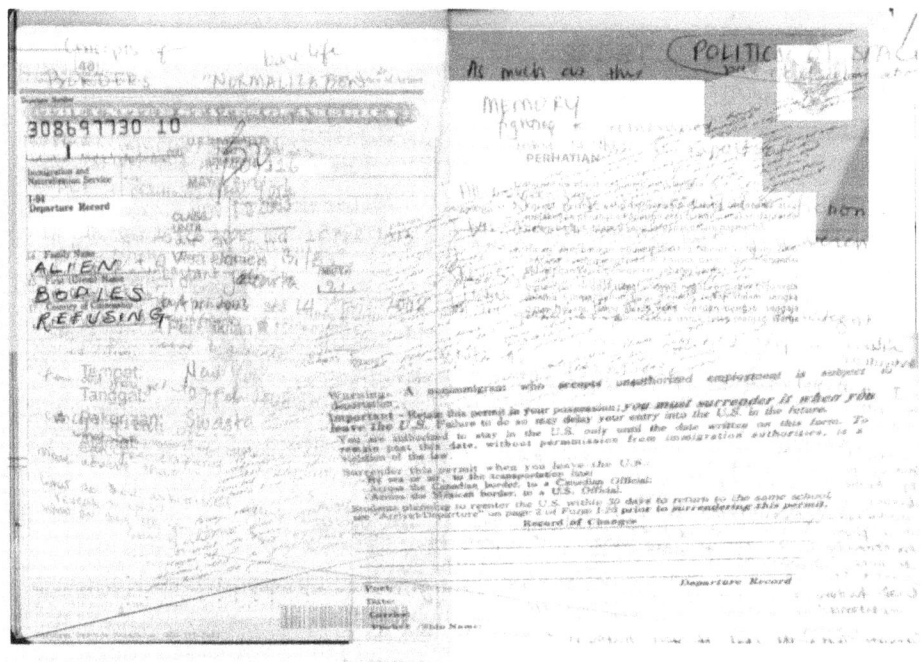

FIGURE 11.1. Image of ten documents. Composited by Angel Sutjipto.

Paranoia

Living in a constant state of; Necessary for survival.

Photographs

In 1850, Harvard Professor Louis Agassiz commissioned daguerreotypes of enslaved people, among them Renty and Delia Taylor. It's 2019, Ms. Lanier and her daughter want the photo of their ancestor Papa Renty freed from the colonial plantation chattel enterprise (Hartocollis 2019).

Harvard Peabody Museum is once again at the center of this debate, after a researcher found the photos again in the museum's attic. In the context of conquest and colonization, photography becomes a "technological device" to "record the remnants of that defeat" (Siegel 2011, 79). What does it mean for a colonial enterprise to fight for the photographs against the wishes of the family members? Amid the lawsuit, Harvard has a new publication based on the photographs of Renty Taylor, among many others, and a proposal for a traveling exhibition planned to launch in 2022. The word traveling leaves a bitter taste in your mouth. You think of all the traveling freak shows in the early nineteenth century that also operated according to the perceived superiority of the able-bodied white race and you remember the names of Saartjie Baartman, Millie and Christine McKoy, and wonder: who gets to decide what is "preserved" (memory/family history) for whom, and why? Your ears remember the voice of poet Diana Ferrus when she read the line, "I've come to take you home—"[14] (See: Home).

In a conversation with A, you talked about why one takes photos of people, of buildings, of objects, and things. How "capturing" moments, a person in a moment, from an archival stance could embody all the racist, sexist, heteromasculine, colonial, ableist practices. But capturing can also mean a way for us to grasp at time. Trying to capture things we cannot. Creating our own dissenting, queer archives.

You love photos. You love taking photos of flowers, of the moon, of random signs and notes on the street, sidewalks, and buses. When you were younger, you had an emergency bag you would grab in case of an ICE raid or a house fire. It was heavy from photos you wanted to take. You realize that you are afraid of losing your memory. You are afraid that the years of stress and anxiety will erase your memories, memories of people, of places, of moments. You take photos to remind yourself of the beauty and joy in the present moment. Your technological devices are always alerting you to buy more storage. You hoard memories and you are learning: sometimes letting go is also an important lesson.

T:

Time

"Control people's time and you control their reality," one of your mentors will say. For those of us who are targeted by the state—Black bodies, Indigenous bodies, migrant bodies, queer bodies, disabled bodies—we have a complicated relationship to time.

A lifetime stolen/

serving time.

A lifetime walking/

the tightrope of blurred memories,
dreams, and hopes that persist.

A lifetime running/

> out of time: to find a job to pay for the lawyer, to file the application, to enroll the children in school, to schedule a doctor's appointment, to file an appeal.

When time is all we have/when time is taken from us by white supremacy, settler-colonialism, xenophobia, homophobia, and ableism—we invent new joyous ways to steal our time back. We are time-travelers.

Trains[15]

Filmmaker Miko Revereza said in an interview: "On the train, everyone is telling their neighbor their life story. You get to see what modern fugitivism looks like and how mundane it looks. . . . We travel along the same arteries as the constant flow of commodities—countless shipping containers in passing: lumber, coal, corn, rice, french fries, pharmaceuticals, phosphate, gravel, footwear. . . . " (Cronk 2019).

As you buy the Amtrak ticket, you remember recent reports from networks of concerned friends and comrades: Border Patrol agents started to check identifications, again.[16] You remember the Chinese labor running under the tracks of the Transcontinental Railroad. You remember how Chinese im/migrants concocted subversive networks for identifications to make a life in the white settler land; they were called "Paper Sons." You worry about your mother taking a cross-country trip from the West Coast to the East Coast of this stolen land for your college graduation. You regret, for a moment, attending college so far away.

On February 19, 1942, with Executive Order 9066 signed by FDR, more than 120,000 Japanese Americans were forcibly removed from their homes to military barracks, traveling hundreds of miles on trains to camps. In the picture by Clem Albers, Cold War politics does a good job separating US cruelty from the same racist mechanisms that justified all genocide that happened before. Even just two months before this photo, Nazi leadership, under the guise of resettlement and "deportation," filled their freight trains en route to "killing centers" via the European rail system.

You wonder about the list of items inside those shipping containers that Revereza listed: the lumber, coal, corn. Who tended the lands before extraction, and who works the land, under whose command, whose labor is exploited, whose temporary work visa expired, who is standing in front of the hot boiling oil making the french fries, timing between the frozen chicken patties while the children at home anxiously wait for dinner, who is skipping a trip to the doctor's because insulin prices went up again, how many

FIGURE 11.2. Two photos by Clem Albers dated 1942. Left photo with the inscription "Los Angeles-Japanese leaving." Right photo with the inscription "Santa Anita, B-414, Japanese Arrival from San Pedro." Central Photographic File of the War Relocation Authority Series, 1942 – 1945 Records of the War Relocation Authority, 1941–1989 (Record Group 210), National Archives.

overtime hours get uncounted for the im/migrant seamstresses working on a shipment deadline, which parts of the electrical boards came from China or Tijuana?

You learned in a college classroom about Karl Marx's concept of commodity fetishism and wonder how Western liberal consumers are unable to see workers from the Global South as full human beings. As in, even the category of "worker" is abstracted through labor theories, preference for success stories, and exceptionalism.

W:

Wellness[17]

"And how temporary is temporary when the damage is thousands of years? It's damage so permanent in terms of environment and spirit, there's no way to pay for it."—Marshallese elder[18]

As the coronavirus spread, and the xenophobia resurfaced, your appa reads the newspapers on rich, first-world countries sending sponsored planes to fly out their citizens safely (and contained) out of China. It made you think of the Vietnam War, and how the US military personnel fled while the poor war-torn people were left to suffer and die. Your appa says to you, "It's very scary to not have a country of belonging in a world system like this. No national belonging means no national protection. No home place to return, no people or government who will stand up for you. You are lost and left to be treated like life not worth anything." And you think of all the Muslim lives under scrutiny in India, Haitians in the Dominican Republic being stripped of their citizenship, the Central Americans in Mexico, and the immigrant families in Italy. Your appa says to you, "I don't want that for you. Whether it's going back to Korea and reestablishing your citizenship there (socially, culturally, economically, and politically) or gaining citizenship here...." Xenophobic scare of a virus strain made your appa open up his concerns about citizenship, nationality, and belonging. The funny thing about the coronavirus is that, aside from the disproportionate fear mapped onto racialized subjects, microorganisms like virus strains have no national borders or boundaries. And in nations whose health care systems prioritize profit over life, like the United States, people are bankrupted by medical bills if hospitalization is required; otherwise, they pay with their lives. So, you wonder, who will pay for that exclusive plane ride out of China? Who is paying for the medical screenings at the border? Who has health insurance that will cover preexisting conditions rooted in environmental racism, economic discrimination, and imperial history?

Work authorization/working under the table[19]

The racialized migrant upon entry is recognized as a (reserved/always plentiful/disposable) able-bodied laborer; when the existence of one's life is reduced to its labor (authorized or otherwise). See: Transcontinental Railroad; see: Asian American Indentured Laborers; see: Bracero Program; see: United Farm Workers and the Delano Grape Strike; see: how they transplanted laborers from Puerto Rico to Hawaii through deception; see: how after decades of working under the table, the aged migrants with a bad back, a limp, a coughing-fit are deported to an economy that will not receive them kindly. Never kindly.

Also, see: your mother, still working during the pandemic.

In New York City, your mother worked in supermarkets, delis, and restaurants. Places that are always hiring workers, paid in cash at the end of the week. Workers who wouldn't complain about standing on their feet for twelve hours without proper breaks. Workers who wouldn't fuss if they noticed the math didn't add up right. Workers who wouldn't know what a union meant.

Worth

You are worthy of.

Notes

1. In a court hearing of Anne Hutchinson in 1637, she asked John Winthrop where she was being banished. To which Winthrop answered, "Say no more, the Court knows wherefore and is satisfied." Oscar Handlin in his foreword to William Preston Jr.'s *Aliens and Dissenters: Federal Suppression of Radicals 1903–1933* (1963) also mentions the case of Hutchinson.

2. Taken from audio from a mass trial of immigrants presided over by Judge Ronald G. Morgan, in Brownsville, Texas, on May 10, 2018: See https://theintercept.com/2018/05/29/zero-tolerance-border-policy-immigration-mass-trials-children/.

3. The method of theorizing from the bed derives from Khanmalek and Rhodes 2020.

4. Borgeson 2016.

5. "All borders are acts of state violence inscribed in landscape," write activists Alessandra Moctezuma and Mike Davis, as quoted in Harsha Walia's *Undoing Border Imperialism* (2013), 38.

6. The authors conducted an interview with Harsha Walia on the topic of trains for "A Revolutionary Love Letter" podcast on June 4, 2023. Listen here: https://podcasts.apple.com/ca/podcast/interrogating-citizenship-with-harsha-walia-part-1/id1570742392?i=1000615640653.

7. USCIS entry: https://www.uscis.gov/tools/glossary. (Last Accessed: March 2021)

8. Human Rights Watch 2007.

9. The authors conducted an interview with Dr. Alán Pelaez Lopez on the topic of fugitivity for "A Revolutionary Love Letter" podcast on June 20, 2021. Listen here: https://podcasts.apple.com/us/podcast/on-fugitivity-alien-with-alan-pelaez-lopez/id1570742392?i=1000526162381.

10. Georgia House Bill 87.

11. *Hamdi v. Rumsfeld*, 542 U.S. 507 (2004).

12. Private conversation with Lauren Quijano, a community organizer. While this conversation was recorded, the audio quality prevents us from releasing it as a podcast episode.

13. Bello, Kemi. 2014. Letter to My Family of Displaced Peoples.

14. South African poet Diana Ferrus's *A Poem for Sarah Baartman* (1998) is a tribute to the long, painful history of Sarah Baartman. The poem has gained great recognition as it has been read by French politicians and was published into French law to repatriate the remains of Baartman to South Africa in 2002.

15. The authors conducted an interview with Miko Revereza on the topic of trains for "A Revolutionary Love Letter" podcast on September 19, 2021. Listen here: https://podcasts.apple.com/us/podcast/on-trains-with-miko-revereza-part-1/id1570742392?i=1000535900415.

16. In 2017, Syracuse Workers Center and the Syracuse Rapid Response Team organized actions to deter and condemn Greyhound and Amtrak collaborating with Border Patrol and ICE. On February 26, 2019, Mirko Ralli-Falconi faced

deportation after an encounter with two Border Patrol agents at the Syracuse Regional Transportation Center. His Miranda rights were not read upon his arrest and now he is fighting to have evidence tossed out. Read: https://www.syracuse.com/crime/2019/05/peruvian-immigrant-arrested-at-syracuse-bus-station-border-patrol-didnt-read-my-rights.html. August 20, 2019, Mercedes Phelan is a Black, Puerto Rican US citizen profiled by the CBP while riding a Greyhound bus. Read: https://iacenter.org/2019/08/20/im-migrant-rights-activists-fight-cbp-transportation-checks/.

17. The authors conducted an interview with Soultree Camba on the topic of wellness for "A Revolutionary Love Letter" podcast on July 18, 2021. Listen here: https://podcasts.apple.com/us/podcast/on-wellness-with-soultree-part-1/id1570742392?i=1000529218201.

18. Aguon 2008.

19. The authors conducted an interview with Luna X Moya on the topic of work for "A Revolutionary Love Letter" podcast on November 7, 2021. Listen here: https://podcasts.apple.com/us/podcast/on-work-with-luna-x-moya-part-1/id1570742392?i=1000541006272.

Bibliography

Aguon, Julian. 2008. *What We Bury At Night*. Fort Lauderdale, FL: Blue Ocean Press.

Alexander, M. Jacqui. 2005. *Pedagogies of Crossing: Meditations on Feminism, Sexual Politics, Memory, and the Sacred*. Durham, NC: Duke University Press.

Anzaldúa, Gloria. 1987. *Borderlands: The New Mestiza/La Frontera*. San Francisco: Aunt Lute Book Company.

Bello, Kemi. 2014. "Letter to My Family of Displaced Peoples." In *Dreamers Adrift Secrets & Borders: Our Stories Are All We Have*. Youtube video. https://www.youtube.com/watch?v=vDWMRg34jEk.

Borgeson, Isabella. 2018. *Afterearth*, directed by Jess X Snow. Experimental Documentary.

Chae Chan Ping v. United States. 130 U.S. 581 (1889).

Cronk, Jordan. 2019, April 18. "Interview: Miko Revereza." *Film Comment*, Film at Lincoln Center. https://www.filmcomment.com/blog/interview-miko-revereza/.

"Deportation." *USCIS.gov Glossary*, U.S. Citizenship and Immigration Services, www.uscis.gov/tools/glossary. Last Accessed: October 20, 2020.

De Genova, Nicholas. 2013. "Immigration 'Reform' and the Production of 'Illegality.'" In Cecilia Menjívar and Daniel Kanstroom (eds.) *Constructing Immigrant "Illegality": Experiences, Critiques, and Responses*. New York: Cambridge University Press.

Diaz, Natalie. 2020. Postcolonial Love Poem. Minneapolis, MN: Graywolf Press, 2020.

Elliot, Alicia. 2019. *A Mind Spread Out on the Ground*. Canada: Doubleday Canada.

Ellis, Elizabeth. 2018. "The Border(s) Crossed Us Too: The Intersections of Native American and Immigrant Fights for Justice." *Emisferica* 14(1). https://hemisphericinstitute.org/en/emisferica-14-1-expulsion/14-1-essays/the-border-s-crossed-us-too-the-intersections-of-native-american-and-immigrant-fights-for-justice-2.html.

Ferrus, Diana. 2010. "I've Come to Take You Home (Tribute to Sarah Baartman Written in Holland, June 1998)." Black Venus 2010, Temple University Press, p. 213.

Fong Yue Ting v. United States, 149 U.S. 698 (1893).

Fukushima, Annie Isabel. 2019. "Has Someone Taken Your Passport? Everyday Surveillance of the Migrant Laborer As Trafficked Subject." *Biography* 42(3): 561–585. Doi:10.1353/bio.2019.0060.

Georgia (State). 2011, April. Legislature. Assembly. Illegal Immigration Reform and Enforcement Act of 2011. House Bill 87. 2011–2012 Reg. Sess. 14.

Glissant, Édouard. 1990. *Poetics of Relations*. Ann Arbor: University of Michigan Press.

Hamdi v. Rumsfeld, 542 U.S. 507 (2004).

Hannah-Jones, Nikole. 2019. "America Wasn't a Democracy, Until Black Americans Made It One: The 1619 Project." *New York Times (Online)*.

Hartocollis, Anemona. 2019, March 20. "Who Should Own Photos of Slaves? The Descendants, Not Harvard, a Lawsuit Says." *New York Times*. https://www.nytimes.com/2019/03/20/us/slave-photographs-harvard.html.

Human Rights Watch. 2007, July 16. "Forced Apart: Families Separated and Immigrants Harmed by United States Deportation Policy." Report. https://www.hrw.org/report/2007/07/16/forced-apart/families-separated-and-immigrants-harmed-united-states-deportation.

Khanmalek, Tala, and Heidi Andrea Restrepo Rhodes. 2020. "A Decolonial Feminist Epistemology of the Bed," *Frontiers: A Journal of Women Studies* 41(1): 35–58.

Kuhn, Gabriel, ed. and trans. 2010. *Gustav Landauer Revolution and Other Writings: A Political Reader*. Oakland, CA: PM Press.

McMahon, Julie. 2019, May 14, "Peruvian Immigrant Arrested at Syracuse Bus Station: Border Patrol Didn't Read My Rights." *Syracuse.com*, https://www.syracuse.com/crime/2019/05/peruvian-immigrant-arrested-at-syracuse-bus-station-border-patrol-didnt-read-my-rights.html.

Nathan, Debbie. 2019, May 29. "Hidden Horrors of 'Zero Tolerance' Mass Trials and Children Taken from Their Parents." *The Intercept*, https://theintercept.com/2018/05/29/zero-tolerance-border-policy-immigration-mass-trials-children/.

Ng, Fae Myenne. 1993. *Bone*. Westport, CT: Hyperion Press.

Ngai, Mae M. 2004. *Impossible Subjects: Illegal Aliens and the Making of Modern America*. Princeton, NJ: Princeton University Press.

Pratt, Minnie Bruce. 2019, August 20. "Im/migrant Rights Activists Fight CBP 'Transportation Checks.'" *International Action Center*, https://iacenter.org/2019/08/20/im-migrant-rights-activists-fight-cbp-transportation-checks/.

Preston, William, Jr. 1994. *Aliens and Dissenters: Federal Suppression of Radicals, 1903–1933*. Champaign: University of Illinois Press.

Romero, Anthony D. 2012. "School Is for Everyone: Celebrating Plyler v. Doe." ACLU Blog post. https://www.aclu.org/blog/immigrants-rights/ice-and-border-patrol-abuses/school-everyone-celebrating-plyler-v-doe.

Siegel, James T. 2011. *Objects and Objections of Ethnography*. 1st ed., New York: Fordham University Press.

"Smuggled Into Exile: Immigration and Customs Enforcement's Practice of Deporting Non-Citizens without Valid Travel Documents." Families for Freedom. Report. 2015, 30 September. https://familiesforfreedom.org/resources/smuggled-exile-immigration-and-customs-enforcement%E2%80%99s-practice-deporting-non-citizens.(Last accessed: March 2021)

Tuck, Eve, and C. Ree. 2013. "A Glossary of Haunting." In *Handbook of Autoethnography*, 639–658. Walnut Creek, CA: Left Coast Press.

Walia, Harsha. 2013. *Undoing Border Imperialism*. Oakland, CA: AK Press.

Walia, Harsha. 2020. *Border & Rule*. Chicago: Haymarket Books Press.

12

Warrior Butterflies Walking with the Ancestors
Xicanx Indigenous Youth Becoming Leaders of Transformational Justice

CUEPONCAXOCHITL D. MORENO SANDOVAL,
MIRIAM G. VALDOVINOS, ELISA CONTRERAS,
and XOCHITL E. LÓPEZ ANDRADE

Upon landing, the aromas of Mexico's ancient earth immediately traveled bidirectionally into our DNA structure, activating meridians between our bodies and the territory. We, the Anahuakenyxs, traveled for one week to ancestral Mother Lands of Teotihuacan and Tenochtitlan in August 2011. Anahuakenyxs are a collective body of eighteen individuals including grandmothers, high school students (in 2011) and family members, public school educators, and researchers, of which four of us write this manuscript together. Most of us carry the lineages of Mexican Indigenous Nations. We began our journey to Tenochtitlan, also known as Mexico City, together. We arrived at *El Zócalo*, un *ombligo del universo Tenochtitlanteco*, to pay our respects, and to thank the land for receiving us. When we entered this belly button, we made offerings of gratitude for this ancestral territory that continues to teach us so much about living, learning, and dying in the world.

Seeing the *sala de comidas ancestrales* in *El Templo Mayor* helped us realize the nourishment we continue to receive from our ancestors in the foods we still consume across generations. Salmón (2012) asserts that eating the landscape is riddled with food identities and resilience. These foods sealed our relationships to the land, our ancestry, our native science (Cajete, 2005) practices, and each other. Our ancestors domesticated the corn from careful observation and experimentation; from wild grass to the wide varieties of biodiversity of corn that have kept our ancestors alive for centuries (Dunbar-Ortiz, 2014). We are what we eat, we taste what our ancestors tasted, and we commune with the growing of our foods as we continue to live in this world.

Activating ancestral identities for youth promotes firmly rooted agencies toward co-liberation.[1] This research examines the influences and outcomes of an educational pilgrimage to Tenochtitlan[2] and Teotihuacan[3] by the Anahuakenyxs,[4] a collective of Xicanx, Zapotec, Purépecha, and Huichol Indigenous intergenerational organizers. The journey promoted a warrior butterfly (Berlo, 1983; Browder, 2005) spirit, a process of unearthing ancestral knowledge systems (AKS) (Moreno Sandoval et al., 2016) that draw from a fountain of being and knowledge older than colonialism, remembering the old ways of our ancestors in today's context, healing medicine in the face of colonial disdain while nurturing collective dignity and radical love. Ancestral knowledge systems refer to the collective wisdom, beliefs, and practices passed down through generations within a community or culture. These systems often encompass traditional ways of understanding the world, including spiritual, ecological, and societal aspects. In the aforementioned case of communing with food, ancestral knowledge systems on foodways include passing down recipes, knowledge about planting, caretaking and harvesting foods, and food memories, for example.

For us Anahuakenyxs, the warrior butterfly (Taube, 2018; Taube, 2000) spirit is a two-fold process: on the one hand, a warrior spirit is one that honors a spiritual discipline that is needed to survive and thrive in present-day colonization. At the same time, a butterfly is a keen example of transformation. How might a warrior butterfly metaphor inspire the transformative power of dismantling dominant ideologies, healing from intergenerational traumas, and standing with courage to walk a dignifying path of revitalizing ancestral epistemologies? A warrior butterfly 1) acknowledges the continuous impacts of colonial, systemic oppression, 2) engages in sacred warfare to counter internal and external colonial systems, 3) minimizes fear-based ideologies, 4) fosters liberation through a process of unwavering perseverance and transformation, and 5) roots itself in AKS and community.

This research examines a fourteen-year relationship (2009–2023) of implementing a culturally sustaining, community-based research program involving a high school student-led organization, Movimiento Estudiantil Chicanos de Aztlán (MEChA), that partnered with a transnational nonprofit organization, Conservation of the American Pyramids, to design and participate in a 2011 educational journey to the Mother Lands. We conducted a community-centered autoethnographic research study whose findings indicate that Indigenous youth nurtured their co-liberation via connection to their ancestral identities and critical agencies *over time*. We also invited the warrior butterflies who engaged in this work to be co-authors of this work

FIGURE 12.1. "Warrior Butterflies," Tepantitla Mural of Teotihuacan, approximately 450 CE. Photograph by K. Taube.

FIGURE 12.2. Los Anahuakenyxs excavating in Teotihuacan. Photograph by Xochitl Esperanza.

with us. Two responded to our invitation as co-authors. In this chapter, we describe the tenets of culturally sustaining pedagogies, the 2011 educational journey, and its aftermath highlighted in 2020 follow-up interviews.

During our pilgrimage, we were supported by mentors Rudy Dueñas, Jonathan Malagon, and Cueponcaxochitl (author) to define *our own* relationships to Indigenous cultural practices. In our recent conversations with Lxs Anahuakenyxs, we were reminded that access to decolonial knowledge and cultural activation are necessary components of identity formation, agency development, and holistically sustaining health. We emphasize that the pilgrimage catalyzed the continual forming of a chrysalis by youth to assert their passions to be agents of cultural production, conservancy, transformation, and sustainability.

We engaged in educational excursions focused on history, artifacts, museums, and archaeological sites, along with arts, music, and creative activities *in Xochitl In Cuicatl* (Flor y Canto/Flower and Song), and nurturing relationships and community between the Anahuakenyxs and elders. We visited the temples (pyramids) of Teotihuacan and had the great honor of working alongside elders, archaeologists, cultural preservationists, and curators. We were among the ancient guardians of ancestral knowledge encoded in the life-giving force of the butterflies that crossed our paths, the trees that stand tall, and the foods that never consented to colonization. We walked through the sacred sites of Teotihuacan and noticed the warrior butterflies in one of the murals. Some of us spoke about these butterflies and immediately connected to them. This pilgrimage to the Mother Land could not have been possible without the long-standing relationships with the elders who guided us on our journey.

The activities our elders organized were intentionally oriented toward revitalizing AKS in active and creative ways that were healing for many of us. The elders hosting us organized *danza Mexica* lessons that exposed us to a deeper understanding of the history and traditions of *danzantes* as well as the significance of the instruments that are a part of ceremonial dances. We visited a family who were painters in the town of San Juan for multiple generations and taught us how to make and use ancient paint materials. We painted on handmade *papel de amate* and made pottery. During these art lessons, we were given tools that reminded us that we are artists in our own right, and that *arte cura* (art heals). Working the clay with our hands and seeing the oven fire solidify the shape of our creations helped us give life to the color of our warrior butterfly wings. Re-centering AKS advances a decolonial approach to living and learning.

Culturally sustaining education is essentially absent from current public education policy (Paris & Alim, 2017; McCarty & Lee, 2014), and, when present, often under attack (Kunnie, 2010). Curriculum created to address this void is usually situated in Ethnic Studies (De los Ríos, López, and Morrell, 2015/2016; Morrell, Dueñas, Garcia, and López, 2015). Underserved Black, Indigenous, Students of Color (BISOC) routinely face the no-win conundrum of assimilating or acculturating. When a student is pressured to assimilate through dehumanizing school norms, this student is sent overt and covert messages that pressure them to divorce themselves from their community, culture, and self by rejecting their cultural knowledge and participating in Eurocentric approaches to living and learning. While writing this manuscript (October 2022), we experienced pervasive anti-Blackness and anti-Indigeneity from Los Angeles city council members. How can political leaders be held accountable for uplifting Black and Indigenous experiences and scholarship? Culturally sustaining pedagogies offer students a multi-dynamic and multiplicitous means to reclaim AKS and thrive. A culturally sustaining education honors and helps students and their families preserve their wholeness in educational settings (Paris & Alim, 2017) by nurturing an "inward gaze" (McCarty & Lee, 2014). Following the guidance of Cherrie Moraga (2011), we assert that "Our preconquest imaginations offer strategies for building self-sustaining societies today, societies that can disrupt the mass suicide of global consumption, engineered by the empire of the United States" (p. 80). To enact culturally sustaining education, we facilitated a means to connect with AKS through an educational journey to Tenochtitlan and Teotihuacan. This chapter reflects on this experience and follow-up interviews that occurred ten years later with seven of the twelve participants.

Central to revitalizing AKS is keeping the fires of sacred intergenerational relationships burning. These intergenerational stories remind us that our communities are still blooming in the face of unrelenting attempts to colonize and that our communities continue to thrive as warrior butterflies who maintain a sense of dignity in the face of ongoing colonial disdain. The elders guiding this process gave us space to wholeheartedly be ourselves regardless of gender identity, sexuality, cultural identity, and Tribal identity, and to confront conventional Eurocentric standards of beauty. Though conversations about anti-Blackness were not central in our travel experience, because as non-Black Native people born in the United States, we have the privilege to disengage, our group continues to find ways to engage with and counter anti-Blackness and anti-Indigenous actions and rhetoric that plague the communities in which we grew up.

Positioning Ourselves

As four Indigenous muxeres and gender non-conforming individuals, we draw from decolonial Indigenous feminist theories and methods (see Theoretical Framework). We have lived dehumanizing experiences in schools that attempted to erase our cultural and spiritual identities, so it is crucial that we speak and act from authentically rooted scholarship to produce more grounded cultural work.

We introduce ourselves as a way to continue nurturing relationality and transparency in our cultural work. From our positionalities, we engage in the personal, spiritual, and intellectual investment of our place in the world, and our relationships with Earth and our relatives (human and non-human, living and nonliving). It is through this hunger to dignify and nurture our ancestral identities that we share how we navigate the world. These positionalities spawned our growth as *individuals connected to community for co-liberation*.

Cueponcaxochitl (she/they): My name means "blossoming flower" in Nahuatl. The interweaving of my personal, professional, and academic lives has welcomed this creative blending as a decolonizing process of healing from intergenerational wounds. I was invited to co-sponsor MEChA in 2009 at Wilson High School in El Sereno, where five generations of my family have lived. As an undergrad, I studied abroad in Tenochtitlan in 2000, and later (2008) was introduced to ceremonial community in Teotihuacan (Headrick, 2007; Manzanilla, 1996). When I heard the MEChistA students wanted to learn more about their Mexican Indigenous cultures, I contacted the elders in my ceremonial family to meet the students' hunger for learning. Together, we made magic happen.

Miriam (she/her/ella): I was born on the ancestral lands of the Tongva people, now Anaheim, California. My parents migrated from Michoacán, Mexico, in the 1970s. They instilled a cultural pride that included eating ancestral foods, speaking Spanish, and centering a Mexican nationalist sentiment. As a youth, I felt disconnected from my Indigenous roots even though my maternal grandfather was one of our P'urhépecha elders actively involved with *Pueblos Indígenas*. As an adult, I reconnected with my Indigenous lineage. I met Cueponcaxochitl during our undergraduate years, and she introduced me to the Ananhuakenyx group. I embarked on my own healing and "elder-in-training" journey.

Elisa (she/her): I am the oldest daughter of "undocumented" immigrants from Santa Marta Latuvi, Oaxaca, Mexico. I was born in East Los Angeles, California. When I was five months old, my parents and I migrated back to Oaxaca, and six years later, we migrated back to L.A. in El Sereno, and now with two younger sisters. Adapting to school in the United States was traumatic. I was bullied by my peers for not speaking English, and I struggled to see myself as an intellectual. It wasn't until I became involved with Wilson High School's MEChA and other community organizations that I learned about the socially constructed structures that enable the dehumanization my community, my family, and I experience. My parents worked tirelessly to help fundraise for the trip to Tenochtitlan and Teotihuacan in 2011. The trip was a privilege that to this day is denied to my parents and sisters because of dehumanizing immigration policies in the United States.

Xochitl Esperanza (they/them/ellxs): I am a QTBIPOC, Boyle Heights–born Xicanx Indigenx who grew up and attended schools on Tongva lands—in the village 'Ochuunga, now known as El Sereno (90032). Being raised by my maternal grandparents from mixed Indigenous ancestries of central and western Mexico provided an Indigenous Mexican Roman Catholic* upbringing. Mentorship with community grassroots organizers and teachers (like Wilson High School[5] MEChA) helped nourish the importance of cultural weaving and sustainability. The non-linear work with Lxs Anahuakenyxs inspired me to pursue Ethnic Studies at the University of California. I later was invited to participate in a ceremony on Ohlone Lands (the Bay Area), influencing current health equity work and leading me to work in one of the only Native consulting firms in present-day Los Angeles.

It is our honor to share the voices of our ancestors through us with you, as we continue our journey to activate our agencies for the liberation of marginalized youth and peoples throughout Abiayala.[6] Each one of us was (and is) tied to each other by a *mecate*[7] of flowers, nurtured into existence through our relationships with each other and with the Mother Land that called (and calls) us. As two organizers and two youth leaders of transformational justice, we share a unique collective perspective as participants and researchers. As warrior butterflies, we are guided by our collective desire to decolonize our identities (Mignolo, 2009; Moraga, 2011) and participation in our daily lives, especially, as it relates to our periphery to Latinidad and Chicanidad through naming efforts still needed to dismantle settler colonialism, anti-Blackness, and anti-Indigenous sentiments. For example, the Los Angeles community in 2023 found itself grappling with the fact that three of its elected city council members were exposed using anti-Black/anti-Indigenous/homophobic language. Through this, we see these warrior butterflies organizing in the community to create a space for decolonial systems and inclusive representatives.

Theoretical Framework

Our theoretical considerations stem from our cultural intuition (Delgado-Bernal, 1998) as cultural workers in our personal and academic lives, leading by example. From this place, we turn to Native/Indigenous feminisms to guide our work (Green, 2007). It is through engaging Native feminisms as "foundational to our traditional cultures as well as our revitalizations that we can truly build a future with our past" (Risling Baldy, 2018, p. 31). On a community level, Native feminisms can help inspire a commitment to self-determination to dismantle and "confront the normative gendered and sexed bodies that seek to create Indigenous peoples as 'citizens of the state'"

(Risling Baldy, 2018, p. 30). Indigenous feminism draws on core elements of Indigenous cultures—particularly the nearly universal connection to land, through "relationships framed as a sacred responsibility" and predicated on reciprocity and definitive culture and identity (Green, 2017, p. 5). Furthermore, the f-word (feminism) continues to be contested among Native feminists. Luana Ross (2009) reminds us of this tension and the following: "My indigenous/feminism privileges storytelling as a way to decolonize and empower our communities" (p. 50). Here too, we center the participants' narratives as part of our decolonial practices.

Indigenous feminist epistemologies (Arvin, Tuck, & Morrill, 2013) help us examine the relationality embedded in nurturing positively charged identities and agencies of youth into early adulthood. This is a form of disruption to the bodies of knowledge that continue to reify historically oppressed communities as monolithic groups, and particularly as it relates to expanding the educational opportunities of youth, such as Ethnic Studies. Returning to the knowledge from the people where we originate is imperative when we consider identity and agency and the coming-of-age ceremonies during adolescence and adulthood (Risling Baldy, 2018) in collective community relations. Particularly during the critical developmental time in adolescence and young adulthood, elevating youth promotes the revitalization of AKS as it pertains to identities and agencies.

AKS guides one's connection to ancestors, ancestral homelands (places), traditions, beliefs, and assumptions as a decolonizing research framework to demonstrate subjective epistemologies. Smith (1999/2012) delineates the importance of using research methodologies that decolonize our understanding of how knowledge is incorporated in research and lived experiences. AKS brings to consciousness how knowledge systems and social constructs intersect with power systems (such as colonialism) over time. Further, decolonial theories center relational accountability (Wilson, 2008) and require one to recognize the five phases of decolonization (Laenui, 2000), which are rediscovery and recovery, mourning, dreaming, commitment, and action. We focus on rediscovery and recovery, for these set the foundation for the decolonial journey. In this phase, one reflects on culture, language, identity, relationality, and prioritizing "form over substance" to not reify colonial notions of Indigeneity (Laenui, 2000, p. 3).

The centrality of acknowledging and revitalizing AKS in this research inquiry is not interested in engaging in colonial identity politics. Furthermore, we are not interested in proving our Indigeneity or engaging in the often-lauded "oppression Olympics" to determine who is "more Indigenous." Instead, we assert that we all are inheritors of AKS, Earth languages per se, and that one way to be accountable to Earth is to revitalize and apply these understandings in the present and future. Reawakening AKS is our spiritual practice, unrelenting in its approach to transform intergenerational trauma into radical love. The connection to AKS awakens stored genetic memory. Like neurons sending invitations to these primordial ways of being, these moments of *Conciencia Indígena* (Marín, 2009) during and beyond the 2011 pilgrimage are an unending source of energy and focus for the Anahuakenyxs collective members. This connection and remembering of cellular memory while journeying over sacred sites was central to this process of positive nuanced identity formations. Students bridge their present urban Indigenous identities while anchoring to the timeless ancestral intelligence in AKS, pushing against assimilationist praxis and combating cultural amnesia.

Through participating in community-based skills and ancestral knowledge engagement workshops, organizing culturally engaging assemblies (such as Día de Los Muertos), and collaborating with established community centers (including Proyecto Jardín and East Side Café), students deepened relationships to AKS. Before embarking on our trip, youth, their families, mentors, and community members united to organize fundraisers that made the trip possible. In that process, family members experienced their own transformation as they guided their youth, passing on what they learned from our ancestors and what has been passed down for generations.

Method

We use a critical ethnography approach (Villenas & Foley, 2011; Villenas, 2010) to record some of what emerged during our prolonged community engagement ten years after this process began. This approach doesn't intend to produce a holistic understanding of a culture, often the goal of traditional ethnography. We follow a critical ethnography approach often used by Chicanx scholars, which focuses on revealing and eradicating oppressive relations of power (Trueba, 1999; Villenas & Deyhle, 1999; Zarate & Conchas, 2010). This is rooted in a political intent that is praxis-oriented and connected to historical and experiential knowledge. As Villenas and Foley (2011) stated, this work is "a serious political intent to change people's consciousness, if not their daily lives" (p. 176). We reviewed social media archives and conducted interviews with seven of the twelve young adults who participated in this experience.

Ten years after our educational journey, we asked questions like: Remembering our educational trip to Tenochtitlan and Teotihuacan in 2011, how would you describe its impact on your current identity (how you perceive yourself)? Remembering our trip, how would you describe its impact on your current agency (actions)? Various Indigenous forms of knowing (Smith, 1999) came up as part of these *pláticas,* such as claiming, storytelling, celebrating survival, remembering, Indigenizing, envisioning, returning, and creating the spaces that we often have been excluded from. In the next section, we share some of these narratives.

Prayers in the Flesh // Anahuakenyx Youth Leaders

These narratives that the students shared on the pilgrimage are in part due to the magic of a conspiracy for justice—on behalf of generations of ancestral prayers. Ancestral prayers made tangible through the lives of our participants and mentors. This group is composed of: Woodrow Wilson High School seniors Carolina, Elisa, Josue, and Xochitl E., first-year college students Jason and Cynthia, and mentor Xochitl X., community wellness educator and eldest sister of Carolina and Cynthia. The three sisters bring with them the grace and dreams of their ancestors from the Lands of Aguas Calientes and Ensenada, Mexico, down to El Salvador in Central America. Josue and Jason were fulfilling the dreams of their relatives from Nuevo León and Michoacán, México. As a high school teacher, Elisa now guides her students through the reunification of their ancestral identity and agency. Xochitl Esperanza's post-college work centers on healing equity and fostering inter-community relations.

As Xochitl Ximehua expresses, "The work of the Anahuakenyxs staged intergenerational healing." Years later (ten years until the latest interviews), we find ourselves blessed in leading our communities' fulfilling roles inspired by this pilgrimage and demonstrating the warrior butterfly spirit and its transformative power. Carolina and Cynthia uplift and educate the community in financial literacy as a service manager and personal banker. Josue now writes policies in Washington, D.C., that directly address the issues based on equity distribution to uplift the community.

Walking with the Ancestors

The focus of this chapter is the narratives shared during the 2020 interviews. These illustrate how positive identity formation and critical agency continue to be interwoven ten years later. We share the words of Anita, an elder and lead coordinator for our journey to Anahuac:

> They [participants] realized there is an urgency to transform the way each one of us behaves in order to spread Respect, Gratitude, Honesty and Service. The Historical Amnesia and Cultural Trauma we carry for the past 500 years needs to be healed. The healing begins with study and application of our ancestral essence and roots to understand what we carry in our DNA.

As a witness of the participants' transformations, Anita speaks to the healing that students committed to—stepping unapologetically into their power.

Intertwined with our elder's observations, we were beginning and/or continuing our decolonization process.

In 2020, Jason reminds us that "Knowing our hxstory ... is important in the development of [identity and in] understanding other cultures as well. By knowing ourselves we recognize the other. Much like the philosophy of *In Lak 'Ech*." Through this we reflect(ed) on how the center of Lxs Anahuakenyxs organically became aligned with the Mayan philosophy of *In Lak 'Ech* (*In Lak 'Ech, Hala Ken*—I am you, you are me). This is a philosophy paralleling other Indigenous wisdoms, like that of *Avatamsaka Sutra*, or "interbeing" that translates intertribally.

Anahuakenyx students sustained AKS values. Ten years later, Cynthia explains, "When you can connect to the *root* of [our ancestors] and see where the culture is coming from you get a deeper understanding ... and it's beautiful to identify with your own culture—you get to understand yourself more." Ancestral spaces of thought, heart, and spirit honor the intuition in sacred rhythms of development.

Connection to Indigenous Roots

In documenting our developing perspectives and newfound knowledge, we completed pre- and post-trip questionnaires related to group members' reflections about identity, agency, and wellness. Themes that emerged from these reflections included the importance of strengthening our sense of cultural heritage, connecting and understanding our familial ancestries, internal healing, beginning to understand some of our intergenerational traumas, and relating to others.

The experiences leading up to the trip and pearls of wisdom acquired during the pilgrimage cemented the tie to AKS. There is a continued emphasis on honoring all our relations and, as Carolina expresses, a curiosity "to know the true background of our family and ancestors to help us understand why we do certain things." She refers to the trip and her mentor: "Dueñas made me the person I was in high school, [and working with MEChA and the trip] opened the doors that made me who I am today." Jason writes, "It [the trip] helped me decolonize my mind from the narrative school often taught about the underdeveloped or primitive nature of Native Tribes before European conquest." Elisa critically reflects on her people and her ancestral homelands:

> Latuvi exists because my ancestors resisted slavery, we are the descendants of Zapotecs who refused to live under Spanish control and risked their lives by escaping into other parts of the mountains. My ancestors were smart and creative, ... We still are. I learned that Zapotec means "People of the clouds" and I could clearly see why. ... I was back home, breathing

fresh air, drinking fresh water from the river, enjoying fresh corn, *calabazas* [squash], *chícharos* [peas] and *frijoles* [beans] from my grandma's *terreno* [land], living off the land my ancestors left behind, the land my grandma now nurtured in order to nurture us.

Xochitl Esperanza also shares:

> I found a dope teacher Celia Herrera Rodriguez, . . . being able to work with her was awesome . . . opened relationships with more Indigenous *artivists*, and brought an opportunity [to bridge resources to off-campus community], I am appreciative to all the folks out here still committed to decolonization and for their willingness to guide younger generations, you know—we are really siblings. . . . CoVid-19 has reminded me . . . how much they have tried to separate all of our peoples—This is a reminder of how resourceful, how strong [we are] and all these things that we can be.

Reconnecting to their roots, before and during the pilgrimage, allowed students to further explore their ancestral identities and practices after the trip. For Carolina, she was able to recognize herself as a leader, leading to her current successes. For Elisa, she was inspired to go back and reconnect with her ancestral homeland. For Xochitl Esperanza, they continued to seek out Indigenous teachers and nurture unity among Indigenous communities. Through these reflections of the pilgrimage, we see that it is this reunion with ancestral lands that continues to be the fuel for these leaders of transformational justice and their engagement with revitalizing and strengthening their ties to Indigeneity, while we hold ourselves accountable to the historical and contemporary harm that embodies anti-Blackness and anti-Indigenous beliefs.

Power Activation: Becoming Leaders of Transformational Justice

Reconnecting youth to their Indigenous identities reignited the desire to combat assimilationist narratives and root in AKS. By remembering their Indigenous identities, they allowed themselves to grieve with their ancestors and address the heartbreaks with the abundance available today. Josue states, "Seeing these temples still standing in the face of adversity, being immovable inspired me to work for the U.S. Congress, to always push against these injustices that I witness in my life, in my role, in my periphery." Students became critical of social structures that seek to oppress. They began to see themselves as powerful individuals who have the right to interrogate colonial structures of power. Xochitl Ximehua shares:

> This trip helped me become fearless and trust that I have everything I need inside of me. It also chipped away at all feelings of inadequacy of not

being worthy and filled me with: 1) [Sacred] knowledge, 2) trust in myself and my community, and 3) a longing to continue decolonizing and trauma-informed intergenerational healing.

The three things that Xochitl Ximehua identified as transformational have also been integrated in her healing work that includes art-based interventions to address community health and well-being. The reflections of the youth demonstrate that transformational justice leadership may take various approaches, all while dismantling the colonial structures that are reified in the formal education process. Recognizing our positionality within colonial systems, centering in AKS, and leading with the warrior butterfly spirit allows us to reframe the ways colonial structures, such as the Western educational system, can provide a space to interrogate socially constructed and upheld oppressing ideologies.

Recentering Indigenous identities allowed students to reestablish themselves as the leaders that they are and restored their relationship to themselves and their communities. Xochitl Esperanza speaks to their current activism in their communities as government- and state-sanctioned violence is continuously enforced against Black and Indigenous peoples:

> With my friends, trying to figure out what our roles are as light-skinned Indigenous people in a world where a genocide [of BIPOC] started since colonization—but we are not dying in the same ways, so what does it mean to hold these many truths and still support? That's where I feel a lot of my energy has been in [2020].

While this trip to Tenochtitlan and Teotihuacan was a privilege, it is also a reminder of our responsibility in distributing blessings via resources to our communities, as we have learned a nuanced understanding of what it means to be Indigenous and challenge the anti-Blackness permeating our communities.

In the last ten years, each individual has exercised their agency to reclaim spaces for themselves and their communities. This experience directed participants' areas of study in college and career choices. Students transitioned into their new paths determined to challenge colonialism. Josue shares, "Now being in D.C., my aim is . . . to do what I can to inspire younger generations to change the spaces that they are in." For youth who entered college, decolonial knowledge was vital in the manifestation of their agency. Jason writes, "I became the co-chair of Hermanos where I tried to spread my ancestral knowledge to help Latinos graduate from college." Xochitl Esperanza recounts, "I stayed as a main organizer with Xinachtli throughout my five years at Berkeley, up until 2015, and through that, started finding a lot of Indigenous community that really needed that [financial] support."

Reconnecting these first-generation college students to AKS gave them the agency to reclaim their identities as educators, leaders, and activists in new spaces. As warrior butterflies we inhabit these spaces, understanding that the master's tools will never dismantle the master's house—rather, we visit these spaces to gather resources in our active efforts to nourish sustainable spaces and futures. The impact and realizations that students had during the trip shaped their last ten years and current trajectory of their lives. Participants recall their experience as a reunion with agency, and as reclaiming power of their identities. Xochitl Ximehua says, "It has made me as solid and strong as the stone-figure Coatlicue." Elisa asserts, "My history reminds me to live my life of resilience, I know where I come from and will continue to learn who I am." Josue communicates, "This [AKS] allows [me] to preserve and breathe expansively into who I am—this nucleus for lack of a better word—of my ancestors, and of my people, a nucleus that allows me to pay that forward for someone to be able to also chase and reach their dreams." Xochitl Esperanza remembers, "This is who I am, and it's so powerful to be this flower of hope."

Conclusion

In a sense, the Anahuakenyx journey began long before we took off on the plane to Mexico. Our ancestral dreams sparked our collective quest to remember the broken pieces of our ancestral identities. Anahuakenyx student leaders were already on their path to greatness before the Anahuakenyx collective formed. The educational trip provided us with tangible examples of AKS to actively support cultural institutions and form ancestral identities that nurtured the spinal cord of decision-making. *Unlearning* structures of oppression helped reawaken ancestral memories. Through culturally sustaining pedagogies and Ethnic Studies curricula, we engaged in cultural work that promoted positive identity formations. We remind our readers about the background content that we offered at the beginning of the chapter: "schooling is a site of struggle" (e.g. Grande in Feminist Freedom Warriors, 2018). The cultural work that the Anahuakenyxs engaged in sprouted powerful instantiations of critical consciousness and radical love. What did we learn from organizing an educational pilgrimage and its impact over these last ten years? The following illustrate the wisdom gleaned from ten-year reflections on the impact of the journey to the Mother Lands:

1. Unlearning internalized colonization such as anti-Blackness and anti-Indigeneity. Colorism can be normalized in families and communities in a way that is deeply harmful. Unlearning this ideology requires courage to have uncomfortable and necessary conversations

to dismantle these internalized oppressions. The Anahuakenyx collective was bEarthed from the collective hunger to learn about our ancestral roots and make sense of our ancestral identities. In community, we engaged in unlearning and healing from internalized colonization. Like the warrior butterflies and *Coyolxauhqui* continuously teach us, we choose to remember our parts—to be whole, even when others try to fracture our spirits. The decolonial phases of mourning, dreaming, commitment, and action (Laenui, 2000) continue to show up in our daily practices and relationships. We dream for the children in our lives, the future generations, and our journey in becoming our authentic selves. This commitment and action show up in our relationships with one another, our agency, and our leadership.

2. Relationality matters. We answer the call to nurture relationships even through distance and capitalist pressures of individualism—especially as it relates to intergenerational communities of elders, adults, and youth. We nurtured a collective, family-centered movement, to travel to an epicenter that helps imagine worldviews and lifestyles of our ancestors and learn from their mistakes and wrongs. Our relations are not intended to build another form of superiority that encompasses anti-Blackness in service of Indigenous resurgence. We are intentional in fighting white supremacy and anti-Blackness within our relationships in aspiring to show a different path to ourselves, our children, and future generations.

3. #BeAGoodAncestor. Speaking of leading by example, we are all intergenerationally called to heal intergenerational trauma, act from our highest selves, and be accountable to Earth and to one another. Illustrating a warrior butterfly dance in the art of living and learning is like taking on the form of water. The colonial forces could not make our cells forget—these cells carry the oldest of our memories, memories of waters that have flowed through our people's rivers and fallen from their skies since time immemorial. As land-based peoples forcibly removed, we know that cells in our bodies are how we carry home with us. Our intuitive ancestral intelligence is an intangible sustainability tool that helps us play with time. We imagine ourselves connected to the descendants' forthcoming. What memories will we choose to pass on?

In our process of conducting research and writing together, we enjoyed the conversations we had in creating this labor of radical love. We are grateful for this opportunity to reflect on the last decade, to bring breath to our stories, and for this journey of (re)discovery. We thank the Anahuakenyxs for trusting us to share these intimate narratives. We remain committed to exploring the possibilities and conspiring for justice for all our BIPOC siblings. Culturally sustaining pedagogies in Ethnic Studies curricula have the power to shift the normalized epistemologies in the world. Like the International Council of

Grandmothers, we come together as representatives chosen by our ancestors to sit in our roles to heal forward and back, seven generations. When we heal ourselves, we heal the spirits of those who waited years to peacefully sleep.

Notes

1. We describe co-liberation as a process of elevating freedom from systemic oppression of the Earth, humans, and non-humans for the next seven generations.

2. Tenochtitlan was founded as the center of the Aztec Empire, 1325 CE. Now Mexico City's historic center.

3. Teotihuacan is an extensive Mexican archaeological site. At its zenith (450 CE), among the most populated regional areas.

4. Anahuakenyxs are named after Anahuac, meaning "close to the water" in Nahuatl. Together, we are a group of Xicanx Indigenous youth, researchers, elders, and community members ranging from ages sixteen to seventy-two. We named ourselves Anahuakenyxs with a gender neutral "x" signifier to reclaim ancestral identities in ways that promote gender fluidity, and draw from decolonial approaches to living and learning. The term Anahuakenyx speaks back to imposed Eurocentric structures of identity markers such as "Hispanic," "Latino," and "American," all categories that divorce us from deeply rooted ancestral knowledge systems of Anahuac.

5. Woodrow Wilson High School/Wilson High School in El Sereno; also the campus where the Anahuakenyxs met and conspired for justice.

6. Abiayala is a term originated by the Guna Nation meaning "land in its full maturity." It is currently used to refer to Turtle Island, or the Western hemisphere. Using terms like Tenochtitlan, Turtle Island, and Abiayala asserts the self-determination of Indigenous Nations, unlearning Western colonial classifications. See "The Idea of Latin America" (Mignolo, 2009) for further understanding of how colonial concepts like "Latin America" came to be.

7. Translation: rope.

Bibliography

Arvin, Maile, Eve Tuck, and Angie Morrill. "Decolonizing Feminism: Challenging Connections between Settler Colonialism and Heteropatriarchy." *Feminist Formations* 25, no. 1 (2013): 8–34.

Berlo, Janet Catherine. "In the Warrior and the Butterfly: Central Mexican Ideologies of Sacred Warfare and Teotihuacan Iconography." In *Text and Image in Pre-Columbian Art: Essays on the Interrelationship of the Verbal and Visual Arts,* edited by Janet Catherine Berlo, 79, 180. Oxford University Press, 1983.

Browder, Jennifer Kathleen. "Place of the High Painted Walls: The Tepantitla Murals and the Teotihuacan Writing System." PhD diss. University of California, Riverside, 2005.

Cajete, Gregory. *Native Science: Natural Laws of Interdependence*. Santa Fe, NM: Clear Light Publishers, 2000.

Cajete, Gregory. *Spirit of the Game: An Indigenous Wellspring.* Skyand, NC: Kivaki Press, 2005.

Carty, Linda E., Chandra Talpade Mohanty, and Sandy Grande. Feminist Freedom Warriors. (2018). Available online: http://feministfreedomwarriors.org/watchvideo.php?firstname=Sandy&lastname=Grande (accessed on 23 December 2020).

De los Rios, Cati V., Jorge López, and Ernest Morrell. "Critical Ethnic Studies in High School Classrooms: Academic Achievement via Social Action." In *Race, Equity, and Education,* edited by Pedro Noguera, Jill Pierce, and Roey Ahram, 177–198. Springer, 2016.

De los Rios, Cati V., Jorge López, and Ernest Morell. "Toward a Critical Pedagogy of Race: Ethnic Studies and Literacies of Power in High School Classrooms." *Race and Social Problems* 7, no. 1 (2015): 84–96.

Delgado Bernal, Dolores. "Using a Chicana Feminist Epistemology in Educational Research." *Harvard Educational Review* 68, no. 4 (1998): 555–582.

Dunbar-Ortiz, Roxanne. *An Indigenous Peoples' History of the United States.* Beacon Press, 2014.

Green, Joyce. *Making Space for Indigenous Feminism.* (2nd ed.). Winnipeg: Fernwood Publishing, 2007.

Headrick, Annabeth. *The Teotihuacan Trinity: The Sociopolitical Structure of an Ancient Mesoamerican City.* Austin: University of Texas Press, 2007.

Kunnie, Julian. "Apartheid in Arizona? HB 2281 and Arizona's Denial of Human Rights of Peoples of Color." *The Black Scholar* 40, no. 4 (2010): 16–26.

Laenui, Poka. "Processes of Decolonization." In *Reclaiming Indigenous Voice and Vision,* edited by M. Battiste, 150–160. UBC Press, 2000.

Manzanilla, Linda. "Corporate Groups and Domestic Activities at Teotihuacan." *Latin American Antiquity* (1996): 228–246.

Marín, Guillermo. "Pedagogía Tolteca: Filosofía de la educación en el México antiguo." Guillermo Marín Ruiz, 2009. Available online: http://toltecayotl.org/libros/PEDAGOGIA%20TOLTECA%20-%20Guillermo%20Marin.pdf (accessed on February, 16 2019).

McCarty, Teresa, and Tiffany Lee. "Critical Culturally Sustaining/Revitalizing Pedagogy and Indigenous Education Sovereignty." *Harvard Educational Review* 84, no. 1 (2014): 101–124.

Mignolo, Walter D. *The Idea of Latin America.* John Wiley & Sons, 2009.

Moraga, Cherrie. *A Xicana Codex, of Changing Consciousness.* Duke University Press, 2011.

Moreno Sandoval, Cueponcaxochitl D., Rosalva Mojica Lagunas, Lydia T. Montelongo, and Marisol J. Díaz. "AKS: A Conceptual Framework for Decolonizing Research in Social Science." *AlterNative: An International Journal of Indigenous Peoples* 12, no. 1 (2016): 18–31.

Morrell, Ernest, Rudy Dueñas, Veronica Garcia, and Jorge López. *Critical Media Pedagogy: Teaching for Achievement in City Schools.* New York: Teachers College Press, 2015.

Paris, Django, and Samy H. Alim (Eds.). *Culturally Sustaining Pedagogies: Teaching* and *Learning for Justice in a Changing World.* New York: Teachers College Press, 2017.

Risling Baldy, Cutcha. *We Are Dancing for You: Native Feminisms and the Revitalization of Women's Coming-of-Age Ceremonies.* Seattle: University of Washington Press, 2018.

Ross, Luana. "From the 'F' Word to Indigenous/Feminisms." *Wicazo Sa Review* 24 (2009): 39–52.

Salmón, Enrique. *Eating the Landscape: American Indian Stories of Food, Identity, and Resilience.* University of Arizona Press, 2012.

Smith, Linda T. *Decolonizing Methodologies: Research and Indigenous Peoples.* Zed Books Ltd., 1999.

Taube, Karl A. *Studies in Ancient Mesoamerican Art and Architecture: Selected Works by Karl Andreas Taube,* Vol. 1. San Francisco: Pre Columbian MesoWeb Press, 2018. Retrieved from https://www.mesoweb.com/publications/Works1/Taube_Works_v1.s.pdf.

Taube, Karl. "The Turquoise Hearth: Fire, Self-Sacrifice, and the Central Mexican Cult of War." In *Teotihuacan to the Aztecs,* edited by D. Carrasco, L. Jones, and S. Sessions (eds.), 269–340. University Press of Colorado, 2000.

Trueba, Enrique T. *Latinos Unidos: From Cultural Diversity to the Politics of Solidarity.* Rowman & Littlefield, 1999.

Valenzuela, Angela, and Brenda Rubio. *Subtractive Schooling.* The TESOL Encyclopedia of English Language Teaching, 1–7, 2018.

Villenas, Sofia, and Douglas Deyhle. "Critical Race Theory and Ethnographies Challenging the Stereotypes: Latino Families, Schooling, Resilience and Resistance." *Curriculum Inquiry* 29 (1999): 413–445.

Villenas, Sofia A., and Douglas E. Foley. "Critical Ethnographies of Education in the Latino/a Diaspora." In *Chicano School Failure and Success: Past, Present, and Future* (3rd ed.), edited by R. R. Valencia, 192–213. Routledge, 2011.

Villenas, Sofia. "Thinking Latina/o Education with and from Chicana/Latina Feminist Cultural Studies." In *Handbook of Cultural Politics in Education,* edited by Z. Leonardo, 451–476. Sense Publishers, 2010.

Wilson, Shawn. *Research Is Ceremony: Indigenous Research Methods.* Fernwood Publishing, 2008.

Zarate, Maria Estela, and Gilberto Q. Conchas. "Contemporary and Critical Methodological Shifts in Research on Latino Education." In *Handbook of Latinos and Education: Theory, Research, and Practice,* edited by E.G. Murillo, Jr., S.A. Villenas, R. Trinidad Galván, J.S. Muñoz, C. Martínez, and M. Machado-Casas, 90–107. New York: Routledge, 2010.

13

A Red Feminist Manifest
Meditations on Native American Women, Sovereignty Protectors, and the Liturgies of Colonial Violence

LEECE LEE-OLIVER

My Story Starts Here—Reflections on Sovereignty, Protection, and Red Feminism

I come into this moment, writing on the heels of the losses of several of my most near and dear loved ones. Much of what brought me into this work I absorbed from them. I understand, differently today from a few years ago, that we bind ourselves to the living universe around us. We make and remake ourselves in relationship to others and places. I am fortunate for that spiritual understanding. It is a gift. Epistemologically knowledgeable Native American and Indigenous peoples live relationally within a living universe of humans and non-humans, not as a binary, but as a reality. A phrase commonly used, that has made its way to the public's consciousness, "All my Relations," is often misused as a recognition of the human family. Rather, it is an affirmation of our relationships within the broad and interrelated networks of life in the living universe. That epistemological understanding has been a saving grace in times like this. It is with this understanding of an interwoven personhood, space, and place that I write about sovereignty and the protectors and Red feminists whose work is a commitment to all relatives within the living universe. In this essay, I share the long trajectory, from home, to community, to institution that is my epistemological ground as a Red feminist and sovereignty protector. This discursive effort is also one of reclamation and a call to engage tribal sovereignty, locally, spatially, and comprehensively no matter who and where we are. Embrace the protectors, culture bearers, and knowledge keepers whose work is present in the eclipse of modern narratives of feminisms and activism, American exceptionalism, and corporate power and design.

I begin with context and a note. I will use terms, reference people and peoples, and cite sources—too few to reflect the absolutely voluminous number of Native American knowledge keepers. This story is mine. What I share is what I have learned over many years and it still is incomplete.

Red Feminists and Sovereignty Protectors

Native American women, broadly defined, and Red feminist protectors take up a responsibility of protecting and educating others about what Vine Deloria theorized as relationship-to-place (Deloria and Wildcat 2001). At the core of Native American cultural-intellectual systems there is an ethos grounded in the understanding that all members of the living universe coexist in spiritual and pragmatic relationships that are rooted in places. To live in relationship to place is to actualize one's epistemological knowledge in the contexts of homelands, and now states, nations, and global relations, and even in its most core representation, in the self. The boundaries between earth, water, and the cosmos are porous and everything is alive, conscious, and part of the physics of everything. Living with the consciousness of relationship to place requires experiential and observational learning and acting. The generational transference of that knowledge is also part of a praxis lending survival strategies and guidance to future generations. Tribal self-discovery and purpose are mutually produced, and they produce understanding of holistic praxes in ecosystemic life. Having been taught to comprehend the ever adapting social-sacred system when I was a child, it is no wonder that I came to this work—an educator, community worker, and genocide and sovereignty scholar—on a circuitous path to Red/Indigenous feminism as descendant, granddaughter, daughter, sister, and auntie. My own intersectional understanding of the roles of scholarship, education, music, art, writing, oral history, silence, and listening as modes of personal and collective protection come from decades of living happily in the shadows of and running alongside many great protectors, nearly all women. As an academic, my own critical auto-ethnographic cartography of becoming a Red feminist and genocide scholar is rooted in places, people, and the non-human world. It gives me great comfort to connect my work and journey to a genealogy of sovereignty protectors, in all life forms, whose own lives and life works illustrate that we inherit sovereignty as a responsibility and learn to protect all life within the sacred. Strategies are passed forward, back, and across generations for those who, perhaps it is fair to say, are willing to imagine and be a force for building Indigenous futures.

While I would say that none of the epistemology that was imparted to me was time-stamped, and I understand that ethos are passed through family and community members over millennia, it bears noting that my use of the term "protectors" grew out of the clarifying statements made by Lakota protectors at Standing Rock in 2016 and thereafter. Those protectors represent a longstanding leadership praxis in sovereignty movements that existed long before the 2000s. Protection acknowledges the first agreements, treaties, between peoples and non-human relatives, lands, and waters, and these agreements are based in reciprocity and contextual, while also complex (Deloria 2006; Estes 2018). In the 1960s and '70s, the American Indian Movement and Red Power Movement enacted their protection of liberation under sovereign treaties. That is to say that while collaborations were born, civil rights activists focused their efforts rightly on the human scale as they sought and created better forms of communal relationships—human to human, state to citizen, and nation to nation. At the heart of tribal sovereignty movements, the agreements are among Native peoples to live, protect, and be good relatives to all relatives, the life forms that make up the broader cosmic communities that make up the living universe. From fish-ins, to Alcatraz, to the second Wounded Knee, the peoples and places were inextricably linked through sovereign relationality. Not to romanticize the movements, out of necessity Women of All Red Nations (WARN) coalesced in that era, too, out of the realization that the limiting, overbearing, and even violent burden of patriarchy had become an overdetermining factor in Native women's lives and communities. Compounding the epistemic and physical violence that Native women faced, racialization combined with misogyny represented a long-standing colonial legacy that contributed to the erasure of Native American women as leaders and practitioners in sovereignty and solidarity movements. Many of those protectors sought to move into the light and so created new spaces that intentionally pierced the silencing effects of Western feminist essentialism and male domination in their own movements. Laser-focused on protecting life, in all of its cultural, physical, and spiritual manifestations, they created Women of All Red Nations, and many, many localized grassroots efforts still known and unknown by name today, to thwart imperialist and corporate encroachment. They put their bodies on the line and reinvigorated efforts in the 1980s to rail against Reagan's white patriarchal, nostalgia-infused nationalism, crony capitalism, and the legacies of Kissinger's transnational empire by building solidarity with other Native and Indigenous women. In the 1990s, while the public saw what appeared to be the quieting of uprisings, the Bush/Cheney imperialist and global capitalist-era wars saw the immersion of Native American communities in anti-war and anti-corporation sovereignty movements on the ground (LaDuke 1999). Whether they adopted the term "feminism" or not, Native women sovereignty protectors poured themselves into protecting land, water, and human and non-human relatives and raised awareness across the United States and transnationally about the interconnectedness between imperialism, war, and extraction capitalism, and their own potentially slow and subtle death and depletion. Witness to all of this, my own life seemed to welcome me into a purpose—to join in the complex network of Native American women protectors and Red feminists that still is happening today.

On Becoming a Genocide Scholar and Activist

This isn't where it started, but in 1999, I found myself sitting on a Browning, Montana, hillside, eating lunch at a gathering of Native educators. Staring out at the blue sky, broad lands, and high mountains, I sat marveling over some wild horses grazing in the distance. An elder Northern Cheyenne citizen, Steve Brady Sr. quietly sat down a few feet away. We said hello and then he asked if I knew anything about the Sand Creek massacre. I said that I'd only read about it in books written by non-Native peoples, which probably meant that I didn't really know anything about it. Mr. Brady is one of the Northern Cheyenne people who carries the history of the Sand Creek massacre. There are others. It is not my knowledge or right to share their names. Mr. Brady decided to share the oral history of the Sand Creek massacre with me that day, and he did so over five days. When he finished, he said, "Now you can teach it." I will pause to say that the oral history is not mine to tell, and I don't tell it or write about it specifically. In my teaching and dissertation, as I promised Mr. Brady I would, I used my learning to study the intersections of white supremacy and law to interrogate how laws can be written to allow genocidal violence, first by dehumanizing a people and then by legalizing their extermination. I learned and have written in many formats about the laws that impose "Indian" racialization and white supremacy (Lee-Oliver, Dissertation Chapter Two, 2013). The oral history as carried by Steve Brady Sr. has been published for those who wish to read it.

The day he finished sharing the oral history, Mr. Brady impressed on me the importance of telling the true histories of Native tribes and peoples. In many ways, it was an intervention in my understanding about my place in the living universe. I felt hungry to learn more and to expose truths about America's genocidal foundations and ongoing legacies. It became apparent to me over time that the lessons I learned would give me many opportunities to interrogate what it meant in material ways to say that the US empire was built on genocide, and how racist misogyny was a critical tool of disempowerment, for colonizers and imperialists alike. It would be my welcome responsibility to share that knowledge with others, including new generations of willing protectors. In my mind, this became the work—to pass forward real history for the people to understand Native Americans and non-Native genealogies within the context of empire-building. That goal required me to pursue how laws enabled genocidal violence and systemic oppression to be practiced on Native Americans, and to grow my own knowledge about the vast and diverse histories of Native Americans. It sent me into the depths of research into how a term like "Indian" could be created and then discursively used to produce to dehumanize and authorize killing "Indians" while exceptionalizing whiteness. It allows me, still, to overthrow the tropes that enable white supremacy in all its overt and nuanced forms. My learning encouraged me to look for answers to many questions, including the following: (1) How was state-sponsored genocidal violence made legal? (2) How do the hypocrisies of white supremacy extend into Western hegemony? (3) How are the absences of Native American women's lives in all factors of history and contemporary life created, including in feminist scholarship and literature? (4) How can we bring Native American women's leadership, as constants, into the public imaginary and scholarly discourses?

Learning Starts at Home

I was raised by a revolutionary and sat in the company of her contemporaries for decades; I have always been surrounded by strong women. I absorbed their lessons and strategies of action and silence. I knew they'd all experienced state and interpersonal violence and, even as a child, I knew the state had a hand in all of it. Later, I could see systems of violence in homes, communities, and across the nation—wreaked of colonial and imperialistic justifications that naturalized a schema and centralized those valued against the devalued, and those with power against the constructively disempowered. I grew up understanding that trauma reverberated over generations, so when I was gifted the oral history, the abject nature of the violence against women, Elders, and children resonated in my mind and body. As I listened to the oral history of the Sand Creek massacre, the cadence of violence was as clear as it was unrelenting. I started to see the colonial legacy of violence in the contemporary. I read everything I could find to see where and to what degree these details justifying genocidal violence were included. On the journey, I was given Sol Lewis's reprinting of the testimonies of Army troops at Sand Creek, heard by the Joint Chiefs of War of the US Department of War. The testimonies capture verbatim the logic of the perpetrators and colluders in *The Sand Creek Massacre* (Lewis 1973). In those pages, troops recall targeting Native women, children, and Elders as though they were of a different nature than the perpetrators. The perpetrating troops were shameless, gleeful, and unapologetic. The vile ways in which women, children, and Elders at Sand Creek were subjected to being hunted for days, slaughtered, with pieces of their flesh, especially sexualized ones—breasts and scrotum—cleaved off, snatched, and made into pouches for carrying coins or tobacco, or were worn on the saddles and hats of the Army and militia who rode proudly through settler communities as if to parade in their own honor. The history has not escaped the minds of the survivors' descendants like Steve Brady Sr. Many troops and military leaders claimed that they had acted as protectors of "women and children," disregarding the violence on Cheyenne and Arapaho women's and children's bodies. As Colonel Chivington, a minister turned anti-Indian leader in the northern plains, recalled: "[T]he women and children that were killed could not have been saved if the troops had tried.... [T]hey were in the rifle pits with the warriors"; read as Native American men] (Chivington 1865: 1–2). Inherent in destabilizing the virtue of Native women and children is the beginning of the erasure and concomitant vulnerability of Native women, children, and peoples to state and societal violence, and its legacies remain today. As the record shows, there were no "warriors" in "rifle pits." The people had been disarmed as a condition of President Lincoln's acknowledgement of them as a "friendly" and ostensibly protected people (Lewis 1973; Lee-Oliver 2013).

As I read the troops' testimonies and defense of genocide, I could not help but see a long trajectory connecting to the epidemic rate of violence that came to be known as Missing and Murdered Indigenous Women, Girls, and Relatives (MMIWGR). It is clear and apparent that the roots of abject dehumanizing violence erupted in small- and large-scale genocides of Native peoples and, generations later, it is still palpable, active, and a condition of life. The trajectories of genocidal violence travel across time and are embodied in all sides of the generational inheritors later. In our faceted work, resistance to that genocidal violence against Indigenous life and systems is echoed in the shared responsibility among Native American protectors and Red feminists to stop these systems of death. It is felt. That lack of value that we ostensibly embody, that our mothers, grandmothers, and aunties, our peoples all embody/ied, hold lessons that are rife with historical prescience. The racism and misogyny we experience today were birthed in colonialism. It is as if to say that when we know that our own family, lineages, the stuff we are literally made of physically, spiritually, and culturally, brought our relatives face to face with the perpetrators of genocide, we should expect to feel the precarity of our own lives and the necessity to stop it. It is as if we should have known, American life is not for us, and we should hold those truths close now. Sometimes, the things we live and know reveal themselves over time.

I had become a genocide scholar long before I went to university or met Steve Brady Sr. It was concretized when I was ten years old and learned that Nazism had existed, and it grew deeper when I was fourteen and realized the definition of contradiction was comprehensible in the life of Thomas Jefferson. Standing in the kitchen looking out the window, I couldn't make sense of how he was touted in textbooks as the "father" of democracy. I guess I'd had some history class that week. I remember being perplexed by the reality that, as I conceptualized it at fourteen, "he laid down at night with a woman who, by day, he wrote into slavery." By the time I was gifted the oral history of the Sand Creek massacre, I realize I had already been on this journey. I'd made a commitment to speak that truth into the world, and to explain the ways the United States, as an empire, orchestrates racist and misogynistic technologies lay at the foundations of US nation-formation and empires beyond.

Red Feminist Theories and Reclamation

When I entered into the last phase of graduate school, dissertating, I was a pretty well-honed Red feminist. I came with the goal of rewriting the US military's genocidal campaign against Cheyenne and Arapaho women, children, and Elders at Sand Creek and to tell a larger story about how the entrenchment of white supremacist logic and genocide were mutual and instrumental to the liturgy of US nation-formation. In the following, I offer brief analyses and theorizations I grew to understand during and since the writing of my dissertation. I further propose them here as the liturgies of death, in the legal roots of state-sponsored genocide, and the liturgies of life in Native American women protectors' sovereignty work. It has been over many years and long hours of contemplation that the heart of my own scholarly activism bloomed. This work is the basis of my upcoming book project.

In my dissertation, and in many papers before, I sought to unpack the racialization of "Indians" and "squaws" and to expose how racialized and misogynistic technologies subsumed Native American women and girls in tropes that enabled their violation in genocidal violence. I wrote of the ways that these histories necessitated the Tribal Law and Order Act (2010), which was intended to ameliorate the extraordinarily high rate of abduction and homicide of Native American women and girls, Two Spirit, and children (Lee-Oliver 2020, 2013). I built on analyses that understood how white supremacy, as a false logic, embedded colonial narratives about manifest destiny, which invoked a Christian ethos in calls to build empires by militarizing white citizenry (Stannard 1992; Smedley 2007; Omi and Winant 1994; Roediger 2005). Genocide from that perspective, I theorize, can be conceived as part of a larger liturgical practice—considered a sacred part of one's religious obligation to the nation. Practiced as part of nation-formation, I theorize, it is a liturgy of death. Native Americans during the genocidal era of United States and state formations, records indicate, were attuned to the contradictions of white settler expansionist death ethic (Maldonado Torres 2008) and its extractive nature. Tribal leaders and members strategized for survival that intentionally aimed for future-building, and their own liturgies of life emerged. As generations survived and bore witness to the atrocities and the extraordinary leadership of family and communities across Native America, a responsibility to voice and act with respect to this liturgy of life emerged time and again. The praxes can be seen today in the work of women, men, Elders, children, and transgender relatives who live and work in communion with the sacred. Nez Perce Red feminist and scholar Dr. Patricia Penn Hilden recognizes the phenomenon of a spatial consciousness, which she calls the "Red Zone," wherever Native peoples convene to hold fast to protecting Native American epistemologies and sovereignty itself (Penn Hilden 2007). Resolved to bear the personal, family, and community issues that arise from the generational transference of grief, liturgies of life aim to mitigate the fracturing power of the coloniality of being.

I am entirely unsure when exactly the exclusion of Native American women's leadership, intellectualism, or spiritual significance was normalized in mainstream society, but I am sure that the racial misogyny that dehumanized Native women and girls centuries ago, and the imperatives that set the stage for colonial nation-formation, remains in manifestations of modernity today. Whenever I return to the Sand Creek massacre to seek out more evidence, it is never unclear that Native women and girls represented the majority of victims, and that they were intentionally disarmed and left as marks by the US military and government. It is clear that Native American women and girls suffer a secondary relegation to subjugation that creates an entire class of peoples as incommensurable others. That Indigenous gender formation is clearly represented in the military records of troops at Sand Creek. It shows that genocidal violence during territorial expansion intentionally selected women, children, and Elders and that their value within white societal paradigms was minimal to nonexistent. The troops' actions even attest to engaging a death ethic in their own testimonies uttered before the Joint Committee on the Conduct of War, as they illustrated their unapologetic and vile frenzy of genocidal violence at Sand Creek:

> All manner of depredations were inflicted on their persons . . . the men [troops] used their knives. . . . I saw a squaw with her head smashed in before she was killed. Next morning, after they were dead and stiff, these men pulled out the bodies of the squaws and pulled them open in an indecent manner.
>
> I heard one man say that he had cut out a woman's private parts and had them for exhibition on a stick. . . . I also heard of numerous instances in which men had cut out the private parts of females and stretched them over the saddlebows and wore them over their hats while riding in the ranks. (All quoted in Stannard 1992: 132–133)

In its final report, the Joint Committee on the Conduct of War condemned the Sand Creek massacre as a "war crime." It was determined to be not only premeditated, but also gendered, noting the "killing [of] women and children, who were incapable of offering any resistance" (Lewis 1972: x). In the end, no troops, colonels, nor the territorial governor who invited the killing of all Indians as "hostiles," faced repercussions. Instead, the Joint Committee officials condemned the troops for embarrassing the Army by conducting themselves in such a manner while in uniform. The harm, according to officials, was done to the institution of the Army. This example of the systematic silencing of the US military history of domestic genocide can be interpreted as one of the many ways that white supremacist nationalism is created and protected today under the cloak of American exceptionalism (Lee-Oliver 2013).

Sand Creek was not a singular nor anomalous moment in time. It is representative of decades of conquest that overtook the Americas through the abject genocidal eradication of Indigenous peoples, cultures, and sovereignty (Lewis 1973; Brady 1999; Lee-Oliver 2013). The historicization of the Sand Creek massacre exemplifies the discursive power to engender the normalization of Native American death. Because Native Americans were conflated with animals, as George Washington did when he declared Native Americans to be "savage as the wolf," "Indians" became nothing more than that (Williams 2005; Lee-Oliver 2013). Entrenching that liturgy of death in law, one of the most opaque discursive claims cast the so-called "merciless Savage Indian" in the US Declaration of Independence. While the colonial and expansionist projects and futures relied on their ability to disaggregate Native Americans from the broader population, Native women were thus discharged from their Indigenous sovereign selves (Lewis 1973; Brady 1999; Lee-Oliver 2013). The power of that erasure is captured by Sherry Farrell Racette, who explains some of the challenge of overwriting the discursive apparatus:

> Our ability to understand (or even locate) the gender relationships that existed prior to colonization is complicated by an array of overlapping factors: the tumultuous history that separates us from our pasts, gender bias in early historic documents, and the way anthropologists and other scholars conduct research to advance or dispute ideas about gender relations as universal truths (Racette 2010: 28).

Unlike the critiques of early feminists who coalesced their efforts around certain sets of "women's issues," Racette's reflection of "universal truths" responds to a category of women in which Native American women were not formulated. Gender, as the author notes, was a pre-formed concept that did not accept the types of women Native American societies produced. So we find ourselves in the archives, sitting with Elders, revisiting family histories, and at times unable to locate any semblance of "real" Native women's lives. In Red feminist scholarship, specifically, painstaking examinations aim to bring forward historical and contemporary analyses with Native American oral traditions to enable us to make visible how subduing the political potency of Native American women through patriarchal gendered normativity itself is a form of violent conquest—no matter who exacts the practice. It has been surmised that casting Native American women historically through racist and patriarchal norms led Native American women and girls to be perceived as lacking intelligence and morality and, in fact, as "masculine" by their nature. The masculinization of Native women and girls is said to have spawned many forms of sexualized violence (Lee-Oliver 2010, 2013). Historically, Native American women and girls were condemned as threats to the success of colonization because they were loyal to "Indian" men and because Native American women and girls can be progenitors of the "race" as well as sovereign nations. Thus, according to Racette, "colonial strategies of church and state sought to erode the respect for and power of women and problematized female sexuality through shame and exploitation" (Racette 2010: 34). Certainly, the deployment of patriarchal representations of Native American women justified the disregard of their political and social viability, as well as their inherent right to exist. Likewise, American Indian boarding schools based their sterilization practices on that conjecture, to permit laypeople to commit sterilization as part of the liturgical process of eradicating Indians (Lomawaima 2007). The practice of eugenics violated the bodies, spirits, and psyches of Native American children. It is also fair to note that the histories of these "truths" were not largely included, and they were even silenced in abolition, suffrage, and feminist efforts focused on political and civil liberation of others. Many suffragists and early feminists touted themselves as the real "mothers of the nation" (Newman 1999). Examined on a racially gendered axis, where Native women should have found their voices in Indigenous feminisms, instead they found alternative forms of erasure and epistemic violence (Winnemucca Hopkins 2017; Green 1975; Jaimes and Halsey 1992; Lee-Oliver 2013).

As theorists of historical trauma and its legacies have noted, conquest and its multiple forms of violence, including erasure, are demoralizing (Brave Heart 1998). Effectively, to silence historically is to repress the grievances of Native Americans. This legacy, many Native American women activists claim, is at the basis of today's invisibility even inside feminism. Recognizing the patriarchal paradigm and genocidal violence as trans-generational, Maria Yellow Horse Brave Heart (1998) contends that the waves of inhumane violence ensured the enduring legacies of colonial dominance. The intended absolute subordination of Native American peoples resulted in the commensurate super-subordination of Native American women. However, more than just remnants of political and cultural sovereignty remain. Through survivor histories, shared over generations and across cultures through oral histories, new ceremonies and new body politics give life to new modes of resistance. Historical voices, as it turns out, were impossible to suppress. Instead, these histories reemerge in Native American communities and give rise to individual and collective responses—a liturgy of life—to the coloniality of being, knowledge, and systems. Through Native American, Red feminist, decolonial movements today, we find grassroots actions, cultural preservation, community-building projects, and scholarly activism.

Red Feminism: Theorizing Native American Women as Protectors

In part, my aim here is to parse out the ways commitments to personal sovereignty and tribal sovereignty emerge in contemporary Native American women's political modes of resistance and community-building efforts—in liturgies of life. I see certain ethos illuminated and extant threads of Native American women's agency that exist over long historical periods, landscapes, bodies of water, spiritualities, and the sacred that give rise to a consciousness and foundations for movements. The practices, which some might call decolonial, reveal willing agents who rely on and grow their capacities for resistance through their reliance on ancestral models and coalition building. That sense of purpose, which is passed from generation to generation, is something that I theorize as a "politics of hereditary voice." We, those who willingly accept sovereignty work as foundational to our life's purpose, inherit a common responsibility best expressed in our commitment to sovereignty protection. Whether culture bearers who carry and protect Indigenous cultural-intellectual systems of knowledge, or political agents who carry legal knowledge from oral histories to written records related to sovereignty, myriad practitioners can visibly trace their praxes to their cultural-intellectual and sacred systems in a genealogy. Oral traditions are expansive, diverse, and full of examples of those we refer to as the ancestors from whom we learn, carry on the work, and pray that we are accepted and acknowledged as trusted stewards. We find descendants in nineteenth-century autobiographies, like that of Sarah Winnemucca Hopkins, twentieth-century literary activism, and all the way to the organizing of Women of All Red Nations, the National Indigenous Women's Resource Network, and in the work of contemporary scholar-activists-protectors in the feminist formation of Red feminism—networked through long lineages of practitioners. Note that feminism is, in my work, not capitalized. That is intentional to situate Native American women's sovereignty work as the primary mode and feminism as one vehicle for sharing that work beyond community and intertribal networks.

To decolonize and disentangle Native American women from tropes and reveal the traces of the politics of hereditary voice, I learned to illustrate how diverse spheres of Native American resistance converge in strategic formations. The fact of generational transference as a pedagogical mode brings all this together. I assert that an inheritance of colonial legacies leads to a responsibility to confront them, and they shape the liturgies of life in Native American women's sovereignty work. We inherit the purpose and understand that to be a Native American is to accept that "Native" is a verb. The term imparts action, impact, observation, movement, and change. Temporality becomes a way of being. The practice of knowledge sharing and preservation between relatives, communities, and coalitions across time and space is intentional. Across time, tribal leadership relied, and still relies, on collective mobilization to protect sovereignty. Ultimately, an ethic of revolutionary love is inherent in the politics of hereditary voice and sovereignty work, and it is elemental in Native American women's protective pedagogies. The work, in conversation with the historic, enables present and future protectors, culture bearers, and Red feminists to draw on cultural-intellectual praxes and to envision and manifest futures free of colonial and imperial subjugation.

As a decolonial modality, Native American sovereignty movements assert a relation to place, and their reflexive properties are guided by values that support the inherent right to personal sovereignty. As life-affirming modalities within Native American women's sovereignty work, this framework also necessarily affords strategic essentialism (Spivak 1988). Upholding treaties advances their inherent rights to protect peoples, lands, waters, and the sacred within ecosystems and as a whole. In the Native context, what affects Native American peoples in their localities reverberates for all others in their locality. Unique crises shape the experiences, for example, of the Mohawk, the Zapatistas, the Blackfeet, and the Western Shoshone. Yet all these peoples face similar constructs of domination and the deleterious effects of imperial domination. Relatedly, urban Indian centers provide for the displaced, the forcibly removed, the wanderers, and those seeking the new beginnings. These centers, that saw much of their heydays in the 1970s, still exist today, running on shoestring budgets, to meet the promises of treaties to provide health care, education, and community and cultural access points. Native leaders, including the famous like Wilma Mankiller, John Trudell, and Winona LaDuke, and so many others known in their communities, transgress/ed the boundaries of reservation to urban and rural spaces to engage in sovereignty work, to hold and protect the inherent rights of Native peoples. What is lost through the colonial encounter is gained, and reclaimed, through sovereignty work projects like urban Indian centers. Therefore, there is room for coalition building, through an Indigenous decoloniality, that opens the veins of communication for exchanges of shared strategizing and solidarity (Lee-Oliver 2013).

Sovereignty, Red Power, and Red Feminism

Where many of us hope to find solidarity is with other liberation movements. Since the living universe and the responsibility to protect it is an inherited responsibility of Native American protectors, including Red feminists, Native women's work notably understands that sovereignty takes on many forms: bodily, personal, and spiritual. In that sense, this work has a materiality to it. Unfortunately, hegemonic (aka Western) feminism is often challenged as a limited and limiting positionality for feminists and activists of color. In Native America, that feminism does not confront settler colonialism, nor disaster capitalism, nor the larger project of empire-building, all of which continue to uproot the critical interventions of sovereignty work. To that end, Red feminism must be disentangled from Western feminism. The relational elements of sovereignty with Native American women's embodiment of sovereignty, and the violence that continues to be endured in the state's efforts to overthrow them, are well articulated in the Indigenous transnational collection on Red feminism, *Indigenous Women and Feminism: Politics, Activism, Culture* (2010):

> For Indigenous women, colonization has involved their removal from positions of power, the replacement of traditional gender roles with Western patriarchal practices, the exertion of colonial control over Indigenous communities through the management of women's bodies, and sexual violence. ... Although Indigenous women do not share a single culture, they do have a common colonial history, and our conception of Indigenous feminism centres [sic] on the fact that the imposition of patriarchy has transformed Indigenous societies by diminishing Indigenous women's power, status, and material circumstances. (Huhndorf and Suzack, 2010: 2–3)

To comprehend and engage with sovereignty protectors, including Red feminists, feminism as a system of political entities must understand how sovereignty is situated in personal and sacred places and commitments. Then, Native American women and allies can dream together of shared liberation. Likewise, to understand that is to understand how violence against women, girls, and, in the Western sense, transgender people, is about sovereignty. This point of departure is where I began my own work: unpacking the laws that permit (from one side) the colonial regimes and the state to enact genocide, first by constructing a racialized and gendered logic and human hierarchy. Following that trajectory, we can see then that the overrepresentation of white supremacy is enmeshed in the matrixes of the crisis of the Missing and Murdered Indigenous Women, Girls, and Relatives (MMIWGR). The state violence that ensued at Standing Rock in 2016, whether against water protectors, treaty protectors, Elders, or the grassroots community from around the world, was emblematic of the ongoing white supremacist logic embedded in American exceptionalism. For the work of Red feminists and Native protectors to be embraced by Western feminists, tribal sovereignty has to be understood as central to the heart of everything.

Native American women sovereignty protectors have navigated the silences, even in Western feminism, to pierce through and leave evidence for generations to come. Where our erasure seems overwhelming, the work is there. For example, the Mattaponi descendants of Pocahontas and, earlier, Paiute activist Sarah Winnemucca Hopkins, offer two examples of the intentional transmission of histories left for the purpose of offsetting settler overdetermination. The Mattaponi peoples published *The True Story of Pocahontas* in 2007 to bring truth to the life of Pocahontas and her peoples under British colonization and abject violence. It is a brilliant discursive move to offer a translation of the actual oral history, which turns every stereotype and false narrative on its head as early as the 1600s. The oral history also informs us of a Pocahontas who was a skilled diplomat, stunning in her cognition even under the most abjectly violent conditions, and of a Powhatan leadership bent to its knee by the cruelty of the British. Pocahontas was abducted and held captive to manipulate Powhatan leaders, including her father, to take measured steps and give in to British demands. She died in captivity. The book was timed to be out in time to counter Disney's twentieth anniversary of its animated colonizer's reimagining (Custalow and Daniels, 2007; Lee-Oliver, 2020). Likewise, putting words to paper for future generations, Sarah Winnemucca Hopkins accepted the invitation to write her book, *Life Among the Piutes: Their Wrongs and Claims* (1883). At the time, writers and settlers, including so-called "friends of Indians," penned curious diaries and books, typically sponsored by monied settlers, that created and archived fantasy stories that cast Native Americans as "vanishing peoples." Winnemucca Hopkins seized the opportunity to explain the realities of settler avarice and their habitual tendency to devour Native women and children through sexual violence. Winnemucca Hopkins shows, too, that white settlers were often met by the survival strategies of Native American women. She recalled how settler men would rape women and children and, despite the wails of the violated, other settler men would walk by and carry on as if they'd heard nothing. What they heard, I surmise, were the voices of nothingness, nothing more than obstacles, or the "Indian problems," slaves, or resources. Winnemucca Hopkins retells one morning when her mother and auntie strategized an act of refusal:

> Oh, what a fright we all got one morning to hear some white people were coming. Everyone ran as best they could. My poor mother was left with

my little sister and me. Oh, I never can forget it. My poor mother was carrying my little sister on her back and trying to make me run; but I was so frightened I could not move my feet, and while my poor mother was trying to get me along my aunt overtook us, and she said to my mother: "Let us bury our girls, or we shall all be killed and eaten up." So they went to work and buried us, and told us if we heard any noise not to cry out, for if we did they would surely kill us and eat us. So our mothers buried me and my cousin, planted sage bushes over our faces to keep the sun from burning them, and there we were left all day (Winnemucca Hopkins 2017: 11).

Such resistance practices by Native women were ingenious and also replete in the oral histories of Native peoples. The space of this essay is dedicated to Native women's resistance, and so I will leave it to Winnemucca Hopkins, whose quote speaks volumes on the everyday violence of the settler state. Still, though Winnemucca Hopkins is published, I wonder when and where her work or her legacy of public speaking about Native rights and democracy is taught, as a part of the liberation work of women, more broadly. The searing critique of settler inhumanity and ideology and the violations, a century later, rarely make their way into feminist discourses.

Later, by the 1960s and 1970s, when WARN formed, it was in the context of the Native American sovereignty movements on reservations and in urban communities. Survival schools were created in urban Indian centers to grow the consciousness and self-esteem of those living in cities with knowledge of histories, treaties, and strategies. One of the better-known resistance efforts by Native American women that inspired people across the country were the Western Shoshone tribes' Dann sisters. Despite their efforts to be self-determining and maintain economic stability, they found themselves constantly fighting against the illegal confiscation of sheep by Bureau of Alcohol, Tobacco, and Firearms (ATF) agents; it was a practice that obstructed their capacity to make livings and continue living within their homelands and epistemologies—which goes against human rights law and treaties in their actual form. The same oppressive encroachment occurred in more cases than ever made mainstream news. In the 1970s, the longest walks aimed to awaken citizens of the denizens of war that remained underfoot in Native communities—reservation, rancheria, rural, and urban. In that time an emergent Red feminist presence began to expose the long durée of colonial gender violence and disaster capitalism. Today, the scholarly activism in Red feminism is grounded in those grassroots community-building efforts to resist the oppressive state, its coercion, and subjugation.

For people whose sovereignty is the base of their rights claims, allies matter. In these fights for sovereignty, Western feminism could also run the course. With its focus on a non-racialized sexism and equal pay, however, many Western feminists seem unaware of their own impact on Indigenous women's political work, including Red feminists. Second-wave Western feminist Sally Roesch Wagner has addressed this in numerous articles and interviews. She is what I would call an Elder in the mainstream feminist movement who has worked for decades to address the need for anti-racist and sovereignty allyship within feminism. Still today, with sovereignty's vulnerability as a structure of protection, most notably visible in MMIWGR and disaster capitalism, like lithium mining, there is no time to waste. So we go on.

Native Women and Sovereignty Protectors: Life, Land, and Water in the Living Universe

The work of Lakota protector Madonna Thunder Hawk and Seminole water protector and scholar Dr. Melinda Micco offer examples of two protectors whose work exemplifies the liturgy of life and the responsibility to uplift new generations in sovereignty work, amid several of their contemporaries. Uniquely and collectively, their sovereignty work illustrates the strategies, patience, and depth of their own knowledge about sovereignty rights and responsibilities that are the core of the work of protectors.

By the 1970s, Native American sovereignty movements found good company with many in the civil rights movements. Good allies and coalitional partners supported the assertion of inherent sovereignty and all that that entails. Adding layers to the challenge of treaty rights recognition, most Americans lacked even a basic education in tribal sovereignty or histories. Moreover, patriarchal exceptionalism was fomented everywhere. Where civil rights movements, including mainstream feminism, and the Red Power movement exalted either men or white women, Women of All Red Nations (WARN) emerged to take the long-standing traditions of Native American women's political responsibility to the forefront. Madonna Thunder Hawk is known today by many as one of WARN's founders and a Native American movement leader. In this essay, I draw attention to her current project to preserve the history of Native women sovereignty protectors in an archival project, but note that her life work is remarkable as a Native American sovereignty protector.

Over several decades, Madonna Thunder Hawk's name has become synonymous with Native American women's sovereignty work. It should be no surprise that Thunder Hawk herself took notice of so many people involved in fish-ins, the occupation of Alcatraz, and the defense of Lakota peoples at the second Wounded Knee, whose legacies seemed to disappear as time moved on. The invisibility of Native women protectors can be understood as a loss of political history and knowledge. Given the dearth of knowledge about Native women as political figures and sovereignty protectors, Thunder

Hawk and her daughter, Marcella Gilbert, embarked on a project to create a digital visual, oral, and textual archive of Native American women leaders. In an interview on the Laura Flanders Show ("Warrior Women & Wounded Knee at 50: Madonna Thunder Hawk & Marcella Gilbert," 2023), Thunder Hawk and Gilbert explain the basis of the *Warrior Women Project*, an archive of contemporary Native American women sovereignty leaders. Before I go further, I found it particularly important to include Thunder Hawk's and Gilbert's explorations of their own political coming-of-age stories, because they illustrate how the people, not academia, are the tombs of intellectual systems. Their lived experiences as treaty and land protectors have served as life lessons. Growing up, they both learned about the relationship between their tribe, jurisdiction, and rights within the context of the United States; more accurately, they learned about the creation of the United States within the contexts of sovereign tribes. Both Thunder Hawk and Gilbert carry those legal and resistance histories in memory.

In an interview with Nick Tilsen, on Landback for the People (2023), Thunder Hawk tells the story of her childhood and how lessons learned from her relatives shaped her understanding of sovereignty and being Native when she was just a girl. Even though she says that at the time, she "just wanted to listen to rock and roll" and hang out with her grandmother and uncle, the stories her uncle shared with her stuck with her. It seems that her grandmother asking her to help care for her uncle would unfold in a variety of unanticipated ways. As Thunder Hawk listened to her uncle, he shared his generation's frustrations with the carving of US presidents' faces on Mt. Rushmore. Even a brief review of history shows that that mountain is sacred, and erecting emblems of the conquerors atop it is an act of war. For Thunder Hawk, the story resonated. Later, she and her contemporaries decided to climb Mt. Rushmore in protest. That understanding and ethos followed her to Alcatraz, and then to Standing Rock in 2016 (Tilsen 2023).

In her interview with Laura Flanders, "Reflecting on the Fiftieth Anniversary of the Occupation of Wounded Knee" ("Warrior Women" 2023), Thunder Hawk concludes that since there is an absence of scholarship on Native American women's political and community work, we must rely on storytelling and archives built by Native women. She recollected how the media came to the region during the second stand at Wounded Knee and stoked the public to fear an uprising of "Indians," using tropes of "Indian savagery." Rather, she clarifies that it was "grandmothers and respected elders who decided, after years of trying to address corruption on the Pine Ridge Reservation and broken US Government treaties dating back to the original 1890, to take a stand, and that's what they did. The absence of women in the history of that moment, and in the American Indian movement or AIM itself" is remarkable when you know what you know.

Thunder Hawk's daughter Marcella Gilbert, also interviewed, recounts that she was raised in the movement under the guidance of and bearing witness to teachings about sovereignty. As a young person, she watched her mother and community as they responded to the ongoing systematic oppression by the Bureau of Indian Affairs. She experienced how enacting occupations on Native homelands and at Alcatraz, over generations, were acts of sovereignty. Their visibility was intended to educate the public about treaties and the ongoing theft of Native American lands, waters, and rights, and grow new generations of sovereignty protectors. It is important to clarify that while Native American children are often exposed to sovereignty work and educated, they are not expected to take up the work in the same ways. Respect for personal sovereignty and autonomy are embraced in Native American epistemologies, and it shows up in the teaching and passing of knowledge within communities. Gilbert explains how the generational transference of knowledge is accomplished and shares how she was inspired to take on her early role as a representative in the International Indian Treaty Council. She explains what so many Elders talk about today:

> I was handed the 1868 treaty and [told], you need to know this, read it. Why are treaties so important? We learn ... water rights, winters' doctrine ... the relationship of nation-to-nation. What does that mean? What are the obligations that this country has to us? I'm part of a nation that has a very unique relationship with this government, and they're accountable to me. And to learn that as a young person, you know, you're like, "Hey, man, don't mess around with me." It was very empowering to learn that I stood for something in this country ... was so very powerful. [Later] I was a youth delegate [in the International Indian Treaty Council] that got to go on ... the first trip ... we went as a nation to the United Nations, and that work continues today on the Pine Ridge Reservation. (Interview with Flanders 2023)

Even in the depths of militarized oppression, the liturgy of life is found in the teachings of treaties and sovereignty. The ways Native American women come into the work as sovereignty protectors, and the ways exposure to those conversations and bearing witness to state oppression inform generations of children, many of whom adopt that which gives them life—sovereignty—and go on to cultivate community strategies and systems of life-affirming support. This is the heart of the liturgies of life. The praxes are seen in the long history of societies in Native America, before and after colonization and US nation formation, and in urban Indian communities. Turning now, I weave in the work of more Native women, whose sovereignty work began in their youth, to reveal the broad spectrum of Native women leaders and feminists. Survival schools, health clinics, jobs programs, and socio-cultural events, some that were for bonding in communities and others that were for growing public awareness about issues faced by Native Americans, are among the ways that Native American communities, lifeways, and cultural-intellectual systems have been preserved through the liturgies of life and sovereignty affirmation, most often with Native women at the helm. Well-known figures like Anishinaabeg citizen Winona LaDuke and Cherokee citizen and twelve-year Principal Chief of the Cherokee tribe of Oklahoma, Wilma Mankiller, were present throughout numerous movements over time and highlight yet more Native American women while fighting for the inherent sovereignty of all Native peoples. Both of these figures have made critical interventions long before their names became popular in the broader public. For example, Mankiller's contributions to urban Indian sustainability can be found in the Native American Community History Project, an archive of the Bay Area urban Indian history and movement of the 1960s and beyond held in the Bancroft Library at the University of California, Berkeley.

Mankiller's family had been pushed to leave the reservation for one of the nine "urban Indian" designated cities, determined by the Bureau of Indian Affairs and through Department of Interior policies (Mankiller 1993). As a young adult, she engaged in sovereignty work, including building jobs programs for families coming into the urban site in San Francisco, California, as part of ameliorating the failed government promises to provide employment, education, health care, and housing supports to stabilize incoming Native families. The fact that Native American women have always been "at the heart" of Native American sovereignty work, as M. Annette Jaimes shares in *The State of Native America* (1992), shows the commonality of that knowledge and is echoed by Thunder Hawk here:

> [W]e've never had to singly say women should be . . . talked about. We've known that, you know, generation after generation. It's the outside world that doesn't know. We had societies of women that have responsibilities that kept our communities healthy and vibrant and powerful. And, you know, we had to make sure we had a future. We have our culture, we have our way of life, we have our language. What we're trying to do is retain it, retain our right as a people to be Indian. (Interview with Flanders 2023)

For the youth, Thunder Hawk emphasizes the importance of preserving the knowledge, not only broadly about Native Americans, but also preserving the invisiblized women, their names, their actions, and their service to Native people. She says:

> [W]atching the women is amazing, how they handle everything protecting our people and our children's future and fighting. Being warriors in that way. They've passed on. They're gone. And if it wasn't for this archive, a lot of their stories wouldn't be known. And maybe, you know, in families

handed down stories, but generally speaking, because of the way of patriarchy and the way the whole system is set up.... We were totally disregarded and so this archive is very important. It gives our young people the whole history ... it wasn't just the guys; the women toed the line. (Interview with Flanders 2023)

Coalitional work and building ally networks are also critical to sovereignty's success. To bring the point full circle, that sovereignty, land, water, the living universe, and everything that Native American people embody are interconnected. As Thunder Hawk reminds us, "whether it's here in our territory, Dakota, Lakota Territory, or if it's in Palestine, it's an indigenous struggle, and it always starts with the land. The issues never gonna change, because the colonizers ... they're always gonna want your land. And so the movements are like breathing, living things" (Thunder Hawk in interview with Tilsen, 2023). The understanding of the living universe carries us toward a reciprocal relationship and into a commitment to protect the living universe. To do so, alliances built on ethos of protection are necessary. Standing Rock, in 2016, represents the same fight, generations later and, yet, the same ethos and praxes in sovereignty work emerged:

> Standing Rock not only [brought] all of the indigenous people together of this hemisphere but the non-indigenous, too ... I think that's one of the strengths that helps us. Those of us that choose to take on the responsibility of carrying this on and the dedication it takes ... for example, my station in life now, as an elder, ... I work within the community of elders, elderly women, you know, and we have to learn not only how to carry on our teaching from the past, in that our teachings from our ancestors are struck from the oral histories [but they] are streaming online. (Thunder Hawk in interview with Tilsen, 2023)

Sovereignty Work in the Urban Indian Community

Seminole activist, cofounder of the Bay Area IdleNoMore, and professor of Native American Studies, Dr. Melinda Micco found herself far from home in the Bay Area. In 2021, Micco shared her own journey into sovereignty work in an interview with me and Elena Harvey Collins, for our collaborative exhibition titled "All Words Have Roots," a poem by US Poet Laureate and Muskogee citizen Joy Harjo, which inspired an exhibition that explored the ways Native American culture bearers' works are all rooted in land, water, sovereignty, and relational praxes with the living universe (2021). Our conversation centered on her experience as a cofounder of the Bay Area's IdleNoMore organization and the Refinery Walks. In each, she carried on the well-documented practice, a praxis, really, of walking as an act of sovereignty, of protection, of communion with the living universe, speaking for those who are not audible to humankind, and for public education. For her part in the broader scope of sovereignty work, Micco joined others who used their bodies to demonstrate their refusal to allow the ongoing and disastrous practice of oil extraction and all of its facets. Whether historically or today, the impetus to walk as a demonstration of sovereignty and responsibility has roots in the violence of US and state formation and the sacrifices of relatives and ancestors. For Micco, she says, "just in terms of my own family's history... we were marched from the southeast to Oklahoma, so there are tinges of the death march for me in my own family's history." She explains:

> When I went to Florida... I went to where one of our treaties was signed, by myself, just out there, and that's where I felt that strong, strong connection to the land and to the treaty by which we lost that land. So for me, it's an inherent responsibility to all land, whether it's the California Native land, the Ohlone land that I'm living on, all of that is to recognize that all of this came from that spiritual base. For me, the borders, the medicine line, all of those are fabricated entities, made up entities, and they don't really reflect... the sacredness of land, the sacredness of water, air, and everything because of the ways that people have abused and misused it. (Interview with Lee-Oliver and Harvey Collins, 2021)

By the 1970s, the long history of forced "death marches" was an ever-present touchstone in Native American histories, including urban Indian. In the San Francisco Bay Area, home to one of the first urban Indian communities, Native peoples came from far and wide to initiate what would become the first "longest walk" from Alcatraz Island off the coast of San Francisco to Washington, D.C.'s, Bureau of Indian Affairs. The practice of walking also represents a cognitive shift from walking by force, or the state violence intentionally aimed to sever Native peoples from their sovereign homelands and eliminate their rights as sovereigns, to walking as a demonstration of inherent sovereignty. Walking is a call out to the world to take notice and join in efforts to stop disaster capitalism in Native America, that Native America is the basis on which all other forms of U.S. empire are founded, and that the deracination of Native American peoples, epistemologies, and political systems is part and parcel of the systems of oppression faced by any other US resident or citizen. It is not, however, a human-centric action. Rather, it considers the living universe, peoples, lands, waters, and the cosmos, which form our systems of integrated life. Intervening by walking and occupying key places and institutions, like the tar sands, Chevron, and Shell, including refineries in the Bay Area's Richmond, California, Micco and IdleNoMore members walk to bring attention to the environmental impacts of disaster capitalism. They also targeted major institutions, including banks like Wells

Fargo, that cosign and sponsor mega-corporate over-power, including gasoline and oil companies. Micco and the Grandmothers, a transnational Indigenous group of women who commit to work in coalition on issues related to threats against Indigenous sovereignty, engage in occupying spaces and disrupting the flow of commerce, as a means to pressure co-participants—people—whose engagement in disaster capitalism is also a major catalyst of the ongoing deleterious effects of westernity and globalization. They physically put their bodies on the line. Micco explains that as Grandmothers, the hope (though she acknowledges the privilege of hoping as an Elder woman) was that police and others would be less likely to beat or harm grandmothers. They hoped, too, that a political kinship may form, where the growth of allies results. In one walk down a major avenue in San Francisco, followed by the occupation of a Wells Fargo lobby, Micco shares that many people expressed their frustration, but some also experienced a turn toward allyship. She says many asked:

> Why you doing this? They were upset because traffic was slowed down and we were walking, and just kept walking. By the end, we had people honking at us, and, you know, waving and joining our walk. And that in itself is really important, because [we are] a small number. As we are in the Native population in this country, we need our allies. We need people to stand up. But we're the cog that needs to propel the machine in where it's going to go.

The sense of responsibility to be a "cog" is not far reaching. Considering what I also theorize as an inheritance of political voice, Micco and other Native women whose work is an exercise of sovereignty do so as a commitment to protecting a broader holistically representative sovereign. To do so is to live in acknowledgement of our ancestors—all relatives—who also sacrificed, who may be watching, and collective peers and youth, who also may be witness to efforts to protect. Micco says, "If I don't do something, don't say something, or bring the attention to the rest of the world about this, then what kind of modeling will I have done for my children and grandchildren? It's extremely important to carry that on."

After a major malfunction at one of the refineries in the Bay Area sent plumes of toxic smoke and debris into the environment and hundreds of local Richmond residents to emergency rooms, there was little to no notification sent out by the refinery or city officials. The refineries' minimal follow-up about the crisis lasted for days and weeks. In response, IdleNoMore members commenced the "Refinery Walks." Every Sunday, wearing Ribbon Skirts, carrying eagle feathers, smudging as they walked, the grandmothers, youth, and other members walked to demonstrate against the disastrous effects of capitalist extraction. Micco speaks of this impetus for this critical work and its necessity:

> If we can look back at that history, and if people can know that history, then they can understand why we walk, why we do the things that we do. [E]very time there's a flaring [when the refinery processing plant emits excessive and toxic levels of fumes and debris into the air] ... I know the communities that are being affected. [It's] important to realize, too, and keep in your mind: Every step is a prayer. It may hurt, and you may be tired ... but every step is a prayer.

Although Native American women are recognized in reservation and urban communities for their contributions to sovereignty work, there remains a dearth in the literature and popular imaginary about Native American women and girls and their roles in their communities and political interventions. Janet McCloud, Wilma Mankiller, Winona LaDuke, Tillie Black Bear, Madonna Thunder Hawk, Marcella Gilbert, Melinda Micco, and Patricia Penn Hilden are just a few who should be exalted in teachings about sovereignty, democracy, climate change, and environmental protection and, just saying, feminism and women's rights.

Love and Sovereignty—the Other Side of Human-Centered Modernity

I have had the great fortune of being raised by a revolutionary protector, so I have learned of and from many of these Native women leaders and protectors. The absence of acknowledgement I witnessed over the long course of my education made their invisibility appear as a great silencing of their histories and them as role models. They breathe life into people like me—and other kids who become protectors or who seek meaningful lives. Good thing we have stories and oral traditions. They allow us, then and now, to pierce the silence and spread knowledge about the construction of silence and power and to document the critical work of sovereignty protectors and other invisbleized peoples.

There are varied spatial and multi-modal ways that Native American women enact sovereignty work. It is a relational process. Native American literary scholars have long used the spaces of the page to speak from the intimacy of body, home, community, and relation to place, to retrace and recollect for themselves—and the broader public—alternative and positive representations of Native American peoples. Many work through the mode of Red feminism to undo the entanglements of coloniality by speaking back to the public. In her book *Seeing Red: Anger, Sentimentality, and American Indians*, Cari Carpenter says that to reclaim and confront the racialized and sexualized images that linger today is conducive to enacting the love and rage necessary in the work of protectors of all types (2008). Literature, by extension a form of storytelling, is one of the earliest expressions for reaching non-Native audiences, and Native American women authors used "anger and rage" discursively and ideologically through literature to extend their political critiques beyond the limitations of the genres (Carpenter 2008: 7). Voicing anger in literary form, according to Carpenter and other Native writers like Joy Harjo, Louise Erdrich, and Craig Womack, enables the writer to contextualize and reframe the peoples within decolonial counternarratives, therein reanimating Native American political agency, among other themes, through rationalizing anger and rage (Womack 1999; Carpenter 2008).

For Native American peoples, we are only a few generations away from colonial and "American" expansions across the Americas. The reverberations of these violent histories continue to galvanize sovereignty work, which is inherently decolonial. The work resonates across national, tribal, and international borders, and essentialism is widely accepted. It is considered common sense. Today, Native American women on reservations, pueblos, and rancherias, as well as in urban Indian spaces, face the highest rates of murder and sexual assault of any women in the United States (Lee-Oliver 2013). Canadian First Nations women and girls experience similar levels of violence. The violence can be and often is interpreted as part and parcel of the long durée of colonialism. In the most practical sense, Native American women's liturgies of life rely on an ethos grounded in sovereignty and protection. In his own decolonial work and allyship, Nelson Maldonado-Torres reflects the inherent love that is part and parcel of what I identify as the liturgies of life among revolutionaries and protectors:

> For colonized and racialized peoples, identity is always contested since it is tied to a power structure and an imaginary that militates against their very existence. For this reason, questions of liberation and identity are central to philosophical discourses articulated from the position of sub-altern peoples, ... The destabilization of the imperial order of things occurs in thought as well as in praxis. Appeals to love in the face of colonialism and slavery appear more as consistent responses to systems of dehumanization. ... Love, once again, appears as a response to war ... but love is interpreted here as a de-colonizing activity and war as a paradigm. (Maldonado-Torres 2008: 189, 240–252)

Native American women's sovereignty work exemplifies a decolonial liturgy of life. It is made of the right to inherent sovereignty in a living universe, thus a political responsibility that is born with the inheritors of the first treaties and sovereignty in that context. In diverse ways, with intentionality, the Indigenous self is made to disrupt the manifold systems of oppression, the comfort zones of settler nativists, and the imaginary naturalness of the hegemonic order, its imperatives, and its policing forces. Expressions of decolonial, revolutionary, and "fierce love" are foundational to Native American women's sovereignty work (Racette 2010). Therein, the "Red Zone" is revealed, whether on reservations, in rural communities, or in urban "Indian" settings. The reclamation of the Red Zone exemplifies sovereign peoples untethered from US nationalism and, rather, is understood as part and parcel of sacred systems and the great mystery. That is the prime imperative. Native American women's sovereignty work emerges as an ethic of love and strategy, in multiple liturgies of life, to breathe life into and revitalize individuals and collective lifeways in the living universe.

Bibliography

Barbie, Donna. 2001. "Sacagawea: The Making of a Myth," *Sifters: Native American Women's Lives*, Oxford: Oxford University Press.

Bernasconi, Robert. 2002. "Kant As an Unfamiliar Source of Racism," *Philosophers on Race: Critical Essays*, Malden, MA: Blackwell Publishing.

Blackhawk, Ned. 2004. *Violence Over the Land: Indians and Empires in the American West*, Cambridge, UK: Cambridge University Press.

Brady, Sr., Steve. 1999, June. Oral history.

Brave Heart, Maria Yellow Horse. 1998. *The Return to the Sacred Path: Healing from Historical Trauma and Unresolved Grief among the Lakota* (PhD dissertation, Smith College Studies in Social Work, 68(3): pp. 287–305).

Carpenter, Cari M. 2008. *Seeing Red: Anger, Sentimentality, and American Indians*, The Ohio State University Press.

Chivington, John M. 1865. "The Sand Creek Massacre—John M. Chivington's Defense: To the People of Colorado," *Papers, Manuscript of John M. Chivington 1862–1892*, Western History/Genealogy Department, Denver Public Library. http://www.kclonewolf.com/History/SandCreek/sc-documents/sc-chiv-defense.html.

Churchill, Ward. 1997. *A Little Matter of Genocide: Holocaust and Denial in the Americas, 1492 to the Present*, San Francisco: City Lights.

Custalow, Dr. Linwood "Little Bear" and Angela L. Daniel "Silver Star." 2007. *The True Story of Pocahontas: The Other Side of History*, Wheat Ridge, CO: Fulcrum Publishing.

Cutler, Bruce. 1995. *The Massacre at Sand Creek: Narrative Voices*, Norman, OK: University of Oklahoma Press.

Deloria, Philip. 2004. *Indians in Unexpected Places*, Lawrence: University of Kansas Press.

Deloria, Vine. 2006 *The World We Used to Live In: Remembering the Powers of the Medicine Men*. Wheat Ridge, CO: Fulcrum Publishing.

Deloria, Vine, and Daniel Wildcat. 2001. *Power and Place: Indian Education in America*, Wheat Ridge, CO: Fulcrum Publishing.

Eastman, Charles Ohiyesa. 2003. *The Soul of the Indian*, Garden City, NY: Dover Publications.

Estes, Nick. "Honoring Treaties to Understand the Past & Plan for the Future," Pt. 1, *New Mexico in Focus*, PBS, August 24, 2018.

Grande, Sandy. 2004. *Red Pedagogy: Native American Social and Political Thought*, Lanham, MD: Rowman & Littlefield Publishers.

Green, Rayna. 1975. "The Pocahontas Perplex: The Image of Indian Women in American Culture," *Massachusetts Review*, Vol. 27, No. 4, pp. 698–714.

Guerrero, M. A. Jaimes. 2003. "'Patriarchal Colonialism' and Indigenism: Implications for Native Feminist Spirituality and Native Womanism," *Hypatia*, Vol. 18, No. 2, pp. 58–69.

Hanke, Lewis. 1974. *All Mankind Is One: A Study of the Disputation Between Bartolemé de Las Casas and Juan Ginés de Sepúlveda on the Religious and Intellectual Capacity of the American Indians*, De Kalb: Northern Illinois University Press.

Hoig, Stan. 1961. *The Sand Creek Massacre*, Norman: University of Oklahoma Press.

Huhndorf, Shari, and Cheryl Suzack. 2010. *Indigenous Women and Feminism: Politics, Activism, Culture*. Vancouver/Toronto: UBC Press.

Jaimes, M. Annette, and Theresa Halsey. 1992. "American Indian Women: At the Center of Indigenous Resistance in North America," *The State of Native America*, Boston: South End Press.

Kincheloe, Joe L. (ed.). 1998. *White Reign: Deploying Whiteness in America*, New York: St. Martin's Press.

LaDuke, Winona. 1999. *All Our Relations: Native Struggles for Life and Land*, Boston: South End Press.

Lee-Oliver, Leece. 2020. "Pocahontas: Digital Coloniality, Coercive Fiction, and 'Renewing' Western Hegemonic Power," ed. Shearon Roberts, *Recasting the Disney Princess in an Era of New Media and Social Movements*, Lanham, MD: Lexington Books.

Lee-Oliver, Leece. *Contemporary Modernity and "Death Ethics": Antecedents and Impacts of Western Expansion as War in the Northern Plains, 1820–1880* (dissertation, Department of Ethnic Studies, University of California, Berkeley, May 16, 2013).

Lewis, Sol. 1973. *The Sand Creek Massacre: A Documentary History*, NY: Sol Lewis.

Lomawaima, Tsianina. 2007, fall. Lecture notes from her talk on "good" and "bad" "Indians," Department of Ethnic Studies, University of California, Berkeley.

"Madonna Thunder Hawk: A Matriarch of the Movement," interview with Nick Tilsen, Landback for the People, Season 1, Episode 1, NDN Podcasts, accessed September 5, 2023.

Maldonado-Torres, Nelson. 2008. *Against War: Views from the Underside of Modernity*, Durham, NC: Duke University Press.

Mankiller, Wilma, and Michael Wallis. 1993. *Mankiller: A Chief and Her People*, New York: St. Martin's Press.

Marubbio, M. Elise. 2006. *Killing the Indian Maiden: Images of Native American Women in Film*, Lexington: University Press of Kentucky.

Micco, Melinda. 2021, February 19. "Why Are We Walking, What Are We Doing This For?" interview with Leece Lee-Oliver and Elena Harvey Collins, for *All Words Have Roots* exhibition.

Moore, MariJo. 2008. *Birthed From Scorched Hearts: Women Respond to War*, Wheat Ridge, CO: Fulcrum.

Muthu, Sankar. 2003. *Enlightenment Against Empire*, Princeton, NJ: Princeton University Press.

Newman, Louise. 1999. *White Women's Rights: The Racial Origins of Feminism in the United States*, Oxford University Press.

Omi, Michael, and Howard Winant. 2015. *Racial Formation in the United States*, 3rd ed. New York: Routledge.

Ortiz, Simon. 1981. *From Sand Creek: Rising in this Heart Which is Our America*, New York, Thunder's Mouth Press.

Ostler, Jeffrey. 2004. *The Plains Sioux and U.S. Colonialism from Lewis and Clark to Wounded Knee*, New York: Cambridge University Press.

Penn Hilden, Patricia. 2005. *From a Red Zone: Critical Perspectives on Race, Politics & Culture*, NJ: The Red Sea Press, Inc.

Perry, Barbara. 2008. *Silent Victims: Hate Crimes Against Native Americans*, Tucson: University of Arizona Press.

Racette, Sherry Farrell. 2010. "'This Fierce Love': Gender, Women, and Art Making," *Art in Our Lives: Native Women Artists in Dialogue*, Santa Fe, NM: School for Advanced Research Press.

Roediger, David. 2005. *Working Toward Whiteness: How America's Immigrants became White: The Strange Journey from Ellis Island to the Suburbs*. New York: Basic Books.

Sepulveda, Juan Gines de. 1547. *The Second Democrates*, http://www.digitalhistory.uh.edu/learning_history/spain/spain_sepulveda.cfm.

Simpson, Audra. 2007, December 9. "On Ethnographic Refusal: Indigeneity, 'Voice,' and Colonial Citizenship," *Junctures*.

Smedley, Audrey. 2007. *Race in North America: Origin and Evolution of a Worldview*, Boulder, CO: Westview Press.

Spivak, G. C. 1988. "Can the Subaltern Speak?" In *Marxism and the Interpretation of Culture*, edited by C. Nelson and L. Grossberg. Urbana: University of Illinois Press.

Stanciu, Cristina, and Kristina Ackley. 2015. "Introduction: Laura Cornelius Kellogg: Haudenosaunee Thinker, Native Activist, American Writer," in *Laura Cornelius Kellogg: Our Democracy and the American Indian and Other Works*, Syracuse, NY: Syracuse University Press.

Stannard, David. 1992. *American Holocaust: Columbus and the Conquest of the New World*, New York: Oxford University Press.

Stoler, Ann Laura. 2002. *Carnal Knowledge and Imperial Power: Race and the Intimate in Colonial Rule*, Berkeley: University of California Press.

Tohe, Laura. 2000. "There Is No Word for Feminism in My Language," *Wicazo Sa Review*, Vol. 15, No. 2, pp. 103–110.

Trask, Haunani. 1996. "Feminism and Indigenous Hawaiian Nationalism," *Signs: Journal of Women in Culture and Society*, Vol. 21, No. 4.

Troulliot, Michel. 1995. *Silencing the Past: Power and the Production of History*, Boston: Beacon Press.

Wagner, Sally Roesch. 1996, Winter. "Is Equality Indigenous? The Untold Iroquois Influence on Early Radical Feminism," *On the Issues,* Vol. 5, no. 1.

Wallerstein, Immanuel. 2004. *World-Systems Analysis: An Introduction*, Durham, NC: Duke University Press.

"Warrior Women & Wounded Knee at 50: Madonna Thunder Hawk & Marcella Gilbert," interview on *The Laura Flanders Show*, aired February 12, 2023. https://www.youtube.com/watch?v=jr1QBdefxH0&t=26s.

Wilkins, David E. 2009. *Documents of Native Americans Political Development: 1500s to 1933*, Oxford: Oxford University Press.

Wilkins, David E., and K. Tsianina Lomawaima. 2001. *Uneven Ground: American Indian Sovereignty and Federal Law*, Norman: University of Oklahoma Press.

Williams, Robert. 2005. "'The Savage As the Wolf, The Founders' Language of Indian Savagery," *Like a Loaded Weapon: The Rehnquist Court, Indian Rights, and the Legal History of Racism in America*, Minneapolis: University of Minnesota Press.

Winnemucca Hopkins, Sarah. 1883, republished 2017. *Life Among the Paiutes: Their Wrongs and Claims*, Mount Pleasant, SC: Arcadia Press.

Womack, Craig. 1999. *Red On Red: Native American Literary Separatism*, University of Minnesota Press.

14

Not Only an Academic Field, but Also Movements
Advancing Ethnic Studies with Decolonial Feminisms

XAMUEL BAÑALES

Ethnic Studies emerged in the late 1960s as an antidote to oppression. It developed during a charged sociopolitical context in the United States and abroad that included the Cold War, the Civil Rights movement, the Vietnam War, police violence, and the Black, brown, red, yellow, feminist, and gay power activism of the late 1960s (Ordona 2000; Pulido 2006; Biondi 2012; Bañales and Lee-Oliver 2019). As protest and decolonization movements intensified across the globe, so did state repression and violence. One example is in 1968, when the Mexican Armed Forces massacred students, workers, and urban poor who protested the Mexico City Olympics (see Poniatowska 1975)—the same international event where African American athletes Tommie Smith and John Carlos opposed oppression by raising their black-gloved fists (known as the Black Power salute) as the U.S. national anthem played during their medals ceremony (see Edwards 2018).

One exceptional component of Ethnic Studies is that protest movements birthed it (Abdullah 2020), pushing educational institutions and society to be more inclusive and transform. Developing from numerous *movidas* (Espinoza, Cotera, and Blackwell 2018) or movements, and alongside local, national, and global protests, activism created Ethnic Studies out of various regional and ethnic/racial positionalities that were often interconnected but politically unique. Challenging the Western university and society, one of the reasons that the field and movements for Ethnic Studies emerged was as a decolonizing epistemic necessity, serving as a bridge to transcend violence, racism, and other forms of coloniality (Grosfoguel 2012; Bañales and Roaf 2016). The field and movements advocated to think critically about power, oppression, and privilege, enact personal and community empowerment, and inspire activism and social change (Bañales 2019b). Furthermore, Ethnic Studies contributed to a critical consciousness that "seeks to decolonize, desegregate, and de-generate power, being, and knowledge" (Maldonado-Torres 2019, 242), at the intersection of social politics and activism, artistic creation, and intellectual production. Institutionalizing Ethnic Studies disrupted normative academic knowledge and enacted a critical intervention against Eurocentric imperial culture and modern/colonial thought.

To be sure, Ethnic Studies challenged the colonial legacy of the university, but it was also bounded by sociopolitical issues, discourses, and activist strategies of the time. One shortcoming was the limited theorization of race, racism, and colonialism in relation to other constitutive forms of power, like gender and sexuality. Although women of color since the 1960s theorized simultaneous oppressions (see Combahee River Collective 1977; Garcia 1997), including race, ethnicity, class, gender, sexuality, and nation, Ethnic Studies—as well as other disciplines, like Women/Gender/Queer Studies—did not effectively integrate (what would later be called) intersectionality (Crenshaw 1995). Although the field and movements of Ethnic Studies have evolved since their inception, there is still much work to do.

One promise and possibility for the evolution of the field/movements for Ethnic Studies is to center decolonial feminisms. Decolonial feminisms has roots in Latin America as a political struggle and theoretical framework (Lugones 2007 and 2010; Martínez 2019; Pitts, Ortega, and Medina 2020; Martínez and Agüero 2021; Curiel 2021; Espinosa-Miñoso, Lugones, and Maldonado-Torres 2021; Martínez-Cairo and Buscemi 2021) and is in complex interrelation with women of color thought (Pérez 2010; Arvin, Tuck, and Morrill 2013; Velez 2019; Alarcón et al. 2020; Lee-Oliver and Bañales 2023). Given the various contexts and nuances of the theories and praxes, referencing them as decolonial feminisms in the plural is significant. Central propositions of decolonial feminisms include affirming that gender is a construct of modernity/coloniality, expanding the narrow treatment of gender in theories and analyses about decolonization, and centralizing new proposals for resistance, multiplicity, and coalition to defy the logics of categorical, hierarchical, and dichotomous colonial power (Sandoval 2000; Lugones 2007 and 2010; Pérez 2010; Alarcón et al. 2020; Bañales 2023). Therefore, centering decolonial feminisms in Ethnic Studies can contribute to the development and futurity of the field/movements by exposing "what is hidden from our understandings of both race and gender and the relation of each to normative heterosexuality" (Lugones 2010, 742).

Focusing on the field/movements of Ethnic Studies, this essay engages with decolonial feminisms to further transform. It begins by discussing the activist foundations and decolonizing interventions of the field/movements of Ethnic Studies. Then, it examines a U.S. historical context of the mid-twentieth century to underscore the politics of heteropatriarchy within respective discourses and movements of the time. The chapter proceeds by considering the ways decolonial feminisms can serve as a bridge to advance Ethnic Studies. Finally, the essay provides examples of decolonial feminisms integrated into Ethnic Studies curriculum and programming at my current university.

Protest Movements: The Heart of Ethnic Studies

Before World War II, most people attending American universities were historically male and white, invariably children of parents who attended colleges who were most likely children of parents with higher education, and so on down the line (Davis 2010). In the United States and other "Global North" (or "first world") countries, people of European origin have long dominated scholarship and higher education. Subjects such as history, literature, art, and society "were formerly always 'white only' (and usually 'male only'), with other groups considered only as problems, enemies, or outsiders" (Forbes 2008, 59). Since the settler-colonial origins of the United States, when education was mostly rural and organized around agricultural or religious practices, institutions have contributed to epistemological violence, prohibited literacy, and erased the experiences or histories of marginalized populations (see Jackson 2001; Hale 2002; Miranda 2013; War Jack 2019a).

During the 1960s in the United States, many Black, Indigenous, and people of color entered the university as first-generation college students through the GI Bill or recently established state outreach programs like Extended Opportunity Program Services (EOPS). However, once these students were on campus, they encountered a white supremacist, hostile university that reflected society's exclusionary racial power dynamics (Roaf 2019). In response, radical activism, revolutionary art and music, anti-colonial movements, and anti-racist scholarship influenced students—along with professors and communities in struggle—to organize. Black, Chicano/a/x, Asian American, and Native American students and their allies formed the Third World Liberation Front (TWLF) coalition, which went on strike and demanded the institutionalization of Third World studies, first at San Francisco State University (SFSU) and then University of California, Berkeley (Okihiro 2016).

Challenging the structural racism of the university, the TWLF led the longest student strike in the United States at the time through informational picketing, blocking campus entrances, mass rallies, and teach-ins. Arrests, violence, and bloodshed of activists eventually led SFSU and UC Berkeley to create Ethnic Studies in 1969 (Asian Community Center Archive Group 2009; Macias 2019). However, the university betrayed the idea of Third World studies by welcoming a more neutral "race relations" approach to the field, drawing from the Chicago School's sociologically based studies of ethnicity in the early 1900s. Despite this, "the spirit of the global Third World anticolonial struggles for self-determination and antiracism lives on" (Okihiro 2016, 14). The compromise of the name did not stop students at college campuses across the United States from organizing demonstrations and fighting against institutional racism and social inequities, and instituting versions of Ethnic Studies elsewhere (Ginzberg and Dawson 2016; López, Gold, and Sporn 2021).

The movements to institute Ethnic Studies in higher education were a critical intervention. The Western academy is an imperial and corporatized university, whereby scholarship and intellectuals play a central role—wittingly or unwittingly—in legitimizing settler-colonialism and American exceptionalism, as well as rationalizing U.S. repression and expansionism domestically and across the globe (Wallerstein 1997; Chatterjee and Maira 2014; and Grosfoguel, Hernández, and Velásquez 2016). As Sandy Grande argues, the academy is "an arm of the settler state—a site where the logics of elimination, capital accumulation, and dispossession are reconstituted" (Grande 2018, 47). While the university is a contradictory and limiting space (Hames-García 2014), it is also a site where transformative thinking and social change can occur (Oparah 2014). As the Third World Strike demonstrated, college students, staff, faculty, or administrators can occupy a space that may offer many productive opportunities to challenge the university's colonizing structures.

Ethnic Studies has faced many political obstacles and institutional challenges since its inception, including reduced budget allocations, lack of support or autonomy, marginalization of faculty, racist ideologies, and reactionary public policy measures and laws (Scott 2008; Bañales and Roaf 2016; Acosta 2019; Jackson 2019; Khanmalek 2019; Maldonado-Torres et al. 2023). To provide examples of Ethnic Studies struggles, a coalition of students at the University of California, Berkeley, protested budget cuts in 1999 with a hunger strike to support the development of Ethnic Studies and other critical spaces there (Bacchetta 2019; Luna 2019). In 2010, the Arizona legislature passed House Bill 2281, which banned Ethnic Studies courses at the high school level in Tucson (Bañales and Roaf 2016; Acosta 2019). The California State University Task Force on the Advancement of Ethnic Studies issued a report in 2016 that revealed several issues, including that Ethnic Studies units in the CSU were disproportionately affected by the reduction of resources and lacked appropriate institutional support (California State University 2016). The same year, students at San Francisco State University enacted a hunger strike to demand a substantial budget increase for the College of Ethnic Studies (Herrera 2016). In 2017, students at CSU Northridge launched massive protests that halted implementation of the chancellor-mandated Executive Order 1100, which negatively affected the General Education requirement of Ethnic Studies there (see Campbell et al. 2019). In 2020, the "model curriculum" of AB331, which would require that all California high school students complete a one-semester Ethnic Studies course to graduate, was the subject of intense debate, revision, and criticism. Critics claimed that the curriculum was ideological and leftist, and that it privileged identity politics and oppression that failed to include ethnic groups like Jewish Americans (Morrar 2020). In California, controversies emerged in 2023 over how Ethnic Studies should be taught in high schools (Tucker 2023), and in 2025, Assembly Bill 1468—later withdrawn—sought to censor honest discussions of Palestine, colonization, and anti-Arab racism in Ethnic Studies classrooms (CAIR California 2025).

Thus, Ethnic Studies is not only a field of study but also movements that are part of an epistemic decolonizing project for liberation that is unfinished. Reframing Ethnic Studies this way can explain why it continuously faces obstacles and appears antithetical to educational institutions, which are rooted in and contribute to (settler) colonialism and Western imperialism (Chatterjee and Maira 2014; Grosfoguel, Hernández, and Velásquez 2016). Specific to the academy, the university provides countless excuses as to why it neglects to properly support, develop, or institute Ethnic Studies, regardless if there are educational benefits or positive results (Bravo 2020; Donald 2016). It's not unusual for administrators to determine the growth, or measure the "success," of Ethnic Studies by comparing it against more "established" academic disciplines (see Khanmalek 2019). Conventional disciplines are ideologically and structurally positioned to comfortably align with and reproduce Western thought and Eurocentric imperial culture at the university, while Ethnic Studies is often perceived as less rational or rigorous (Maldonado-Torres 2019).

The Mid-Twentieth Century: Politics of Heteropatriarchy

Self-determination, nationalism, and racial/ethnic/class consciousness occupied a foundational role in the emergence of Ethnic Studies. Heteropatriarchal perspectives were dominant within the context of decolonial theories and revolutionary ideas of the mid-twentieth century, which often focused on race and class while eclipsing gender, sexuality, and other forms of power (see Pérez 2010). The privileging of heteropatriarchy was not unique to Ethnic Studies but reflected the social political context and protest movements of the time, which were often plagued with sexist or heterosexist/homophobic undertones or views. For example, Eldridge Cleaver, who was the Prime Minister of Information for the Black Panther Party, wrote an essay titled "Notes on a Native Son," which appeared in his 1968 book *Soul on Ice* (Cleaver 1991). In this essay, Cleaver critiques the author James Baldwin by suggesting that a Black homosexual enacts self-hatred against his own blackness when he has a white lover, declaring that Baldwin adopts Europe as his fatherland (DeGout 1992, 425). Further, Cleaver describes a Black homosexual as someone whose masculinity and manhood has been destroyed and "castrated" by a white man. Cleaver states, "Homosexuality is a sickness, just as are baby-rape or wanting to become head of General Motors" (Cleaver 136; for a discussion on the topic, see Porter 2012). Taken together, these arguments assume that homosexuality is an aberration, and that Black and Queer identities are antithetical.

Alongside homophobia, heteropatriarchy manifested in the Black Power movement, which frequently elevated the leadership of men. Although Black women held prominent positions in ethnic/racial organizations during the time, such as the Black Panther Party (Shames and Huggins 2022), their treatment and participation remain misunderstood, controversial, and the subject of rigorous debate (Alameen-Shavers 2016; Brown 1994; Elaine Brown Reading/Talk 2015; Jennings 2001; Joseph 2009; Josephs 2008). Embracing militant rhetoric and postures in the power movements contributed to male leaders' visibility while female-headed Black families in American society were devalued, such as in the 1965 report by Patrick Moynihan of the U.S. Labor Department (Biondi 2012, 26). An undergraduate at Roosevelt University in Chicago in the mid-1960s, Darlene Clark Hine recalls reading, studying, listening to, and valorizing Black men almost exclusively, such as Muhammad Ali, Malcolm X, and Huey P. Newton. By 1968, she felt that she had developed a "black masculine consciousness" and was unaware of the lack of attention on Black women's experiences (quoted in Biondi 2012, 27).

Heteropatriarchy also overshadowed dynamics in the Chicano movement of the late 1960s. Male leadership often dominated even though many Chicana women were central to organizing. For example, at the Chicano Youth Liberation Conference in March 1969, where over 1,500 people gathered to organize, many women incorporated themselves into the male-centric discussion and rallied to address feminist concerns, such as sexism in families and society (see NLCC Educational Media 1996). Not surprisingly, women's leadership in the movement was often suppressed, and there were many struggles over gender and sexuality (see Blackwell 2011). Despite the internal fissures, Chicanas, like other women of color, continued to align with their respective ethnic/racial organizing, as many did not see themselves represented in the emerging feminist movement of the time, which was largely white and middle class (see NLCC Educational Media 1996).

The politics of heteropatriarchy were also part of the Third World Strike of the San Francisco Bay Area. The Black Student Union (BSU) at San Francisco State University (SFSU), which spearheaded the TWLF (see Roaf 2019), had a defined structure with solid gender divisions. This included a central committee of twelve members of vocal, assertive, and noticeable men. Under the central committee were mostly women who were consigned to supportive positions. Men dominated the visual leadership of the strike, even though many women played important roles in it. As former Third World striker Carmen Carrillo states, "the face of the strike was male, but the engine of the strike was female," alluding to how women served as the backbone of the movement for doing critical work behind the scenes, such as being in charge of a "legal defense fund, bailing people out of jail, and clerical work" (Manzanillo 2018). A case in point is former striker Ramona Tascoe's duties for the BSU at SFSU, which consisted of typing speeches, scheduling meetings, and sending out notices, despite standing on the front lines of activism with men and facing arrests, attending rallies, or walking picket lines (Biondi 2012, 59).

There were exceptions. For example, LaNada War Jack, who was part of the central leadership of the TWFL at UC Berkeley. Reflecting on gender dynamics within TWLF organizing, War Jack states, "I did not have to fight for power or to express my voice since the male leadership generally respected me and wanted to hear my perspective. Although male privilege was evident in certain spaces, the men treated me courteously and acted respectfully" (War Jack 2019b, 35). In 1970, Huey P. Newton, co-founder of the Black Panther Party, publicly expressed support for the Women's Liberation and Gay Liberation movements through a published letter and speech (Porter 2012). In a different context, the radical Filipino American organization *Katipunan ng Demokratikong Pilipino* (KDP) of the 1970s included queer members in leadership roles (Bañales 2019c). While instances of gender and queer inclusion existed in racial and ethnic movements of the 1960s–1970s, they were limited and often overshadowed by broader patterns of exclusion.

Despite the strong leadership and active participation of queer people and women of color during the Civil Rights era and ethnic/racial power movements, heteropatriarchal norms and structures continued to dominate. Consider how sexism or homophobia in the Civil Rights movement kept remarkable activist Bayard Rustin in the shadows due to his gay sexual orientation (Gates Jr. 2013), silenced prominent Black women at the 1963 March on Washington (Civil Rights Pioneer Gloria Richardson 2013; Weaver n/d), and limited or undermined the influence of Ella Baker and others (Wong 2017; Urban 2002). Writing about her identity during this time, Audre Lorde states, "Over and over again in the 60s I was asked to justify my existence and my work, because I was a woman, because I was a lesbian, because I was not a separatist, because some piece of me was not acceptable. Not because of my work but because of my identity" (Lorde 2007, 143).

Efforts to integrate these identities faced shortcomings during civil, racial, and nationalist movements. In addition, the limitations of race and class politics in the feminist and gay liberation movements were widespread (see García 1997; Ordona 2000; Bañales 2019c). Unfortunately, leadership in racial/ethnic, gender, or sexuality movements frequently viewed feminists/Queer/Trans people of color as traitors, often rejecting, uninviting, or making them feel unwelcome to participate (Ordona 2000; Jessi 2007; Bañales 2019c). As a result, embodying an identity and politics at the crossroads of simultaneous oppressions during the 1960s came with many challenges and exclusions.

Decolonial Feminisms As a Bridge

Anti-imperialist male leaders and thinkers of the mid-twentieth century, such as Malcolm X, Che Guevara, Mao Zedong, and Frantz Fanon, inspired many with their ideas to engage in radical social change, including activists of color who fought to create Ethnic Studies. Given the context, their interventions were critical at the time. However, due to the absence of thorough feminist or intersectional analyses, their ideas of revolution and movements offered masculinist interpretations of race, nation, and class, and arguably limited understandings of liberation. Consequently, Ethnic Studies mistakenly was understood as a discipline that narrowly focuses on national, racial/ethnic, and class identities (Grosfoguel 2012). Such a limited focus created myopias in the field of Ethnic Studies, which to this day have not entirely been resolved. One critique is that Ethnic Studies scholars may consider gender and sexuality but often do not comfortably integrate the topics in their frameworks, while some avoid them altogether, frequently believing that they belong solely to the realm of Women, Gender, and Queer Studies. On the other hand, many of the latter disciplines believe that race, class, and colonialism are not at the crux of those fields. Without a doubt, centering a feminist and/or queer/trans politics in Ethnic Studies, and, on the flip side, centralizing race, class, or colonialism in Women, Gender, and Queer Studies, are problems that these fields struggle with (see Ferguson 2004; Chávez-García and Brown 2005; Hames-García 2011; Arvin, Tuck, and Morrill 2013; Durazo 2014; Galarte 2014, 2021).

Fortunately, there have been significant developments in the fields. Since the 1960s, Ethnic Studies, Gender Studies, and other critical fields have grown and adjusted to changing contexts and configurations, such as centralizing the topics of intersectionality, transnationality, and decoloniality. In doing so, programs and scholarship have articulated the work of decolonial thinking and praxis around race, ethnicity, gender, sexuality, and/or nation (see McLaren 2017; Sueyoshi 2019; Bacchetta 2019; Fukushima 2019; DiPietro, McWeeny, and Roshanravan 2019; DiPietro 2025). Serving as a bridge between scholars of modernity/coloniality and U.S. women of color thought (Maese-Cohen

2010), decolonial feminisms have expanded theories of modernity/coloniality to move beyond the narrow treatment of gender in analyses about decolonization and/or the lack of serious engagement with women of color thought and theories of intersectionality (Lugones 2007 and 2010; Pérez 2010; DiPietro 2024; Salas-SantaCruz 2024). That is, decolonial feminisms highlights the limitations of decolonial theories, including the heavy privileging of male-centric perspectives and lack of engagement with women of color activism and scholarship. Decolonial feminisms also include Native/red feminisms, which calls attention to settler colonialism, heteropatriarchy, and/or sovereignty in critical theorizing and practice (Arvin, Tuck, and Morrill 2013; Lee-Oliver 2019; Whitebear 2023). Moreover, Decolonial Trans* Feminism "represents a critical intersection of thought that interrogates the intersections of coloniality, power, and racialized gender identities within a framework of decolonial feminism[s]" (Salas-SantaCruz 2025, 16).

Decolonial feminisms draw and build on earlier foundations of women of color feminisms and queer of color thought, which has contributed to creating a literary method that bridges the personal with the political, theoretical, creative, and spiritual. The method includes critical scholarship, poetry, prose, political analysis, fiction, storytelling, autobiography, and other forms of creative writing that often examined one's own life (Hull et al. 1982; Moraga and Anzaldúa 1983; Pérez 2010). In doing so, women of color rejected dominant intellectual criteria that relegated the disclosing of the personal into something substandard. Laura E. Pérez argues, "Women of color's autobiographical writing and locating of self within scholarly texts has often staked a claim to theory and philosophizing itself, but through a consciously different protocol than that imposed by academia or literary canons yet knowingly positioning these as alternative archives of knowing and being" (Pérez 2010, 127). Similarly, Juana María Rodríguez argues that foundational women of color feminist texts like *This Bridge Called My Back* "rejected established academic and literary precepts by combining personal essays, poetry, multilingual writing, history, and artwork that theorized the texts of lived experience" (Rodríguez 2003, 30).

In addition, women of color feminist methodologies included multi-issue and coalition-building approaches to politics and organizing. Women of color in the United States worked in solidarity and linked struggles across colonial borders by recognizing the similarities of their racialized, economic, gendered, and sexualized oppression among themselves and with women in the third world (see Sandoval 2000; Lugones 2003; Bacchetta 2010). Since traditional intellectual spaces historically excluded women of color, many spoke for themselves and their communities about the distinct and similar ways that they experienced oppression in the United States (Pérez 2010). As Emma D. Velez argues, "Women of color have long emphasized the importance of coalition to collective struggle against a matrix of systems of oppression" (Velez 2019, 391). Reflecting this perspective, women of color sought liberation by working in coalition to challenge domination and oppression in the United States and abroad.

Reflecting these earlier foundations, decolonial feminisms provide critical analysis to understand struggles for liberation, including the protest context that birthed Ethnic Studies and other movements. Furthermore, decolonial feminisms contribute to imagining futures that transcend ontological, epistemological, and transnational borders to shape new horizons. Finally, decolonial feminisms center creative methodologies, such as solidarity coalitional work, self-reflection, action, and art (Lugones 1987; Sandoval 2000; Pérez 2007, 2010, and 2019; Fujiwara and Roshanravan 2018; Mohanty and Carty 2018; Alarcón et al. 2020; Bañales 2023; Bravo and Figueroa-Vásquez 2023; Fukushima 2023; Lee-Oliver and Bañales 2023; Maese 2023). Thus, decolonial feminisms are critical to Ethnic Studies, Gender Studies, Queer Studies, and other fields for advancing critiques of colonialism and heteropatriarchy while offering critical engagements that advocate for creative and coalitionary approaches to solidarity and liberation movements within and beyond academia in the United States and elsewhere. Like other radical traditions that challenge colonial, racial, and gendered hierarchies, decolonial feminisms offer a generative framework by which to contribute to the unfinished project of liberation.

Advancing Ethnic Studies with Decolonial Feminisms

When the California State University at Stanislaus (CSU Stanislaus) hired me as an assistant professor of Ethnic Studies, the expectation was to serve as a faculty member who contributed to a program that was primarily centered on race/ethnicity. Regrettably, the program was not only outdated but also on the verge of falling apart (Rivera 2013; Ruiz 2013). Although I was a pre-tenured professor, disrupting the normative assumption of my position as a faculty member and of what constitutes Ethnic Studies became critical. Rather than abiding by respectability politics of following established protocol and procedures or treating Ethnic Studies as only an academic discipline, one of the ways that I rejected these norms was by making my position and the field relevant to the regional community and by centering decolonial feminisms in curriculum and pedagogy. It was imperative to enact academic refusal through this intervention, not as a passive retreat or withdrawal but rather understood as an active instantiation of being and doing that is radically different from the norm. Drawing from Black radicalism (abolitionism) and critical Indigenous Studies (decolonial theorization), Sandy Grande argues that refusing the university makes available "more possibilities for coalition and collusion within and outside the university" (Grande 2018, 47). Refusing the university can include "rejecting liberal theories of justice [and recognition] that center respect for cultural difference over critiques of power" (50). Academic refusal can also mean imagining life beyond settler state, white supremacy, and their institutions, and to work "within, against, and beyond the university-as-such" (50).

The consequences of refusing the university, which involved social isolation, administrative retribution, struggles with self-worth, and potential job loss were clear. However, colonizing educational institutions already consider Ethnic Studies as illegitimate (Cacho 2010), which renders its practitioners suspect regardless of whether they challenge or refuse the status quo. Thus, as an Ethnic Studies scholar committed to social change, I chose to maintain my integrity by refusing the university, as I encountered countless structural problems from the beginning of my tenure. For example, although CSU Stanislaus is a Hispanic Serving Institution with about 10,000 enrolled students, of which over 50 percent are "Hispanic," most of the full-time faculty and administrators are white. The university is in a region called the Central Valley of California, which has deeply entrenched socioeconomic problems (Gilmore and Gilmore 2003; González 2017). Furthermore, the history and contemporary context of the area includes the Ku Klux Klan (Rodríguez 2012) and white supremacists, including Nathan Damigo, who founded Identity Evropa and was a former student at CSU Stanislaus (Austin 2016). Along with poor air quality and other harmful environmental factors (Palm 2023), the Central Valley—including CSU Stanislaus—severely lacks community centers and artistic spaces, events, or festivals that center historically marginalized populations or social justice matters.

When I started the faculty position as an assistant professor in the fall of 2016, the campus climate felt tense, as white supremacy intimidations appeared on and off throughout the academic year. One of the main problems was that the Ethnic Studies program had been neglected over time and there was almost nothing on campus (or in the region) to affirm the identities, experiences, histories, or contributions of marginalized populations. Despite not having many resources, much support, or even tenure, and often against (disobeying) the will of administrators, I worked with like-minded campus members to enact critical events that centered culture and organizing. Rather than only focusing on following the guidelines of the tenure process in a traditional way, suspending the guiding principles and expectations of the process became important. Instead, the priority was to institute a variety of annual events on and off campus, such as Day of the Dead (Día de Muertos), Indigenous Peoples Day, Ethnic Studies conference, Race and Power film festival, and other critical events (see Santos and Olmos 2017; Váldez 2017; Dunlap 2018; Gaxiola 2018; Sánchez 2018; and Bustos 2021).

These events advanced a decolonial feminist framework by centering women/Queer/Trans of color identities, experiences, and epistemologies in at least three ways. First, in the initial years of the events, Jazz Díaz, whose artwork is grounded in a decolonial feminist aesthetic, created most of the flyers and promotional materials (see Díaz 2019). Second, each of the events included women/Queer/Trans of color speakers, films, and/or workshops, such as Reverend Dr. Trinity Ordona (see Bañales 2019c), who was a keynote panelist in the 2018 Ethnic Studies conference. Finally, the programming integrated intersectionality in ways that disrupted normative assumptions of race, culture, gender, and/or sexuality. To highlight one example, I'll discuss the Day of the Dead event, which draws from the holiday celebrated in Mexico (and elsewhere) that culminates on November 2.

The atmosphere of the Day of the Dead events that the Ethnic Studies Department at my campus hosts is colorful and festive, as the lives of ancestors are remembered and celebrated with food, altars, and community. When the Chicano/a/x community popularized this holiday in the United States during the 1970s, cultural and social justice politics became central to the celebrations (Marchi 2009). In the Chicano/a/x tradition, students in Ethnic Studies classes that I taught called attention to social justice issues in creative ways through the altars they created for the event. For the 2018 Day of the Dead event, a variety of critical topics were depicted in the altars, including the unjust killings of Black and Brown people by police and the many unfair deaths of migrants crossing the US-Mexico border. Alongside, students also created altars that focused on the discriminatory deaths of women/Queer people of color, such as Missing and Murdered Indigenous Women (MMIW), Translatina migrants who died under Immigration Customs and Enforcement (ICE) custody, and the Orlando Pulse nightclub massacre in 2016, where the majority who were murdered were of Puerto Rican and Latinx backgrounds (see Figures 14.1, 14.2, and 14.3).

The Day of the Dead events combine critical pedagogy while also addressing many of the pressing needs of students and community members in the region. These events foster a sense of cultural affirmation and belonging, providing spaces where participants can honor ancestral traditions while engaging in meaningful discussions on social justice and collective healing. In particular, the events contributed to revamping Ethnic Studies courses by centering not only popular education (see Freire 2000) and community responsive approaches (Tintiangco-Cubales et al. 2019), in which dialogue and critical learning connect with community engagement and praxis, but also feminist decolonial methodologies and activist histories that shape the field.

Learning about the origins of Ethnic Studies, which involved the TWLF and student-led Third World Strike, along with other factors, such as engaging in close mentorship and establishing connections with community

FIGURE 14.1. Ethnic Studies students created this altar to honor the Missing and Murdered Indigenous Women. Photograph by Xamuel Bañales.

organizations, invigorated many students to feel empowered and work toward action. As such, part of academic refusal involved using the classroom and university in creative ways to help mobilize students' and community members' efforts to enact social change (see Bañales and Roaf 2016; Bañales 2019a). One example of this took place at the beginning of the spring semester of 2019, when white supremacist posters of Identity Evropa resurfaced on campus. Outraged students in an Ethnic Studies course that I taught created a coalition with activist organizations at CSU Stanislaus and members of the

FIGURE 14.2. Ethnic Studies students created this altar to honor Roxana Hernandez and Victoria Arellano, two trans migrants who died under ICE custody. Photograph by Xamuel Bañales.

FIGURE 14.3. Ethnic Studies students created this altar to honor those who died in the Orlando Pulse nightclub massacre. Photograph by Xamuel Bañales.

regional community to spark a semester-long protest campaign on campus that incorporated "teach outs" every Tuesday afternoon, which was referred to as #TransformativeTuesdays. The mobilizing campaign of #TransformativeTuesdays refused the "business as usual" attitude and approach of the university, which had failed to appropriately address and resolve the white supremacy on campus. As a result, students, faculty, and other supporters called attention to the inequities on campus through protest (see Dunlap and Dias 2019). In addition, Queer/women students and faculty of color led this campus protest movement, contrasting with the ethnic/racial organizing of the 1960s, which often relegated them to the margins. The pressure eventually pushed the university to enact structural change, which included hiring faculty, counselors, and administrators of color with an emphasis in social justice training, and funding permanent campus-wide murals to reflect the historical and contemporary experiences of Native American, Black, Chicano/a/x-Latino/a/x, and Asian American and Pacific Islander communities. The first installment was the Chicano/a/x-Latino/a/x mural in the fall of 2019 (First Installment 2020). Departing from popular ethnic murals of the 1960s and 70s that depict heteronormative or nationalist themes (Jackson 2009), the first mural at CSU Stanislaus centered land and healing. Additionally, there is an abstract visual reference to Xochipilli, who was the Mesoamerican deity of flower, song, dance, and creativity (see Renteria 2018) and has been interpreted as the patron of male homosexuality (Greenberg 1990, 165).

During the spring 2021 semester, refusing the university by further enacting decolonial feminisms continued. In 2020, the California governor approved then-assembly member Dr. Shirley Weber's AB1460, which made Ethnic Studies a graduation requirement across the California State University system starting in the fall of 2021. The academic year of 2020–2021, then, was particularly tough for Ethnic Studies scholars in the CSU system, since the process of implementing AB1460 became a battle with the chancellor's office and the CSU Academic Senate (see Maldonado-Torres et al. 2023). Adding to this challenge was the stress of the COVID-19 pandemic, and the fatigue of online teaching and learning. Furthermore, at CSU Stanislaus, the annual Ethnic Studies event for Black History Month in February was targeted and zoom-bombed by racists (Tonarelli 2021). At the same time, anti-Asian violence gained widespread attention and police killings of Black and other marginalized people continued.

Midway through the spring 2021 semester, Ethnic Studies faculty and students reached a point where institutional and social tensions culminated. In one of my classes, in which the curriculum centralizes decolonial theory and women of color feminisms, the idea of protesting emerged again. After several discussions, and limited by COVID-19 restrictions, students decided to write love letters in favor of Ethnic Studies. To voice their anger and frustrations, students enacted a decolonial feminist approach of centering love, which initiates "from below," works between those rendered "other" by hegemonic forces (Sandoval 2000), and serves as a practical and theoretical model for healing the wounds of coloniality (Ureña 2017). Unlike colonial love, which is based on "an imperialist, dualist logic, dangerously fetishizes the beloved object and participates in the oppression and subjugation of difference," decolonial love "promotes loving as an active, intersubjective process, and in so doing articulates an anti-hegemonic, anti-imperialist affect and attitude that can guide the actions that work to dismantle oppressive regimes" (Ureña 2017, 86). As Yomaira C. Figueroa contends, decolonial love is "central to imagining a radical repair/reparation in the modern/colonial world" and "is part of what fuels the work of decolonization as a political and social project" (Figueroa 2015, 44).

Consequently, a group of students took the lead to organize a decolonial love letter campaign. The campaign included Ethnic Studies students and alumni who emailed letters to supportive administrators, staff, and faculty. Rather than adding to the tensions experienced on campus and in society, students enacted affirming strategies to highlight the struggles of Ethnic Studies in ways that invited support rather than resistance and antagonism. The results were positive, as the campaign helped students feel inspired about enacting social change in creative ways. The letters also demonstrated that Ethnic Studies is part of a field/movements of struggle as much as it is about decolonial love, joy, and pleasure (see Brown 2019; Campbell et al. 2019; Negrón-Muntander 2020; Bañales 2023). Because the class in which this strategy emerged centered decolonial feminisms, it opened new possibilities for thinking and action, and the love letters infused Ethnic Studies at CSU Stanislaus with generative meaning.

Conclusion

White supremacy, heteropatriarchy, and (settler) colonialism continues in the twenty-first century in higher education and elsewhere. The U.S. university, especially post-9/11, has become a charged space for debates about various topics, including democracy, freedom, citizenship, patriotism, and nationalism (Chatterjee and Maira 2014). In addition, the growing privatization of the public university is progressively putting students into exorbitant amounts of debt and making it harder for people to access higher education (McClanahan 2011). Academic freedom is increasingly undermined (Pettit and Stripling 2022), while critical pedagogy, scholarship, and theory are delegitimized (Cacho 2010; Brown 2022; García-Peña 2022; Truong 2022). At the same time, oppressive logics —including those of warfare, nationalism, racism, sexism, heterosexism, and ableism—are deeply embedded in the U.S. academy, reflecting the broader structures of modern/colonial society (Chatterjee and Maira 2014; Sandoval et al. 2016). Within this context, educational institutions repeatedly attempt to thwart, stifle, whitewash, or co-opt Ethnic Studies (see Sandoval et al. 2016; War Jack 2019b; Dong 2019; García-Peña 2022; Robertson 2022).

Furthermore, the contemporary sociopolitical context points to the increasing need to support and expand Ethnic Studies more than ever. As the Black Lives Matter movement and viral videos demonstrate, summoning law enforcement can have dire consequences for minoritized populations. This type of racism is not part of isolated incidents but is systemic, reflecting the global Right turn and ongoing resurgence of white supremacy in the United States and abroad. COVID-19 has further revealed anti-Asian hate and racism, as well as the disproportionate effects of structural inequities in health care, employment, housing, and labor practices, especially for Black, Indigenous, and people of color. Movements of #SayHerName, #MeToo, Land Back, reparations for slavery, and other forms of decoloniality are pressing. The ongoing destruction of sacred sites, colonialism in places like Puerto Rico and Guam, the trafficking of women and others into informal economies of service and sex, the rise of Islamophobia, the relentless targeting of marginalized communities—including Indigenous nations, Black populations, and trans, gender non-conforming, and non-binary people across the planet—the caging of displaced migrants, the separation of families, the abuse and forced sterilization of those in detention in the United States, and the gentrifying removal of those who reside in underserved neighborhoods, many of which are undocumented, impoverished, neurodivergent, and/or with disabilities: these are among the urgent reasons why centralizing decolonial feminisms in the fields and movements of Ethnic Studies is vital for confronting and transcending systemic violence rooted in colonial, racial, and gendered hierarchies (Bañales and Lee-Oliver 2019; Lee-Oliver and Bañales 2023).

As the origins and developments of the Ethnic Studies field/movements demonstrate, substantial collective pressure from students, faculty, and community members pushed educational institutions to shift priorities, including allocating resources and enacting generative policies. Strengthening intergenerational relations and strategic mobilization were necessary in the struggle to defend, build, and multiply Ethnic Studies, and activist organizing will continue to be crucial for the ongoing survival and growth of the field/movements (see Bañales 2012; Khanmalek 2019). Although mobilizing efforts comes with many challenges, solidarity and bridge-building are critical as demographic shifts occur and the inner workings of colonial society reward and seduce people to conform. Fortunately, advancing Ethnic Studies with decolonial feminisms can forge deep transformations in which radical healing, love, joy, and pleasure move us further toward new futures and liberatory horizons.

Bibliography

Abdullah, Melina. "Institutions Didn't Birth Ethnic Studies, Movements Did: The Long Struggle for the Nation's Second College of Ethnic Studies." *Ethnic Studies Review* 43, no. 1 (Spring 2020): 5–11.

Acosta, Christina. "Gonzalez v. Douglas: Overturning the Ban on Ethnic Studies in Arizona." *Ethnic Studies Review* 42, no. 2 (Fall 2019): 115–130.

Alameen-Shavers, Antwanisha. "The Woman Question: Gender Dynamics within the Black Panther Party." *Spectrum: A Journal on Black Men* 5, 1 (2016): 33–62.

Alarcón, Wanda, Dalida María Benfield, Annie Isabel Fukushima, and Marcelle Maese. "Guest Editors' Introduction: 'World'-Making and 'World'-Travelling with Decolonial Feminisms and Women of Color." *Frontiers: A Journal of Women Studies* 41, no. 1 (2020): x–xxi.

Arvin, Maile, Eve Tuck, and Angie Morrill. "Decolonizing Feminism: Challenging Connections between Settler Colonialism and Heteropatriarchy." *Feminist Formations* 25, no.1 (Spring 2013): 8–34.

Asian Community Center Archive Group. "Third World Strike." In *Stand Up: An Archive Collection of the Bay Area Asian American Movement 1968–1974*, 43–60. Berkeley: Eastwind Books of Berkeley, 2009.

Austin, Nan. "Turlock University Copes with White Supremacy Uproar." *The Modesto Bee*, October 13, 2016. https://www.modbee.com/news/local/turlock/article108125847.html.

Bacchetta, Paola. "Decolonial Praxis: Enabling Intranational and Queer Coalition Building." In *Qui Parle: Critical Humanities and Social Sciences*, edited by Peter Skafish, vol. 18.2 (Spring/Summer 2010): 147–192.

Bacchetta, Paola. "Public Talk at the Fiftieth Anniversary of the TWLF at UC Berkeley." *Ethnic Studies Review* 42, no. 2 (Fall 2019): 158–161.

Bañales, Xamuel. "The Future(s) of Ethnic Studies is in its Past(s) . . . and in the Surrounding Possibilities." *nineteen sixty nine: an ethnic studies journal* 1, no.1 (2012): 10–22.

Bañales, Xamuel. "Building Community, Decolonizing Spirituality, and Women of Color Feminism: Applying Gloria Anzaldúa in and out of the Classroom for Healing and Empowerment." In *This Bridge We Call Communication: Anzaldúan Approaches to Theory, Method, and Praxis*, edited by Leandra H. Hernández and Roberto Gutierrez-Perez, 291–311. New York: Lexington Books, 2019a.

Bañales, Xamuel. "Commemorating 50 years of Ethnic Studies." *NACLA Report on the Americas* 51, no. 3 (Fall 2019b): 232–235.

Bañales, Xamuel. "Rev. Dr. Trinity Ordona, A Queer Filipina American Activist Scholar: Her Journey from Political Revolutionary to Human Evolutionary." *Ethnic Studies Review* 42, no. 2 (Fall 2019c): 68–82.

Bañales, Xamuel. "A Conversation with Favianna Rodriguez: World-Making through Decolonial Feminist Artivism." *Feminist Formations* 35, no. 1 (Spring 2023): 154–194.

Bañales, Xamuel and Leece Lee-Oliver. "Guest Editors' Introduction, Fifty Years of Ethnic Studies: Foundations, Challenges, and Opportunities." *Ethnic Studies Review* 42, no. 2 (Fall 2019): 7–14. https://doi.org/10.1525/esr.2019.42.2.7.

Bañales, Xamuel and Mary Roaf. "The Battle to Decolonize Knowledge: Theories, Experiences, and Perspectives Teaching Ethnic Studies in Arizona." In *White Washing American Education: The New Culture Wars in Ethnic Studies*, ed. by Denise M. Sandoval et al., 69–94. Santa Barbara, CA: Praeger Publishers, 2016.

Biondi, Martha. *The Black Revolution on Campus*, Berkeley: University of California Press, 2012.

Blackwell, Maylei. *¡Chicana Power!: Contested Histories of Feminism in the Chicano Movement*. Austin: University of Texas Press, 2011.

Bravo, Kent. "Study: ethnic studies curriculum tied to increased graduation, retention rates." *SF State News* (December 14, 2020). https://news.sfsu.edu/news-story/study-ethnic-studies-curriculum-tied-increased-graduation-retention-rates.

Bravo, Stephany, and Yomaira C. Figueroa-Vásquez. "Reflections: On Strike MoMA, Caribe Fractal and Decolonial Feminisms as Political Arts Practice." *Feminist Formations* 35, no. 1 (2023): 30–46.

Brown, Adrienne Maree. *Pleasure Activism: The Politics of Feeling Good*. Chico, CA: AK Press, 2019.

Brown, Elaine. *A Taste of Power: A Black Woman's Story*. New York: Anchor Books, 1994.

Brown, Sarah. "She was denied tenure at Harvard. But She's not done fighting for Change in Academe." *The Chronicle of Higher Education* (July 29, 2022). https://www.chronicle.com/article/she-was-denied-tenure-at-harvard-but-shes-not-done-fighting-for-change-in-academe.

Bustos, Yoselin. "The 4th Annual Ethnic Studies Conference: Alliance and Decolonization." *The Signal*, April 20, 2021. (Last accessed on May 20, 2025). https://csusignal.com/9339/news/academics/the-4th-annual-ethnic-studies-conference-alliance-and-decolonization/.

Cacho, Lisa Marie. "But Some of Us Are Wise: Academic Illegitimacy and the Affective Value of Ethnic Studies." *The Black Scholar* 40, no. 4 (2010): 28–36.

California State University Task Force on the Advancement of Ethnic Studies. Report, January 2016. https://www2.calstate.edu/impact-of-the-csu/diversity/advancement-of-ethnic-studies/Documents/ethnicstudiesreport.pdf.

CAIR California. "AB 1468 Withdrawn After Public Outcry, AB 715 Emerges as New Threat to Civil Rights." May 13, 2025. (Last accessed May 19, 2025). https://ca.cair.com/press-release/ab-1468-withdrawn-after-public-outcry-ab-715-emerges-as-new-threat-to-civil-rights/.

Campbell, Malik, Kelly De Leon, Martha D. Escobar, Dezzerie González, Rocio Rivera-Murillo, and Tracy M. Sadek. "Ethnic Studies as Praxis: The Movement against Racism at California State University, Northridge." *Ethnic Studies Review* 42, no. 2 (Fall 2019): 131–150.

Chatterjee, Piya and Sunaina Maira, eds. *The Imperial University: Academic Repression and Scholarly Dissent*. Minneapolis: University of Minnesota Press, 2014.

Chávez-García, Miroslava and Monica Brown. "Women's Studies and Chicana

Studies: Learning from the Past, Looking to the Future." In *Women's Studies for the Future: Foundations, Interrogations, Politics*, edited by Liz Kennedy & Agatha Beins, 143–155. Piscataway, NJ: Rutgers University Press, 2005.

"Civil Rights Pioneer Gloria Richardson, 91, on How Women Were Silenced at 1963 March on Washington." *Democracy Now!*, August 27, 2013. https://www.democracynow.org/2013/8/27/civil_rights_pioneer_gloria_richardson_91.

Cleaver, Eldridge. *Soul on Ice*. New York: Dell Publishing, 1991.

Combahee River Collective. "'The Combahee River Collective Statement' (1977)." In *Available Means: An Anthology of Women's Rhetoric(s)*, edited by Joy Ritchie and Kate Ronald, 292–300. University of Pittsburgh Press, 2001. https://doi.org/10.2307/j.ctt5hjqnj.50.

Crenshaw, Kimberlé. "Mapping the Margins: Intersectionality, Identity Politics, and Violence Against Women of Color." In *Critical Race Theory*, edited by Kimberlé Crenshaw, Neil Gotanda, Gary Peller, and Kendall Thomas. New York: The New Press, 1995.

Curiel, Ochy. "Decolonial feminism in Abya Yala." *Multitudes* 84, no. 3 (2021): 78–86.

Davis, Jeff. *The First-Generation Student Experience: Implications for Campus Practice and Strategies for Improving Persistence and Success*. Sterling, VA: Stylus Publishing, 2010.

DeGout, Yasmin Y. "Diving the Mind: Contradictory Portraits of Homoerotic Love in Giovanni's Room." *African American Review* 26, no. 3 (Autumn, 1992): 425–435.

Díaz, Jazz. "Art and Ethnic Studies: Decolonizing Expressions for Critical Awareness and Transformation." *Ethnic Studies Review* 42, no. 2 (Fall 2019): 173–179.

DiPietro, Pedro, Jennifer McWeeny, and Shireen Roshanravan. *Speaking Face to Face: The Visionary Philosophy of Maria Lugones*. New York: SUNY Press, 2019.

DiPietro, PJ. "Coloniality of Gender." *Kohl: A Journal for Body and Gender Research* 11, no. 1 (30 December 2024): 5–5. (Last accessed on March 5, 2025). https://kohljournal.press/coloniality-gender.

DiPietro, PJ. *Sideways Selves: Travesti and Jotería Struggles Across the Américas*. Austin: University of Texas Press, 2025.

Donald, Brooke. "Stanford study suggests academic benefits to ethnic studies courses." *Stanford News*, January 12, 2016. https://news.stanford.edu/2016/01/12/ethnic-studies-benefits-011216/.

Dong, Harvey. "Ethnic Studies on its Fiftieth Anniversary," *Ethnic Studies Review* 42, no. 2 (Fall 2019): 62–67.

Dunlap, Nicole. "Climate Change and Colonialism Panelists Describe the Aftereffects of Recent Disasters." *The Signal*, March 20, 2018 (last accessed March 5, 2025). https://csusignal.com/9751/stan-state-news/climate-change-and-colonialism-panelists-describe-the-aftereffects-of-recent-disasters/.

Dunlap, Nicole and Kristen Dias. "Teach Out Protestors Rally Solutions to Combat Campus White Supremacy." *The Signal*, February 27, 2019 (last accessed March 5, 2025). https://csusignal.com/9140/stan-state-news/teach-out-protestors-rally-solutions-to-combat-campus-white-supremacy/.

Durazo, Ana Clarissa Rojas. "Decolonizing Chicano Studies in the Shadows of the University's 'Heteropatriracial' Order." In *The Imperial University: Academic Repression and Scholarly Dissent,* edited by Piya Chatterjee and Sunaina Maira, 187–214. Minneapolis: University of Minnesota Press, 2014.

Edwards, Harry. *The Revolt of the Black Athlete: 50th Anniversary Edition.* Urbana: University of Illinois Press, 2018.

Elaine Brown Reading/Talk. Anonymous 2015 (last accessed on March 5, 2025). https://video.alexanderstreet.com/watch/elaine-brown-reading-talk.

Espinoza, Dionne, María E. Cotera, and Maylei Blackwell, eds. *Chicana Movidas: New Narratives of Activism and Feminism in the Movement Era.* Austin: University of Texas Press, 2018.

Espinosa-Miñoso, Yuderkys, María Lugones, and Nelson Maldonado-Torres, eds. *Decolonial Feminism in Abya Yala: Caribbean, Meso, and South American Contributions and Challenges.* New York: Rowman & Littlefield, 2021.

Ferguson, Roderick A. *Aberrations in Black: Toward a Queer of Color Critique.* Minneapolis: University of Minnesota, 2004.

Figueroa, Yomaira C. "Reparation As Transformation: Radical Literary (Re)-imaginings of Futurities through Decolonial Love." *Decolonization: Indigeneity, Education & Society* 4, no. 1 (2015): 41–58.

"First Installment of Mural Project Reflects Focus on Social Justice." Anonymous February 13, 2020 (last accessed March 5, 2025). https://www.csustan.edu/news/first-installment-mural-project-reflects-focus-social-justice.

Forbes, Jack D. "Ethnic or World Studies: A Historian's Path of Discovery." In *Ethnic Studies Research: Approaches and Perspectives*, edited by Timothy P. Fong, 59–92. Lanham, MD: AltaMira Press, 2008.

Freire, Paulo. *Pedagogy of the Oppressed.* New York: Continuum, 2000.

Fujiwara, Lynn and Shireen Roshanravan. *Asian American Feminisms and Women of Color Politics.* Seattle: University of Washington Press, 2018.

Fukushima, Annie I. *Migrant Crossings: Witnessing Human Trafficking in the U.S.* CA: Stanford University Press, 2019.

Galarte, Francisco J. "Transgender Chican@ Poetics: Contesting, Interrogating, and Transforming Chicana/o Studies." *Chicana/Latina Studies* 13, no. 2 (Spring 2014): 118–139.

Galarte, Francisco J. *Brown Trans Figurations: Rethinking Race, Gender, and Sexuality in Chicanx/Latinx Studies.* Austin: University of Texas Press, 2021.

García, Alma M. *Chicana Feminist Thought: The Basic Historical Writings.* New York: Routledge, 1997.

García-Peña, Lorgia. *Community As Rebellion: A Syllabus for Surviving Academia As a Woman of Color.* Chicago, IL: Haymarket Books, 2022.

Gates, Jr., Henry Louis. "Who Designed the March on Washington?" *The Root* (August 19, 2013), https://www.theroot.com/who-designed-the-march-on-washington-1790897781.

Gaxiola, Steven. "New Downtown Art Space Has Social Justice Focus." *The Signal*, November 5, 2018 (last accessed March 5, 2025). https://csusignal.com/9865/la-letra-n/new-downtown-art-space-has-social-justice-focus/#modal-photo.

Gilmore, Ruth Wilson and Craig Gilmore. "The Other California," In *Globalize Liberation: How to Uproot the System and Build a Better World*, edited by David Solnit, 381–396. San Francisco: City Lights Books, 2003.

Ginzberg, Abby and Frank R. Dawson. *Agents of Change*. (American Documentary, 2016), film.

González, Genevieve. "Constrained Inclusion: Access and Persistence Among Undocumented Community College Students in California's Central Valley," *Journal of Hispanic Higher Education* 12, no. 2 (2017): 105–122.

Gordon, Lewis R. "Shifting the Geography of Reason in an Age of Disciplinary Decadence." *Transmodernity: A Journal of Peripheral Cultural Production of the Luso-Hispanic World* 1, no. 2 (Fall 2011): 95–103.

Grande, Sandy. "Refusing the University." In *Towards What Justice?: Describing Diverse Dreams of Justice in Education*, edited by Eve Tuck and K. Wayne Yang, 47–65. New York: Routledge, 2018.

Greenberg, David F. *The Construction of Homosexuality*. Chicago, IL: University of Chicago Press, 1990.

Grosfoguel, Ramón. "The Dilemmas of Ethnic Studies in the United States: Between Liberal Multiculturalism, Identity Politics, Disciplinary Colonization, and Decolonial Epistemologies." *Human Architecture: Journal of the Sociology of Self-Knowledge* 10, no. 1 (Winter 2012), 81–89.

Grosfoguel, Ramón, Roberto Hernández, and Ernesto Rosen Velásquez E.R., eds. *Decolonizing the Westernized University: Interventions in Philosophy of Education from Within and Without*. Lanham, MD: Lexington Books, 2016.

Hale, Lorraine. *Native American Education: A Reference Handbook*. Santa Barbara, CA: ABC-CLIO, 2002.

Hames-García, Michael. "Queer Theory Revisited." In *Gay Latino Studies: A Critical Reader*, edited by Michael Hames-García and Ernesto J. Martínez, 19–45. Durham, NC: Duke University Press, 2011.

Hames-García, Michael, "Which Way Forward? The Corporate University As a Site of Contradiction." In *The Truly Diverse Faculty: New Dialogues in American Higher Education*, edited by Stephanie A. Fryberg and Ernesto Javier Martínez, 89–96. New York: Palgrave Macmillan, 2014.

Herrera, Jack. "10-day Hunger Strike = Victory for SFSU Students." *USA Today*, May 22, 2016. https://www.usatoday.com/story/college/2016/05/22/10-day-hunger-strike-victory-for-sfsu-students/37417869/.

Hull, Gloria T., Patricia Bell Scott, and Barbara Smith, eds. *All the Women are White, All the Blacks are Men, but Some of Us Are Brave: Black Women's Studies*. New York: The Feminist Press, 1982.

Jackson, Carlos. *Chicana & Chicano Art: ProtestArte*. Tucson: University of Arizona Press, 2009.

Jackson, Cynthia L. *African American Education: A Reference Handbook*. Santa Barbara, CA: ABC-CLIO, 2001.

Jackson, Shirley A. "Oregon's K-12 Ethnic Studies Bill." *Ethnic Studies Review* 42, no. 2 (Fall 2019): 180–195.

Jennings, Regina. "Africana Womanism in the Black Panther Party: A Personal Story." *Western Journal of Black Studies* 25, no. 3 (2001): 146–152.

Jessi, Gan. "'Still at the Back of the Bus': Sylvia Rivera's Struggle." *Centro Journal* XIX, no. 1 (2007): 124–139.

Joseph, Peniel E. "The Black Power Movement: A State of the Field." *Journal of American History* 96, no. 3 (December 2009): 751–776.

Josephs, Samuel. "Whose Revolution Is This? Gender's Divisive Role in the Black Panther Party." *Georgetown Journal of Gender and the Law* 9, no. 2 (2008): 403–426.

Khanmalek, Tala. "Looking Back (and Inward), Moving Forward: A Roundtable on Ethnic Studies." *Ethnic Studies Review* 42, no. 2 (Fall 2019): 99–114.

Lee-Oliver, Leece. "Situating Native American Studies and Red Feminisms." *Ethnic Studies Review* 42, no. 2 (Fall 2019): 196–209.

Lee-Oliver, Leece and Xamuel Bañales. "On Decolonial Feminisms: Engagement, Practice, and Action." Special Issue, *Feminist Formations* 35, no. 1 (Spring 2023).

López, Gisely Colón, Tami Gold, and Pam Sporn. *Making the Impossible Possible*. (Grito Production, 2021), film.

Lorde, Audre. *Sister Outsider: Essays & Speeches*. Berkeley, CA: Crossing Press, 2007.

Lugones, María. "Playfulness, 'World'-Travelling, and Loving Perception." *Hypatia* 2, no. 2 (Summer 1987): 3–19.

Lugones, María. *Peregrinajes/Pilgrimages: Theorizing Coalition Against Multiple Oppressions*. New York: Rowman & Littlefield Press, 2003.

Lugones, María. "Heterosexualism and the Colonial/Modern Gender System." *Hypatia* 22, no. 1 (Winter 2007): 186–209.

Lugones, María. "Toward a Decolonial Feminism." *Hypatia* 25, no. 4 (Fall 2010): 742–759.

Luna, Jennie M. "1999 twLF at UC Berkeley: An Intergenerational Struggle for Ethnic Studies," *Ethnic Studies Review* 42, no. 2 (Fall 2019): 83–98.

Macias, Ysidro. "Liberating a Colonized Mind: Activism, Ethnic Studies, and the Great Spirit," *Ethnic Studies Review* 42, no. 2 (Fall 2019): 40–48.

Maese, Marcelle. "Lxs Caravanerxs and Nonsecular Protest: Rethinking Migrant Family Separation with Un llanto colectivo." *Feminist Formations* 35, no. 1 (2023): 268–292.

Maese-Cohen, Marcelle. "Introduction: Toward Planetary Decolonial Feminisms." *Qui Parle: Critical Humanities and Social Sciences* 18, no. 2 (Spring/Summer 2010): 3–27.

Maldonado-Torres, Nelson. "Ethnic Studies As Decolonial Transdisciplinarity." *Ethnic Studies Review* 42, no. 2 (Fall 2019): 232–244.

Maldonado-Torres, Nelson, Xamuel Bañales, Leece Lee-Oliver, Sangha Niyogi, Albert Ponce, and Zandi Radebe. "Decolonial Pedagogy Against the Coloniality of Justice." *Educational Theory* 73, no. 4 (2023): 1–21.

Manzanillo, Alexis. "Fierce women drove 1968 student strike." *Golden Gate Xpress*, November 14, 2018. https://goldengatexpress.org/85522/latest/news/fierce-women-drove-1968-student-strike/.

Marchi, Regina M. *Day of the Dead in the USA: The Migration and Transformation of a Cultural Phenomenon*. New Brunswick, NJ: Rutgers University Press, 2009.

Martínez, Silvana. "Feminismo Comunitario: Una propuesta teórica y política desde Abya Yala." *Servicios Sociales y Política Social* XXXVI (119) (Abril 2019): 21–33.

Martínez, Silvana and Juan Agüero. "Cartography of Southern Feminisms: Contributions of Decolonial Feminisms and Community Feminisms." *International Social Work* 00.0 (2021): 1–13.

Martínez-Cairo, Bárbara and Emanuela Buscemi. "Latin American Decolonial Feminisms: Theoretical Perspectives and Challenges." *Amérique Latine: Histoire et Mémoire* 42 (2021).

McClanahan, Annie. "The Living Indebted: Student Militancy and the Financialization of Debt." *Qui Parle: Critical Humanities and Social Sciences* 20, no. 1 (2011): 57–77.

McLaren, Margaret A., ed. *Decolonizing Feminism: Transnational Feminism and Globalization*. Lanham, MD: Rowman and Littlefield, 2017.

Mignolo, Walter D. "Epistemic Disobedience and the Decolonial Option: A Manifesto." *Transmodernity: A Journal of Peripheral Cultural Production of the Luso-Hispanic World* 1, no. 2 (Fall 2011): 44–66.

Miranda, Deborah A. *Bad Indians: A Tribal Memoir*. Berkeley, CA: Heyday, 2013.

Mohanty, Chandra Talpade and Linda E. Carty, eds. *Feminist Freedom Warriors: Genealogies, Justice, Politics, and Hope*. Chicago, IL: Haymarket Books, 2018.

Moraga, Cherríe and Gloria Anzaldúa, eds. *This Bridge Called My Back: Writings by Radical Women of Color*, 2nd ed. New York: Kitchen Table Press, 1983.

Morrar, Sawsan. "Controversial ethnic studies draft approved by California commission, moves to final round." *The Sacramento Bee*, November 20, 2020. https://www.sacbee.com/news/local/education/article247293984.html.

Negrón-Muntaner, Frances. "Decolonial Joy: Theorising from the Art of Valor y Cambio." In *Theorising Cultures of Equality*, edited by Suzanne Clisby, Mark Johnson, and Jimmy Turner, 171–194. New York: Routledge, 2020.

NLCC Educational Media. *Chicano! History of the Mexican American Civil Rights Movement*, episode 1 (Los Angeles, CA, 1996), film.

Okihiro, Gary Y. *Third World Studies: Theorizing Liberation*. Durham, NC: Duke University Press, 2016.

Oparah, Julia C. "Challenging Complicity: The Neoliberal University and the Prison-Industrial Complex." In *The Imperial University: Academic Repression and Scholarly Dissent*, edited by Pia Chatterjee and Maira Sunaina, 99–121. Minneapolis: University of Minnesota Press, 2014.

Ordona, Trinity A. "Coming Out Together: An Ethnohistory of the Asian and Pacific Islander Queer Women's and Transgender People's Movement of San Francisco." PhD diss., University of California at Santa Cruz, 2000.

Palm, Iman. "Bakersfield Ranks No.1 in Cities That Have the Worst Air Pollution in the Nation, Study Says." *KGET.com*, March 14, 2023. (Last accessed March 5, 2025). https://www.kget.com/news/local-news/bakersfield-ranks-no-1-in-cities-that-have-the-worst-air-pollution-in-the-nation-study-says/.

Pérez, Laura E. *Chicana Art: The Politics of Spiritual and Aesthetic Altarities.* Durham, NC: Duke University Press, 2007.

Pérez, Laura E. "Enrique Dussel's *Ética de la liberación,* U.S. Women of Color Decolonizing Practices, and Coalitionary Politics amidst Difference." *Qui Parle: Critical Humanities and Social Sciences* 18, no. 2 (Spring/Summer 2010): 121–146.

Pérez, Laura E. *Eros Ideologies: Writings on Art, Spirituality, and the Decolonial.* Durham, NC: Duke University Press, 2019.

Pettit, Emma and Jack Stripling. "Inside the Academic-Freedom Crisis that Roiled Florida's Flagship." *The Chronicle of Higher Education* (September 6, 2022). https://www.chronicle.com/article/inside-the-academic-freedom-crisis-that-roiled-floridas-flagship.

Pitts, Andrea J., Mariana Ortega, and José M. Medina, eds. *Theories of the Flesh: Latinx and Latin American Feminisms, Transformation, and Resistance.* New York: Oxford University Press, 2020.

Poniatowska, Elena. *Massacre in Mexico,* trans. by Helen R. Lane. New York: The Viking Press, 1975.

Porter, Ronald K. "A Rainbow in Black: The Gay Politics of the Black Panther Party." *Counterpoints* 367 (2012): 364–375.

Pulido, Laura. 2006. *Black, Brown, Yellow, & Left: Radical Activism in Los Angeles.* Berkeley: University of California Press.

Rivera, Carla. "Cal State's Ethnic Studies Programs Falter in Changing Times." *Los Angeles Times*, October 30, 2013. https://www.latimes.com/local/la-xpm-2013-oct-30-la-me-college-ethnic-20131031-story.html.

Roaf, Mary. "Trailblazing a Movement: An Interview with Black Student Union Co-founders Jerry Varnado and James Garrett." *Ethnic Studies Review* 42, no. 2 (Fall 2019): 15–26.

Roaf, Mary. "Breakdowns to Breakthroughs: Participating in a Decolonial Black Feminism Program." *Feminist Formations* 35, no. 1 (2023): 5–17.

Renteria, Jose Alejandro. "Xochipilli: Unveiling the Spiritual Concepts of a Nahua Deity." Master's thesis, San Diego State University, Spring 2018.

Robertson, Katie. "Nikole Hannah-Jones Denied Tenure at University of North Carolina." *The New York Times*, July 15, 2022. https://www.nytimes.com/2021/05/19/business/media/nikole-hannah-jones-unc.html.

Rodríguez, Alicia. "The Kern County Klan Local KKK members, including Bakersfield's police chief, were outed 90 years ago." *Bakersfield Californian,* May 7, 2012. https://www.bakersfield.com/opinion/the-kern-county-klan-local-kkk-members-including-bakersfields-police-chief-were-outed-90-years/article_13d6d2c8-494b-5c8a-a766-c2944fb0f1d6.html.

Rodríguez, Juana María. *Queer Latinidad: Identity Practices, Discursive Space.* New York: New York University Press, 2003.

Ruiz, Olivia Barragán. "Ethnic Studies threatened at CSU Stanislaus." Vida en el Valle (Fresno, CA), November 13, 2013. Page A1.

Salas-SantaCruz, Omi. "Colonial Gender Continuum." *Kohl: A Journal for Body and Gender Research* 11, no. 1 (December 29, 2024): 2–2. (Last accessed March 5, 2025). https://kohljournal.press/colonial-gender-continuum.

Salas-SantaCruz, Omi. "Decolonial Trans* Feminism." *Kohl: A Journal for Body and Gender Research* 11, no. 1 (January 11, 2025): 16–16. (Last accessed March 3, 2025). https://kohljournal.press/decolonial-trans-feminism.

Sánchez, Marina. "Indigenous Peoples' Day Event Honors Heritage of Native People." *The Signal*, October 17, 2018 (last accessed March 5, 2025). https://csusignal.com/9911/campus-culture/indigenous-peoples-day-event-honors-heritage-of-native-people/.

Sandoval, Chela. *Methodology of the Oppressed*. Minneapolis: University of Minnesota Press, 2000.

Sandoval, Denise M., Anthony J. Ratcliff, Tracy L. Buenavista, and James R. Marín, eds. *"White" Washing American Education: The New Culture Wars in Ethnic Studies* (2 volumes). Santa Barbara, CA: ABC-CLIO, LLC, 2016.

Santos, Francely and Vanessa Olmos. "First Annual Ethnic Studies Conference Hosted at Stan State." *The Signal*, April 3, 2017 (last accessed March 5, 2025). https://csusignal.com/8847/campus-culture/first-annual-ethnic-studies-conference-hosted-at-stan-state/.

Scott, Otis L. "Ethnic Studies: Preparing for the Future," In *Ethnic Studies Research: Approaches and Perspectives*, edited by Timothy P. Fong, 17–32. New York: Altamira Press, 2008.

Shames, Stephen and Ericka Huggins. *Comrade Sisters: Women of the Black Panther Party*. New York: ACC Art Books, 2022.

Sueyoshi, Amy. "Redefining Higher Education: Reflections on Queer Ethnic Studies." *Ethnic Studies Review* 42, no. 2 (Fall 2019): 225–231.

Tintiangco-Cubales, Allyson, Rita Kohli, Jocyl Sacramento, Nick Henning, Ruchi Agarwal-Rangnath, and Christine Sleeter. "What Is ethnic studies pedagogy?" In *Rethinking Ethnic Studies*, edited by R. Toltekca Cuauhtin, Miguel Zavala, Christine Sleeter, and Wayne Au, 20–25. Milwaukee, WI: Rethinking Schools, 2019.

Tonarelli, Samantha. "Zoom Bombing of the Black Power STILL Matters Event." *The Signal*, March 17, 2021.

Truong, Debbie. "After O.C. school district bans critical race theory, it faces Cal State Fullerton backlash." *Los Angeles Times* (Oct. 19, 2022).

Tucker, Jill. "California ethnic studies classes are sparking controversy as mandate looms." *San Francisco Chronicle* (March 20, 2023).

Urban, Dennis J. "The Women of SNCC: Struggle, Sexism, and the Emergence of Feminist Consciousness, 1960–66." *International Social Science Review* 77, no. 3/4 (2002): 185–190.

Ureña, Carolyn. "Loving from Below: Of (De)colonial Love and Other Demons." *Hypatia* 32, no. 1 (2017): 86–102.

Váldez, Jesús. "Ethnic Studies hosts its 3rd annual Día de los Muertos Celebration." *The Signal*, November 6, 2017 (last accessed March 5, 2025). https://csusignal.com/8961/la-letra-n/ethnic-studies-hosts-its-3rd-annual-da-de-los-muertos-celebration/.

Velez, Emma D. "Decolonial Feminisms at the Intersection: A Critical Reflection on the Relationship Between Decolonial Feminisms and Intersectionality. *The Journal of Speculative Philosophy* 33, no. 3 (2019): 390–406.

Wallerstein, Immanuel. "The Unintended Consequences of Cold War Area Studies," *The Cold War and the University: Toward an Intellectual History of the Postwar Years*, edited by Noam Chomsky et al., 195–231. New York: New Press, 1997.

War Jack, LaNada. *Native Resistance: An Intergenerational Fight for Survival and Life*. Brookfield, MO: Donning Company, 2019a.

War Jack, LaNada. "Native Americans and the Third World Strike at UC Berkeley," *Ethnic Studies Review* 42, no. 2 (Fall 2019b): 32–39.

Weaver, Meghan. "'Freedom!': Black Women Speak at the March on Washington for Jobs and Freedom." The Martin Luther King, Jr. Research and Education Institute, n.d. https://kinginstitute.stanford.edu/freedom-black-women-speak-march-washington-jobs-and-freedom.

Whitebear, Luhui. "Resisting the Settler Gaze: California Indigenous Feminisms." *Feminist Formations* 35, no. 1 (2023): 97–116.

Wong, Stephanie. "Why Do We Learn So Little about Ella Baker? The Answers are Wrapped Up in Sexism, Leadership and Ego." *Act Build Change* (blog), December 9, 2017. (Last accessed March 5, 2025). https://actbuildchange.com/ideas/why-do-we-learn-so-little-about-ella-baker.

Conclusion

K. MELCHOR QUICK HALL, ANNIE ISABEL FUKUSHIMA, CHANDRA TALPADE MOHANTY, and LINDA CARTY

To conclude, co-editors Fukushima and Hall, and senior scholars Mohanty and Carty, reflect on the collaborative processes that have resulted in this collection and the connected feminist scholars, to share lessons learned. Rooting in this history, we articulate individual and collective visions for decolonial feminism.

In an earlier conversation while working on the book in its early manifestation, we reflected during a Zoom call about the decolonial feminists we are, as people connected to each other, familial (chosen and otherwise) and community based. We are a people sustained by indigenous lands, where home is "about people," as Chandra stated. And as we work toward decolonial feminisms, Linda reminded us of the tensions of belonging that we may feel. She shared, "I'm part of the world, but I feel. I don't feel connected to where I spent most of my life at all, not at all. In an American context I don't necessarily feel connected here, not yet anyway. It's just something new that's happening to me now, so I always say I'm a citizen of the world. And I find home wherever that is, then do the work that I need to do there because I always—I will always find people who are part of that work doing it themselves." Our multiple conversations via Zoom, some in person in New Jersey, in San Antonio, Texas, some that even preceded the emergence of the book—made their way into our conversations about decolonial feminisms. K. Melchor reminded us that decolonial feminisms are people—people with names, people who we find shaping our own lives. K. Melchor conveyed, "I remember Marie Claire in Martinique, I remember Nellie in Punta Piedra Honduras. They're all these names that come to mind: Sadio in Zinguichor Senegal, and Janice Smith on First Street [in Washington, DC]. There are all these names that come to mind." Decolonial feminisms are not a straight line. They have multiple points of connections for people, shaped by departures that carry us in our work in different directions. Chandra described her own journeys in decolonial feminisms as "crisscrossing. And of course, the reason you connect with people is because you as an individual have been doing similar work in the past, right? And then that becomes a real basis for connection and then for continuing work, so it's kind of like these spirals. When I think about my own genealogy there have been people and movements and ways of . . . thinking, ways of organizing, that have, you know, constantly been a part of my entire trajectory." As we discussed how decolonial feminist genealogies are embedded in community as a praxis, we were also reminded of the silence and pain that decolonial feminisms endeavor to speak to, and also may not fully be able to name. Annie reflected on han, "a pain that Koreans say they endure in silence, and so I think about how my family, then, and my mother actually literally—she holds a lot of stuff in. And so I see that getting passed on, and so, then thinking about what it means to not talk about things, and hold it in. . . . I've been thinking a lot about those things, the things we don't talk about or . . . that haunt conversations, or they haunt our realities and the next generation, or even our communities." Therefore, as this anthology has sought to name and speak to decolonial feminisms, we recognize the plurality of decolonial feminisms that may not find its way in this anthology, and the issues, tensions, and lived realities that may continue to haunt our communities through ongoing coloniality.

Therefore, this chapter is presented as a roundtable discussion, among the co-authors and the voices of our students. In writing the conclusion, we thought it important to make even more of our community visible, especially earlier scholar-activists. We wanted to know what they might say about genealogies and futures. With that idea in mind, we reached out to other transnational feminists and asked them the following two questions: (1) What are the practices that sustain you within feminist community and struggle at this time? (2) What lessons, tools, and strategies from the past are you carrying forward in your praxis? In this concluding chapter we have woven together excerpts from their responses. Our goal is to emphasize that a decolonial feminist genealogy is one that is ongoing in time and space, that we look not only to a past to understand how a decolonial feminist praxis and theory are being formed and by whom, but also to the ongoing moving line of a "present."

We start here with a one-sentence introduction to the transnational feminists who shared their perspectives.

- Kristian Contreras is a Cultural Foundations doctoral candidate in the School of Education at Syracuse University.
- Sandra Del Rio Madrigal is a graduate of the University of Utah.
- Marla Goins is an August 2020 PhD graduate of the Ohio State University Department of Teaching and Learning.

- Keish Kim is a Comparative Literature doctoral student at Harvard University, and a graduate of Syracuse University.
- Maegan Shanks is a Deaf Black feminist doctoral candidate in American University's School of International Service.
- Taveeshi Singh is a doctoral student in the Social Science Program at Syracuse University, and a Democratizing Knowledge scholar.
- Tangerine Vei is a doctoral candidate in Education, Culture & Society at the University of Utah.

We have put their responses in conversation with one another, even though each of the contributors sent their responses directly to one of the co-authors of this chapter. The goal was to explore themes among the responses, rather than to simply repeat their answers. In that sense, we are putting their ideas into conversation to think through the future(s) of transnational feminist communities.

Sustaining Feminist Communities of Struggle

Implied in the term "feminist community" is resistance to something patriarchal. In that sense, we wanted to ask specifically about that tension that is a community that has come together to struggle against a form of oppression. Some of the transnational feminists focused on how being in community made them feel, while others focused on mechanisms or structures of the community. Of course, as feminist scholar-activists we know that these two things are not unrelated, fighting as we do against long-standing institutions designed to make womxn feel small. However, below we mirrored that emphasis on feeling and structure as a way to group the responses of those surveyed.

Feeling Spiritually Grounded, Understood, and Nurtured

Marla Goins is sustained through prayer, protest, and dialogue. Prayer and worship are daily practices that give her spiritual grounding and strength for ongoing Black feminist struggle. For Maegan Shanks, what sustains her within feminist community and struggle is understanding and preserving identities, with attention to how disability can be viewed as a verb (in international education). When Kristian Contreras thinks of "sustaining" herself and others, images of tending a garden come to mind, as people reshape and rebuild the world around us; what sustains her is the feeling of being nurtured and poured into, a unique offering of feminist friendships at a time when many systems are working to make one feel alone.

Pedagogy, Praxis, and Mutual Aid

Tangerine Vei finds that working with other activist educators, through critical participatory action research, while asking difficult questions about pedagogical practices, (re)creates critical consciousness and enacts transformative healing; this collaborative work inspires and sustains her in times of painful polarization. As a creative writer who finds that social media facilitates connection and community, Sandra Del Rio Madrigal has discovered that online discourse and visuals have supported intersectional and decolonial feminist reflection and praxis, in that it draws her attention to agency within the margins of society. Similarly, Keish Kim has participated in online groups that write, watch movies, and dance together, which reminds her to nurture the potential for joy.

Taveeshi Singh believes that people need to rely more on social institutions for survival and support, since systems of domination and oppression are crises of human relationality. The practice that sustains her is training her attention toward how she and members of her various communities exist in relationship to each other, often exemplified through mutual aid practices that build solidarity-based networks to address community needs. Similarly, checking in on a routine basis, sometimes sending meals or gift cards, has been a critical care practice for Keish Kim. Redistributing money from institutions, passing along work gigs, and filling up community fridges have been small but essential practices, in Kim's effort to take care of her neighbors. Most importantly, her community centers love, reminding one another to be kind and compassionate with themselves and others. Saying, "I love you, friend" has been sustaining her.

Lessons, Tools, and Strategies for Feminist Praxis

For our second question about the mechanisms of feminist praxis, we wanted to share more of the stories of those surveyed. In that way, the many and varied manifestations of feminist praxis become visible. Thus, in the following paragraphs, we give a short highlight from the response of each of the transnational feminists who shared their thoughts with us.

Finding Unbuntu in Brazil

Through Goins's fieldwork with Black women teacher-activists in São Paulo, she learned that the Ubuntu philosophy was foundational to participants' epistemologies. Ubuntu means "Eu sou porque nós somos," or "I am because we are." The concept highlights the interconnectivity of humanity and recognizes that compassion is critical for us to sustain ourselves, our communities, and humanity at large. As a scholar-activist of the Black diaspora, Goins infuses the Ubuntu philosophy into her pedagogical praxis as a way to understand the inherent and holistic value of the communities where she works.

Bridging Disability and Language Justice Frameworks

In her praxis, Shanks centers intersectional analysis, citing Black feminist scholars such as Kimberlé Crenshaw, Patricia Hill Collins, K. Melchor Quick Hall, and Moya Bailey. She is looking to create greater education access for Deaf students, which is both a question of disability (or different abilities) and language justice. Ultimately, she looks forward to greater integration of Deaf perspectives into a Black feminist praxis that should inform international (and transnational) education norms.

Teaching and Learning with Latina Feminists

As an activist educator, Vei regularly faces the challenges of facilitating uncomfortable teaching and learning processes. With María Lugones, she learns that to teach is to listen deeply to what is (un)said. Listening deeply means that she practices holding her own world in suspense and endeavoring to delight in the unknown. Gloria Anzaldúa helps her to cultivate the skills of the nepantlera—the artist/activist who both embodies and facilitates transformation through ongoing inner work and public acts.

Recognizing the Liberatory Power of Decolonial Imaginaries

Del Rio Madrigal observes that, for Chicana/o/x populations in the United States, a decolonial imaginary assists the diaspora in dismantling displacement. Recognizing the structured erasure of anyone who deviates from the normative narrative leads to critical action that moves us toward decolonization. By considering communities' capabilities and accomplishments, we can create a more inclusive environment for all people, both socially and economically, through the possibility of creative and intellectual work. One must acknowledge and respect the work done within historically erased communities. The path toward liberation is paved through collaboration.

Finding Feminist Texts and Friends

Contreras sees her community's wisdom and value reflected through poetry, prose, dance, photographs, film, and friendship. (Re)visiting texts and multimedia resources allows her to rekindle the desire to continuously fight for herself and her comrades. Feminist friendships grounded in solidarity help her hold on to the truth; she is deserving and whole. As she remains open and grateful for her mentors and kindred spirits, her community is able to bloom.

Doing Everyday Mutual Aid

Singh considers historical examples of mutual aid in the United States, Global South, and around the world, in places where it sometimes has existed by other names. Three principles of mutual aid across different contexts include identifying and building intentional networks of support, voluntary exchange of resources, and an ethics of care. Adopting these mutual aid principles into her day-to-day life, among her peer groups, in mentoring students, and teaching about them in the classroom, has been critical for Singh to sustain herself within feminist community and struggle. Singh asks, "What does feminism do if not challenge and expand our imaginations about what is possible in the world?"

Making Contemporary Feminist Legacies

Recently, Minnie Bruce Pratt told Kim, "be in your own historical moment." At the time, Kim was engrossed in replicating the kind of feminist gatherings and collaborations she saw in the *This Bridge Called My Back* anthology. Alongside that, she was reading the collaborative writing of *Yours in Struggle*, and passages from *Charting the Journey*. Through centering these histories, she had been carrying the lessons of cross-coalitional organizing, theorizing, and writing. These texts reminded Kim of the importance of de-centering US exceptionalism and highlighting the power of intersectional and transnational organizing. Taking into consideration what she is still learning from the past, and with Minnie Bruce's reminder, Kim is learning to respectfully and critically apply these lessons to the present moment. As she learns with new generations of students, she embraces the powerful tool of listening through care, leaving room for mistakes and transformation. Most importantly, transnational feminist work requires that we hold multiple histories, migrations, and transformations simultaneously.

Precarious Midpoints

Although we have reached the end of this text, we hope that these lessons and legacies will inspire more action and activism in the academy and beyond. A global coronavirus pandemic has unearthed many things, some good and some bad. We have been reminded how easily one can be trapped inside the home under patriarchal rule that is described as safe on popular media outlets. The conditions of racial capitalism have made visible who counts as a human, as workers labored in dangerous conditions in the face of the global pandemic. Also, we have revitalized, expanded, and enhanced mutual aid (and cooperative economy) practices of generations past that have been central to the survival of our communities. This book emerges in print form during an era following a contentious election where higher education, learning environments, and words such as diversity, inclusion, and equity are under attack. These words are not radical; in fact, diversity has been understood to not further justice (Ore et al. 2021) and "diversity, equity, and inclusion" are insufficient terms that are unable to describe the colonial and racial capitalist systems. However, the visible attack on speech (Sachs and Young 2025) and campus coalition efforts to support Palestine (Kim and Mulkoff 2025), going hand in hand with the closing of governmental institutions in the United States (Wolf 2024), means that we are entering a new sociopolitical era that calls for the deep necessity to contend with frameworks, praxis, and methodologies that foster a way to envision a present and future beyond the existing system.

Despite the outcome of this election (or other elections around the world), transnational feminists intend to build networks that will allow us to survive in spite of the most neglectful governments and patriarchal cultures. Leveraging power where we have it, we work through these institutions (when possible) and around them (when necessary). The excerpts shared above highlight some of the ways that we do that; and we continue to innovate, as technologies and conditions change. We hope that this anthology will serve as inspiration to feminists everywhere, especially those who are struggling against a particularly challenging confluence of conditions, designed to relegate them to the corners of society. It is with this community of scholar-activists that we write.

References

Kim, Scarlet, and Daniel Mullkoff. "We're Fighting Back Against Efforts to Intimidate Professors into Silence." *ACLU*, January 10, 2025. https://www.aclu.org/news/free-speech/were-fighting-back-against-efforts-to-intimidate-professors-into-silence.

Ore, Ersula, Kim Wieser, and Christina V. Cedillo. 2021. "Symposium: Diversity is Not Enough: Mentorship and Community-Building as Antiracist Praxis." *Rhetoric Review* 40 (3): 207–56. https://doi.org/10.1080/07350198.2021.1935157.

Sachs, Jeffery Adam, and Jeremy C. Young. "For Federal Censorship of Higher Ed, Here's What Could Happen in 2025." *Pen America*, January 2, 2025. https://pen.org/for-federal-censorship-of-higher-ed-heres-what-could-happen-in-2025/.

Contributors

ANNIE ISABEL FUKUSHIMA, Associate Professor, Ethnic Studies Division, School for Cultural and Social Transformation, and Associate Dean, Undergraduate Studies, University of Utah

K. MELCHOR QUICK HALL, Resident Scholar, Women's Studies Research Center, Brandeis University

ESTHER OLUWASHINA AJAYI-LOWO, Assistant Professor, Women and Gender Studies, Texas Christian University

ANA CAROLINA ANTUNES, Assistant Professor, Gender Studies, University of Utah

XAMUEL BAÑALES, Associate Professor and Chair, Ethnic Studies, California State University, Stanislaus

AZZA BASARUDIN, Associate Professor, Women's, Gender, and Sexuality Studies at California State University, Long Beach

TINA BEYENE, Associate Professor and Academic Advisor, Department of Gender and Women's Studies, California State University, Northridge

LINDA CARTY, Associate Professor Emerita, African American Studies, Lesbian, Gay, Bisexual, and Transgender Studies, Syracuse University

ELISA CONTRERAS, Leader of Anahuakenyx Collective, Educator at School of Social Justice, Miguel Contreras Learning Complex

JANICE CINDY GAUDET, Assistant Professor at Campus Saint-Jean and Canada Research Council Chair in Métis Kinship and Land-Based Wellness

LYNN HAMPTON, Director of Diversity, Equity and Inclusion at Kenyon College

Contributors

AMANDA JURNO, Researcher and Professor, PhD by the Federal University of Minas Gerais

EUN-JIN KEISH KIM, Assistant Professor, American Studies and English, Rutgers University, Newark

SHIREEN KEYL, Associate Professor, Cultural Studies, School of Teacher Education and Leadership at Utah State University

LEECE LEE-OLIVER, Associate Professor of Women's, Gender and Sexuality Studies and Director of American Indian Studies at California State University, Fresno

MONIQUE LEMOS, Founder and CEO, TOPO @topofutures

XOCHITL E. LÓPEZ ANDRADE, Leader of Anahuakenyx Collective, Community Health and Sustainability Advocate

TRICIA McGUIRE-ADAMS, Assistant Professor, Education, University of Ottawa; Tier II Canada Research Chair, Indigenous Ganandawisiwin (Good Health) Sovereignties

SYLVIA MENDOZA AVIÑA, Assistant Professor, Mexican American Studies, Race, Ethnicity, Gender and Sexuality Studies Department, University of Texas at San Antonio

AKANKSHA MISRA, Assistant Professor, Department of Gender and Women's Studies at the State University of New York, Plattsburgh

CHANDRA TALPADE MOHANTY, Distinguished Professor, Dean's Professor of the Humanities, Women's and Gender Studies, South Asian Studies, Syracuse University

CUEPONCAXOCHITL D. MORENO SANDOVAL, Associate Professor of Native American and Mexican Indigenous Studies, Stanislaus State, Organizer and Co-learner of the Anahuakenyx Collective

BRUNO MORESCHI, Postdoctoral Fellow, Faculty of Architecture and Urbanism, University of São Paulo; Senior Researcher, Center for Arts, Design and Social Research

RACHEL AFI QUINN, Associate Professor, Comparative Cultural Studies and Women's, Gender & Sexuality Studies, University of Houston

ANGEL SUTJIPTO, Freelance Writer

MIRIAM G. VALDOVINOS, Associate Professor of Social Work, University of Denver, Graduate School of Social Work, Organizer and Co-learner of the Anahuakenyx Collective

LYDIA ZAKEL, MA in Geography, Indiana University

Index

a number, in the migrant glossary/vernacular, 206
Abdullah, Melina, 269
Abu-Lughod, Lila, 145–146, 150, 188
Abu-Sitta, Salman H., 90–93
academic labor, 31–46; Black and women of color as adjunct/contingent faculty, 31, 33–46, 49–62; COVID-19 pandemic and, 49–62; Indigenous women and decolonial feminist praxis, 64–79; praxis of solidarity for adjunct/contingent faculty, 33–46, 53–56 (*see also* praxis of solidarity); racial opportunity cost in, 31–33, 44, 61–62; reconciliation labor of Indigenous female scholars in Canada, 7, 64, 65–66, 68–74, 76; structural violence in the neoliberal university, 42–43, 51, 61–62 (*see also* neoliberal university)
Academic Women's Association, 65
Acosta, Christina, 272
activists/activism: campus activism, 32–33, 36, 38; civil rights, 110, 243, 256; community activism, 5, 235–236; Ethnic Studies and, 269–272, 275–277, 280–281, 286; importance of, 2, 59; mapping and counter-mapping and, 89–90, 94; migrant workers and, 104, 106, 108, 110–112, 114–115, 116; in praxis of solidarity, 34; Red Feminism and, 241, 243, 247, 250–251, 253–255, 260; social media and, 130–137; women's rights and, 178–179; working with children, 159
Adichie, Chimamanda Ngozi, 185–186, 188, 189
Adıvar, Halide Edib, 169–170n5
African Americans: Black homosexuality and, 274; Black Power movements, 58, 269, 273, 274; Civil Rights movement, 58, 110, 124–125, 209, 243, 256, 275; enslavement and, 6, 58, 204, 209, 214–215, 246–247, 286. *See also* anti-Blackness racism; Black and women of color scholars; Black Lives Matter (BLM) movement
Afzal, Ahmed, 135–136
Agarwal-Rangnath, Ruchi, 280
Agassiz, Louis, 214
Agha, Zena, 96–97
Agüero, Juan, 270
Ahmed, Leila, 145–146
Ahmed, Sara, 50, 52, 53
Aikman, Sheila, 170n9
airports, in the migrant glossary/vernacular, 204–205
Ajayi-Lowo, Esther O., 9, 175–199
Akanksha, Misra, 159
Al Ahad research collective, 143–144, 148–152
Alameen-Shavers, Antwanisha, 274
Alarcón, Wanda, 4, 270, 278
Albers, Clem, 216, 217

Alcatraz occupation, 243, 256–258, 261
Alexander, M. Jacqui, 5, 146, 168, 176, 207
Ali, Muhammad, 274
alien bodies like atoms, in the migrant glossary/vernacular, 205–206
Alim, Samy H., 226, 227
Al-Nada, Palestine, 85–88, 96–100; Decolonizing Architecture Art Residency (DAAR) and, 96, 98–101; described, 88, 96
Alvaredo, Facundo, 158
Amazon Mechanical Turk (AMT), 6, 15–28; anonymity as possible advantage for workers, 25–26; children and childcare, 20, 22–25, 27; creation of, 17–18; domestic work and, 15, 21–23; gender and, 18–23, 24–27; general problems of workers, 20–21; Human Intelligence Tasks, 15, 17, 20–27; methodology, 19; nature of, 16–17; sites in study, 16; sleep and, 23–24; source of worker pseudonyms, 28; worker characteristics and locations, 18–20; worker pay, 20–21; work seen as non-work, 24–25
American Indian Movement (AIM), 243, 257
Amireh, Amal, 145
Anahuakenyx collective, 223–226, 229, 231–238, 238n4
ancestral knowledge systems (AKS), 9, 224–227, 230–236
Anderson, Kim, 67–68
Andrews, Walter G., 164
anger, power of, 58–61
anti-Asian racism, 205–206, 207, 216–218; Chinese "Paper Sons," 216; COVID-19 pandemic and, 1–2, 54, 61, 217–218, 284, 285–286; Japanese internment camps, 216
anti-Blackness racism: basis in the United States, 34; countering and unlearning, 59, 227, 229, 236–237; harm of, 34, 234; impact on communities, 1–2, 227, 235; misogynoir (Bailey) and, 7, 33, 37–46; patriarchy and, 37–46, 227; perpetuation of, 34; spirit murder and, 7, 33, 41–46; universities and, 44

anti-Indigeneity: countering and unlearning, 227, 229, 236–237; harm of, 234; impact on communities, 227; patriarchy and, 227; perpetuating, 34; universities and, 44
Antunes, Ana Carolina, 8, 143–156, 144
Antunes, Ricardo, 18, 20
Anzaldúa, Gloria, 2–3, 5, 34, 204, 277, 301, 302
appear, notice to, in the migrant glossary/vernacular, 206–207
Archibald, Jo-Ann, 65
Arizona, banning of Ethnic Studies by legislature (2010), 272
artificial intelligence (AI). *See* Amazon Mechanical Turk (AMT)
Arvin, Maile, 66, 230, 270, 276–277
asexual persons. *See* LGBTQIA+ persons
Ashar, Sameer M., 146
Asian American Feminisms and Women of Color Politics (Fujiwara and Roshanavan), 127–128
Asian Americans. *See* anti-Asian racism; South Asian Youth in Houston United
Asian Community Center Archive Group, 271
Atanasokski, Neda, 19, 22, 27
Atatürk, Mustafa Kemal, 164–165
Austin, Nan, 279
Aydin, Cemil, 169–170n5

Baartman, Saartjie (Sarah), 215, 219n13
Bacchetta, Paola, 272, 276, 277
Bahng, Aimee, 4, 52
Bailey, Moya, 37, 40, 301
Baker, Ella, 275
Balagopalan, Sarada, 160, 168, 170n9
Baldwin, James, 274
Bañales, Xamuel, 9–10, 269–270, 269–295, 272, 275, 277–280, 284–286
Barlow, Tani E., 171n13
Barman, Jean, 67
Bartkowski, John P., 150
Basarudin, Azza, 7, 49–63, 149
Bastin, G., 18
Battiste, Marie, 66
bed, in the migrant glossary/vernacular, 207

Bedard, Renee, 65, 73
Behng, Aimee, 52
Beirut, Lebanon. *See* Migrant Center (Naba'a, Beirut, Lebanon)
Bello, Kemi, "Migrate to Me," 213
Benfield, Delida María, 4, 270, 278
Bent, E., 147
Berik, Günseli, 170–171n2
Berlo, Janet Catherine, 224
Beyene, Tina, 7, 49–63
Bhattacharya, Himika, 149
Bilge, Sirma, 150
Biondi, Martha, 269, 274, 275
bisexual persons. *See* LGBTQIA+ persons
Black, Indigenous, and People of Color (BIPOC): erasure/invisibility of BIPOC feminist scholars, 33–46, 49–62, 65, 79; solidarity in the Black Lives Matter movement, 53. *See also specific ethnic groups*
Black and women of color scholars: adjunct/contingent academic labor of, 33–46, 49–62; black feminist theory and, 122, 123–125; COVID-19 pandemic and, 49–62; praxis of solidarity and, 33–46, 53–56 (*see also* praxis of solidarity); racial opportunity cost in white supremacist schooling, 31–33, 44; reconciliation labor of Indigenous female scholars in Canada, 7, 64, 65–66, 68–74, 76
Black Bear, Tillie, 263
Black Lives Matter (BLM) movement, 1–2; Black Lives Matter in college courses, 36–37, 52, 58–59; Ethnic Studies and, 285–286; George Floyd's murder and, 49–50, 53, 58, 60; history foregrounding, 53, 58; power of anger and, 58–61; uprisings in, 49–50, 53, 58, 124
Black Panther Party, 273, 274, 275
Black Power movements, 58, 269, 273, 274
Blackwell, Maylei, 269, 274
boats and ships, in the migrant glossary/vernacular, 207–208
bodily modification: female genital cutting (FGC), 180–181, 185, 187, 192–194; piercings, 144, 149–150; tattooing, 144, 149–150, 152; transgender surgery, 163, 164
borders/binaries, 1, 8, 85, 88, 90, 146–147, 160, 165, 168, 208
Bose, Sumantra, 169–170n5
Brady, Steve, Sr., 244, 246, 249
Braithwaite, Ann, 196n1
Braun, Virginia, 181, 194
Brave Heart, Maria Yellow Horse, 250
Bravo, Stephany, 278
Brazil: Group on Artificial Intelligence and Art (GAIA, Brazil), 6, 15–28; Ubuntu philosophy and, 301
Brice-Heath, Shirley, 108
Brocket, Tom, 86
Browder, Jennifer Kathleen, 224
Brown, Adrienne Maree, 285
Brown, Elaine, 274
Brown, Monica, 276
Brown, Sarah, 285
Brown v. Board of Education, 209
Bruce Pratt, Minnie, 302
Bruno, Fernanda, 16
Buenavista, Tracy L., 285
Bullock, Katherine, 145–146
Bunge, William, 89
Burciaga, Rebeca, 33, 35
Bureau of Indian Affairs (BIA), 258, 259, 261
Burman, Erica, 160, 168, 170n9
Burrell, Jenna, 16
Burst of Light (Lorde), 64
Buscemi, Emanuela, 270
Bush, George W., 243
Bush, Laura, 145–146
Bustos, Yoselia, 279

Cacho, Lisa Marie, 279, 285
Cainkar, Louis A., 145
Cajete, Gregory, 223
California State University: Ethnic Studies at California State University at Stanislaus, 278–285; Task Force on the Advancement of Ethnic Studies Report, 272
Camba, Soultree, 220n16
Campbell, Laura, 86
Campbell, Malik, 52, 272–273, 285
camps, in the migrant glossary/vernacular, 208, 216, 217

Campt, Tina, 148
Canada, 64–79; reconciliation labor of Indigenous female scholars in Canada, 7, 64, 65–66, 68–74, 76; Truth and Reconciliation Commission of Canada Call to Action, 69–70
capitalism/capitalist patriarchy: disaster capitalism and, 253, 255–256, 261–263; diversity, equity, and inclusion (DEI) and, 43–44, 303; imperialist white supremacist capitalist patriarchy, 176, 243–244, 261–263; Women's and Gender Studies and, 176, 178, 184, 194
care / care work, 7, 53, 57–59, 66, 68, 124, 133, 302
Caribbean peoples: US imperial powers and, 207–208; "Wet Foot, Dry Foot" policy (1995), 207
Carlos, John, 269
Carpenter, Cari M., 263–264
Carrillo, Carmen, 275
Carter, Jimmy, 207
Carty, Linda E., vii–xiv, 2, 5, 34, 236, 278
Casey, Edward S., 162
Castañeda, Claudia, 160
Castells, Manuel, 28
Çayır, Kenan, 167
Cedillo, C. V., 303
Césaire, Aimée, 2
Ceyhan, Müge Ayan, 167
Chae Chan Ping v. United States, 205
Chancel, Lucas, 158
Chatterjee, Partha, 164, 169n3
Chatterjee, Piya, 52, 272, 273, 285
Chávez-García, Miroslava, 276
Cheney, Dick, 243
Chicano Youth Liberation Conference (1969), 274
Child, Brenda, 67
childcare, Amazon Mechanical Turk and, 20, 22–25, 27
children's sensual experiences, 8–9, 157–171; author identity and positionality, 169–170n5; central role of schooling and, 160–162, 165–168; child sexual abuse prevention and, 159; colonial modernity and, 161–162;

comprehensive sexuality education (CSEd) in Turkey and India, 157–168, 168–169n2; Indigenous and Native perspectives on, 161–162, 164, 170n8; LGBTQIA+ persons and, 163–164, 168; menstruation and, 163–164; nature of, 158; similarities across cultures, 158, 165–168; teleologies of the adult national body and, 162–168; tensions in fieldwork, 159
Chivington, John M., 246
chosen family, in the migrant glossary/vernacular, 208–209
Chowdhury, Elora, 149, 150
citizenship, in the migrant glossary/vernacular, 209–210
Civil Rights movement, 58, 110, 124–125, 209, 243, 256, 275
Clark, Septima, 124–125
Cleaver, Eldridge, 273–274
coalitions, 2–4, 33, 79, 122–127, 151, 152, 251–252, 270–272, 277–278, 302–303
Coelho, Paulo, 110
Collins, Patricia Hill, 19, 27, 301
colonialism: children's sensual experiences and colonial modernity, 161–162; citizenship and, 209; colonial notions of other/othering and, 177; components of, 1; dismantling, 229; Ethnic Studies and, 273 (*see also* Ethnic Studies); impact of, 204; Indigenous challenges to, 65, 70, 76, 253; legitimizing, 272; mapping in, 85–88, 89–90; prevalence of, 285
Combahee River Collective (CRC), 34, 124, 270
Comparative Race and Ethnic Studies (CRES) course, 32–33, 37–46
Conchas, Gilbert Q., 231
Conley, Valerie J., 31
consciousness, 3–5, 79, 230, 231; ancestral knowledge systems and, 230; critical, 114, 236, 270, 300; oppositional, 62; of the "other," 108; racial/ethnic/class, 37, 108, 273, 274; Red Feminism and, 241, 242, 248, 251, 255; spatial, 105–106
Contreras, Elisa, 9, 223–240, 302
Contreras, Kristian, 298, 299

Cotera, María E., 269
counter-mapping: as a decolonial spatial practice, 7–8, 85–87, 89–90; in Miska (Palestinian village), 93–96, 100; nature of, 86–87, 89, 100–101; participatory action research (PAR) and, 93–96; in Sataf, Israel (village in historic Palestine), 87, 89, 90–93, 100
COVID-19 pandemic, 194–195; anti-Asian racism and, 1–2, 54, 61, 217–218, 284, 286; Black and women of color scholars and, 49–62; course on relationship between knowledge and power, 56–61; decolonizing pedagogy and, 49–62; Indigenous and Native perspectives, 234; inequities and crisis of care during, 1–2, 49–56, 52, 57, 61–62, 158; love letters in Ethnic Studies class, 284–285; political turmoil during, 49–50; politics of crisis in the neoliberal university, 51–52; power of anger and, 58–61; Secondary Street Trauma (SST) of educators, 61–62; South Asian Youth in Houston United (SAYHU) and, 120–121, 123, 128, 130–134, 136–137; working during, 218. *See also* Black Lives Matter (BLM) movement
Cowen, Michael, 169n3
Cozman, Fabio G., 17, 19, 20, 21
Crary, Jonathan, 16, 24
Crenshaw, Kimberle, 184, 270, 301
critical ethnology approach, nature of, 231
Critical Participatory Action Research (CPAR): future directions, 300; in *The Hijab Project*, 8, 143–152; nature of, 143
Cronk, Jordan, 216
Crul, Maurice, 145
Crunk Feminist Collective (CFC), 123–124
culturally sustaining pedagogies, 226–227, 236
Curiel, Ochy, 270
Custalow, Linwood "Little Bear," 254

Damigo, Nathan, 279
Daniel, Angela L. "Silver Star," 254
Das, Arpita, 161
Davis, Angela Y., 19, 23, 26, 57
Davis, Jeff, 271
Davis, Mike, 219n5
Davis, Shardé M. Black, 32, 37
Dawson, Frank R., 272
Daya Houston, 120
De Beauvoir, Simone, 19
decolonial feminisms: anti-racist theory and, 3; as bridge, 276–278; coloniality as theory and practice, 2–3; colonial modern gender system and, 4; contributors to, 2; decoloniality as unfinished project, 2; Ethnic Studies and, 270–271, 278–285; formation of anthology on, 5–10; future directions for, 3–4, 298–302; Indigenous women and, 4, 64–79; legacy of theories and theorists on, 5; methodological approaches in, 3, 6; Migrant Center and (*see* Migrant Center [Naba'a, Beirut Lebanon]); multiple meanings of genealogies, 5; rejection of colonial systems and binaries, 4; resistance in theory and practice of decolonizing, 3; roots in Latin America, 270; subjectivity of multiple selves and realities in, 3–4; tensions between transnational feminisms and decolonialism, 4; time as a construct in, 3–4, 5. *See also* Red/Indigenous feminism
Decolonizing Architecture Art Residency (DAAR) and, 96, 98–101
De Genova, Nicholas, 210
DeGout, Yasmin Y., 274
De Leon, Kelly, 52, 272–273, 285
Delgado Bernal, Dolores, 33, 35, 229
Deloria, Vine, 242, 243
De Los Rios, Cati V., 226–227
Del Rio Madrigal, Sandra, 298, 300, 301–302
Democratizing Knowledge Project (DK Project), vii–viii, xiv, 2, 5–6
deportation, order of: Border Patrol and, 219n15; families separated and migrants harmed by US deportation policy, 211; in the migrant glossary/vernacular, 210; migrants harmed by, 211; to unrelated places, 211

Desai, Jigna, 149
Deyhle, Douglas, 231
DiAngelo, Robin, 38, 41
Dias, Kristen, 281
Díaz, Jazz, 280
Diaz, Natalie, 211
Difallah, Djellel, 18–19
D'Ignazio, Catherine, 19
DiPietro, Pedro J., 276
disability, intersectionality and, 299, 301
domestic work, Amazon Mechanical Turk, 15, 21–23
Dong, Harvey, 285
Dong, Madeleine Yue, 171n13
Dorion, Leah, 67
Dosekun, Simidele, 147
Dueñas, Rudy, 226–227
Dunbar-Ortiz, Roxanne, 223
Dunlap, Nicole, 279, 281
Durazo, Ana Clarissa Rojas, 276
Dussel, Enrique, 2
Dyer, Hannah, 157–158

Edney, Matthew, 86, 87, 101
Edwards, Harry, 269
Edwards, Kirsten T., 32
Ekbia, Harold R., 22
Elaine Brown Reading/Talk, 274
Elliot, Alicia, 208
Ellis, Elizabeth, 210
emperor turning people into ghosts, in the migrant glossary/vernacular, 211
empire state, in the migrant glossary/vernacular, 211
environmental destruction, 158, 261–263, 279
Erasmus, Georges, 72
erasure/invisibility: of African Americans, 9, 274, 275 (see also Black Lives Matter [BLM] movement); of BIPOC feminist scholars, 33–46, 49–62, 65, 79; deviation from the normative narrative and, 301–302; honor killings and, 178, 185, 187, 192–194; of immigrants, 8, 9; of Indigenous/Native peoples, 9, 65, 243, 246, 249–251, 253–254, 256–257, 263, 280, 281; misogynoir as spirit murder, 33, 37–41; of Palestinian villages, 86–88, 90–91, 97–98, 100–101; of South Asian Texans, 126; in Turkish history, 160, 165. *See also* genocide
Ergenc, Ceren, 158
Escobar, Arturo, 147–148
Escobar, Martha D., 52, 272–273, 285
Espinosa-Miñoso, Yuderkys, 5, 270
Espinoza, Dionne, 269
Estes, Nick, 243
Ethnic Studies, 269–286; banned by Arizona legislature, 272; at California State University at Stanislaus, 278–285; challenges to colonial legacies in, 269–270; Comparative Race and Ethnic Studies (CRES) course, 32–33, 37–46; culturally sustaining education and, 226–227, 236; decolonial feminisms and, 270–271, 278–285; need to support and expand, 285–286; politics of heteropatriarchy and, 273–278, 285–286; protest movements in origins of, 269–270, 271–273; refusing the university and, 278–284
eugenics, 250
Evans, David T., 158

Facebook, 125, 130, 131
Falcón, Sylvanna M., 148, 151, 152, 184
families separated and migrants harmed by US deportation policy, in the migrant glossary/vernacular, 211
Fanon, Frantz, 2, 276
Federici, Silvia, 19, 21–22, 24
Feldman, Keith P., 145–146
Fels, John, 85
female genital cutting (FGC), 180–181, 185, 187, 192–194
feminisms. *See* decolonial feminisms; Red/Indigenous feminism; transnational feminisms
Feminist Freedom Warriors (Mohanty and Carty, eds.), 2, 34, 236, 278
Ferguson, Roderick A., 276
Ferguson Teaching Collective, 52
Ferrus, Diana, 215, 219n13
Fierros, Cindy Ochoa, 35
Figueroa-Vásquez, Yomaira C., 34, 278, 284

Filgueiras, Vitor, 20
Fine, Michelle, 94, 143, 151
Finkelstein, Martin J., 31
Finn, Ed, 18, 20
Flaminio, Anna, 67
Flanders, Laura, 256–260
Flores Carmona, Judith, 33, 35
Floyd, George, 49–50, 53, 58, 60
Foley, Douglas E., 231
Fong Yue Ting v. United States, 205–206
Fonow, Mary Margaret, 184, 195
food: as a basic need, 31, 112; native/ancestral foods, 109, 166, 223–224, 226, 228
Forbes, Jack D., 271
Ford, James, 51
Fortna, Benjamin C., 160
Fox, Madeline, 143, 151
Frazier, Demita, 34, 124
Fredericks, Bronwyn, 66
freedom: academic, 285; and agency, 148; feminist freedom warriors, 2; hijab use and, 145, 148; and individualism, 145
Freire, Paulo, 51, 280
fugitive status, 211–212
Fujiwara, Lynn, 127–128, 277–278
Fukushima, Annie Isabel, 3, 4, 177, 213, 270, 276, 278, 298
futurity, decolonial feminisms and, 3–4, 298–302

Gabel, Chelsea, 65
Galarte, Francisco J., 276
García, Alma M., 270, 275
Garcia, Veronica, 226–227
García-Peña, Lorgia, 285
Gates, Henry Louis, Jr., 275
Gaudet, Janice Cindy, 7, 64–81, 67, 68, 69; "Keeouykaywin: Interrupting Coloniality," 74–75; "The Lining of Our Wellness Bundle" (with Ward, and McGuire-Adams), 78–79; "Poetic Interlude" (with Ward), 72
Gaudry, Adam, 65, 66–67
Gaxiola, Steven, 279
gay persons. *See* LGBTQIA+ persons
Gender Studies: capitalist patriarchy in Women's and Gender Studies, 176, 178, 184, 194; erasure of BIPOC feminist scholars and, 49–62. *See also* Women's and Gender Studies (WGS)
genocide: of Indigenous/Native peoples, 9, 65, 235, 242–251, 253–254, 261–263, 280; in Nazi Germany, 216; Orlando Pulse nightclub massacre, 280, 283; of Palestinians, 2, 85, 97–98
Ghosh, Suresh Chandra, 160
Gilbert, Marcella, 256–258, 263
Gillespie, Tarleton, 19
Gilmore, Craig, 279
Gilmore, Ruth Wilson, 279
Ginzberg, Abby, 272
Giroux, Henry, 51
Giving Voice project, 68–70, 75
Glenn, Evelyn Nakano, 5
Glissant, Edouard, 203, 204
Global North, Women's and Gender Studies and, 176–183
Global South: children's sensual experiences and, 8–9, 157–171; economic and social development of, 147; perspective on Amazon Mechanical Turk, 16; Women's and Gender Studies and, 176–183; women's rights oppression in, 178. *See also* South Asian Youth in Houston United (SAYHU)
Goins, Marla, 299, 301
Gold, Tami, 272
Goldthree, Reena N., 52
González, Dezzerie, 272–273, 285
González, Genevieve, 279
González, González, 52
Google Survey, 131–132
Gordon, Lewis, 2
Granados, Guadalupe, 52
Grande, Sandy, 236, 272, 278–279
Gray, Mary L., 19, 20, 22
Green, Joyce, 66, 229, 230
Green, Rayna, 250
Greenberg, David F., 284
Grewal, Inderpal, 146–147, 148, 182, 193, 195
Grohmann, Rafael, 18
Grosfoguel, Ramón, 3, 269–270, 272, 273, 276
Grosz, Elizabeth, 3–4

grounded theory, 106
Group on Artificial Intelligence and Art (GAIA), 6, 15–28
Guantánamo Bay, in the migrant glossary/vernacular, 212
Guevara, Che, 276
Guy-Sheftall, Beverly, 52

Ha, Trinh Minh, 146
Hale, Lorraine, 271
Hall, K. Melchor Quick, 1–11, 297–303, 301
Halsey, Theresa, 250, 259
Hames-García, Michael, 272, 276
Hammonds, Evelyn, 52
Hamoğlu, Şükrü M., 169n4
Hampton, Lynn, 7, 31–48, 35; Black Lives Matter college course and, 36–37; Comparative Race and Ethnic Studies (CRES) course and, 32–33, 37–46; testimonio, 34, 36–46
Hamzeh, Manal, 35
Handlin, Oscar, 218–219n1
"hanging out" / hangouts, 149–151, 152
Hannah-Jones, Nikole, 209
Haraway, Donna, 16, 19
Harjo, Joy, 260
Harris, Jake, 33
Hartocollis, Anemona, 214
Harvard Peabody Museum, 214–215
Harvey Collins, Elena, 260, 261
Hatem, Mervat F., 150
Haynes, Chayla, 37
Headrick, Annabeth, 228
heart storms, 72, 73, 76, 77
Henning, Nick, 280
Hernández, Ellie, 2–3
Hernandez, Oscar, 16
Hernández, Roberto, 272, 273
Hernández, Tanya Kateri, 34
Herrera, Jack, 272
heteromation, 22
The Hijab Project, 8, 143–152; *Al Ahad* research collective and, 143–144, 148–152; data collection and method for study, 144; described, 143, 151–152; expectations of study, 149–152; Islamophobia and, 8, 143–146, 151, 152; participants in, 144; politicization of the veil, 145–146; transgressive solidarity and, 148–152; transnational girlhood studies and, 146–152

Hinduism, 126; children's sensual experiences and, 160–162, 164, 170n6. *See also* South Asian Youth in Houston United (SAYHU)
Hine, Darlene Clark, 274
Hoff, Pamela Twyman, 31–32, 33, 39, 40
home: feminist pedagogy as (Mohanty), 51, 57–58; in the migrant glossary/vernacular, 212–213
homophobia, 127, 273–274, 275
honor killing, 178, 185, 187, 192–194
hooks, bell, 51, 53, 176
Hopkins, Lucy, 168
Huggins, Ericka, 274
Huggins, Kristen S., 32
Huhndorf, Shari, 67, 253
Hull, Gloria T., 277
Human Intelligence Tasks (HITs), 15, 17, 20–27
Human Rights Watch, 160–161
Hussein, Leyla, 187–188, 194
Hutchinson, Anne, 218–219n1
Huws, Ursula, 18

Identity Evropa, 279, 281
IdleNoMore, 260–262
immigration. *See* migrant/immigrant community
Immigration Act (1965), 125, 209
Immigration and Customs Enforcement (ICE), 208, 215, 219n15, 280–282
Immigration Reform and Enforcement Act (2011), 211–212
imperialist white supremacist capitalist patriarchy, 176, 243–244, 261–263
India. *See* children's sensual experiences
Indigenous/Native persons, 64–79; Bureau of Indian Affairs (BIA), 258, 259, 261; challenges to settler colonialism, 65, 70, 76, 253; children's sensual experiences and, 161–162, 164, 170n8; counter-mapping as decolonial practice and, 89–90; COVID-19 pandemic and, 234;

disaster capitalism and, 253, 255–256, 261–263; displacement on their own land, 208; erasure of Indigenous peoples, 9, 65, 242–249, 250–251, 253–254, 256–257, 263, 280, 281; genocide and, 9, 65, 235, 242–251, 253–254, 261–263, 280; Giving Voice project, 68–70, 75; Indigenization in Canadian universities, 7, 65–69; Indigenous feminisms as conceptual framework, 4, 66–68, 229–231, 253 (*See also* Red/Indigenous feminism); Missing and Murdered Indigenous Women, Girls, and Relatives, 246, 253–254, 256, 280, 281; Native American sovereignty movements, 242–243, 261, 253–258, 260; "Native" as a verb, 252; poetry and narratives in, 64–65, 68–79; reconciliation of female scholars in Canadian universities, 7, 64, 65–66, 68–74, 76; resistance and sovereignty movements, 242–243, 253–258, 260–263; testimonio and, 35; Tribal Law and Order Act, 247; urban communities and, 259, 260–263; in Women's and Gender Studies, 182–183. *See also* Xicanx Indigenous youth

Indigenous Women and Feminism (Huhndorf and Suzack), 253

Instagram, 125, 130, 131

International Council of Grandmothers, 237–238, 262

International Indian Treaty Council, 258

International Organization for Migration, 207

intersectionality: of black and South Asian experience, 123–125, 138n9 (*see also* South Asian Youth in Houston United [SAYHU]); COVID-19 pandemic and, 54–56; Crenshaw and, 184, 270, 301; cross-coalitional organizing and, 302; in decolonial feminist framework, 279–280; disability and, 299, 301; domestic, 184; transnationalism in Women and Gender Studies pedagogy, 175–176, 183–184, 187–188; of white supremacy and law, 244–245; women of color thought and, 270, 276–277

intersex persons. *See* LGBTQIA+ persons

Ipeirotis, Panos, 19

Irani, L., 19

Islamophobia, and *The Hijab Project* and, 8, 143–146, 151, 152

Ismail, Qadri, 93

Israel: displacement of Palestinians, 2, 85, 86, 90–98, 100; maps of Palestine, 86; military destruction in Gaza (2014), 96, 98; occupation of Palestine, 86–88; ongoing destruction of Gaza, 98; Sataf, Israel (village in historic Palestine), 85–93, 100; withdrawal of military and citizens from Gaza (2005), 98

Israel, Jonathan, 169n3

Jackson, Carlos, 284
Jackson, Cynthia L., 271
Jackson, Shirley A., 272
Jaimes, M. Annette, 250, 259
James, Allison, 158
Jarrett, Kylie, 19
Jefferson, Thomas, 246
Jennings, Regina, 274
Jessi, Gan, 276
Johnson, Kaley, 33
Johnson, K. R., 146
Joler, Vladan, 15, 28
Joseph, Peniel E., 274
Joshi, K. M., 170n7
joy, in the migrant glossary/vernacular, 213
Jurno, Amanda, 6, 15–30

Kabeer, Naila, 170–171n12
Kadman, Noga, 86
Kalpakh, Mehmet, 164
Kandiyoti, Deniz, 165, 169n3
Kaplan, Caren, 146–147, 182, 195
Karahalios, Karrie, 97
Kasaba, Reşat, 169n4
Kaya, Nurcan, 161, 167
Keating, AnaLouise, 185, 186
Keating, Cricket, 5

Keish Kim, Eun-Jin, 9, 203–222, 299, 300
Kelley, Robin D. G., 125
Keyl, Shireen, 7–8, 103–119
Khanmalek, Tala, 219n3, 272, 273, 286
Khoja-Moolji, Shenila, 144, 147–148
Kidwai, Saleem, 164
King, Martin Luther, Jr., 110
Kissinger, Henry, 243
Kitch, Sally L., 184, 195
Klein, Lauren F., 19
knowledge, relationship to power, 56–61, 112, 113–114
Kohli, Rita, 280
Kouzmin, Alexander, 146
Krishnaswamy, Revathi, 160
Kuhn, Gabriel, 210
Ku Klux Klan, 279
Kumar, Krishna, 160
Kundnani, Arun, 145
Kunnie, Julian, 226

labor: academic (*see* academic labor); automation of (*see* Amazon Mechanical Turk [AMT]); domestic labor, 16, 24–25, 27, 104–105; emotional labor, 25–26, 38, 66, 68, 74, 136; invisible labor of faculty of color, 51–52, 61; migrant laborers (*see* Migrant Center [Naba'a, Beirut Lebanon]); resistance and, 6–7
LaDuke, Winona, 243, 252, 259, 263
Laenui, Poka, 230, 237
land: borders and, 1, 8, 85, 88, 90, 146–147, 160, 165, 168, 208; colonization of (*see* colonialism); displacement in Palestine (*see* Palestine); displacement of Indigenous peoples, 208; Japanese American internment during World War II, 216, 217; mapping (*see* mapping); Turtle Island (Abiayala), 5, 203, 210, 238n6
Landauer, Gustav, 210
LaRocque, Emma, 65, 67
Las Tesis, 2
Latina Feminist Group, 35
Latina/o/x/e / Chicana/o/x persons: Day of the Dead celebrations, 279–280; heteropatriarchy of the Chicano movement, 274; Orlando Pulse nightclub massacre, 280, 283; teaching and learning processes with, 301; testimonio and (*see* testimonio). *See also* Black and women of color scholars
Lawrence-Zúñiga, Denise, 115
Lebanon. *See* Migrant Center (Naba'a, Beirut, Lebanon)
Lee, Laurie Thomas, 146
Lee, Tiffany, 226, 227
Lee-Oliver, Leece, 9, 244, 246, 247, 249, 250, 252, 254, 261, 264, 269, 270, 272, 276–278, 284, 286
Lefebvre, Henri, 168
Lemos, Monique, 6, 15–30
Lewis, Sol, 245–246, 248–249
LGBTQIA+ persons: Black homosexuality and, 273–274; children's sensual experiences and, 163–164, 168; COVID-19 pandemic and, 56; homophobia and, 127, 273–274, 275; SAYHU and, 123–124, 128, 134, 135–136, 137; transgender surgery and, 163, 164; violence against transgender people, 253, 282; Xicanx Indigenous youth and, 227–229
liberatory theory, 4
Life Among the Piute (Winnemucca Hopkins), 254–255
Lloyd, David, 1
Lone Star Muslims (Afzal), 135–136
López, Gisely Colón, 272
López, Jorge, 226–227
López Andrade, Xochitl E., 9
Lorde, Audre, 53, 64, 124, 275
Lorenz, Chris, 51
Lorenz, Danielle, 65, 66–67
love: love letters in Ethnic Studies class during the COVID-19 pandemic, 284–285; in Red/Indigenous feminism, 263–265
Love, Bettina L., 41
Love, Erik, 145
Low, Setha M., 115
Lowawaima, Tsianina, 250
Lugones, María, 3, 5, 6, 149, 150, 152, 168, 177, 270, 277–278, 301
Luna, Jennie M., 272

Macey, Marie, 145
Macias, Ysidro, 271
Maese, Marcelle, 278

Maese-Cohen, Marcelle, 4, 276
Maira, Sunaina Marr, 52, 122, 272, 273, 285
Malagon, Jonathan, 226
Malcolm X, 110, 274, 276
Maldonado-Torres, Nelson, 2, 3, 5, 247, 264, 270, 272, 273, 284
Mani, Braj Ranjan, 170n6
Mankiller, Wilma, 252, 259, 263
Manoff, Einat, 94
Manzanilla, Linda, 228
Manzanillo, Alexis, 275
Maoz, Ifat, 93
Mao Zedong, 276
mapping, 85–101; as act of return for Palestinians, 87–88; Al-Nada reconstruction, 85–86, 87, 88, 100; of architecture, 88, 96–101; counter-mapping as a decolonial act, 85–87, 89–100; decolonial praxis in trying to undo, 85, 96–100; Miska reconstruction, 85–86, 88, 93–96, 100; nature, 87, 89; participatory action research (PAR) and, 85, 87, 88, 93–96; Sataf (Israeli village in historic Palestine) reconstruction, 85–93, 100; in settler colonialism, 85–88, 89–90; state governments and, 86–87; tools for, 88
Maracle, Lee, 66
Marchi, Regina M., 280
Marín, Guillermo, 231
Marín, James R., 285
Marshall, Paul A., 147
Martínez, Carla, 52
Martínez, Silvana, 270
Martinez-Cairo, Bárbara, 270
Marx, Karl, 217
Massey, Doreen, 87, 116
Mavroudi, Elizabeth, 95
McCarty, Teresa, 226, 227
McClanahan, Annie, 285
McCloud, Janet, 263
McGuire, Patricia D., 65
McGuire-Adams, Tricia, 7, 64–81, 67, 68, 69; "The Lining of Our Wellness Bundle" (with Gaudet and Ward), 78–79; "Niceness Is Not Kind," 70
McLaren, Margaret A., 276
McMichael, Philip, 169n3
McWeeny, Jennifer M., 276

Medina, José M., 270
Mehta, Purvi, 171n13
memory. *See* erasure/invisibility; migrant glossary/vernacular
Mendez, X., 3
Mendoza, Breny, 193
Mendoza Aviña, Sylvia, 7, 35
Menon, Priya, 160
menstruation, 163–164
Mexican Indigenous Nations. *See* Xicanx Indigenous youth
Micco, Melinda, 256, 260–263
Mignolo, Walter D., 2, 3, 229, 238n6
Migrant Center (Naba'a, Beirut, Lebanon), 103–118; author identity and positionality, 107–108; Dakshi, 104, 106, 109–110; data collection tools, 107–108; as decolonial feminist space, 104–105, 108–110, 114–115; described, 103–104, 106, 108–110; establishment of, 104, 108, 114, 115; Fakira, 106, 107–108, 110–111, 113–114, 115; feminization of labor migration and, 104–105; horizontal vs. vertical help and, 110–111; Irene, 106, 111; juxtaposition of contentious space and, 104–105; Laurencia, 106, 111–112, 113; participant observation, 107–108; resistance of migrant domestic workers and, 105; as space of learning and knowledge production, 111–114, 116; spatial theory of (in)justice and, 8, 105–106, 116; Suba, 104, 106, 109–115; Tamkin, 106–108, 110–111, 114–116; Thomas, 106, 112; voluntourism and, 110–111, 113–114
migrant glossary/vernacular, 203–220; airports, 204–205; alien bodies like atoms, 205–206; a number, 206; appear, notice to, 206–207; bed, 207; boats and ships, 207–208; border/binaries, 208; camps, 208; chosen family/calderas that hold, 208–209; citizenship, 209–210; deportation, order of, 210–211; emperor turning people into ghosts, 211; empire state, 211; families separated and migrants harmed by US deportation policy, 211; Georgia, fugitive status in, 211–212; Guantánamo Boy, 212; home,

migrant glossary/vernacular (*continued*)
212–213; joy, 213; "Migrate to me" (Bello), 213; palimpsests, 214; papers, 213–214, 216; photographs, 214–215; time, 215–216; trains, 216–217; wellness, 217–218; work authorization/working under the table, 218; worth, 218

migrant/immigrant community: COVID-19 pandemic and, 55; deportation and, 210–211, 219n15; erasure/invisibility of migrants, 8, 9; fugitive status and, 211–212. *See also* Migrant Center (Naba'a, Beirut, Lebanon); migrant glossary/vernacular; South Asian Youth in Houston United (SAYHU)

"Migrate to me" (Bello), in the migrant glossary/vernacular, 213

Mihesuah, Devon, 66

Mikkonen, Enni, 143–144, 147

military: displacement and erasure of Indigenous peoples, 9, 65, 208, 242–249, 250–251, 253–254, 256–257, 263, 280, 281; genocide in Nazi Germany, 216; genocide in Palestine, 2, 85, 97–98; United States intervention in the Middle East and Asia, 145–146; United States intervention in the Southwest Asia and North Africa (SWANA) region, 104–105, 107–108. *See also* war

Milland, Kristy, 19

A Mind Spread Out on the Ground (Elliot), 208

Miranda, Deborah A., 271

Mirza, Heidi Safia, 145

Miska, Palestine, 85–86, 88; countermapping in reconstruction of, 93–96, 100; described, 88, 94; participatory action research in reconstruction of, 93–96, 100

misogynoir, 33, 37–46; nature of, 7, 37–38, 40; as spirit murder, 7, 41–46

Misra, Akanksha, 8–9, 157–174

Missing and Murdered Indigenous Women, Girls, and Relatives (MMIWGR), 246, 253–254, 256, 280, 281

Moctezuma, Alessandra, 219n5

Modi, Narendra, 126

Mohanty, Chandra Talpade, 5, 31, 145–146, 148, 168, 176, 278, 297–303, 298; *Feminism Without Borders,* 51, 57, 193, 195; *Feminist Freedom Warriors* (Mohanty and Carty, eds.), 2, 34, 236, 278; feminist pedagogy as home and, 51, 57–58; power-knowledge nexus and, 113–114; "Under Western Eyes," 176, 183

Molina, Natalia, 34

Monture-Angus, Patricia, 65–67

Moosa-Mitha, Mehmoona, 148

Moraga, Cherrie A., 34, 227, 229, 277, 302

Morell, Ernest, 226–227

Moreschi, Bruno, 6, 15–30, 17, 19, 20, 21, 23

Morgan, Ronald G., 219n2

Morrar, Sawsan, 273

Morrell, Ernest, 226–227

Morrill, Angie, 66–67, 230, 270, 276–277

Movimiento Estudiantil Chicanos de Aztlán (MEChA), 224–225, 228–229, 233

Moya, Luna X., 220n18

Moya, Paula, 3

Moynihan, Patrick, 274

Mukherjee, Debashree, 122

Mukherjee, Jashodhara, 160

Mulkoff, D., 303

Muslims: children's sensual experiences and, 160, 164–165; Miska, Palestine reconstruction and, 85–86, 88, 93–96, 100; xenophobia and, 217–218. *See also The Hijab Project*

mutual aid, principles of, 302

Nagar, Richa, 134, 168

Najmabadi, Afsaneh, 170n10

Narayan, Uma, 176, 195

Nardi, Bonnie A., 22

narratives and poetry. *See* poetry and narratives

Nash, Jennifer C., 148, 152, 184

National Indigenous Women's Resource Network, 251

National Women's Studies Association (NAWSA), 138n7, 194–195

Native American Community History Project (archive), 259
Native Americans. *See* Indigenous/Native persons; Red/Indigenous feminism
Naylor, Lindsay, 98
Nazism, 216, 246
Negrón-Muntaner, Frances, 285
neoliberal university: Black and women of color as adjunct/contingent faculty, 31, 33–46, 49–62; Codes of Wellness, 68, 70, 74–76; COVID-19 pandemic and, 49–62; decolonial practice in, 33–46, 53–56, 61–62, 64–79; education-industrial complex and, 51–52; Ethnic Studies (*see* Ethnic Studies); Gender Studies (*see* Gender Studies); inequities for students in, 51–52, 53–56, 57, 61–62; neoconservatism and, 52; power of anger and, 58–61; reconciliation of Indigenous female scholars in Canada, 7, 64, 65–66, 68–74, 76; resistance to the neoliberal ethos, 53, 56–61; structural violence in, 42–43, 51, 61–62; Women's and Gender Studies (*see* Women's and Gender Studies [WGS])
New Digital Worlds (Risam), 134–135
Newman, Louise, 250
Newton, Huey P., 274
Ng, Fae Myenne, 213
Ngai, Mae M., 206
Nickel, Sarah, 66
Niyogi, Sangha, 272, 284
NLCC Educational Media, 274
Notion (project management app), 131
Nzinga, Sekile M., 31, 37

Oakley, Ann, 23
Okazawa-Rey, Margot, 124–125
Okihiro, Gary Y., 271, 272
Olkowski, Dorothea, 170n11
Olmos, Vanessa, 279
Olympic Games (1968), 269
Omi, Michael, 247
Oparah, Julia C., 272
Ordona, Trinity A., 269, 276, 280
Ore, E., 303
Orlando Pulse nightclub massacre, 280, 283
Orr, Catherine M., 196n1
Ortega, Mariana, 5, 270
Osei-Kofi, Nana, 52
Osher, Steven A., 146
Osler, Audrey, 145
other/othering: "blessed" status of US vs. "oppressed others," 180–181, 185–186, 192, 195; colonial notions of, 177; consciousness of, 108; COVID-19 pandemic and, 284; Muslims and, 145; violent suppression of voices of non-privileged in, 158
Öz, Mine Eder Özlem, 167

Palestine, 85–101; Al-Nada reconstruction, 85–86, 87, 88, 100; author identity and positionality, 88; counter-mapping and, 7–8, 85–87, 89–93; Gaza genocide (2023), 97–98; genocide in, 2, 85, 97–98; Israeli ethnic cleansing (1948), 2, 85, 86, 90–98, 100; Israeli military destruction in Gaza (2014), 96, 98; Israeli occupation, 86–88; Miska reconstruction, 85–86, 88, 93–96, 100; Palestinian Land Society (PLS), 90, 93, 95; restrictions of aerial imagery, 96–97; Sataf (village in historic Palestine) reconstruction, 85–93, 100; settler colonial mapping and, 85–88, 90
palimpsests, in the migrant glossary/vernacular, 214
Palm, Iman, 279
Pandit, Eesha, 123–124
Paniagua, Diego, 52
papers, in the migrant glossary/vernacular, 213–214, 216
Pappe, Ilan, 90–91
Paris, Django, 226, 227
Parisi, Laura, 176, 177, 179, 182, 193, 194
participant observation. *See* children's sensual experiences
participatory action research (PAR): in mapping and counter-mapping in Palestine, 85, 87, 88, 93–96, 100; nature of, 93, 100–101. *See also* Critical Participatory Action Research (CPAR)
Pasquinelli, Matteo, 15, 28
Patel, Sharifa, 177

Patil, Vrushali, 184
patriarchy: anti-Blackness racism and, 37–46, 227; anti-Indigeneity and, 227; heteropatriarchy and, 66, 122, 271, 273–278, 285–286; imperialist white supremacist capitalist patriarchy, 176, 243–244, 261–263; power of anger and, 58–61; in Women's and Gender Studies (WGS), 176, 178, 184, 194. *See also* Black Lives Matter (BLM) movement; neoliberal university
Pelaez Lopez, Alán, 219n8
Peluso, Nancy, 89
Penn Hilden, Patricia, 248, 263
Pereira, Gabriel, 17, 19, 20, 21
Perez, Emma, 2
Pérez, Laura E., 2, 270, 273, 276, 277–278
Pérez Huber, Lindsay, 33, 35
Perreault, Jeanne M., 67
Petti, Alessandro, 98–99
Pettit, Emma, 285
Pew Research Institute, 144
Philipose, Liz, 149
photographs, in the migrant glossary/vernacular, 214–215
piercings, bodily, 144, 149–150
Piketty, Thomas, 158
Pinto, Alvaro Vieira, 28
Pitt, Cassady, 146
Pitts, Andrea J., 270
pláticas, 6, 7, 33–36, 43–45
Plyler v. Doe, 209
Pocahontas, 254
poetry and narratives, 64–79; "Being Bold and Living Boldly," 64–65; "Creating Sister Scholar Relationships and Reflecting on the Risks of Emotional Labor," 70–74; "Enacting Codes of Wellness," 74–78; "'Giving Voice,' Our Broader Research Paper," 68–70, 75; heart storms, 72, 73, 76, 77; "Keeouykaywin: Interrupting Coloniality" (Gaudet), 74–75; "The Lining of Our Wellness Bundle" (Gaudet, Ward, and McGuire-Adams), 78–79; "Niceness Is Not Kind" (McGuire-Adams), 70; "Nîci-iskwêwak" ("My Fellow Sisters") (Ward), 71; "Poetic Interlude" (Gaudet and Ward), 72; storytelling and, 9, 230, 231–232, 257, 263–264
Poiger, Uta G., 171n13
police violence: George Floyd and, 49–50, 53, 58, 60; Indigenous protests and, 262; teaching about, 36, 49–50, 53, 58
Ponce, Albert, 272, 284
Poniatowska, Elena, 269
Porter, Ronald K., 274
power: activation in transformational justice, 234–236; of anger, 58–61; asymmetrical power relations and, 149; relationship to knowledge, 56–61, 112, 113–114
Prashad, Vijay, 51
Pratt, Minnie Bruce, 214, 302
praxis of solidarity: for Black and women of color as adjunct/contingent faculty, 33–46, 53–56; components of, 44–45; method for study, 34; pláticas in, 6, 7, 33–36, 43–45; poetry and narratives in (*see* poetry and narratives); racial opportunity cost and, 31–33, 44, 61–62; reconciliation of Indigenous female scholars in Canada, 7, 64, 65–66, 68–74, 76; testimonio in (*see* testimonio); transgressive solidarity and, 148–152
predominantly white institution (PWI), 31–46
Preservation Project (digital archive), 130, 132
Preston, William, Jr., 218–219n1
Prout, Alan, 158
Przybylo, Ela, 177
Pulido, Laura, 269

queer persons. *See* LGBTQIA+ persons
Quijano, Anibal, 3, 6
Quijano, Lauren, 219n11
Quinn, Rachel Afi, 8
Quiquivix, Linda, 97
Quraishi, Usma, 125

Racette, Sherry Farrell, 249, 250, 265
racial opportunity cost, 31–33, 44, 61–62
racism. *See* anti-Asian racism; anti-Blackness racism; anti-Indigeneity
Rackow, S. H., 146

Radebe, Zandi, 272, 283
Ralli-Falconi, Mirko, 219n15
Ramamurthy, Priti, 171n13
Rankin, Katharine N., 148
Rao, Nitya, 170n9
Ratcliff, Anthony J., 285
Read, Jen'nan Ghazal, 150
Reagan, Ronald, 243
Red/Indigenous feminism, 241–265, 276–277; allies and, 253, 255–256, 262; author identity and positionality, 241–247; Indigenous feminisms as conceptual framework, 4, 66–68, 229–231, 253; love and sovereignty in, 263–265; Missing and Murdered Indigenous Women, Girls, and Relatives, 246, 253–254, 256, 280, 281; "Red Zone" and, 248, 265; Sand Creek massacre, 9, 244, 245–249; Standing Rock and, 242–243, 253–254, 257, 260; theoretical background, 247–252; tribal sovereignty protectors and, 241–249, 251–265; Western feminism vs., 253–256; Women of All Red Nations and, 243, 255, 256; Wounded Knee Occupation and, 243, 256–260. *See also* decolonial feminisms
Red Power Movement, 243, 253–256
Ree, C., 203
relationality: transgressive solidarities and, 148–152; in transnational girlhood studies, 147–149
Renteria, Jose Alejandro, 284
reproductive justice, 134; female genital cutting, 180–181, 185, 187, 192–194; sexual violence against women, 105, 187, 250, 253, 254, 264; sterilization and, 250, 286
resistance: in decolonial feminism, 3; "hanging out" / hangouts as, 149–151, 152; Native American sovereignty movements, 242–243, 253–258, 260–263; pláticas in, 6, 7, 33–36, 43–45; poetry and narratives in, 64–79; praxis of solidarity in, 33–46, 53–56 (*see also* praxis of solidarity); racial opportunity cost of, 31–33, 44, 61–62; reconciliation of Indigenous female scholars in Canada, 7, 64, 65–66, 68–74, 76; self-care as (*see* self-care); subversive tools in, 6, 9, 176, 276; testimonios in, 7, 34, 36–46; wellness as an act of, 65–79; to Western narratives about Muslim women (*The Hijab Project)*, 143–152; to white supremacist academic violence by adjunct/contingent faculty, 33–46, 49–62. *See also* Red/Indigenous feminism
Revereza, Miko, 216, 219n14
Rhodes, Heidi Andrea Restrepo, 219n3
Ribeiro, Djamila, 19, 27
Richardson, Gloria, 275
Ríos-Rojas, Anne (Anna), 135
Risam, Roopika, 123, 134–135
Risling Baldy, Cutcha, 229–230
Rivera, Carla, 278
Rivera-Murillo, Rocio, 52, 272–273, 285
Roaf, Mary, 269–270, 271, 272, 274, 280
Robertson, Katie, 285
Rodgers, Yana Van Der Meulen, 170–171n12
Rodríguez, Alicia, 279
Rodríguez, Juana María, 277
Roediger, David, 247
Romero, Anthony D., 209
Rose, Tricia, 33
Roshanravan, Shireen, 127–128, 276, 277
Ross, Luana, 230
Ross-Sheriff, Fariyal, 148
Roy, Arundhati, 62, 158
Roy, Srila, 168
Ruiz, Olivia Barragán, 278
Rustin, Bayard, 275

Sachs, J. A., 303
Sacramento, Jocyl, 280
Sadek, Tracy M., 52, 272–273, 285
Saez, Emmanuel, 158
Salas-SantaCruz, Omi, 276, 277
Salman, Yasmin, 91–93
Salmón, Enrique, 223
Sánchez, Marina, 279
Sand Creek massacre, 9, 244, 245–249
Sandoval, Cueponcaxochitl D. Moreno (Chela), 2, 5, 9, 193, 224, 226, 270, 277–278, 284
Sandoval, Denise M., 285

Sandvig, Christian, 97
San Francisco State University (SFSU), 271–273, 274–275
Santos, Francely, 279
Sarkar, Tanika, 161
Sataf, Israel (village in historic Palestine), 85–86; counter-mapping in reconstruction of, 87, 89, 90–93, 100; described, 88, 91
Saxena, Sadhna, 170n7
Scarlett, K., 303
Schuster, Jack H., 31
Scott, Joan Wallach, 145–146
Scott, Otis L., 272
Scott, Patricia Bell, 277
Scott-Clayton, Judith, 51
Segalo, Puleng, 94
Seguino, Stephanie, 170–171n12
self-care, 44, 71; "Being Bold and Living Boldly" (poem), 64–65; Codes of Wellness in the university, 68, 70, 74–78; COVID-19 pandemic and, 56–61; decolonial care, 66; poetry and narratives in, 64–79; resisting isolation, 68–69, 70, 72–74, 78; stress relief and, 75–76; wellness as an act of resistance, 65–79
Seltzer, Rick, 52
Serdar, Ayşe, 167
settler colonialism. *See* colonialism
sexuality: comprehensive sexuality education (CSEd) in Turkey and India, 157–168, 168–169n2; sexual violence against women, 105, 187, 250, 253, 254, 264. *See also* LGBTQIA+ persons; reproductive justice
Shames, Stephen, 274
Shanks, Maegan, 299, 301
Shenton, Robert W., 169n3
ships and boats, in the migrant glossary/vernacular, 207–208
Siegel, James T., 214
Singh, Taveeshi, 299, 300, 302
Sinha, Mrinalini, 164
Slack, 126, 127, 130–132, 133
sleep, Amazon Mechanical Turk, 23–24
Sleeter, Christine, 280
Smedley, Audrey, 247
Smith, Barbara, 34, 277
Smith, Beverly, 34

Smith, Linda Tuhiwai, 2, 230, 231
Smith, Tommie, 269
social justice: feminization of labor migration and, 104–105; transformational justice and Xicanx Indigenous youth, 224–227, 229, 232, 234–236, 237. *See also* reproductive justice; South Asian Youth in Houston United (SAYHU); Women's and Gender Studies (WGS)
social media and digital tools, 120–128, 130–137
Soeller, Gary, 97
Soja, Edward W., 105
Somel, Selçuk Akşin, 160
Song, M., 148
Soul on Ice (Cleaver), 273–274
South Asian Youth in Houston United (SAYHU), 8, 120–139; black feminist theory and, 122, 123–125; COVID-19 pandemic and, 120–121, 123, 128, 130–134, 136–137; feminist community building, 122–130, 132–137; Generation Z and, 122, 128, 134–135; LGBTQIA+ community and, 123–124, 128, 134, 135–136, 137; origins at the University of Houston, 120–121, 123–124, 138n1; Preservation Project (digital archive), 130, 132; social media and digital tools, 120–128, 130–137; "South Asian" as term, 121–122; Virtual Summer Institute (VSI), 121, 123, 127–128, 130–131, 132–134, 136–137
space/spatial analysis: of migrant worker knowledge production in Lebanon, 103–118; in reconstruction of Palestine, 85–101; time and, 6–8, 105, 116, 121, 204
spirit murder, 7, 41–46
Spivak, Gayatri Chakravorty, 145, 197n7, 252
Sporn, Pam, 272
Spotify, 133
Sriprakash, Arathi, 168
Srnicek, Nick, 19
Stacey, Jackie, 160, 168, 170n9
Standing Rock, 242–243, 253–254, 257, 260
Stannard, David, 247–248

The State of Native America (Thunder Hawk), 259–260
Stephens, Monica, 85
storytelling, 9, 230, 231–232, 257, 263–264
Stoudt, Brett G., 143, 151
Street, Brian V., 108
stress relief: Codes of Wellness and, 68, 74–78; Secondary Street Trauma (SST) of educators and COVID-19 pandemic, 61–62; in self-care, 75–76
Stripling, Jack, 285
subaltern, as term, 197n7
Subramanian, Shreerekha, 124
subversive tools, 6, 9, 176, 276
Sueyoshi, Amy, 276
Sundar, Pavitra, 122
Suri, Siddharth, 19, 20, 22
Sutjipto, Angel, 9
Suzack, Cheryl, 66, 67, 253
Swarr, Amanda Lock, 168
Switzer, H., 147

Tambe, Ashwini, 4
Tamkin (feminist organization in Lebanon), 106–108, 110–111, 114–116
Tascoe, Ramona, 275
tattooing, 144, 149–150, 152
Taube, Karl A., 224
Taylor, Renty, 214–215
Telling to Live (Latina Feminist Group), 35
temporality/time: in the migrant glossary/vernacular, 215–216; space and, 6–8, 105, 116, 121, 204; transformations and, 98
testimonio: basis in radical Latin American traditions of decolonial resistance, 35; of Lynn Hampton, 34, 36–46; misogynoir and, 7, 33, 37–41; nature of, 35; pláticas of Sylvia Mendoza Aviña in witnessing, 6, 7, 33–36, 43–45; spirit murder and, 7, 41–46
Texas, South Asian Youth in Houston United (SAYHU), 8, 120–139
Texas India Forum, 126
Texas Woman's University (TWU), 178–179
Thayer, Millie, 4, 146, 148

Third World Liberation Front (TWLF) / Third World Strike, 271–273, 274–275, 280–285
This Bridge Called My Back (Moraga and Anzaldúa, eds.), 277, 302
Thomas, Deborah A., 148
Thomas, Lynn M., 171n13
Thorne, Kym, 146
Thunder Hawk, Madonna, 256–260, 263
Tilsen, Nick, 257, 260
Timmerman, Christiane, 145
Tintiangco-Cubales, Allyson, 280
Tonarelli, Samantha, 284
Torre, María Elena, 143, 151
Townsend, Justine, 86
trains, in the migrant glossary/vernacular, 216–217
transformational justice: power activation in, 234–236; Xicanx Indigenous youth and the warrior butterfly spirit, 224–227, 229, 232, 234–236, 237
transgender persons. *See* LGBTQIA+ persons
transnational feminisms: children's sensual experiences and, 8–9, 157–171; concept of transnationalism, 175–176; theorizing labor in, 6; transnational girlhood studies, 146–152 (see also *The Hijab Project*); Women's and Gender Studies and, 9, 175–197. *See also* South Asian Youth in Houston United (SAYHU)
Treleaven, Sarah, 65
Tribal Law and Order Act (2010), 247
Triplett, Nicholas, 51
Trudeau, Daniel, 90
Trudell, John, 252
Trudy, 33, 34, 37
Trueba, Enrique T., 231
Trump, Donald, 49–50, 54, 126
Truong, Debbie, 285
Truth and Reconciliation Commission of Canada Call to Action, 69–70
Tubaro, Paolo, 18
Tuck, Eve, 66–67, 97, 203, 230, 270, 276–277
Tucker, Jill, 273
Tuhiwai-Smith, Linda, 66

Turkey. *See* children's sensual experiences
Turtle Island (Abiayala), 5, 203, 210, 238n6
24/7 (Crary), 16
Twitter, 17, 125, 130, 131

Uber, Equipe, 16
United Nations (UN): Convention on the Elimination of Discrimination against Women (CEDAW, 2008), 178; international human rights laws, 178; new state of Israel and, 90; UN Relief and Works Agency (UNRWA), 98; UN Women, 168–169n2
United States: "American dream" and, 166–168; basis in anti-Blackness, 34; "blessed" status vs. "oppressed others," 180–181, 185–186, 192, 195; Bureau of Alcohol, Tobacco, and Firearms (ATF), 255; Bureau of Indian Affairs (BIA), 258, 259, 261; Citizenship and Immigration Services (USCIS), 210; Civil Rights movement, 58, 110, 124–125, 209, 243, 256, 275; Customs and Border Protection (CBP), 208, 216, 219n15; Declaration of Independence, 249; Department of Defense, 24; Department of Homeland Security (DHS), 206, 211; Department of Labor, 274; genocide and Indigenous / Native peoples, 9, 235, 242–251, 253–254, 261–263, 280; Immigration Act, 125, 209; Immigration and Customs Enforcement (ICE), 208, 215, 219n15, 280–282; intervention in the Middle East and Asia, 145–146, 207; intervention in the Southwest Asia and North Africa (SWANA) region, 104–105, 107–108; oppression of people within borders of, 184; structural oppression in, 34; students from Turkey and India and, 158; Turtle Island (Abiayala) and, 5, 203, 210, 238n6; US-centered worldview of students and, 180, 181–182; War on Terror, 145–146; "Wet Foot, Dry Foot" policy for Caribbean peoples, 207; women's rights and, 178. *See also* South Asian Youth in Houston United (SAYHU); Xicanx Indigenous youth
University of California, Berkeley, 271–273
University of California, Los Angeles (UCLA), 49–62
University of Houston, 120–121, 124. *See also* South Asian Youth in Houston United (SAYHU)
University of São Paulo, Artificial Intelligence Center (C4AI), 16
Urban, Dennis J., 275
Ureña, Carolyn, 284
Utah Museum of Contemporary Art. *See The Hijab Project*

Váldez, Jesús, 279
Valdovinos, Miriam G., 9, 223–240
Valentine, Gill, 92–93
Vanderwaeren, Els, 145
Vanita, Ruth, 164
Vanner, Catherine, 147, 148
Vei, Tanjerine, 177, 299, 300, 301
Veiga, Cynthia, 160
veiling. See *The Hijab Project*
Velásquez, Ernesto Rosen, 272, 273
Velez, Emma D., 122, 124, 270, 277
Venzant Chambers, Terah T., 32
Verhaeghe, Amy, 177
Villenas, Sofia A., 33, 35, 231
Vora, Kalindi, 19, 22, 27

Wagner, Sally Roesch, 256
Walia, Harsha, 208, 219n5
Walker, Rafael, 50
Wallerstein, Immanuel, 272
Wang, Bo, 148
Wankhede, Harish S., 170n6
war: genocide in Nazi Germany, 216; genocide in Palestine, 2, 85, 97–98; Japanese American internment during World War II, 216, 217; self-care as warfare, 53; United States intervention in the Middle East and Asia, 145–146, 207. *See also* military
Ward, Jennifer, 7, 64, 68, 69, 75; "The Lining of Our Wellness Bundle" (with Gaudet and McGuire-Adams),

78–79; "Nîci-iskwêwak" ("My Fellow Sisters"), 71; "Poetic Interlude" (with Gaudet), 72
War Jack, LaNada, 271, 275, 285
warrior butterfly spirit, and Xicanx Indigenous youth, 224–227, 229, 232, 234–236, 237
Warrior Women Project, 256–257, 256–258
Washington, George, 249
Weaver, Meghan, 275
Weber, Shirley, 284
Weems, Lisa, 147
Weinbaum, Alys Eve, 171n13
wellness: as an act of resistance, 65–79; Codes of Wellness in the university, 68, 70, 74–78; in the migrant glossary/vernacular, 217–218. *See also* self-care
White, Jenny B., 161
Whitebear, Luhui, 277
White Fragility (DiAngelo), 38, 41
white supremacist academic violence: misogynoir and, 7, 33, 37–41; resistance by adjunct/contingent faculty members, 49–62; spirit murder and, 7, 41–46; structural violence in the neoliberal university, 42–43, 51, 61–62; Third World Liberation Front (TWLF) / Third World strike and, 271–273, 274–275, 280–285
white supremacy: "hanging out" / hangouts in racialized communities and, 149–151, 152; oppression of people of specific nationalities, 184; race and gender of minoritized groups and, 148–151; Women's and Gender Studies (WGS) and, 176, 184, 194
Wieser, K., 303
Williams, Patricia, 33, 41
Williams, Robert, 249
Wilson, Angela, 66
Wilson, Christo, 97
Wilson, Matthew, 85
Wilson, Shawn, 230
Winant, Howard, 247
Winnemucca Hopkins, Sarah, 250, 251, 254–255
Winner, Langdon, 19
Winthrop, John, 218–219n1
WMA (white male administrators): adjunct/contingent faculty members and, 37–46; Comparative Race and Ethnic Studies (CRES) course, 32–33, 37–46; misogynoir and, 37–41; spirit murder and, 41–46
Wolfe, Patrick, 1
Womack, Craig, 264
Women of All Red Nations (WARN), 243, 251, 255, 256
Women's and Gender Studies (WGS), 175–197; author identity and positionality, 178–179, 180; capitalist patriarchy in, 176, 178, 184, 194; challenges with teaching, 179–181; concept of transnationalism and, 175–176, 182–183; ethics and, 193; expertise and, 194–195; Global Current Events Assignments (GCEA), 189–192; in Global North vs. Global South, 176–183; intersectionality and, 175–176, 183–184, 187–188; method for study, 177–178; oppressive practices, 178, 180–181, 185, 187, 191, 192–194; prospects of teaching, 181–182; significance of transnational approach, 182–183, 185; strategies for teaching, 185–195, 197n5; teachable resources and materials, 189–193, 197n5; transnationalism in, 175–176, 179–195
Wong, Stephanie, 275
Wood, Denis, 85
Woodcock, Jamie, 19
Woodrow Wilson High School, 228, 229, 232, 238n5
work authorization / working under the table, in the migrant glossary/vernacular, 218
worth, in the migrant glossary/vernacular, 218
Wounded Knee Occupation, 243, 256–260
Wynter, Sylvia, 2, 6

Xicanx Indigenous youth, 223–238; Anahuakenyx collective and,

Xicanx Indigenous youth (*continued*) 223–226, 229, 231–238, 238n4; ancestral knowledge systems and, 9, 224–227, 230–236; author identities and positionalities, 227–229; foodways and, 223–224, 228; LGBTQIA+ community and, 227–229; method for study, 224–227, 231–234; Movimiento Estudiantil Chicanos de Aztlán, 224–225, 228–229, 233; pilgrimage to Teotihuacan and Tenochtitlán and, 223–227, 228–229, 231–232, 235; theoretical framework for study, 229–231; transformational justice and, 224–227, 229, 232, 234–236, 237; warrior butterfly spirit and, 224–227, 229, 232, 234–236, 237

Yang, K. Wayne, 66–67, 97
Young, J. C., 303

Zakel, Lydia, 7, 85–102
Zarate, Maria Estela, 231
Zaytoun, K. D., 4
Zochrot, 93–96
Zoom, 8, 120, 123, 131, 133, 136–137
Zucman, Gabriel, 158
Zyskowski, Kathryn, 19

The University of Illinois Press
is a founding member of the
Association of University Presses.

Composed in 10.5/13 Mercury Text
with Caecilia display
by Jim Proefrock
at the University of Illinois Press

University of Illinois Press
1325 South Oak Street
Champaign, IL 61820-6903
www.press.uillinois.edu